JAPANESE WOODEN BOATBUILDING

和船

I0891803

和船

Japanese Wooden Boatbuilding

Douglas Brooks

Floating World Editions

Published by Floating World Editions, Inc.
26 Jack Corner Road, Warren, CT 06777

Text and all images not otherwise credited
© by Douglas Brooks

Protected by copyright under the terms of the International Copyright Union; all rights reserved. Except for fair use in book reviews, no part of this book may be reproduced for any reason by any means, including any method of photographic reproduction, without permission of the author.

First edition 2015
First paperback edition 2021

Printed in China
ISBN: 978-1-953225-00-9

Author and publisher gratefully acknowledge the generous and continuing support of the United States-Japan Foundation, and grant administration assistance provided by the Shelburne Craft School. Special thanks to James F. English, Jr. for his generous contribution.

To Catherine,
for always believing in my work,
and for being with me every step of the way.

Praise for *Japanese Wooden Boatbuilding*

"This is a magnificent study. Its minuteness and clarity of detail will fascinate not only wooden boat builders, but anyone interested in the craftsmanship and culture of an earlier Japan. "

— James F. English, Jr., Director Emeritus of Trinity College and Mystic Seaport Museum

"This entrancing book reveals a world of sleek, practical forms perfected over centuries, of dedicated craftsmanship practiced today by just a few. Douglas Brooks's precious record of that world is dense with information, beautifully designed, and highly readable."

— Louise Cort, Curator, Smithsonian Institution

"A bible of the small wooden boat evolution."

—Dick Wagner, Founder, Center for Wooden Boats

"An insightful and enchanting window into the remarkable microcosm of Japan and its boatbuilding traditions."

— Tom Morse, *Ocean Navigator*

"An invaluable record of vanishing watercraft and the ways in which they are made, and a compelling record of a personal journey of discovery. Lavishly illustrated and lovingly wrought, it belongs on the shelf of anyone with more than a passing interest in the craft of wooden boat building. "

— John Summers, *WoodenBoat* magazine

Also by Douglas Brooks

Building the Nagara River Ubune with Boatbuilder Nasu Seiichi (Funadaikou Nasu Seiichi to Nagaragawa no Ubune o Tsukuru), translated by Chieko Wales, Department of Intangible Cultural Heritage, Tokyo National Research Institute for Cultural Properties, 2020 (text in Japanese; forthcoming in English)

Ayubune, museum monograph written with Riko Okuyama, Mizunoki Museum of Art, Kameoka, Japan, 2014 (text in Japanese and English)

Sabani: Building an Okinawan Fishing Boat, translated by Koji Matano, Wooden Boat Center, Takashima, Shiga, Japan, 2014 (Japanese only)

Construction Record of Sabani, the Traditional Okinawan Fishing Boat (Okinawa no Dentouteki Gyosenl Sabani Kenzou Kiroku), Museum of Maritime Science, Tokyo, Japan, 2011 (text in English and Japanese)

"Ships of the Japanese Coastal Trade," in *Shipwrights Annual*, Anova Books, United Kingdom, 2010

"Bezaisen: Japan's Coastal Sailing Traders," in *Sailing into the Past*, Seaforth Publishing, United Kingdom, 2009

The Tub Boats of Sado Island: A Japanese Craftsman's Methods (Shokunin no Gihou: Sado no Taraibune), Kodo Cultural Foundation, Sado Island, Japan, 2003 (English and Japanese)

Contents

Mr. Kazuyoshi Fujiwara of Tokyo, the author's third teacher, drawing a boat on a plank of wood.

Terms & Illustrations

We have endeavored to make this text user-friendly for the broadest readership, not only those with an interest in wooden boats and woodworking, but also in Japanese crafts and their position and prospects in a modern society. To aid the non-boatbuilding reader, English technical terms are explained or illustrated on first usage and thereafter when critical for comprehension. Japanese terms are italicized upon first use and typically when newly introduced in later chapters. Japanese spelling is according to the modified Hepburn system but without macrons, long vowels indicated by an additional a, o, or, u as appropriate. Note that boatbuilding terms may reflect dialect or craft jargon, so may appear in non-standard romanization. As well, some terms may be used only for a particular boat, in a limited region, or by a single builder. An extensive Glossary-Index is provided to clarify these specific usages and to guide the reader to more detailed context in the main text.

Calligraphy for *wasen*, meaning "Japanese-style boat," on jacket and part-titles by Haruko Hayashi. Jacket front shows a *tenmasen*, a cargo boat that traditionally plied the canals of Tokyo, built by the author and Mr. Kazuyoshi Fujiwara in 2002. Title page shows the graceful lines of the *sabani*, the iconic fishing boat of Okinawa, built by the author and Mr. Ryujin Shimojo in 2009. Part I photo (p. 6) shows Mr. Kazuyoshi Fujiwara setting a plank angle using a plumb bob. Part II photo (p. 82) shows the two lower planks being bent into place at the stern of the *chokkibune*, a replica Edo-period water taxi. Jacket back shows the bow transom of a sabani, with the dovetail fastenings made famous by the boatbuilders of Okinawa. Map on p. x by Rhumb Line Maps. Unless otherwise indicated, all photos and drawings are by the author, and copyright © Douglas Brooks. Drawings of the boats can be found on the following pages:

All dimensions in the book are given in *shaku* unless otherwise noted; a conversion table for this and other traditional measurements is on page 13.

Renderings of boats are not suitable for construction. Scale drawings for building them, including lines and construction details, are available for purchase from the author at: douglasbrooksboatbuilding@gmail.com

Wooden Boats Built in Japan by the Author

Douglas Brooks' research travels, to meet and interview traditional boatbuilders, have taken him to all forty-seven prefectures of Japan. The dates and locations of his nine apprenticeships and the names of his teachers are shown below, as are boats he has built for institutions and exhibitions.

Approximately 1 : 9,000,000. Azimuthal Equal-Area projection, centered on Tokyo. Datum WGS84.
Map first created in 2015, updated in 2020. Made by Rhumb Line Maps.

Acknowledgments

When asked about my work, two questions predominate: "How did you get into boatbuilding?" and "Why Japan?" The answer to both is a confluence of favorable circumstances, great luck, and inspiring people.

My father was a house carpenter, so I grew up surrounded by tools, which I used with his guidance and blessing. He was also an avid fisherman. Our family kept a small boat and almost every summer weekend saw us fishing together in Long Island Sound. It was only natural that I gravitated toward wooden boatbuilding, and my father's intense interest in my work and his constant support never wavered.

A semester-long undergraduate program at Mystic Seaport Museum led to an internship with one of the Seaport's boatbuilders. This gave me a taste of the craft and also solidified my interest in traditional boats. After graduating I moved to San Francisco, worked briefly in a venerable west coast boatyard, and then took a position at San Francisco Maritime National Historical Park.

Nobu Hayashi, my roommate at the University of Oregon, had been entreating me for nearly ten years to visit his native country. To be honest, I was not particularly drawn to Japan, but in 1990, immediately after telling Nobu I had left my job at the maritime museum, an envelope arrived from him. Inside was a plane ticket with a note that simply said, "Now you have no excuses." My first day in Tokyo, Nobu helped me find a traditional boatbuilder. Listening to him interpret the boatbuilder's life story opened up a world I had never imagined, one that leads directly to the story told here.

So many people and institutions have helped me with my research that this book feels more like a collaboration. More importantly, each believed in my work; their encouragement was every bit as important as their support. Kazumi Muraki interpreted most of my early interviews with craftsmen and introduced me to several boatbuilders. Shunichi Yamamoto provided me with my first overview of Japanese boatbuilding based on his own travels and research. Hearing my desire to study with a craftsman, he introduced me to two men who would both later become my teachers.

Tetsuaki Nakagawa became one of my first contacts and friends on Sado Island. Yoko Arakawa helped with letters, translation, and continues actively to support my work. Taka Higuchi was my apprentice, assisted my research, and offered important insights on building tub boats, *taraibune*. Kanjiro Homma generously shared his time and expertise from his years as a cooper. Atsushi Sugano helped make the publication of my first book possible through the Kodo Cultural Foundation. Toshio Sato generously shared his research on these boats. Chieko Wales was more than a translator; she was also a superb editor of my first book. Kazunori Tanaka organized my first boatbuilding exhibit in Japan, building a tub boat at the Niigata Prefectural Museum of History.

In Urayasu, Mr. Kikuchi, director of the Urayasu Museum and his staff, including Kazuaki Onoue and Isao Nagai, were generous hosts. Keiju Kurozumi interpreted almost daily for me as we built the *bekabune,* and he also contributed photographs, including his unique images of Urayasu taken in the era before its wooden fleet vanished. In addition, he translated documents and articles that provided historical background on the boat. Natsuhiko Hirayama also interpreted, offered advice, and became a close friend.

David Sheldon enthusiastically embraced my work and introduced me to the Freeman Foundation, which led to my first research grant. Graeme Freeman worked with me and coordinated three grants from the foundation, allowing me to study Japanese at the Middlebury College Summer Language School and then spend a year in Japan and apprentice with two boatbuilders. I cannot exaggerate the significance of this early gift and the Freeman Foundation's support. It opened all the doors that followed and it is fitting the *chokkibune* we built was christened in Mrs. Freeman's name.

In Tokyo various staff of the Koto-ward office helped host my *chokkibune* project. Yoshiko Ogura, Yeorge Tanaka, Yoshie Otani, and Kozo Tominaga all helped to make the project a success. Tomizo Saito and the entire membership of Wasen Tomo no Kai lent their enthusiastic support. Madoka Oshio and Patrick Utley became our friends there, and have opened their home to us on subsequent trips to Japan.

In Aomori, Masaaki Kon helped arrange my apprenticeship to build the *shimaihagi* and has been generous in sharing his own research on Tohoku boats. Toshikatsu Hanabe, the only other English speaker in our village, offered indispensable advice and support. He also contributed historic photographs to the text, along with his reminiscences of his work as a fisherman in his youth. Yuhei Yamada graciously shared with me his research on Hokkaido boatbuilding. Ariyuki Abe, former director of the Michinoku Traditional Wooden Boat Museum, supported my follow-up research on Tohoku boats.

Over the years I have been fortunate to meet other curators, researchers, and boatbuilders from a variety of backgrounds whose work dovetailed with my own. They have each supported my research in myriad ways with introductions, suggestions, advice, recommendations, and clarifications. They include Stuart Frank, Hisayasu Hatanaka, Higashi Norikazu, Fumitaka Nomura, Juin Saito, Asahitaro Nishimura, Satoshi Kitamura, Louise Cort, Lyles Forbes, Hideto Hatano, Yasutani Nishida, Takashi Tsuda, Yasuo Takeuchi, Atsushi Doi, Kumi Makino, Osamu Monden, Kyoko Miyazawa, Tomenoshin Niinuma, Azby Brown, Hayato Sakurai, Chiharu Tao, Tetsuhiro Matsui, Toshihiko Shibafuji, Fumio Iwabuchi, Mamiko Kariyasu, Akiho Yazaki, Takumi and Yoshiko Suzuki, Yutaka Masuyama, Ralph Samuelson, and Len Brackett.

Others who have contributed historic and contemporary photographs, not specifically mentioned elsewhere, include Meguru Tada, KAZI publications, Mamoru Okubo, Yorio Hamaguchi, Noriko Iida, Linda Ohama, Louisa Cameron, Dane Owen, Robert Critchley, George Kochi, Sergeant Emery Ruffin USMC, Hiroyuki Asato, and Kim Sajik.

It took three years of fundraising and negotiations to organize my Okinawa apprenticeship to build the *sabani*, and it would never have happened without the work of a variety of contacts, including Nobuyuki Kobori, Yoichi Yabe, Taiki Fukunaga, Kazuhiro Nishimura, and Yousuke Yamashiro. Tsunemasa Shimabukuro became a daily visitor to our workshop, assisting along with my teacher's son Tomio Shimojo. Others who contributed to my follow-up research, answering questions about sabani and Okinawan culture, include Aya Oshiro, Yoji Mori, Kyoko Kunioka, Tsugaru Ryosuke, Kaoru Soehata, and Dr. Wayne Lawrence. The Okinawan project was funded by the Center for Wooden Boats in Seattle, the Museum of Maritime Science in Tokyo, and the Asian Cultural Council in New York City. The boat now participates in the annual sabani races.

Ongoing support for my work has also come from the Nippon Foundation in Tokyo, whose staff include Akira Maeda, Kenji Ikeuchi, Tetsuro Yoshida, and James Huffman. Fiscal agents here at home who have helped administer my grant funding include the Shelburne Craft School and Frog Hollow, Vermont State Craft Center. William Brooks, former director of Frog Hollow, helped guide me through the implementation of my first grant. His expertise and advice helped shape my subsequent fundraising.

I have relied on various friends for both translation of written work and confirmation of esoteric terms. These people come from diverse and eclectic backgrounds and all have contributed to my understanding of the Japanese language, including the nuances of kanji, Japan's notorious regional dialects, and boatbuilding terms. The text and glossary of this book would be much poorer without their assistance. My thanks to Kyoko Fukuda, Tsuneo Imai, Austin Moore, James Huffman, Dr. Wayne Lawrence, Masashi Kutsuwa, and William de Lange. Koji Matano was particularly helpful translating boatbuilding terms based on his own work in Japan building Western boats. For almost twenty years Yuriko Danaher has provided me with excellent professional translation.

David Janes and the board of the United States-Japan Foundation provided the publishing grant for this book. They have shown both patience and faith throughout this long process. Ray Furse was the very first publisher I spoke with after receiving the grant; he was honest and forthright about the rewards and pitfalls of bringing a specialized book to today's commercial market. He urged me to talk to other publishers and wished me well. In retrospect his openness should have convinced me on the spot to partner with him, but its not surprising that I ultimately returned to Floating

World Editions to make this book a reality. His editing, translating, and publishing expertise have made this book far more than I imagined it could be. Michelle Landry, the book's designer, made the contents beautiful, while my wife Catherine was steadfast as a loving critic, confidante, and advisor. James F. English, Jr. contributed both enthusiasm and financial support for this book, along with his 1946 photographs of Sado Island.

For my teachers I reserve my strongest words of appreciation. These five boatbuilders opened their homes and workshops to me and shared the secrets of their craft. I am humbled by their consummate skills, their commitment to their work, and their generosity of spirit.

Koichi Fujii
Nobuji Udagawa
Kazuyoshi Fujiwara
Seizo Ando
Ryujin Shimojo

The research that informs this book spans over twenty years of interviews, readings, and inspections of boats, but mostly it is drawn from the experiences of working directly with five boatbuilders. The craft of Japanese boatbuilding is essentially a part of folk culture, and does not lend itself readily to formal academic treatment. Hence its techniques, terminology, and designs are varied and fluid, dependent upon particular personalities and environments. I have endeavored to recount what I have learned as accurately as possible, and I take full responsibility for any errors and omissions.

The author, photographed in 2014 while building an *ayubune*, or river fishing boat, at the Mizunoki Museum in Kameoka, Japan. *Photo copyright Kim Sajik.*

Introduction

My first trip to Japan was in 1990, at the invitation of my former college roommate, a native of Hiroshima. He was living in Tokyo at the time, and on my first day in Japan he took me to the Asakusa district to see a large temple complex popular with tourists. I vaguely remembered that Asakusa was where one of Tokyo's last boatbuilders lived and worked. He had been profiled in an American magazine, and I suggested to my friend that we try to look him up.

We succeeded in finding Sano Shipyard and meeting Mr. Ichiro Sano and his son. Though they were working on a modern wooden sloop at the time, the elder Sano assured me that he had spent most of his working life building traditional work boats. He added that he was an eighth-generation boatbuilder.

Eight generations of boatbuilders. This stuck in my mind the rest of the trip, tempered by my growing awareness of the culture of wooden crafts to be found in Japan, and the traditions of master and apprentice that nurture them. Meeting Mr. Sano led me to seek out other boatbuilders, and as I spoke to them a common thread emerged of a craft with amazingly skilled practitioners but almost no apprentices. Even so, I still didn't fully grasp how completely this accumulated knowledge could potentially vanish.

On my second trip to Japan, in 1993, I met a boatbuilder in Kochi City. At that point, I had met about half a dozen boatbuilders. Mr. Hiromitsu was nearing retirement age and, despite having apprenticed with his father, like most traditional craftsmen today, he had never taught an apprentice. As he showed me his drawings, all done on planks of wood, he began by sorting them, saying, "These are my grandfather's drawings, and these are my father's, and these are mine." A Japanese maritime historian, who had brought me to Kochi to meet Mr. Hiromitsu, was whistling in amazement.

I too was initially stunned by the wealth of documentation being spread out before us, but looking more closely I saw a problem: the drawings were incomplete. In fact, it was impossible to build a boat from any of them. The builder had recorded the profile of each boat, and a plan view (width) of the bottom plank, but that was all. The drawings did not record the plan view at the chine and sheer, nor the shape of the transom.[1] I mentioned that the drawings shown were unusable without those crucial dimensions. After a pause, Mr. Hiromitsu looked at me and confirmed what I had said. I opened my notebook and asked him what the missing dimensions were. "I cannot tell you," he said. "Those are my secrets."

Later, over tea at Mr. Hiromitsu's home, I again broached the subject of his secrets. I explained to him that I was living in America and I could never be a threat to his work. In fact,

Mr. Hiromitsu with his plank drawings. Behind him is one of his boats under construction.

A close-up of Mr. Hiromitsu's drawings. They contain only profile views, rendering them useless to anyone but the builder himself, who had memorized all the missing information.

probably no one could be a threat to him; he was the last boatbuilder of the region and his handful of customers were the few elderly fishermen still interested in owning wooden boats. As we talked, it seemed as though he was just then realizing that fact and its implications. Finally, he began to tell me some of the ratios he used in laying down the lines of his boats. More than once he paused, shook his head and said, "You don't understand how hard this is. It is really unthinkable to tell you these things."

I think of Mr. Hiromitsu, and other men like him who would later become my teachers, as the last generation of traditional boatbuilders. In the aftermath of World War II, with Japan's manufacturing capability shattered, most of these men followed their fathers to work in boatbuilding, an industry comprised of mostly small, family-run shops that had been in business for generations. At the outset of their careers, their tools and techniques would have been instantly familiar to their great-grandfathers. Three of my five teachers did not use power tools until the mid-1950s, and my other two teachers did not have electricity until the mid-1960s.

In America the war precipitated the abrupt demise of traditional boatbuilding, but in Japan, paradoxically, it actually extended the craft one more generation. American industry was quick to adopt new technologies and new materials such as aluminum, plywood, and epoxy resins, all direct results of wartime industrialization. Individual boatbuilders could not compete against the economies of scale of large producers that began making boats out of various "miracle" materials.

Meanwhile, Japan's manufacturing rise, delayed by one war, would soon be boosted by the country's proximity to two others. The Korean War created an instant demand for Japanese manufactured goods, spurring the rebuilding of factories and infrastructure. The Vietnam War furthered the nation's meteoric economic growth. Through the 1960s Japan's economy grew annually by more than ten percent, and the country became the world's second largest economy in 1968, less than twenty-five years after the devastation of Hiroshima and Nagasaki.

My teachers' children, like me all born around 1960, were the first generation to benefit from the enormous boom in the Japanese economy that began during their childhoods. This heralded a complete makeover of the Japanese economy, a surge in university enrollment, and a massive expansion of urban corporate and manufacturing jobs. Urban areas expanded exponentially as these opportunities lured tens of millions from the countryside to the city, a migration that continues to this day. Mass-produced boats made of fiberglass (known as FRP in Japan) became widely available and began to replace traditional wooden fishing fleets. Three of my teachers went out of business before 1980, while another was forced to begin building fiberglass boats. Ironically, only my first teacher, who built the primitive-looking tub boat, remained active until his death in 1999. In the face of their own shrinking opportunities, none of my teachers encouraged their sons to apprentice with them.

After my earliest trips to Japan I was determined to document the work of at least a few of the craftsmen I had met. But by my third trip I realized that interviewing boatbuilders was a completely inadequate approach. The craftsmen I met had just rudimentary drawings, if any at all. They depended instead on their patterns and memorized ratios and dimensions. Most importantly, they had learned by working alongside a master. How could I pretend to document their work via a series of interviews?

And then a master invited me to be his apprentice.

This unique opportunity, and subsequent apprenticeships, allowed me to get inside the craft and record the process of building five types of Japanese boats. I am particularly fascinated by the methods these craftsmen use to design their boats. These secrets are the heart of building the traditional boat (*wasen*) and compelled boatbuilders to memorize them in very creative ways. The parochialism of Japanese crafts is such that each craftsman's system is unique. Recording how they designed their boats is as important as the secrets themselves, and an essential element of the culture of the craft. Therefore, I dispense with Western conventions of naval architecture in this book and instead document their designs using the methods my teachers used. This includes abandoning the standard practice of dividing boats into evenly spaced stations, and using *shaku*, the traditional measuring system.

I am regularly asked two questions regarding my research: Why didn't boatbuilders record what they know, and why were they willing to reveal their secrets to me?

The answer to the first question is the need for secrecy. Knowledge and skill were the craftsman's capital and these not only had to be guarded from the prying eyes of competitors but also doled out carefully over time to deserving apprentices in return for their hard work and loyalty. Like most traditional crafts, boatbuilding has been sustained by this system in which apprentices learn by obedience, observation, trial, and repetition, all under the direct tutelage of the master over a long period, in this case usually six years. This same, time-honored system nurtured Japan's last generation of boatbuilders, who could not imagine any other way for their craft to be transmitted.

The author taking photographs during the construction of a *sabani* in Okinawa. Documenting the craft via notes, drawings, photographs, and video was a concept only grudgingly accepted by the craftsmen profiled. *Photo copyright George Kochi.*

The author looking at drawings with Mr. Kihei Sekizuka, the last boatbuilder on the Agano River. This former house carpenter apprenticed with the previous boatbuilder on the river, after realizing that no one else would be inheriting those skills. *Photo copyright Catherine Wood Brooks.*

The answer to the second question follows from the first. The boatbuilders I have met understand better than anyone the amount of knowledge that will be lost in a world with no apprentices. My interest in their work served as the catalyst for my relationships with them. My third teacher, Mr. Kazuyoshi Fujiwara, regarded his talents as the accumulation of four generations of his family's work. My teachers may have made rational choices in discouraging their sons from entering the workshop, but they are all fiercely proud of their accomplishments. In talking to craftsmen throughout Japan, I have also sensed from them a poignant sadness, borne of the realization that they inhabit a world in which their extraordinary skills are no longer understood, appreciated, or wanted. I represented a final chance for them to pass these skills on.

That said, while my teachers supported my research each expressed strong doubts about the efficacy of publishing the results. I can understand their hesitation. Mature craftsman who dedicated six years of their lives to an apprenticeship, and then a lifetime mastering their craft, are not likely to believe that all they knew could be recorded in a book. My teacher in Okinawa regularly pointed to my camera and notebook while admonishing me, saying that although recording his work was fine, I had to "train my eye." In the Japanese context, what we call "learning" might better be called a "practice," in the sense that religious devotion or meditation is a practice. The knowledge is visceral and unconscious; not rational or reducible.

The intuitive nature of crafts is deeply ingrained in the Japanese cultural psyche and, in my experience, researchers have shared boatbuilders' views regarding documenting the process. This has left them treating the boats as artifacts, divorced from the skills that created them. Despite several major Japanese collections of historic boats, I have found almost no research on the techniques of the craft itself.[2] What documentation does exist has been done by just a handful of individual researchers recording the work of isolated boatbuilders. I know of no researchers who have actually worked side-by-side with craftsmen as I have done.

In this book I chronicle my apprenticeships with five boatbuilders over the course of fifteen years (1996, 2001, 2002, 2003, and 2010). I have traveled to forty-five of Japan's forty-seven prefectures, met scores of boatbuilders and interviewed them about their work. I learned that the master-apprentice relationship, which successfully sustained traditional boatbuilding for hundreds of years is, in fact, a very fragile loop. Missing just one generation of apprentices, the craft now finds itself in crisis. The numbers bear witness: of over fifty boatbuilders I have met and interviewed, fewer than ten taught apprentices. For four of my five teachers I am their sole apprentice. All of the boatbuilders I have met are now over seventy years old. In 2000 the Nippon Foundation of Tokyo conducted a nationwide survey of those with experience in traditional boatbuilding and listed 214 men with an average age of sixty-one. On this book's publication in 2015 that average age, assuming they all remain alive, is seventy-six.[3]

The research that forms the basis of this book began late one night in 1995. I was headed to Sado Island, along with an interpreter, to interview Mr. Koichi Fujii about his life and work building barrels and tub boats. On the ferryboat ride from the mainland to Sado, I confessed to my interpreter that I was becoming frustrated. This was my third visit to see and talk with Mr. Fujii, and yet it seemed clear to me I needed to work alongside him in order to really document his work. Since I had established a strong relationship with him, I had decided that I would ask if I could build a tub boat with him.

My interpreter was horrified by the idea that I might ask Mr. Fujii to become his apprentice. It was unthinkable, she said, first because I was a foreigner. She was certain he would never entertain the notion of teaching me. I was disappointed, but I trusted her, and we spent two days with Mr. Fujii and his wife, specifically watching him split bamboo and braid the hoops that hold tub boats together. Making the hoops is the most difficult part of building these boats, and the experience of just watching was frustrating. Mr. Fujii worked quickly and quietly, sitting in the parking lot across from his shop, braiding bamboo hoops at a furious speed. I couldn't make sense of how he braided them, even though I would step as closely as I could, taking photographs while he braided, dodging as he snapped a forty foot tail of bamboo across the lot. As animated and charming as Mr. Fujii could be sitting at the table with a cup of green tea, while working he refused to describe or explain what he was doing. When he finished we posed for a photo holding a giant traditional ripsaw, with his exquisite bamboo hoops at our feet. I was no closer to understanding how to make them.

We said our goodbyes that afternoon and my interpreter and I returned to our small inn. We planned to leave on the first ferry early the next morning. At about midnight, the innkeeper came to my interpreter's room and woke her. She in turn woke me. There was a terrible rainstorm pounding the building and my first thought was the inn was flooding. "Mr. Fujii is in the kitchen!" my interpreter exclaimed, as she rushed past my room. I followed her, stumbling down the steep steps to the first floor. My next thought was that something terrible had happened to Mrs. Fujii.

I found both Mr. and Mrs. Fujii in the kitchen. Mrs. Fujii was silent, focusing a concerned gaze toward her husband. Mr. Fujii's hands shook like a leaf. He managed to blurt out an apology for waking us up, and then he began talking directly to my interpreter, occasionally giving me a nervous glance. I waited. Cups of tea were served which, after quick nods to our host, everyone ignored. Mr. Fujii kept talking, desperately explaining something. Suddenly he finished, his eyes wide and now turned on me. My translator sat back in her chair and gasped. She caught her breath and said to me, distilling all Mr. Fujii had said into a single sentence. "He wants you to come back and be his apprentice!"

I do not know how long Mr. Fujii and I had both been thinking about working together, but now he was fearful I would turn him down. As a master, he was taking a chance making such a request. If I turned him down it would be an enormous loss of face for him. Conversely, his request could be interpreted as making a demand of me, and my refusal could be seen as an insult. By Japanese rules of propriety, he probably would have felt worse for embarrassing me than because of any shame it brought on himself. Only one answer could save us both.

I accepted his invitation on the spot. I tried to control my elation, but mostly I was dumfounded at the ironic turn of events. Mr. Fujii smiled broadly, but before he departed, he grew serious again, and handed me an envelope. When my translator explained this was a cash gift, presented in case we never saw each other again, I immediately tried to give it back. Having just accepted his offer to teach me, I had no intention of taking his money. I also thought refusing the gift was a way of reassuring Mr. Fujii that I would return. My translator shook her head quickly: it was better to take it, to let the protocol play out, even if to me it seemed unfair. When the Fujiis slid open the door to leave I was suddenly conscious again of the wind and rain pounding the inn. In Japan one waves goodbye until the guests disappear from sight. The innkeeper, my interpreter and I crowded into the doorway, waving. The Fujii's little white truck vanished almost immediately in the gale.

* * *

In 2003, at the end of my project in Tokyo, I was introduced to two of Japan's leading maritime scholars. Our intermediary had seen me on television and, knowing the two scholars personally, felt it was important we all meet. Both men had researched and published books on Japan's maritime legacy, which I had seen. Both were aware of my work, and they asked me what the point of my research was. I responded that my goal was to document the *craft* of traditional boatbuilding by working directly with masters. They said they saw no purpose in this.

The senior researcher explained, "These are uneducated men and besides, they have no records and no documents that you can study." I pointed out the man I was working with at that moment, Mr. Kazuyoshi Fujiwara, was a fourth-generation boatbuilder. He learned his skills directly from his father, and it was all but certain he knew methods passed down from his grandfather, and perhaps his great grandfather. Wasn't there some value to documenting such an accumulation of skills?

Both men shook their heads. What I was recording was worthless, they said, because there was no documentation to begin with. It could not be confirmed or annotated, nor substantiated in any scholarly way. I agreed in the strictest sense they were right, but I argued that what I was recording was folk knowledge, an oral tradition consisting of the accumulated wisdom of four generations of craftsmen.

The senior scholar leaned forward, looking at me very seriously. "You cannot call yourself a serious researcher doing what you are doing. Don't listen to people who don't have documents." I thanked the two men for their time and left.

The next day was a Monday, and I was back at work building a boat with Mr. Fujiwara. At break time I asked him if he knew the two scholars I had met the day before. He didn't, but he was very interested to learn they were maritime scholars. He asked me what we had talked about. I gave him only a bare outline of the conversation, omitting anything I feared might sound offensive to him. He listened carefully, and when I was finished he admonished me, his voice rising, "Brooks-san. Don't waste your time talking to people who don't know how to drive a nail!"

This division isn't new or surprising. Academics and craftspeople differ in many ways beyond their perspectives on their work. They often are from different educational backgrounds and different social classes, with different life experiences. In some ways these lines are starker in Japan, where a classic cultural motif is the conflict between the priest and the samurai: one a person of mind and spirit; the other a person steeped in action and the world.

This book is about driving nails. The problem I see with the academic's approach is the quest for certainty, and the narrowness that arises from this quest. My teachers were at once clear products of something we call a tradition of Japanese boatbuilding, but they were not trapped by it. At first glance their work can seem hidebound and anachronistic, yet they lived through times of enormous change, and they demonstrated incredible flexibility and perseverance.

In this book I try to be as faithful as I can to each teacher's processes, techniques, and even language. All of my teachers told me, in the strongest terms, that I needed to go beyond them, to assert myself as an individual craftsman. For them it was a matter of pride, and none of my arguments about the goal of recording precisely their techniques for posterity seemed to resonate with them. In essence they insisted on seeing me as part of their tradition, the next generation. They saw no value in documenting their craft like an artifact. Intuitively they understood that their craft lived and breathed just as surely as their own bodies did.

This is the story of how they drove the nail.

Notes

1 The chine is the corner where the upper and lower planks join and the sheer is the top edge of the top plank (see page 9 drawing). The transom is the panel forming the aft part of the hull.

2 A nationwide survey found a total of 1,627 historic boats held in 625 museums. Japan's largest boat collections are held by the Seto Inland Sea Folk History Museum in Takamatsu (Setonaikai Rekishi Minzoku Shiryoukan); the Toba Sea Folk Museum in Ise (Toba Umi no Hakubutsukan); the Michinoku Traditional Wooden Boat Museum in Aomori (Michinoku Hoppou Gyosen Hakubutsukan); the Osaka Maritime Museum (Naniwa no Umi no Jikuukan); and the Museum of Maritime Science in Tokyo (Fune no Kagakukan). Unfortunately, several of these museums have closed their doors due to financial difficulties, although their supporters have plans for reopening them.

3 The survey was conducted by the Tokai Fisheries Science Association (Tokai Suisan Kagaku Kyokai) and the Toba Sea Folk Museum (Toba Umi no Hakubutsukan).

Part I
Fundamentals

Three boats on a riverbank on the island of Shikoku, used for catching a popular river fish called *ayu*. Their hulls are framed only with horizontal beams; the boxes inside the hulls are live wells to hold the catch.

1

Design, Measurement, and Layout

Traditional Japanese wooden boats (*wasen*) are the product of a shared heritage and follow a pattern of development that is broadly similar across the country. They generally do not have vertical keels like their counterparts in the West. Most have instead a horizontal plank keel, generally twice the thickness of the side planking. This planking for the bottom runs longitudinally, and in larger boats is composed of multiple planks edge-nailed together. In some cases the plank keel, called the *shiki*, is reinforced with internal floor timbers that are nailed or through-bolted. The shiki often has a joint aft, at which point the keel rises at a shallow angle to the transom. In rare cases there is a similar joint forward, with the keel rising slightly toward the stem. With or without these breaks in the keel, the vast majority of keel planks bend at least slightly, giving the bottoms some rocker.

The hulls of these boats are hard chine, that is, the joint between the garboard (lower) planks and the side planks is a knuckle. It could almost be described as lapstrake, since the top plank usually overlaps the top edge of the garboard by a small amount. The name for this type of construction is called *wakizuke,* or *wakizukuri*, literally "side construction," from *waki* meaning "side" and *zukuri* a form of the verb *tsukuru,* "to build." A rare variant has the planks meeting flush to one another, and is called *nokkezukuri*, *nokkeru* meaning "to put one thing on top of another." In my second apprenticeship I built a boat using this unusual form of construction (see Chapter 10).

In larger boats, the panels that make up the bottom and planking are sometimes composed of more than one piece of wood. The boards that make up these planks (also called strakes) are edge-nailed together, sometimes with no internal framing to fasten them to. Planks are fastened to each other where they meet at the chine, in some cases using a type of clench nail. Typically, above the chine the top plank stands nearly vertical for most of its length.

Internal framing in most Western boats forms the structure around which the boat is built. In the Japanese tradition, framing is added after the outer hull is assembled. Frames are either a few large, grown frames (cut from the natural curve of the tree), or athwartship beams that are tenoned into the sides of the hull and shouldered on the inside of the planking. The exposed tenons are wedged from outside the hull. Despite this framing, the hull planking of traditional boats is thick, nearly twice as thick as a Western boat of the

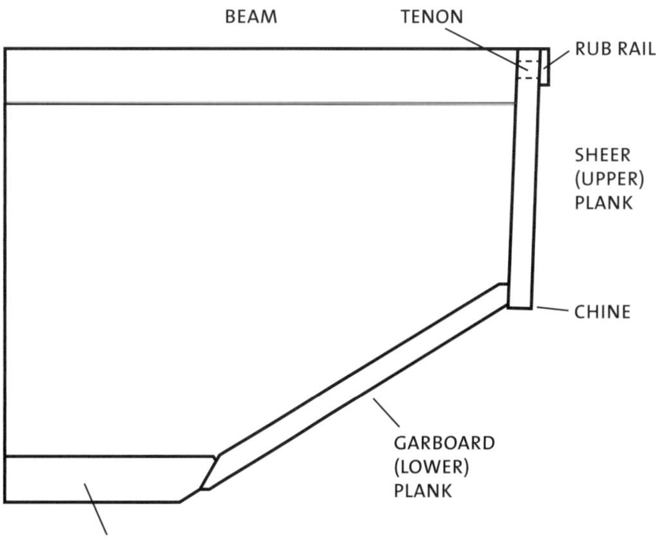

Half-hull cross section showing typical wasen construction. The plank keel is horizontal, made up of one or more thick boards. The garboard (lower) plank meets the sheer (upper) plank creating a knuckle (chine). The upper plank overhangs the bottom plank slightly. Hulls are stiffened by beams, shouldered and through-tenoned into the upper planking.

A collection of *isobune,* small inshore craft popular in the northern Tohoku region. These boats are semi-dugouts, featuring thick, carved bottoms with plank sides. Note the single pair of frames amidships, cut from natural crooks. *Photo copyright Masaaki Kon.*

A builder's plank drawing, showing the boat's profile, expanded transom, and angles for the garboard plank. Without a plan view it is impossible to build a boat from this drawing. The missing dimensions are the boatbuilder's secrets.

same size. The use of thick planking in wide strakes means Japanese boats are longer and narrower, since the material simply cannot be bent to the extent that the narrower and thinner planking of Western boats can.[1]

Other boatbuilding traditions exist, of course. In 1994 I interviewed Mr. Hirotaka Hatakeyama, who specialized in dugout canoes, and had made three as late as 1965. In the northern regions of Tohoku and on the Sea of Japan in rural areas it is still possible to see semi-dugouts being used—fishing boats with bottoms carved out of large baulks of timber fastened together—with vertical side planks added to complete the hull. In Hokkaido the indigenous Ainu made dugout and bark canoes, and their earliest planked boats featured sewn planking. The semi-dugout *sabani* of Okinawa still survives, barely, with at least one man still building them (see Chapter 13). Sabani evolved from the dugout and still retain many elements of semi-dugout construction, including the use of wooden dovetail keys to fasten the planking.[2]

Plank Drawing

When boatbuilders have left a record of their work, the information is usually drawn on a plank of wood. These plans are called *itazu*, or *itazumen,* meaning "plank drawing." Temple and house carpenters also preferred to draw their work on a plank rather than on paper, perhaps because in addition to being a readily available material in the workshop, a plank was also a far more durable medium in a harsh environment. For two of the five boats I have built, my teachers and I worked from itazu; my other three teachers worked without drawings; instead they relied entirely on patterns made of wood or plywood, and memorized dimensions.

Secrecy is endemic to Japanese boatbuilding. At the heart of the craft is knowledge of the dimensions, angles, and ratios of the boats, which the boatbuilder must safeguard. Outside of a family line of boatbuilders, no two craftsmen use the same system for laying down the lines of a boat. In the West there is a standardized system of design that is easily understood throughout the craft, but in Japan dimensions have always been closely guarded secrets. Original drawings are usually incomplete, and can often be interpreted only by the boatbuilders who drew them; boatbuilders' systems for memorizing dimensions are likewise personal, following no standard rules.

In 2005 I had the opportunity to visit a shipyard in Aomori where workers were finishing a replica of an Edo-period sailing ship (see Chapter 14). *Michinoku-maru* is a near replica of the type of coastal sailing trader that once numbered in the thousands. Four of these replicas have been built since the early 1990s, all by one shipwright, who has dedicated the latter half of his career to researching and building these long-vanished vessels. At about one hundred feet in length and one hundred tons displacement, *Michinoku-maru's* construction was a massive undertaking, involving a team of elderly boatbuilders and shipwrights gathered from throughout northern Japan. Still, the sole drawing guiding her construction was drawn on wood—in this case a ten-foot long sheet of plywood—which hung on the wall of one of the shipyard's sheds.

In 2003 I researched the extent of the use of itazu when my wife and I traveled eight thousand miles along the Japanese coastline and up several river valleys. The purpose of the trip was to seek out boatbuilders, conduct interviews, and photograph their work. Our trip ranged from Hiroshima to Hokkaido and I spoke with over forty boatbuilders along the way. All of these men were elderly and most were semi-retired. I asked each to see their plank drawings. I discovered

A plank drawing used for roof sheathing in a shrine in Aichi Prefecture.

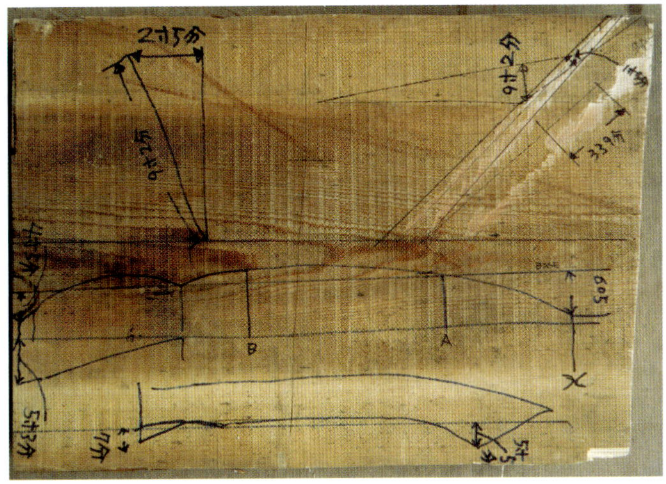

Not a scale drawing, but the layout of a plank by Mr. Kazuyoshi Fujiwara. He did many sketches while building the *chokkibune*, but never drew on paper, always on a scrap of wood.

that in the center of the country, the areas around Tokyo (known as Kanto) and Osaka (Kansai), most boatbuilders used plank drawings, but as we drove north toward Hokkaido their use dropped off. In Tohoku, at the northern end of the main island, and throughout Hokkaido, I met no boatbuilders who used drawings. As well, none of the river boatbuilders I have met to date, ten in all, uses plank drawings, and these men span the entire country from Kyushu to Hokkaido. All boatbuilders are familiar with the tradition of plank drawings, but those who didn't use them told me that they built their boats *kan de,* or "by intuition." At best these latter craftsmen were guided by designs passed down from their teachers, a few patterns, and their memories.

Plank drawings are always, in my experience, drawn to 1/10th scale, and consist of a profile view of the boat showing the bottom, sheer, and chine. They *sometimes* include a half-breadth plan view of the bottom plank and an expanded transom. Some boatbuilders also record the angle of the bottom plank at one or two stations. Even with this information one could not build a boat from most of these drawings; a builder would need the half breadth at the chine and sheer to have enough information for a replica. It is very rare to find a boatbuilder whose plank drawings are complete. The missing information on these drawings is sometimes recorded elsewhere (in some cases on the back of the drawing) but most often it is memorized by the boatbuilder. This information is essential, and without it the drawing is basically useless for construction.

The typical drawing has just two or three stations. Even the largest boats I have built, upwards of thirty feet in length, are constructed based on no more than three stations between the stem and transom. Stations are not evenly spaced as is the convention in the West. The middle station is generally located at the point of maximum beam (width) of the vessel. The two other stations, fore and aft, are located at critical points derived from the boatbuilder's experience, or perhaps a convention passed down from his master.

The small number of stations may seem odd, but it is important to remember these boats are built with much thicker planking material than Western boats for a given length, and the individual strakes are much wider. There is a corresponding limit to the amount of hull shape that the builder can achieve working within this tradition. Also, most wooden boatbuilders today represent the end of long traditions, in some cases stretching back hundreds of years. The methods for laying down the lines of a boat have been refined to the point of maximum simplicity.

"Station" can be translated various ways, depending on the region. In Tokyo Mr. Udagawa called them *yokozumi,* which means, literally, "half-breadth line." Mr. Ando in Aomori called them *toubun,* which means "bisection," while in southern Hokkaido some boatbuilders use the term *kanaba.*[3] The most common convention, almost certainly due to the heavy reliance on memorization, is that the forward and aft station locations will be symmetrical. Because the plank keel is the basis for most of the layout of the boat, the forward station is located by measuring aft from the base of the stem, while the aft station is located by measuring forward from the base of the transom. Over and over again I have seen boatbuilders use the same dimension to locate these two points, though of course the value of that dimension varies between builders.

For the reasons described, the plank drawing presents a decidedly mixed bag for the researcher. A boatbuilder in Wakayama, in his nineties, gave me one of his grandfather's plank drawings. At the time it struck me as too precious a document to accept, until I examined it closely and realized that it would be impossible to replicate the boat it represented. Ultimately the plank drawing and the craftsman who drew it are inseparable, since the builder is the only person who can interpret the drawing. The only way to crack the code is to link a particular drawing with the boat that was built from it, using the boat to provide the missing information. Plank drawings have been collected, sometimes by the hundreds, by museums throughout Japan, but it is an unfortunate irony that most of them can no longer be used to build a boat.

Another challenge is that the 1/10th scale of these drawings necessarily creates a certain amount of inaccuracy, since it is too small to scale dimensions with absolute certainty. Even the finest inkline presents a large margin for error when scaled full size. My two teachers on Tokyo Bay used their plank drawings as a starting point for construction and then as a rough guide as we built. Working with Mr. Udagawa building the *bekabune*, a small boat used to gather seaweed (see Chapter 10), the drawing was mostly an exercise in showing me how it was done, since he had built over three hundred of these boats in his career. I never once saw him refer to the drawing in the course of our work; he had long ago memorized all the information we needed.

A cove full of fishing boats, all built by Mr. Iwabuchi and most since destroyed in the tsunami of March, 2011. The broad concrete ramp allows the boats to be easily pulled from the water each day.

Mr. Fujiwara and I built an Edo-period *chokkibune* that he designed specifically for our project (see Chapter 11), so we referred fairly often to his drawing. But as the boat took shape we used the drawing less; it became more important to make things fit rather than slavishly follow a design. This actually caused some trouble at the end of the project. One Saturday I decided to loft, full size, the chokkibune we had just launched. I used the dimensions I had taken from the boat, so my full-size drawing represented the boat *as built*. When Mr. Fujiwara saw the lofting he told me that I had made several mistakes (he was right about one) but we disagreed about some of the dimensions on my lofting. He insisted they were wrong, and he kept referring to the dimensions as he had scaled them off his original drawing. What he didn't realize was how much some of these dimensions had changed in the process of building the boat and fitting the planks. Trimming, beveling, and fastening had significantly altered the shape of the boat. For me it raised an important question: Should I record the boat's shape as Mr. Fujiwara intended it, or as it actually existed?

My argument with Mr. Fujiwara over dimensions made me recall something he had said to a newspaper reporter in an interview at the outset of our project seven months earlier. In describing how he designed and built boats he told the reporter, as an afterthought, "All in all, Japanese boatbuilding is really quite primitive." In a way he was right, although "primitive" has connotations unfair to the overall level of skill and refinement of technique embodied in the craft. Japanese boatbuilding might be better described as improvisational: drawings and traditional dimensions are the starting point, but the builder ultimately relies on his eye, his experience, and his skills to get the boat right. My two teachers who used drawings only followed them to a certain point in the process. Beyond that, intuition and experience guided them.

It is important to remember that just a few generations ago, at the twilight of traditional boatbuilding in the West, craftsmen would have used systems as ad hoc and individualized as Japan's last boatbuilders use today. A builder of peapods on the coast of Maine, for example, would have carved a half model and scaled off his mold shapes; more than likely he would not have lofted the lines full size. Once he had a mold setup he might have done nothing more than shift the distances between molds to build peapods of different sizes.[4] The efficient builder would have also made patterns for almost every part of the boat, as well as jigs to speed up production. Each of these methods and improvements would have been personal, and unknown to another boatbuilder working further down the coast.

For new designs, boatbuilders often talk about a system they call *wari* or *wariai*, which means "proportion." Wari is the length-to-beam ratio for a boat, or sometimes length, breadth, and depth. The chokkibune that Mr. Fujiwara designed in 2002 was based on a single historic photograph. The image provided many of the construction details, but Mr. Fujiwara relied upon proportions passed down from his father to derive all the other relevant dimensions.

An even rarer design tradition relies on a physical dimension of the boat's operator. The span, or distance from fingertip to fingertip of one's outstretched arms, is *hiro*. Boatbuilders use the term *hitohiro*, or "person's span." My first teacher, who built tub boats, told me that in the years before many fishermen fiberglassed their tub boats (adding a layer of fiberglass to the exterior of wooden boats was seen as a way to preserve them) it was common for an owner to carry the boat on his head. He said in those days builders calculated that the largest tub boat a man could carry was one in which the length equaled the owner's span.[5] Builders designed boats accordingly. While traveling the coastline of the Noto Peninsula on the Sea of Japan I met a boatbuilder who told me that his fishing boats were based on a distance of three times the owner's span, and that this figure determined the length of the plank keel.[6]

Another dimension derived from the body is the distance between one's outstretched arm and one's chin. This dimension is based on the position of an archer having fully drawn a bow and arrow. In Urayasu the makers of paddles (a separate craft from boatbuilding) used this dimension to determine the correct size paddle for each user.

The careers of today's elderly boatbuilders spanned the era of human powered craft to powered boats. Historically, one of greatest catalysts to the design development of working boats has been the introduction of marine engines. While a surprising number of inshore fishing boats to this day are still powered by oars, sculling oars, and paddles, boatbuilders did have to adapt traditional designs for inboard and outboard engines. Mr. Udagawa used the term *mochi* to refer to an adjustment made to a traditional boat design, such as widening or deepening the lines to accommodate an engine. This term likely comes from the verb *mochiageru*, meaning "to lift up."

Measurement

The dimensions used throughout this book are given using the traditional system of *shaku*. This system is part of an

A boat from the Noto Peninsula known locally as a *tenmasen*, with dimensions based on the span of the owner.

Traditional Dimensions and Western Equivalents

10 rin = 1 bu	1 bu = 3.03 mm	1/8 in
10 bu = 1 sun	1 sun = 30.3 mm	1 and 3/16 in
10 sun = 1 shaku	1 shaku = 303 mm	11 and 15/16 in
6 shaku = 1 ken	1 ken = 1.82 m	5 feet 11 and 5/8 in
10 shaku = 1 jou	1 jou = 3.03 m	9 feet 11 and 3/8 in

entire range of traditional measures for distance, area, volume, and weight known as the *shakkanhou*. The system originated in China and spread throughout Asia reaching Japan by the eighth century. Though Japan officially adopted the metric system just after World War I, many traditional measures are still in use. Tatami makers, house carpenters, and boatbuilders use a system called *kanejaku*, while kimono makers use a system called *kujirajaku* (1 shaku in the kimono makers' kujirajaku equals 1.25 kanejaku).[7]

Shaku is a decimal system. Each shaku is divided into ten *sun* and each sun divided into ten *bu*. Bu are further divided into ten *rin* but the smallest dimension that woodworkers use is five rin, the equivalent of half a bu (about 1/16th of an inch). Far from being obsolete, the shaku system is still used by traditional craftsmen in Japan and measuring devices in shaku are readily available for purchase. Shaku is also a very comfortable system to use for one accustomed to working in feet and inches, since one shaku is just one-sixteenth inch less than a foot. Two larger dimensions are the *ken*, equivalent to six shaku and *jou*, or ten shaku.

House carpenters commonly use ken and jou to measure buildings as well as property dimensions. The only boatbuilder I know to use these terms was my fourth teacher. Mr. Ando used a stiff batten one ken long marked off in one shaku increments. Not owning a tape measure, his longest measuring device was this tool he called a *jougi*.[8]

Most published research in Japan records traditional boats using the metric system. The discrepancy between the measuring system used by craftsmen and the one used by researchers has resulted, in my view, in a tragic oversight. Boatbuilders face the challenge of memorizing many secret dimensions, often by using whole, half, or quarter numbers: 12 shaku, 1.75 shaku, 2.5 shaku, 5 sun, 5 bu, and so on. By abandoning the measuring system used by the boatbuilders themselves—converting 12 shaku to 3.636 meters, for instance—researchers obscure the craftsman's ingeniously simpler system. Furthermore, most lines drawings created by researchers of traditional boats use the Western method of dividing the hull by equally spaced sections, ignoring the stations used by the boatbuilders.

In 2005 I was invited by the Michinoku Traditional Wooden Boat Museum (Michinoku Hoppo Gyosen Hakubutsukan) to come to Aomori to research their collection. I set about taking the lines off (measuring the shape of) an inshore fishing boat of the same type that I had built with my teacher in 2003. The boat had been built in the same village where I worked. The builder had retired not long after

Mr. Seiichi Nasu, the last builder of *ukaibune* (cormorant fishing boats) in Gifu Prefecture, used these two patterns when piloting nail holes to check the proper angles.

my teacher established his own shop. He was long dead, and of course he had left no written record of his design.

I started by removing the floorboards so I could measure the shape of the keel. I planned on dividing the hull into evenly spaced stations and measuring hull cross sections at each one. When I got the floorboards out, however, I noticed a faint ink line across the bottom near the bow. I measured from the line to the base of the stem: 2.5 shaku. The simple number was my first clue that this point must mark the builder's forward station. In keeping with tradition I knew the builder probably set his aft station the same distance forward of the transom. I moved aft, butted my tape against the transom and pulled it 2.5 shaku. There, faintly visible across the bottom, was another ink line. I found his third station at the most likely place: the point of maximum beam. Furthermore, measuring heights and breadths at these stations I kept getting easy to remember values: 1.75, 2.25, 3.0 and so on. I had essentially rediscovered the builder's secret dimensions.

Each particular builder developed his own method for laying down the lines and memorizing the dimensions of his boats. These personal systems are an important element of folk culture in themselves. In the West a lines drawing records the shape of a boat and nothing else; in Japan the craftsman's tricks, secrets, and ratios reveal something about each boatbuilder's personality.

As I measured the museum's boat that day, I felt as though the boatbuilder was somewhere in the room watching me rediscover his secrets. To Westerners, used to working from plans based on absolute dimensions, this system can seem random and chaotic. But if the construction of Japanese boats is improvisational, their designs are deeply personal. When talking with boatbuilders one is likely to hear stories about how a fisherman recommended a slightly modified shape, or how a pattern was passed down from the boatbuilder's father. Boatbuilders reminisce about how they connived to steal crucial dimensions from their masters, and how they then developed methods to keep the secrets themselves. Other craftsmen simply say, "That's the way my family always did it."

Another pillar of Western boat design is the primacy of the dimensions of overall length, breadth, and depth of a boat. A Western boatbuilder, for example, sets up the backbone (stem, keel, and transom) based on the design's *overall* length. For Japanese boatbuilders, the foundational longitudinal measurement is the length of the *shiki*, the bottom keel plank. The keel plank is the starting point of the building process and everything derives from it. The stem

Mr. Nasu holding his pattern and preparing to cut a nail hole in the bottom of a boat.

Mr. Nasu used no drawings whatsoever when building his boats. These sticks, with small pieces of wood mortised in them, were the patterns used to bevel the planking.

and transom are set up based on known angles to the keel plank. Therefore, there is no need for boatbuilders to know overall length because it has no relationship to construction. The result is that most boatbuilders cannot accurately tell you the exact length of the boats they build.

For boatbuilders, a more fundamental expression of the length of a boat is the distance at the sheer line from the hood end of the sheer plank to the inside face of the transom. These points are crucial in deriving plank shape and many boatbuilders I have spoken to express the "length" of a hull as this dimension. In fact this value can be as much as three feet less than the actual overall length.

In some regions the "length" of a boat is the length of the keel plank. Sometimes the size of a boat can be even more confusing. In 2001, when I was building a boat at the Urayasu Museum, I asked a group of retired fishermen about a replica net-boat my teacher had built. I guessed the boat was easily over thirty feet long, and inquired about its exact length. The fishermen replied that it was a six-shaku boat—just under six feet. I repeated my question and the conversation went back and forth until finally one of the fishermen said, "We size a boat by its beam [width] here in Urayasu." Most likely this tradition developed because one of the most important products of Urayasu was *nori*. This type of seaweed is raised on nets set on poles in the bay. Strict rules dictated the width between rows of nets, and this governed the beam of the boats used in the harvest; hence Urayasu fisherman sized any boat based on this crucial dimension.

Some of Mr. Fujii's patterns for barrels, buckets, and tub boats.

Patterns

The word *kata* is used to refer to "mold" or "pattern," and many boatbuilders also use the term *kataita,* which is literally "pattern plank." Every boatbuilder I have spoken with relies on patterns. In the West, patterns usually outline the shape of particular parts. In Japan patterns typically supplement the plank drawing or the boatbuilder's memorized dimensions by providing the shape of crucial angles, bevels, and curves; rarely are they copies of parts. Exceptions to this practice among my teachers were Mr. Ando, who used a stem pattern, and Mr. Shimojo, who saved many of his offcuts as crude patterns. All of my teachers however, used patterns for bevels, plank angles, stem and transom rake, nail spacings, and curves.

In the case of those boatbuilders who do not use plank drawings, patterns are the only physical record of the craftsman's designs. Unfortunately for the researcher, these patterns are usually not labeled, so while they may constitute

Mr. Iwabuchi's patterns, marked with the name of each cove, corresponding to a boat type, and three heights.

a fairly comprehensive record of the shape of the boat, only the boatbuilder can decipher their use.

Mr. Koichi Fujii built his tub boats entirely from patterns, which he called *kaikata. Kai* indicates "shell-shaped" or "spoon-shaped," and is very descriptive of these patterns, which look like a sickle blade. The edges traced the inside and outside curvature of the staves, as well as the bevel of the edges. I have since learned that Mr. Fujii's kaikata were the standard patterns of the coopering trade. Tub boats are oval, therefore my teacher and I used two kaikata for the staves: one for the more tightly radiused ends of the boat and another for the sides.

When I had the opportunity in 2002 to do additional research on the tub boats of Sado Island, I spoke with a builder of conventional boats. He had worked with his father and uncles building small fishing boats, either 19 or 21 shaku in length. He said they used only a single pattern for the curved stem, one for each model, and all other dimensions were memorized. Given that they built hundreds of boats (many of which are still in use) in just two variants it is not hard to believe that they could commit all the necessary information to memory. Had their boats not featured a graceful curved, tapering stem, I doubt they would have used any patterns at all.

Mr. Udagawa made new patterns when we began to plank our small Tokyo Bay seaweed boat. He cut short pieces of scrap planking to a standard width, and from a square end marked back a known distance. He then cut to a line drawn from one corner to his mark, creating a beveled end. This pattern, when laid on the bottom of the boat and held at right angles to the edge, showed us the proper angle for the garboard plank. These patterns required him to remember the dimensions of two legs of a triangle, a method that dozens of boatbuilders have described to me for recording angles. He made similar patterns showing the angle of the stem and transom. In a practice unique among boatbuilders I have met, Mr. Udagawa discarded these patterns as soon as we were finished with them. He told me that this was his habit, as a pattern could be stolen by a competitor.

The Karakuwa region of Iwate Prefecture[9] consists of a small peninsula enclosing a bay. The shoreline is very rocky and beautifully studded with cliffs and coves, all framed in overhanging cedars, offering perfectly protected harbors. When I visited in 2005 I found each cove filled with wooden fishing boats, most of which had been built by the man I was visiting. Mr. Fumio Iwabuchi had worked alone for nearly sixty years building boats for the local fishing communities. He guessed he had built over five hundred boats. When I asked him about his designs he first told me that he built three distinct kinds of boats, but a moment later he added that he built eighteen kinds of boats. When I asked him to explain, he said there were actually eighteen different versions of the three basic types. Each cove, he said, had unique characteristics: different wave heights and frequencies, the angles of their launch ramps[10] and so forth, and therefore each cove required a slightly different shape of boat. When I asked him about plank drawings he smiled and pointed to the wall.

Eighteen long, narrow strips of wood were hanging on nails, like so many old-fashioned yardsticks. Each had the name of a cove written at the top and just three marks. Mr. Iwabuchi looked at me, still smiling, and asked, "Do you understand those?" Each stick was about a meter long and the markings were concentrated near the top. I really had only one idea, taking into account the length of the sticks and considering what sort of dimensions in a boat would be grouped in threes, so I told him that I thought that they rep-

The author lofting (drawing full size) the *chokkibune*. As a reference, the author used Mr. Fujiwara's 1/10th scale plank drawing, visible in the foreground. *Photo copyright Catherine Wood Brooks.*

resented heights of the sheer from the plank keel at three points: the highest dimension representing the bow, the lowest point the height amidships and the intermediate dimension the height at the transom.

The stunned look on Mr. Iwabuchi's face told me that I had guessed correctly. Having worked in isolation all his life I am sure that he thought his system was safe from outside interpretation, and certainly safe from a foreigner! My answer was a bit of a wild hunch, albeit one based on my experience, and if nothing else it taught me that I had learned enough to think like a Japanese boatbuilder.

Notes

1 Japanese boatbuilders traditionally used an open flame to pre-bend planks off the boat, a technique used throughout Asia. Theoretically, if the wood has a high enough moisture content, this method should be as effective as the steam bending practiced in the West. However, I know one shipwright in Japan who has used both methods to bend planks and says steam bending is superior.

2 Dovetail keys were also used by boatbuilders in Akita Prefecture; on the Agano and Mogami rivers; and on the Noto Peninsula, all rural regions on the Sea of Japan.

3 I have not found the origin of this last term, although in one form it can mean a horizontal metal bar.

4 When I worked in the Small Boat Shop of San Francisco Maritime National Historical Park, Paul deFur, a volunteer, took the lines off the museum's Monterey fishing boat *Wetton,* which had been built on Fisherman's Wharf by Dominic Labruzzi in 1923. When the lines were laid down full size, deFur noticed how flat the waterlines were amidships. Research revealed that *Wetton* was a bit longer than Labruzzi's stock boat and he lengthened his vessels by making a gap in the center of his mold setup. As for the unfairness of the hull, one might simply fall back on the old adage, "The fish don't care."

5 This is just one of the ways that fiberglassing these boats changed the craft. Carrying even an un-glassed tub boat on one's head would seem a formidable task, but old photographs show that in fact this was done. Today the mostly elderly fishermen and women on Sado tip the tub boats on their sides and roll them.

6 It should be noted that I took these craftsmen at their word, that is, that they actually used measurements of their customers in building boats. I am certain that this is true in the case of the tub boat, and from the way that the others described the process it seemed plausible. I later learned that the hiro in Japanese is like the fathom in English: based originally on the human form it came to possess a standard value. The English fathom is six feet, and the Japanese hiro is 5.965 feet (5 feet 11 and 19/32 inches), almost exactly one ken.

7 *Kujirajaku* actually means "whale shaku" because its early measuring devices were made of baleen.

8 Not to be confused with the 10-shaku measurement called *jou*. *Jougi* means "wooden ruler."

9 The Karakuwa region boasts one of the most beautiful coastlines of Japan. Unfortunately, it was devastated by the March 11, 2011 tsunami, which damaged or destroyed over ninety percent of its fishing boats.

10 Rarely are small boats moored or docked. Even the smallest fishing villages have broad concrete ramps, built by the government, and boats are pulled out of the water when not in use. Formerly boats were hauled up on beaches.

A keel of joined planks for a cormorant fishing boat in the center of Mr. Seiichi Nasu's workshop in Gifu Prefecture. Note the absence of workbenches and sawhorses.

2

Workshop and Tools

Workshop

To a Westerner a boat shop in Japan might seem like a storage space or a barn. The *shigotoba* (literally, "workplace") has no evident workbenches or sawhorses and, even today, few large power tools.[1] A visitor might see a collection of saws hanging on a wall, along with various wooden patterns. Most of the tools would be stored in the small, simple rectangular boxes favored by Japanese craftsmen.

Two elements of the shop, both integral to the way traditional boats are built, would probably escape notice: the floor and ceiling. The floor would likely be dirt and the ceiling supported by a framework of heavy beams. If the building were steel-framed, the beam running down the length of the shop would be padded with wood. This is because small boats are built right side up. The builder begins by laying timbers on the dirt floor for the keel plank to rest on. The keel plank is held in place by posts wedged between it and an overhead beam. Fixed in this way, the plank becomes the starting point for construction. Eventually all the other parts of the boat will be braced, at least temporarily, against the ceiling, the floor, and sometimes the walls. A dirt floor is preferred because props can get a better grip on hard clay than on a smooth plywood or concrete surface. If necessary the boatbuilder can drive a stake into the dirt floor to anchor the end of a prop or to fix the blocking under a boat.

The keel plank and stem of our chokkibune were propped directly over large baulks of timber on the shop floor. They remained braced this way until the boat was finished.

Hanging the first plank on the chokkibune meant propping it from above, below, and even to the side of the shop. *Photo copyright Tomizo Saito.*

In lieu of props, a river boatbuilder in Yamagata holds the keel plank in place with two large stones, a method the author has seen used by another builder.

Photo showing traditional carpenters at work. Two use a saw and adze, holding the work with their feet, while a third planes a beam resting on a trestle. *Photo courtesy Dane Owen.*

The shop floor is reminiscent of the *doma*, the rammed earth floor seen in traditional farmhouses. In this space, lower than the wooden floor of the living area, rougher work could be done under shelter, while in bygone days part of the area might have served as a stable. In 2006 I interviewed the last boatbuilder of the Gokase River valley in Kyushu. His original home and shop were demolished to make way for road widening, yet when he rebuilt his shop, a modern steel building, it still had a dirt floor.[2]

The beamwork supporting a boat shop roof may often appear overbuilt for apparent loads; this is because far more force may come from below, as the boatbuilder wedges a stout prop against the keel plank of a boat. When I worked with Mr. Fujiwara in Tokyo, our shop was a prefabricated building erected on the grounds of the Koto-ward City Hall, as Mr. Fujiwara had lost his own shop to fire many years earlier. When it came time to set the keel plank, the strain was too great for the building's frame, and we could hear the metal roof panels beginning to bend.

Where Western boatbuilders use clamps, Japanese boatbuilders rely on props and wedges. Typically, hanging a plank on a boat requires short props from underneath braced against the plank's bottom edge for support; these oppose props from the ceiling braced against the plank's upper edge, which together pinch the plank in space. Other props bear on the inside face of the plank to force the proper flare, while more props press against the outer face, spreading out from the boat to meet the walls of the shop, or bear against posts set in the floor. Any strong, fixed surface of the shop can potentially serve as a secure base for props. Only two of my four teachers used modern screw clamps, and in those cases only one or two were employed to hold the hood end of planks to the stem.

My teachers called these props *tsukaibou*, or *tsuzu*. The first term can be translated loosely as "useful post;" the second even my teacher could not give me the derivation of. In my last four apprenticeships we made our props from scraps, usually the long, narrow waste left from cutting planking. Mr. Udagawa took the time to teach me that the ends of the props had to have all four corners beveled so they would not split as they were driven in place, and one of my jobs as apprentice was to make props as they were needed, cutting them to length and using a chisel to bevel the ends. Mr. Ando had one very heavy prop he saved and used for much of his career. This post was used to brace the keel plank in place and he had marked various heights on it to serve as reference marks later in setting the angle of the stem and transom. The prop was, in effect, a kind of marking pattern.

All of my work off the boat, including cutting and preparing planks, and fashioning the stem, transom, beams, floorboard, etc., was done on the shop floor. Though I have seen workbenches in a small number of boat shops, none of my teachers used one. Toshio Odate, in his book *Japanese Woodworking Tools: Their Tradition, Spirit and Use* (Linden Press, 1998), describes how craftsmen use a beam as a planing bench.[3] Such beams often have one end resting on the floor and the other held about waist high by a trestle. Part of their usefulness is that they can be adjusted for different kinds of work and are portable. In my case, the "workbench" consisted of timbers on the shop floor. These measured nine-by-nine centimeters in cross section, the Japanese equivalent of the American four-by-four.[4] In Tokyo my teacher took several of these nine-by-nines about a meter long and mounted very small pillow blocks on either end, in effect making several very low sawhorses. Our work rested on these horses, just a few inches off the shop floor, and I sat or kneeled as I worked. He had two horses with large notches cut in them where we could rest a plank on edge, fixing it firmly to the horse with a wedge.

My first teacher, Mr. Fujii, worked seated at a block of wood that he used as a bench. Called a *kezuridai*, or "planing bench," it was identical to the type of bench used by many craftspersons when working on small-scale wood projects. It had a stop at the end closest to the user, which the pulling action of the plane held the work firmly against.[5] Since this was my first apprenticeship, using the kezuridai introduced me to the remarkable degree of physicality required in traditional Japanese crafts. I do not refer to strength—building small boats rarely requires much brute force—but to the flexibility and agility required to work on the floor. Mr. Fujii, for instance, used his bare feet to clamp the work when he joined the edges of planks. Once, talking to him about various tools, we discussed the adze. He grabbed his adze and a block of wood and, holding the block with his bare foot, began swinging furiously. I watched in horror as saucer-sized slices of wood flew from a spot right in front of his toes. All of my teachers were adept at holding a timber in place with one foot while sawing or swinging an adze or axe.

I cannot overemphasize the difficulty, for those who have never worked this way, of sawing stock at one's feet, bent over at the waist, or of planing an entire plank by hand from a crouch, advancing painfully like a crab. All of my teachers could comfortably work this way, bent double at the waist for long stretches, while I had to continually shift from my knees to a seated position and back.

Traditional Japanese carpenters' pants are called *matahiki*, and while they are very tight in the legs they fasten by wrapping around the waist and are tied off with cords. The crotch is extremely roomy (the name literally means "crotch cloth"), allowing the wearer complete freedom of movement. Today one can see matahiki worn by participants in festivals, traditional musicians, and rickshaw drivers in the tourist areas of Kyoto and Asakusa. Japanese construction workers today wear a type of large knickerbockers called *nika zubon* (knicker pants), which my teacher in Aomori also wore. The amount of loose cloth in these trousers seems inherently dangerous to me but again, it provides great freedom of movement.

For footwear, Mr. Fujii only wore *zouri*, rice straw sandals he made himself. My other teachers all wore sneakers or *tabi*.

The author working with his teacher in Tokyo. All work was done on beams resting on the shop floor, hardly a comfortable position for those used to working at a bench. *Photo copyright Tomizo Saito.*

Mr. Ando using an axe to cut the stem of the *shimaihagi* to shape. He is wearing the knickers and toe shoes favored by carpenters and construction workers.

The universal work shoes of Japan, tabi consist of calf-length canvas toe socks with thin, soft rubber soles. They are worn by boatbuilders, house carpenters, and even construction workers on highrises. The ability to be nimble and feel the surface underfoot is thought to contribute more to safety than protecting the feet with heavy leather or steel-toed boots.

A foreigner working at a traditional craft is a veritable magnet for the Japanese media, and I've been interviewed many times. I am invariably asked, "What is the most difficult thing about Japanese boatbuilding?" I've responded in many ways, referring initially to techniques that are unknown in the West, or to some peculiar tool I had never used before. However, one day in 2002 when I must have been particularly sore, I suddenly realized what the greatest challenge really was. I told that interviewer, and every interviewer since, "Working on the floor."

In the previous chapter I mentioned Mr. Hatakeyama, builder of dugout canoes in Akita Prefecture. He had completed three dugouts in 1965, keeping one for himself that he used for fishing until about 2000. In 1990 a local Shinto shrine arranged to have him build one last *marukibune*, (literally, "log boat") so that the entire process could be documented on video. He was in his seventies when I interviewed him in 1994 and he mentioned that women were forbidden to enter his shop. He was the first and only boatbuilder to tell me of any kind of restriction on who could enter a workshop.[6]

He went on to explain if a woman entered the shop, or worse, touched any tools, the boatbuilder would have to hire a Shinto priest to purify the space by saying prayers and spreading salt. Yet I know three boatbuilders, two of whom were my teachers, whose wives were essential to their work, assisting their husbands throughout the boatbuilding process. At the end of the interview I asked Mr. Hatakeyama what the shop was now being used for, since he was no longer building boats. He replied that he had converted it into a beauty shop for his daughter. He said this without a trace of irony, and was slow to understand my joke that it was going to take a lot of salt to restore it to a boat shop.

Tools

In all my apprenticeships the boats have been constructed primarily using hand tools, or *dougu*. The materials for each boat arrived rough sawn from the sawmill and from there my teachers and I used power tools very sparingly. While building the tub boat, I saw Mr. Fujii use a hand-held circular saw to rough-cut a few extra staves, and the last thing we did before completing the boat was to bore two holes for a rope oarlock using an electric drill. Otherwise the entire project was finished completely by hand. In Urayasu, Mr. Udagawa had me cut out all the planking for the bekabune using a handsaw and I planed all parts of the boat from rough stock with a hand plane. As we were close to completing the boat, the museum hosting the project gave us a small bandsaw they had purchased for our shop. When Mr. Udagawa told me to cut out the mast partners for our boat with it, I actually objected, saying that since we had come this far working entirely by hand we should see it through to the end that way. He repeated his order and I didn't argue with him, but our bekabune was literally ninety-nine percent hand-built.

With Mr. Fujiwara we used a few more power tools, but again, by Western standards modern tools seemed nearly absent. Instead of using stationary power tools, planking and other parts of the boat were rough-cut using a circular saw. We occasionally used a hand-held electric planer to remove the milling marks from our material, but every piece of the boat still received its final finish with a hand plane. We also had an electric drill on hand, but that was the extent of our power tools.

In Aomori Mr. Ando and I used the same assortment of portable electric hand tools. The only stationary power tool we used was a bandsaw, and only occasionally. His shop had a large joiner and some other stationary equipment, but these tools were rusty from disuse and covered with piles of lumber. Mr. Ando made no effort to use them. He did, however, use a *maigiri*, a hand-operated drill, when he needed to make a small pilot hole; this was easily the most ancient mechanical tool I have seen used in Japan.

Mr. Shimojo in Okinawa was forced to use power tools because of a stroke that had nearly paralyzed his left side. He used a hand-held electric planer and an angle grinder with a sanding disk to shape the semi-dugout sabani we built together, while I often used his hand tools. We had a bandsaw we used mostly at the end of the project for milling parts, along with a stationary planer we used only a few times. Several times during the project Mr. Shimojo reminded me he had built most of his one hundred sabani using just a few hand planes, chisels, and an adze that he had made from the leaf spring of a U.S. Army vehicle.

The lack of power tools was probably due both to circumstances and tradition. The last generation of traditional boatbuilders came of age in the years during and just after World War II. The country had been completely devastated, and modern power equipment would have been all but unknown outside of major cities. When such tools did become available they would have been prohibitively expensive.

The author, right, with Taka Higuchi building a taraibune at the Niigata Prefectural Museum of History in 2002. *Photo copyright Niigata Prefectural Museum of History.*

Few Westerners can appreciate the level of deprivation in postwar Japan: the country experienced almost widespread famine in the late 1940s and the standard of living for most Japanese did not begin to improve until the 1960s. Mr. Udagawa, who lived and worked within ten kilometers of downtown Tokyo, was advised by a visiting relative in 1955 to get a bandsaw. He did, and although there were six boat shops in his fishing community with well over a thousand boats, his bandsaw was the first power tool in Urayasu. Across the Arakawa River in Tokyo proper, Mr. Fujiwara and his father didn't buy their first power tools—a hand-held planer and circular saw—until 1959. They never owned a bandsaw or any stationary power tool. Before the war, most boatbuilders would have been working in circumstances that had remained unchanged for generations.

Japanese hand tools are justifiably famous throughout the world. In the last thirty years Western woodworkers have come to appreciate them for their excellent quality and their ability to produce fine work, even though most Japanese tools available in the West are machine made and mass-produced. In Japan, and in a handful of Japanese tool stores in the West, high quality hand-made tools are available, but at premium prices. All of my teachers considered it essential they use the finest hand tools they could afford. For crucial tools like planes, saws, and chisels, they used only tools with hand-forged blades. In the West, mass-produced hand tools have been in use for so long that woodworkers have little or no frame of reference to compare them in quality and cost to the finest hand-made tools.

In the spring of 2002 I found myself, ironically, with my own "apprentice." Mr. Fujii, who taught me how to build tub boats, had passed away in 1999. Since I had been his only apprentice, his death prompted a discussion locally of how to preserve this craft. When approached by the Kodo Cultural Foundation, I expressed my willingness to teach someone from Sado Island all I had learned. As a result I spent several weeks with Taka Higuchi, a carpenter from Nibo Village, and together we built two tub boats. The Kodo Cultural Foundation partnered with the Niigata Prefectural Museum of History in Nagaoka City, and Taka and I built the first of our tub boats at the museum in conjunction with a large exhibition about these unique boats.

On a day off from our work Taka suggested we drive to Sanjo City, one of the two most famous tool-making centers in Japan (Miki City is the other). Many crafts are found concentrated in particular regions, and one could tell Sanjo was a tool center from the smell of burned metal in the air, distinctly noticeable even at the outskirts of town. Taka had dealt with a tool broker in Sanjo for purchasing his best hand tools. We started by visiting the broker at his home, and he gave us directions to some of the finest shops for saws, chisels, and planes.

The first shop we visited was more of a high-end hardware store, with a complete selection of hand and power tools. We looked around, and finally left without buying anything. Once back in Taka's truck he muttered in disgust, "I hate it when they do that." I had no idea what he was talking about, but Taka asked me if I had noticed the way the shopkeeper had treated us. I said he was maybe a bit aloof, but I didn't notice anything unusual. "He ignored us," Taka said, "because he didn't know us." He explained that professionals buy their tools from a single source, and more than likely their fathers bought their tools from the same store. This shopkeeper was used to recognizing his customers, many of whom may have had a relationship with his family stretching back three or more generations. In essence, we were nobodies, and not worth his time or attention.

Taka's explanation shed light on an interesting experience I had on my first day in Japan in 1990. I arrived in Tokyo and my college roommate, Nobu Hayashi, a native of Hiroshima, took me sightseeing. I had the name of a Tokyo boatbuilder who had been featured in a short article in *WoodenBoat* magazine some years earlier. We located his workshop, and at the end of an immensely informative visit I asked him where he bought his tools. He gave us the name of the shop and drew us a map.

When we arrived we found no showroom, only a wooden door with a smaller door inset at eye level. We knocked and the smaller door snapped open. My friend explained our reason for visiting to a pair of eyes glaring out from the small hatch. The man behind the door asked what I wanted to buy and I replied that I was curious and might I just look? Without a word the door snapped shut, and neither door was ever opened.

If this seems like a poor business strategy, it is perhaps best to think of Japanese tool stores for professionals as akin to exclusive boutiques. With the rise in popularity of Japanese tools, Westerners have learned the best tools are quite expensive. However, nothing can prepare a foreigner for the cost of the *very best* Japanese hand tools. Working with Mr. Udagawa in Urayasu in 2001, I noticed he had two new handsaws of a special type used only by boatbuilders. He had ordered them, he said, because he felt it was important I be trained on the best tools. I asked how much they cost. Mr. Udagawa took one saw in each hand and said, waving his left hand, "This one cost 70,000 yen (at the time approximately $700) and," now waving his right hand, "this one cost 80,000 yen ($800). I was as shocked as Mr. Udagawa was nonplussed.[7]

The second shop Taka and I visited in Sanjo City was well known among craftsmen, and sold nothing but handsaws. The walls were hung with hundreds or different types of saws, from rough blades used to fell trees to the finest saws used by furniture makers. I knew I probably couldn't afford to buy anything, and sure enough, the least expensive saw was priced at three hundred dollars. I was suddenly much more interested in the customer service, and even I could pick up the cues.

The staff, a well-dressed middle aged man and woman, made absolutely no effort to greet or help us. I finally decided to inquire about boatbuilding saws. "Why do you want to know that?" the man asked. I explained I was an American boatbuilder, and was about to explain my work when the woman cried out, "I saw you on television last night!" Taka and I had been on the evening news the night before, and our minor celebrity status suddenly changed the mood in the store.

The man ordered the woman to fetch the blacksmith from his forge in back and soon we were all engaged in an animated conversation about boatbuilding saws. The blacksmith, who was in his seventies, was the father of the store manager. He told me Sanjo's last saw maker specializing in boatbuilding saws had recently retired, but he assured me that he would be happy to make me any type of saw. I thanked him, but before we could go the older man ordered his son to lay a selection of saws on the copy machine and make Xeroxes of their shapes, to make it easier for me to order what I wanted. I knew I could never afford his work, but we appreciated their interest and attention.

Saws

Boatbuilders depend on a particular type of saw I have not seen in any other woodworking trade. Common types of saws come to a squared-off end, but the back of boatbuilding saws tapers down to a point. These saws are used for a fitting technique called *suriawase* (see Chapter 5); the narrow point allows the boatbuilder to remove the saw easily from tight joints. Boatbuilders have two or three versions of this saw, each with a finer set of teeth.[8] My five teachers used almost no other type of handsaw in their work. If they did, these were basic, mass-produced *ryouba*-style saws (rip teeth on one edge and cross cut teeth on the other) bought from local hardware stores or home centers. Like all Japanese saws, boatbuilding saws cut on the pull stroke and have slightly smaller teeth at the tip to facilitate starting a cut.

My teachers called these saws *nokogiri,* which is the common name for small handsaws. They are becoming very hard to get, and their disappearance is linked to the general decline in the craft of traditional boatbuilding. The blacksmiths who make tools and nails specific to boatbuilding have become harder to find than the boatbuilders them-

A selection of boatbuilding saws, from top to bottom: a new saw with very fine teeth for finishing a seam; an older saw showing the effects of years of sharpening; a saw with aggressive teeth for the initial fitting of plank seams.

Mr. Fujiwara's collection of tsubanomi, curved and straight, in a variety of sizes to pilot various sizes of boat nails. The name comes from the tsuba (hilt) at the handle, which the user hits to knock the chisel out of the work.

selves. When I have asked for boatbuilding saws at high quality tool stores, the shopkeepers often do not even know there are specialized saws for the craft. However, there is nothing that would prevent a competent saw maker from making one.

Chisels

Boatbuilders use a standard set of carpenters' chisels, or *nomi,* in their work. These are usually finely made blades of laminated steel with short handles of Japanese oak with steel ferrules. Craftsmen use a regular steel hammer to hit their chisels, not a wooden mallet as is customary in the West. I am accustomed to using my chisels in a variety of ways, sometimes holding them like a pencil, if necessary, when doing fine work, but my teachers all insisted the chisel always be struck with a hammer. My Tokyo teacher stressed that I had to hold the chisel in a fist-like grip and he objected strongly when I pushed it, even though I felt I had more control doing so. The largest Western paring chisel, the slick, is not found in the Japanese boat shop. The Japanese variant, called *tsukinomi*, are used only by house and temple carpenters.

The most unusual chisel, one central to traditional boatbuilding is the *tsubanomi,* or "sword-hilt chisel," used to cut pilot holes for boat nails. A boatbuilder may have a variety of these chisels, some curved, some straight, and even a special version with a concave tip; his collection will match in size the range of nails he uses. The long, narrow chisel used primarily to make pilot holes for boat nails has a double-beveled point. The boat nails, which are made of flat-stock steel, require rectangular holes. Initially, the nail hole is cut by hammering the chisel point into the plank and then carefully wedging out the material. With the final blows the chisel is driven through the material. The heavy poll at the base of the handle (the "sword-hilt" of the name) is struck with a hammer with an upward motion to drive the chisel back out of the work.

My tub boat teacher had just one tsubanomi, a small version that matched the bamboo pegs he used to join his planking. My two teachers on Tokyo Bay built a range of boats, and both had large collections of tsubanomi in a variety of sizes. In the foothills of Gifu Prefecture the last builder of cormorant fishing boats had a peculiar variety of tsubanomi that looked like small pickaxes, with the handles intersecting the steel at a right angle.

Every boatbuilder I have talked with insists the tsubanomi is unique to boatbuilding, and for years I accepted this as true. However, in 2003 I visited Boso no Mura, a large open-air house museum near Narita City outside of Tokyo. The museum had a mockup of the roof construction of a *kura,* or fireproof storehouse, and displayed the tools of the carpenter's trade, including several tsubanomi. Since carpenters also used nails hand-made from square or flat-stock steel in traditional building, it makes sense they would also have used the type of chisel boatbuilders used to pilot rectangular holes.[9]

Planes

Remarkable for its simplicity, the *kanna* is simply a blade held by a wedge in a block of wood. Until the Industrial Revolution, Japanese and Western planes were nearly identical in terms of materials except for the wedge, usually made of wood in the West and iron in Japan. But the era of mass-produced planes led to innovations in the West such as an all-steel body and threaded mechanisms for adjusting

A selection of planes, from top to bottom: a standard plane; a specialty plane for tuning the soles of plane bodies, and a curved bottom plane.

blade depth. Wooden planes do survive in the West, often specialty planes made by boatbuilders for specific tasks such as hollowing the inside face of planking.

Kanna lack an adjustment mechanism, and while that may seem a disadvantage, in fact they are easy to adjust. The blade is first set to nearly the working depth with a few taps of the hammer, and then the wedge is tapped in until it is just back from the blade's edge. Next, the plane is turned upside down and the user sights down the bottom while tapping the blade. Once the edge appears above the throat opening the user tests the depth of cut. If it is too great, the upper corner of the back of the plane body is struck, which retracts the blade. If the cut is too light, the blade is tapped a bit more. The blade is aligned by tapping either back corner of the blade. I have noticed that once my teachers have set up a plane to their satisfaction, they generally leave it alone until the blade has to be removed for sharpening.

Mr. Udagawa made a point of segregating his planes, having one or two adjusted for a more aggressive cut and one set for the final finish. He called this latter plane *shiage*, which means "finishing touches." It conveys exactly the sense of the English terms "finish plane" or "finishing tool." Despite its basic components, the Japanese plane can do remarkably fine work. Mr. Udagawa in particular took great pride in showing me how he could draw his finish plane the length of a sixteen-foot plank, creating a single long shaving so thin it was translucent. Sandpaper is a Western import, although Japanese used sharkskin in the same way. Still, in traditional carpentry the final finish is made using a very sharp hand plane.

My tub boat teacher used two planes: a conventional plane and a hollowing plane, called a *maruganna*, for hollowing the inside faces of the tub boat's staves. My other teachers had no more than four or five standard planes, with

Two views of the *wakitori*, an unusual plane rarely used by boatbuilders, which Mr. Fujiwara used to finish the curved, inside face of boat planking.

perhaps a rabbet plane for finishing grooves along the edge of boards. In Tokyo, Mr. Fujiwara had, in addition to the standard planes and a rabbet plane, a very small plane he jokingly referred to as *akachan* (the baby), as well as a unique plane for smoothing hard-to-reach surfaces. This tool, called a *wakitori,* consisted of a blade identical to the Japanese marking knife, set in a thin piece of wood; I had never heard of it and have only seen one since, at a Tokyo flea market, where I promptly bought it.

The blades of the finest kanna are hand-forged, laminated steel. The very best blades bear the blacksmith's name marked in the steel. For collectors, these signatures confirm the value of antique tools, and experienced tool dealers at flea markets have books listing famous blacksmiths and prices for their tools. I find myself priced out of the true professionals' tool stores in Japan, but over the years I have been able to buy older tools at flea markets and in antique shops, reliable sources also for boatbuilders in the West. My teachers have also generously given me tools. To my knowledge none of my teachers procured tools from anyone but a family member or a professional tool store.

During my second trip to Japan I visited Nobu Hayashi in Hiroshima, who took me to the Dambara section of his native city. Shadowed by a small hill called Hijiyama, it was the only neighborhood in the city center to have survived the full force of the atomic blast. In the midst of modern Hiroshima, Dambara was an amazing glimpse of prewar Japan. In its narrow streets and tiny, wood-framed houses and shops one could still find musty antique shops and impossibly tiny restaurants. My friend and I ate in one that had just three stools for customers, and specialized in a regional dish called *okonomiyaki,* a grilled pancake layered with cabbage, pork, and octopus. After lunch he took me to an antique shop where I found a plane blade in a well-used wooden body. Next to it sat a wooden plane body in good shape with no blade. The price tag on the blade said 3,500 yen, about 35 dollars.

I brought these items to the shop owner, who was talking to my friend. Since I spoke almost no Japanese at the time,

I asked Nobu to tell the owner I wished to buy the blade and the functional plane body. The owner took the blade from me as Nobu talked. He replied, and I could see Nobu's eyebrows lift. "He says you can't have it." I asked Nobu to find out why. They conversed, with Nobu asking very softly and the shop owner answering in short, harsh words.

"He says the plane blade was made by one of the greatest blacksmiths of the Hiroshima region. He says it is not for just anyone to have. He will only sell it to someone who deserves it." At first I cynically thought this must be a sales pitch. Nobu and the owner continued to talk. The answer was always the same: he wasn't selling this plane to just anyone. Finally I said to Nobu, "Tell him I'm a boatbuilder."

His answer was immediate. "He says you can have it," Nobu said with a smile. The turnaround was so bizarre, I assumed that surely the story of "the greatest blacksmith" was not true.

A few days later Nobu and I were sitting in the home of a boatbuilder on the Inland Sea. I had met Mr. Watanabe previously, and Nobu had agreed to go with me to see him again and interpret for my interview with him. As we were winding down our conversation we turned to the subject of buying tools, and I asked Nobu to tell him about our experience buying the plane in the antique store. Mr. Watanabe roared with laughter, "Who ever heard of buying tools in an antique store? That's ridiculous." The plane happened to be in Nobu's car so I went to get it, hoping Mr. Watanabe could unravel the mystery of this strange transaction. He looked at the plane blade and fell silent, his eyes bulging. "This was made by the greatest blacksmith of the Hiroshima region!" he said, falling back in his chair. "What did you pay for it?" I told him. "It's worth at least ten times that," he replied.

Sharpening Stones

Like handsaws, waterstones, called *toishi,* have become very popular in the West. Westerners are more used to synthetic sharpening stones, as opposed to natural stones mined from the mountains. One of my teachers used natural stones, and the best can be the most expensive tool in a woodworker's toolbox. This cost is in proportion to the importance craftsmen place on extremely sharp tools. A dull tool is simply not tolerated and using one is absolutely unthinkable.

Many accounts of traditional apprenticeship describe weeks, even months, of doing nothing but sharpening. In my case, each of my teachers showed me the rudiments of sharpening and then watched me and tested the results. Once they were satisfied we moved on to building the boat. Even so, my early teachers had to remind me when it was time to sharpen the tools; I was not accustomed to such high standards for sharpness, and left to my own devices I would have probably worked two or three times as long with a tool before feeling it was necessary to hone the blade. My teachers had no tolerance for a less-than-perfectly sharpened blade.

To use the waterstone, one places it in a shallow mortise on a wooden block. The block is long enough to rest across a reservoir filled with water. Mr. Fujii sharpened at a concrete basin equipped with a faucet. My other teachers used various sorts of recycled basins, from square cooking oil tins to, in one case, a kitchen pot. Each teacher had several stones of different grits and quality, and when they weren't being used they rested immersed in the basin of water. Usually one wooden holder sufficed for all the stones, but Mr. Fujiwara glued his oldest stones to blocks of wood when they became too thin and fragile.[10]

The material for all my projects started as a pile of roughsawn lumber. Some wood was subsequently shaped using a hand-held power plane, but except for the sabani, all parts of the boats were given a final finish with hand planes. It was generally my job to finish plane these large surfaces. When it came to the planking, my teachers insisted a newly sharpened plane was only sufficient to dress one side of a plank. Sharpening became a task punctuating almost every day in the shop.

Most of my teachers did not let me sharpen the tools they used, except when first teaching me how to sharpen. Obviously, I was responsible for sharpening my own tools. Only Mr. Ando treated me like the traditional apprentice of yore; I was solely responsible for the care and maintenance of all the tools in the shop. At the outset of the project, I spent

Mr. Fujiwara's waterstones. On the right is a natural stone, cut from a mountain near Kyoto. It is the single most expensive tool he owns.

the first several days rehabilitating all of the tools, none of which had been used for over twenty years.[11] On many days Mr. Ando and I worked in a round robin of newly sharpened and freshly dulled tools. When he handed me a plane or chisel, I was expected to have a sharp replacement ready for him. This would sometimes go on for hours at a stretch.

I noticed all of my teachers used copious amounts of water in washing the stone during sharpening. I mention this because Western instructions for how to use waterstones often direct the user to let a slurry of stone particles build up on the surface of the stone as an aid to sharpening. This made sense, and for years that is how I used my artificial waterstones. I was surprised to see my teachers constantly washing their stones with lots of fresh water while sharpening, never letting *any* residue build up.

The key to getting a sharp edge is a steady hand. Unlike their inflexible directives for using chisels, each of my teachers had his own way of gripping the tool for sharpening, but none insisted I do it their way; the results were all that mattered. Each held the blade in his right hand with the thumb underneath and the four fingers on top, pressing the bevel flat to the stone. The left hand steadied the right. They started by pressing the back of the bevel to the stone and then carefully rocking the edge forward until the bevel lay flat. At the moment the edge touched the stone, the blade would expel the water underneath it. This indicated the blade was at the precise angle for sharpening.

Mr. Fujiwara told me to take precisely thirty strokes on the bevel before turning the blade over to take five strokes on the back. The initial sharpening raises a burr at the blade's edge; the passes on the back take this burr off, leaving the edge slightly sharper. This process is repeated until the blade does not seem to get any sharper, and then a finer stone is used.

A pair of sumitsubo, one with a bamboo pen resting on it. Both were made by their owners, both *sukiyadaiku,* or teahouse carpenters, from Kyoto.

Sharpening took place on the floor or ground, in a kneeling position. My teachers relied on just two grades of stone to bring a blade back to life, though it is important to remember that blades were not allowed to get very dull in the first place. A nick in a blade required a great deal of work to repair. In my shop I might use a grinder or a belt sander to quickly remove metal, but my teachers resorted to their coarsest stone and lots of elbow grease, usually mine.

One of the great advantages of synthetic waterstones is how easily they can be flattened. Getting a sharp edge requires honing a perfectly flat bevel and back on the blade. A stone that has been worn hollow, or grooved, simply cannot do this. Synthetic waterstones are relatively soft, and they can be rubbed on a flat, abrasive surface and restored fairly easily. In my shop I use a piece of coarse wet/dry sandpaper soaked in water and laid on a sheet of tempered glass to flatten my stones. A concrete block also works well.

Inkline

One of the iconic tools in the woodworker's collection is the *sumitsubo,* literally, "ink pot." One sees beautifully carved hardwood sumitsubo in museums, sometimes featuring motifs of dragons or tortoises. It is said that a woodworker would show his skill by making a particularly ornate sumitsubo. While all my teachers had sumitsubo, theirs were commercial versions.[12] This particular tool shows the most influence of modern Japan on traditional tool design. Hardware stores sell brightly colored, plastic sumitsubo, featuring spring-loaded lines that retract automatically, an inkwell that seals shut so it cannot spill, and even a holster for hanging the tool on one's belt.

Whether modern or ancient, the sumitsubo consists of a line wound around a wheel, and when pulled, the line passes through a wad of cotton soaked in water-based ink. A small steel pin set in wood or plastic is attached to the end of the line, and is used to anchor the line to the work. Because the sumitsubo puts down a very fine black line, those familiar with the Western chalkline will immediate recognize it as a highly accurate marking tool. The ink is permanent, however, and in boatbuilding all layout is done on rough lumber, since the ink can only be removed by planing.

The sumitsubo is also often used like a plumb bob. In fact, my teachers all depended on a hanging vertical line for setting planks, stems, and so on, but none of them owned a true plumb bob. Instead they hung their sumitsubo or, in one case, a large boat nail tied to a string.

Mr. Fujiwara used his sumitsubo to demonstrate one of the most interesting and difficult layout techniques I have seen. When we had finished hanging the top planks we needed to mark a fair curve along the plank's top edge. He pinned the end of his sumitsubo string to the plank at a point next to the stem and then held the string taut at a point about six feet aft. The middle of the string stood several inches away from the curved face of the plank. He had a point marked on the plank and, holding the string he quickly moved it in a tight circle, releasing it at the top. Instead of snapping the line he was essentially throwing it under tension. Amazingly, the string hit his mark, leaving a fair curve through all three points.

A boatbuilder might wonder why he didn't use a batten to draw this line. A batten would need to have been pinned to the hull, which would have taken more time. In truth, I was so amazed by what he had done I failed to question the reasons behind his method; I suspect that this was something his father had taught him. He had always done it this way, and that was explanation enough. Although he tried to teach me to do it, for him it had become a completely unconscious technique. He was at a loss for words to explain how he did it, and I never managed to get it right.

In addition to an inkline for marking, the boatbuilder uses a *sumisashi*, a bamboo pen that is dipped into an inkwell. The marking edge is cut on a sharp bevel (biased depending on whether the user is right or left handed) and the bamboo is carefully split with a sharp chisel to form stiff hairs at the tip. As the edge dulls with use it is possible to re-cut and split the end. My teachers rarely used pencils or pens.

Carpenter's Square

The *sashigane*, also known as *kanezashi* or *magarigane*, is used for much more than marking right angles. The sashigane has two legs, one 1.6 shaku long and the other .75 shaku, but of equal width, 5 bu (1.5 cm), narrow compared to a Western square. Most, possibly all, boatbuilders incorporate this width in their pantheon of secret dimensions. If a timber requires beveling, for example, it is easy for the builder to lay one leg of the square even with the edge and then strike a line along the inside, creating a five bu setback. There are a myriad of small dimensions I saw my teachers lay out using the width of the square as a guide. This freed them from memorizing many dimensions for various details of their boats.

Mr. Ando preparing to mark a plank using his sashigane, a flexible square made of thin steel, and sumisashi, a bamboo pen with a split, beveled tip. Beside him is his sumitsubo, and inkline that doubles as an inkpot for the pen.

The legs of the sashigane are not made of flat steel, as are Western squares. Instead they have tapered edges that do not touch the work; this prevents the ink from smearing when using the edge to mark a line with the sumisashi. The legs are also extremely flexible, giving one the ability to bend the square into a tight space.

Rule

The most important tool in my apprenticeships and research was my tape measure, graduated in the traditional shaku measuring scale. My teachers appreciated its convenience, but inexplicably, only one of them owned one.

Instead, my first teacher relied entirely on patterns and a length of string for the measure and layout of his tub boats. He told me that it was a particular challenge for him to learn from his own teacher, who, he said, measured everything with his fingers. My remaining teachers relied on their squares for small measurements, including scaling dimensions from drawings, and for longer lengths they had *jougi*, measuring sticks of either 6 or 10 shaku, which they made themselves. These were just straight pieces of cedar, about one inch square, marked off in 1-shaku increments.

Mr. Fujiwara adjusting the angle of a plank using the sagefuri. He reads the horizontal dimension between the string and the stick, which is determined by the plank angle.

Plumb Bob

Boats are comprised of myriad angles. Plank keels have beveled edges; stems and transoms are mounted at particular slopes; planking may flare out from the hull, stand vertically, or cant inward with tumblehome.[13] For boatbuilders, none of these angles are expressed in degrees. Instead, most use a very simple, homemade tool called a *sagefuri*. In older dictionaries sagefuri is defined as a pendulum, while the modern definition is plumb bob.

The sagefuri consists of a straight piece of wood about 2 shaku long, perhaps 5 bu square in section, with a string holding a weight (often a large boat nail) attached at one end. This is laid against the face of a plank, perpendicular to its edge, and extended so that a mark made exactly 1 shaku back from the string end clears the edge of the plank. With the weighted string hanging plumb, the builder takes his carpenters square and, holding it level, measures the horizontal distance from the string to the 1-shaku mark. For a plank leaning further outward, this distance would be greater; for a more upright plank, this distance would be smaller. By knowing and memorizing this horizontal dimension, the boatbuilder can check the angle of any plank and replicate it.[14]

My experience with this tool began with my third teacher, Mr. Fujiwara. Mr. Udagawa made individual patterns out of scrap wood to set plank angles for the small seaweed boat he and I built, although he said he used the sagefuri, which he called *hakarigata* (literally, "measuring pattern") when building larger boats. Interestingly, when I asked Mr. Fujiwara what he called this tool, he said as far as he knew it didn't have a name. A boatbuilder on the Nagara River in Gifu later told me this was a sagefuri, and other boatbuilders I interviewed used this term as well.

Notes

1 One of my teachers told me an old term for a boat shop was *kariya,* but I cannot find any evidence for this except a definition as "temporary structure," so this usage may be purely local. Another boatbuilder called his riverside shop in the mountains of Gifu a *koya,* which means "shed." Along rural stretches of the coast one can still find small boathouses, simply roofs supported by poles, called *funagoya,* literally, "boat shed."

2 The main storage building for over fifty boats in the collection of the Toba Sea Folk Museum in Ise has a rammed earth floor. Originally conceived as an aesthetic element, reminiscent of traditional storehouses, the museum discovered a climate control system was unnecessary for the space; the clay floor absorbs and releases moisture with seasonal changes in humidity, maintaining perfect moisture content for the artifacts housed there.

3 Toshio Odate apprenticed as a young man in Japan with a *tategushi*, or shoji maker, and it was very common in this trade to work at the customer's home. Mr. Odate

has written numerous articles on Japanese woodworking containing fascinating reminiscences of his own apprenticeship.

4 And, like the American four-by-four, they measure three and one-half inches square in section.

5 Mr. Fujii also had among his tools a rare form of workbench used by coopers known as the *hara-ate*. The user actually wears his beautifully sculpted block around his abdomen (*hara* means stomach) and it provides backing for the work and protection as the cooper uses his drawknife.

6 Although the wife of Mr. Shimojo, my teacher in Okinawa, played an active role in the boat shop, he told me that in his youth women were strictly forbidden from getting into a fishing boat.

7 Since that conversation I have made it a point to ask woodworkers about their sources for tools and their cost. In 2002 I asked Mr. Fujiwara what his most expensive tool was. Most he had inherited from his father and grandfather, but he pointed to a new sharpening stone, which he said cost 110,000 yen ($1,100 at the time). Of course, not all boatbuilders spend such sums on tools, but it is important to understand that these men see themselves and their work worthy of the best tools they can afford.

8 Mr. Udagawa referred to his boatbuilding saws for rough work as *chuume* and for finer work as *koba*, from *chuu* (middle, medium) and *ko* (small, fine).

9 Azby Brown, author of *The Genius of Japanese Carpentry: The Secrets of a Craft* (Tuttle Publishing, 1985, 2014) told me his first teacher, a temple carpenter, kept a tsubanomi in his toolbox, and that square-shank spikes are used in temple carpentry, particularly for rafter framing.

10 He had a stone no more than an 1/8 inch thick glued to a wooden block, but given what he may have paid for the stone it was worth the effort. Of the $1,100 stone he bought for our project, I joked that each time I pushed a blade across it, I cost him 100 yen.

11 My Freeman Foundation grant allowed Mr. Fujiwara and Mr. Ando to come out of retirement to teach me. Neither man had built a boat in over twenty years before we worked together.

12 Craftsmen in the West would sometimes build elaborate tool chests as a demonstration of their skills. My first day on the job in Tokyo Mr. Fujiwara had me build myself a tool box in the traditional Japanese style: a simple rectangular box nailed at the corners with a sliding lid. When I told him of the tradition of ornate tool chests he scoffed at the idea, calling it a waste of time and materials. This attitude is not unusual in Japan, where materials are more precious, and most craftsmen, struggling to make a living, had no time to indulge themselves. Their one indulgence might be to fashion an elaborately carved sumitsubo.

13 In Western and Japanese boats, tumblehome is seen at the stern, where the upper planks pass vertical and lean inward at the transom. In an interesting parallel, the Japanese term for this is *kaeru*, which means "to return home."

14 A researcher who studied boatbuilding in southern Shikoku told me this horizontal measurement is called *hiraki*. If the distance is eight sun, for example, the boatbuilder will refer to the resulting angle as "8-sun hiraki."

Mr. Kazuyoshi Fujiwara (foreground middle) confers with a logger while selecting timber for the chokkibune we built in 2002. *Photo copyright Tomizo Saito.*

3

Wood

Japan is blessed with extensive softwood forests that have traditionally supplied the carpentry and boatbuilding trades. Cedar, or *sugi* (*Cryptomeria japonica*), has served as the predominant boatbuilding timber, used primarily for planking but often for stems, transoms, and framing as well. While it is almost unknown in the West to find a traditional boat made entirely from a single type of wood, it is possible to find many Japanese boats made entirely of cedar.

Sugi grows throughout the country, with one of the most famous varieties being Miyazaki cedar from the prefecture of the same name, prized for its quality and strength. It is also called *obisugi*, named after Obi, a small town in the prefecture (now part of present-day Nichinan City) that began intensive forestry during the Edo period (1603–1868) to revitalize the economy. Miyazaki cedar is preferred by the boatbuilders of Okinawa, an island chain that was deforested long ago.[1]

Another term for cedar is *benkousugi. Benkou*, or *benkouzai*, refers to the process of sawing two flat faces on opposite sides of the log. The reason for this is two-fold: it makes the logs easier to stack for transport, and it allows the craftsman to get an idea of the quality of the material. Today the term typically refers to a high quality cedar.[2]

Sometimes planking is of wood specific to the region where the boats were built. The last builder of cormorant fishing boats, in the mountains of Gifu in central Japan, planked all his boats in local *maki,* referring to *kouyamaki*, or Japanese umbrella pine (*Sciadopitys verticillata*); maki is also used to refer to other conifers.

In the West the most common species used for the backbone and frames of boats is oak. Two common types of oak (*kashi*) in Japan are *shirakashi* and *akagashi* (white oak and red oak); they are typically used for paddles and oars, as well as plane bodies and tool handles, but not in the construction of boats. Instead, hinoki, or Japanese cypress (*Chamaecyparis obtusa*) is most often used for framing. Prized by craftsmen for temples, houses, and furniture, it is generally too expensive for the planking of a fishing boat and better suited for beams and sawn frames, where its density gives it greater strength and the ability to hold fastenings. In Tokyo we used hinoki for the stem, transom, sheer planks, and rub rails.

In Aomori the sawn frames of our boat were from a wood my teacher called *hiba,* which in modern dictionaries is considered a synonym for hinoki, while older dictionaries define it as temple juniper (*Juniperus rigida*). Hiba is also a term used to refer to *asunaro* (*Thujopsis dolabrata*), yet another timber very similar to hinoki. In Urayasu we used *kaya* (*Torreya nucifera*), or nutmeg, for beams and the stem.

A Japanese cedar felled in the forests of Ibaraki Prefecture. *Photo copyright Tomizo Saito.*

This dense, marvelously fragrant wood grows well in a vast wetland near Urayasu, but I have never seen it used by boatbuilders anywhere else.[3] In fact, my Tokyo teacher, living just a few miles west of Urayasu, did not use it.

Each of my teachers procured his materials in a slightly different way. My tub boat teacher, Mr. Fujii, bought his cedar directly from a local sawmill, and together we harvested the bamboo for the boat's braided hoops from a grove directly behind his house. My teacher in rural Aomori had the material for our boat harvested on family land. In Tokyo and Urayasu my teachers worked through lumber brokers, although in both cases they personally went to the forest to select the trees. Mr. Udagawa called the lumber broker a *yamashi*. In earlier days this term meant "a person of the mountains" and referred to a logger, a lumber merchant, or a miner. In more recent times the definition has changed to describe an adventurer or a swindler. Mr. Udagawa seemed to prefer the latter definition, and he told me that the relationship between timber broker and boatbuilder was often strained—one trying to inflate the value of the materials and the other pressing to reduce the price.

Old photo shows logs being cut into planks with the *maebiki oga*, a traditional ripsaw. The wide blades of these saws helped them track in a straight line. *Photo copyright Dane Owen.*

An enormous cedar was required for this marukibune, built in 1990 to document the work of Japan's last dugout builder.

Boatbuilders adhere to a variety of traditions governing the selection of timber and its preparation, but as a general rule trees are felled in the winter and, after sawing, the planking is left to air dry for one year. In some cases, craftsmen and sawyers follow an obscure zodiac called *hassen* governing exactly when timber can be cut.[4] Trees are measured at eye level, a process called *medoori,* from *me* (eye) and *tooru,* (to pass through); the circumference of the tree at this height is the tree's measurement. Mr. Udagawa, brought out of retirement to build replica boats for the Urayasu Folk History Museum, procured an enormous cedar ten feet in circumference. He had the log cut into two ten-meter long sections at the base and one six-meter section at the top. From the two lower sections he built two replica *utasebune*, each over thirty feet long, and from the top section he built five smaller *bekabune*, each about fifteen feet long. The tree was 280 years old.

These days logs are sawn on modern bandmills but in the past special craftsmen called *kobiki* were hired to saw them by hand. One end of a log would be propped on a trestle so the sawyer could pass the blade through, working from above or below. Kobiki did not traditionally use a two-man saw, rather a relatively short one-man saw with an extremely wide blade. Called *maebiki,* sometimes *maebiki oga*, these saws are capable of cutting remarkably thin planks out of long logs. The deep body of this saw acts like a keel, ensuring the saw cuts in a straight line.

The era of the kobiki is well within the memory of today's boatbuilders. The builder of dugout canoes required an enormous cedar for his boat. The Shinto shrine sponsoring the project found a tree and had no problem finding elderly loggers to fell it for their documentary video. The loggers then built a sled on site and wedged one end of the log aboard. The idea was to skid the log down the mountain through the snow. At this point the project was forced to give up on tradition, as the gang of elderly men was only able to move the log part way down the mountain before spring snowmelt stopped them. A bulldozer and cables were finally used to deliver the log to the shrine, where a kobiki sawed the log by hand into an enormous square timber. At this point the boat builder took over, and proceeded to hollow and shape the timber entirely with hand tools.

Boatbuilders have their wood flat sawn and then typically sticker the planks in the shape of the log for at least one year. In my experience, it is a universal practice to use the wood symmetrically from the log. The *shiki*, or keel plank, is taken from the widest plank at the center of the log. The two garboard planks are taken from the two planks on either side of the center. The next two planks outward from the center are used for the top planks. This practice makes sense since the material from the center of the log is the widest, but all the boat builders I have talked with instead give as a reason the importance of the parts of the boat being symmetrically aligned with the tree itself. This corresponds closely with principles of Japanese architecture, with strong beliefs that wood for certain building components should come from trees grown on particular cardinal slopes of a mountain.

Of all my teachers, Mr. Shimojo in Okinawa took most seriously the idea that the orientation of the wood in nature governs its use in boatbuilding. He required the butt ends (corresponding to the base of the tree) of all our material be oriented facing the bow. This, he said, was for strength, as the wood near the roots could better absorb the shock of sailing into a sea. The only teacher who took some exception to the symmetrical use of material was Mr. Udagawa. We followed this rule for the keel and garboards of our seaweed boat, but he insisted that we use the clearest wood in the log for the top planks. Those were chosen solely for their beauty.

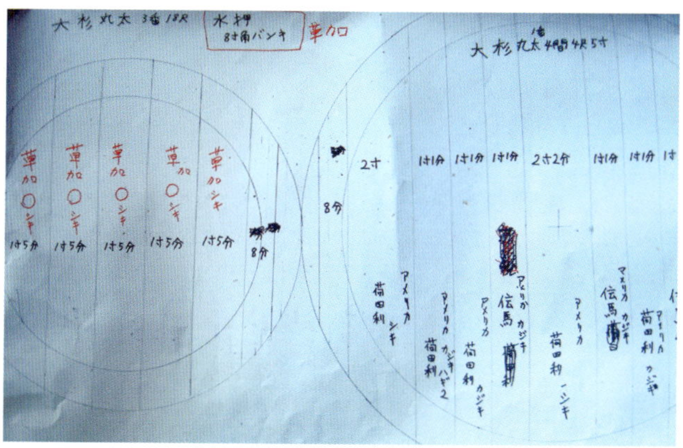

Mr. Fujiwara's instructions to the sawmill, showing the thickness of the planks he wanted. Boatbuilders use the sawn material in the boat starting symmetrically from the center of the log. *Photo copyright Tomizo Saito.*

A bandsaw mill sawing planking for the chokkibune. *Photo copyright Tomizo Saito.*

I have an alternate theory regarding this preference for symmetrical usage. As noted, planking thicknesses are much greater than in Western boats of the same size. As a result, it is much more difficult to manipulate the shape of the material when installing a pair of planks on a boat. Planks taken symmetrically from the log are more likely to bend to the same curve, resulting in a fairer hull.

Another universal rule states the heart sides of all planks in the boat should face the same direction, in or out. Boatbuilders understand that the sapwood is the least rot resistant. In the case of sea boat, it is advantageous to make sure the sapwood encounters salt water, which will help preserve it. For freshwater craft, this rule depends on whether the boatbuilder believes the greatest threat of rot comes from rainwater or from the waters the boat operates in. A boat put under cover daily, or kept in a boathouse, might have the vulnerable sapwood to the inside.

Mr. Fujii, whose tub boats operate in salt water, oriented the bottom planks and staves so that most of the heartwood was on the outside of the hull facing the sea. This was in contradiction to his original training as a cooper; in barrel-making the heartwood is on the inside of the barrel. For him, the rule was consistent whether making boats or barrels: the heartwood faces the liquid.

Notes

1 In 2007 I interviewed a boatbuilder in Miyazaki Prefecture. When I asked if he built boats from this prized local wood, he scoffed, saying "I couldn't afford it. The Okinawans bought it all."

2 A rarer term for benkou-style sawing of logs is *taiko ochi,* referring to the profile of a taiko drum, with its two flat faces connected by rounded sides.

3 The most common use of kaya is for making boards for the game of go. Today the tree is protected in many areas.

4 The only direct experience I have had with hassen is when building tub boats. See Chapter 9 for more on how this zodiac governs the selection and cutting of bamboo.

Beams supporting the hull of the chokkibune. The lower beams were later covered with floor-boards running the length of the hull.

4

Fastening

There is much less internal framing in traditional Japanese boats than in Western boats. Most Western boats are built on a framework consisting of a backbone (keel) and ribs (frames) to which planking (strakes) are attached to form a hull. Most Japanese boats have little internal framing; a strong hull is attained through the use of thicker planking. With little or no framing to attach the planking to, boatbuilders rely instead on edge-fastening the planks to each other, and the craft has developed a variety of specialized tools and techniques for this purpose.

Most traditional boat designs have just two strakes per side after the keel plank. In boats up to about twenty feet the builder can usually find material wide enough to make all of these strakes from single planks. In larger boats, these individual strakes must be composed of several planks joined together. Building wider strakes from their constituent planks is all done on the shop floor. Only when the entire strake is completed is it fitted and hung on the boat.

One unusual type of framing found in Japanese boats are horizontal beams spanning the hull. In the West timbers crossing the hull for support are usually integral to another element of the structure, such as thwarts (seats) or beams supporting a deck. In Japan many types of boats have hulls supported solely by beams with no other internal framing. The bekabune and the chokkibune rely on a series of horizontal beams shouldered against the planking. Their tenons pierce the hull and are wedged to hold them. The hull of the semi-dugout sabani is framed with beams placed at the gunwales.

Western nautical archaeology has uncovered boats edge-fastened with floating wooden tenons (those of the Romans, among others), but beyond this there is simply no counter-

An early yacht built in Hong Kong, imported into the United States and now lying in a boatyard in Noank, Connecticut. Though the planking is fastened to sawn frames and bulkheads, the planks are also edge-nailed to each other.

Close-up of the boat above showing the edge-nailing of the planking. The nail heads are set into simple notches chiseled into the inside face of the planks.

(Left) The heads of the wire nails used in the Hong Kong boat are offset to one side, as are those of Japanese boat nails. (Right) Edge nail in a sailing canoe from Madagascar. *Photo copyright Osamu Monden.*

A selection of copper nails, a mooring ring, and copper tacks, all used in building the chokkibune. Scale increments are sun, about 1 3/16".

part in the West to the practice of edge-nailing large planks to one another.[1] Like many elements of Japanese culture, it is safe to assume these techniques came in some form from China or Korea, either directly or as a native development of earlier foreign influences. However, significant differences exist between Japanese boatbuilding and that of mainland Asia.

In shipbuilding, the Chinese relied on closely spaced bulkheads to which planks were fastened. Some have surmised the Chinese developed the watertight bulkhead based on observation of the regular solid sections within the tubular structure of bamboo. This raises the question of why this technique does not appear in Japan, a culture both familiar with the properties of bamboo and greatly influenced by China. Except for an occasional live well in a small fishing boat, traditional Japanese boats are not sectioned off at all and, at least during the Edo period (1603–1868), even traditional ships had no bulkheads.

I have seen several Chinese-built small boats in which long nails of flat steel are driven though the planking. Rather than penetrating directly into the edge of the bulkhead, the nail shank instead lays along the face of the bulkhead with its tip clenched into the face. This Chinese method is at least reminiscent of, if not the inspiration for the Japanese method of clench-nailing planking.

In Korea an innovation of tongue and groove, or planks edged with shiplaps, was employed. Boatbuilders fastened their planking with trunnels (wooden pegs, or dowels, from the words "tree-nail") inserted from the outside of one plank to the inside of the adjacent plank, at a steep angle through the plank seam. It is certainly plausible that Japanese boatbuilders were exposed to these techniques and then refined them in significant ways.[2] Mr. Osamu Monden, a Japanese filmmaker who has researched boatbuilding and fishing traditions throughout Asia, Polynesia, and the Indian Ocean, has seen boats edge-nailed in places as far-flung as India and Madagascar.[3]

Nails

The common term for nail is *kugi*. Japanese boat nails are made of flat steel or copper stock. They are hand made, and there may be only one company left in all of Japan able to produce even limited quantities. My Tokyo teachers purchased nails from the Omura Bussan Company of Yokohama. In Aomori, my teacher ordered his nails from Yamato Shokai in Onomichi, near Hiroshima. The difficulty in finding boat nails highlights a problem facing traditional boatbuilding: the decline in the craft is exacerbated by the disappearance of craftsmen able to produce the related tools and materials.

While working with Mr. Fujiwara in Tokyo in 2003, an old man came to visit our workshop. I remember noticing the fine new camera that shook in his hands as he took photographs. After watching in silence for a long time, he approached and said, "I made your nails." The man was Mr. Iijima, the blacksmith from Omura Bussan Company in Yokohama. Speaking to me directly, he added, "I've known about you a long time. I made the nails you used in Urayasu."

Mr. Fujiwara was acquainted with Mr. Iijima because, in addition to our nails, he had ordered for me a set of *tsubanomi*, the special chisels for piloting nail holes. The two craftsmen bowed to each other and Mr. Fujiwara ordered me to make coffee and clean the ashtray. Mr. Iijima seemed very pleased with the attention and he relaxed while we took our break. Later, as he prepared to leave, he said to me, laughing, "You'd better hurry and keep building more Japanese boats. I'm not getting any younger."

A complete selection of the galvanized iron nails used for the chokkibune.

The angled head of the kasakugi, or umbrella nail, used by the builder of cormorant fishing boats in Gifu Prefecture.

Two years later I visited Omura Bussan in Yokohama and learned Mr. Iijima had just passed away at age eighty-four. He had made boat nails for the firm for close to seventy years, working until the day he died. This small metal fabrication shop that had been supplying boat nails since 1930 was now selling out its boat-nail inventory. The owner explained, "The younger guys weren't interested in learning."[4]

Mr. Omura explained that his firm's boat nails were made of soft iron (Japan Industrial Standard SS400) and galvanized. Mr. Iijima had produced a full line of boat nails, including some rare types of copper nails. There seems to be no shortage of differences between Kansai (Osaka) and Kanto (Tokyo) culture, and boat nails are no exception. One detail Mr. Omura shared was that nails from Osaka had a semicircular point, while Tokyo nails had an angled point.

I have collected many Japanese boat nails over the years, most gifts from boatbuilders and some pulled from derelict boats. I had one older nail tested by a laboratory, which labeled its hardness as "very soft" at 69.4 HRB scale. The nail was composed of iron (98.5%), with traces of manganese (.91%), carbon (.153%), silicon (.049%), nickel (.038%), sulphur (.024%), chromium (.021%), and phosphorous (.012%). Overall this iron nail would be considered soft, low carbon steel.

In 2006 I visited the last builder of cormorant fishing boats on the Nagara River in Gifu Prefecture. He used a special boat nail with an angled head he called *kasakugi,* literally, "umbrella nail." Although he still had work from time to time (hundreds of thousands of visitors come to Gifu City every year to watch cormorant fishing) he had lost his source for these nails. He told me he had resorted to

The senior blacksmith at Omura Bussan, a machine shop in Yokohama, formerly one of the few firms in Japan manufacturing boat nails. *Photo copyright Tetsuhiro Matsui.*

pulling nails out of several of his older boats that had been wrecked in a typhoon.

There exists a large variety of boat nails, with different names, varying lengths, types of head, head size, and so on. Most are forged from flat stock, thus square or rectangular in cross section, with the head folded over to one side.[5] They taper in both side dimensions and end in a blunt point. Holes are always piloted for these nails using a special set of chisels, as the nails are too soft to drive through wood. In general, nails used to join planks together in a single plane, such as assembling the keel plank, or building up a side plank out of two or more narrower planks, use a small-headed nail. The nail head is buried in a pre-cut mortise that will later be plugged.

Nails used to join different parts of the boat together, such as fastening the lower plank to the keel, or the planking to the transom, have larger heads that are exposed, although the head itself is set into a shallow mortise on the surface of the plank. In some cases nail heads are protected by copper covers or putty. In other specific situations, such as fastening the rub rails to the sheer plank, boatbuilders may use a copper clench nail, also with a large, exposed head offset to one side of the shaft. These nails pass through the rub rail and sheer plank (see Clench-Nailing below), to emerge at the top of a shallow mortise carved on the inside face of the planking, where the protruding tip is then bent over to hook back into the plank.

Older boat nails have shafts tapering gradually from the head to the point, but the nails I have used more recently have shafts tapered over the lower half. Only Mr. Fujiwara was critical of these modern nails, insisting the old nails were better. Modern nails are galvanized; the older ones are not. The tips of the nails are rounded rather than pointed, again because the holes are piloted carefully for the length of the nail.

In the 1990s, Professor Kumi Makino, former research scientist at the Lake Biwa Museum, documented the work of Lake Biwa's last shipwright, Mr. Sanshiro Matsui. The boatbuilder claimed to have soaked his iron nails in seawater before using them, believing the rusted surface gave the nails better holding power.[6]

Another type of fastening, seen commonly in the Tohoku region of northern Japan, is the *kasugai,* or staple.[7] Most Tohoku small craft have large sawn frames supporting the planking, and these frame ends are usually fastened with a square staple that wraps around the frame head, with the legs passing through the planking to the outside of the hull where the tips are then clenched.

Staples were also used extensively for fastening planking on the large coastal sailing vessels that were developed during the Edo period. These ships shared many of the design and construction principles of Japanese small craft (see Chapter 14). Their hulls were frameless, relying instead on athwartship beams shouldered through the hull. The staples were used in conjunction with edge-nailing, with the staples fastened from inside the hull, spanning plank seams and tying them together.

A host of names for boat nails are used throughout Japan, but most can be lumped into one of two categories: small-headed nails used to fasten planks together edge-to-edge, in which the head is buried in a shallow mortise and covered with a plug (*umeki*), and large-headed nails used to join different parts of the boat together (strake-to-strake,

Nail Types

Small-Headed Nails

otoshikugi From one meaning of *otoshi*, a protruding wooden pin for locking doors, these are the smallest of nails, about 2 sun.

nuikugi *Nui* means to pierce with a needle as in sewing, from the verb *nuiawaseru*, to sew.

bouzukugi Likely descriptive of the head of the nail, a *bouzu* being a Buddhist priest, with a shaved head.

happakugi Another small nail (about 2 sun), *happa* meaning "leaf," although not every boatbuilder I have met has used this term for this nail, and all have pronounced it "sappa" instead of the standard Japanese pronunciation.

Large-Headed Nails

toorikugi From the verb *tooru*, "to pass through."

kashirakugi These nails have the largest heads, *kashira*, typically set in shallow mortises on the outside of planking, sometimes covered with sheet copper. There are three head shapes:
- *ichougashira* or "ginko leaf head"
- *marugashira* or "rounded head"
- *kakugashira* or "square head"

kaiorekugi A large-headed, although not necessarily large, nail used to fasten a cap rail, for instance.

kasakugi Literally "umbrella nail," with a flat head at a forty-five degree angle to the shank. I have seen kasakugi only in the cormorant fishing boat. They are used to fasten the edge of the bottom plank to the bottom boards. The slope of the heads roughly matches the angle of the garboard plank.

Other Nail Types

dounokugi Copper nail used for clench nailing, *dou* meaning copper.

aikugi Headless nail pointed at both ends, used to edge fasten planks end-to-end by inserting them into the endgrain of two planks being joined lengthwise. I have only seen these used by a river boatbuilder on the Agano River in Niigata Prefecture.

kasugai A staple, either as a fastening or a clamp (dog).

takekugi Bamboo nail.

hirakugi Literally "flat nail," in fact a headless nail like the aikugi, above.

strake-to-keel, strake-to-transom, etc.). Large-headed nails pass through one plank and into the edge of another.

The chart at left lists terms for a variety of nails, gleaned from many boatbuilders over the years and certainly far from exhaustive. For precise definitions of many of them, I am indebted to Mr. Tetsuhiro Matsui, who for years now been researching and publishing papers on the subject of Japanese boat nails. Mr. Matsui has traveled throughout Japan interviewing boatbuilders and blacksmiths while cataloging regional types of nails.

Wood and Bamboo Fastenings

In several widely dispersed parts of the main island of Japan I have come across wooden fastenings in the form of dovetail keys bridging the seam between planks. The keys are set half the depth of the planking and alternate inside and outside the boat along the plank seam. In some places they are called *tsuzumi,* named after the two-headed drum they resemble. I have seen a small river boat from the Mogami River in Yamagata Prefecture in a museum collection fastened with dovetail keys. I met the last boatbuilder of the Agano River in Niigata Prefecture, who used these fastenings on small river boats. He called them *chikkin,* the local dialect for *chigiri*, from the verb *chigiru*, meaning "to unite" or "to put together." Chigiri is also the name of a wooden spool for thread used in a loom consisting of an axle flanked by large ends, a shape similar to the fastening.

In 2003 I met a father and son on Noto Peninsula, Ishikawa Prefecture, who had been commissioned by a museum to build a replica *chijibune*, essentially a dugout fashioned from large timbers fastened together. These boats are direct descendants of true dugouts, and while the chijibune looks primitive, the elder boatbuilder had made them in the early part of his career before making them out of fiberglass. The planks of the chijibune were fastened with dovetail keys.

By far the most widespread and continued use of dovetail keys in a single region is in building the sabani, the traditional fishing boat of Okinawa, also originally a dugout. When local supplies of large trees were exhausted, the sabani evolved to become either a semi-dugout (a carved bottom with plank sides), or entirely plank construction. Perhaps the remoteness of Okinawa made metal fastenings prohibitively expensive, or the skills required to build dugouts naturally made craftsmen disposed toward wooden fastenings. Whatever the reason, even today the sabani are primarily fastened with dovetail keys, which in the local Okinawan dialect are called *huundu*.[8]

Dovetail key fastenings visible on the hull of an old chijibune, Noto Peninsula, Ishikawa Prefecture.

Wood and bamboo fastenings, from top to bottom: the dovetail key known variously as the huundu, tsuzumi, or chigiri; a bamboo nail from Okinawa; and a small bamboo nail used in building tub boats. Scale increments are sun, about 1 3/16".

The only nails we used in building the taraibune of Sado Island were made of bamboo. These small fastenings, pointed on both ends, act like dowels fitted between planks. Their purpose is to loosely hold parts of the boat together until the hoops securing the staves are fitted. Sabani builders in Okinawa use longer pieces of split bamboo like nails, pinning boat parts together prior to installing huundu.

Nailing

In Chapter 2 I introduced the tsubanomi, or sword-hilt chisel, the tool used by boatbuilders to cut holes for their unique nails. Tsubanomi come in a variety of sizes to suit the various nail lengths and widths, and a typical boatbuilder might have a dozen or more of them. Some are for specific purposes, such as clearing out holes, while others are curved to cut the proper-sized pilot holes for different nails and

Mr. Nasu hitting into the wood and rotating his square-pointed chisel to create rounded nail holes. He hits the wooden handle with a wooden mallet to back the chisel out of the planking. *Photo copyright Tetsuhiro Matsui.*

Mr. Nasu's square pointed chisels he calls mojiri, including versions with a handle and without.

plank widths. While all of my teachers were fastidious about sharpening tools, I only saw one of my teachers ever sharpen a tsubanomi, and even then he simply took a file and made a couple of passes on each edge. Two of my teachers also regularly dipped the points of their tsubanomi in oil to make them easier to withdraw from the wood.

Mr. Nasu, the builder of cormorant fishing boats, had a unique tool he called a *moji*, or *mojiri*. This was a square-tipped chisel with a hole in the center for inserting a T-handle. He used this tool to make his nail holes, hitting the back of the chisel and rotating the tool with the handle after each hammer blow. In this way he piloted a crude round hole for his nails. I have not seen this tool elsewhere in Japan but Mr. Matsui, the nail researcher, assured me they were used by other craftsmen. G. R. G. Worcester also mentions them in his book on Chinese boatbuilding, *The Junks and Sampans of the Yangtze* (Naval Institute Press, 1971).

Edge nails enter through a shallow mortise cut to a depth of about one-third to one-half the plank's thickness. The sides of the mortises flare slightly, narrowing to the width of the nail head. Once the mortises are cut the plank is stood on edge, wedged tight in notches cut into the short sawhorses on the floor of the shop. A pilot hole is then chiseled from the plank edge back to the base of the mortise. It is crucial that the hole provide a snug fit, as the nail will have no holding power in an oversized hole. To accomplish this a chisel of the proper size is held upright in one hand and its point placed about 1/4" to one side of the center mark for the hole; it is tapped lightly and then hit on the hilt to withdraw it. The chisel is then moved 1/4" to the other side of the mark and tapped again. This time the chisel is tilted back so the point of the tsubanomi levers out a small chunk of wood between the two cuts. This leaves a small rectangular hole that should match very closely the size of the shank of the nail. The chisel is held upright again, this time biased just slightly to one corner of the hole. It is struck two or three times, usually enough to see it emerge from the base of the mortise. Finally, the hilt is struck in a direction away from the work to remove the point.

The other plank is clamped on edge the same way and the bottom of the nail hole is piloted using the same method.

Tip of a tsubanomi laid over a nail, showing how the proper tool should compare in size. The boatbuilder chisels a hole slightly less than the length of the nail.

A cross section showing a small-headed nail used to join planks edge-to-edge. Note the slight curve of the nail and the angled base of the mortise.

Mr. Fujiwara and the author cutting pilot holes in the planking. *Photo copyright Tomizo Saito.*

With the holes finished, the two plank seams are ready for final fitting, called *suriawase* (see Chapter 5), after which they can be nailed together. Prior to nailing, with the planks clamped a final pass would be made with a curved tsubanomi to ensure the alignment of the entire pilot hole.

Boat nails come from the blacksmith perfectly straight, but they must be curved slightly for use. To create the proper curve Mr. Udagawa would lay one nail on the shop floor like an anvil, and another on top of it. Striking the top nail he would bend it to the curve he wanted. Mr. Fujiwara placed his nails on a small anvil and hit them solidly along the middle of the shank. The ends would lift up as the metal was stretched.

Working with Mr. Udagawa, Mr. Fujiwara, and Mr. Ando, it was my job to curve the nails. From all three my introduction to the task consisted of a quick demonstration and a request to get started bending more. I would do my best to make nails with the proper curve, but I recall Mr. Fujiwara initially throwing more than half of them back at me with a simple corrective: "Wrong!" He was driving nails very quickly, and I was not producing proper nails fast enough to keep up. I soon lost my concentration and felt like I was just hammering nails, handing them to him and hoping for the best. Finally he stopped and took the time to coach me in some detail. They needed only a slight curve to set smoothly into the pilot holes; I was bending them too much. I quickly traced the shape of a correctly curved nail and kept it in front of me as a guide.

Like their ingrained ability to bend nails to the correct curve, these three craftsmen could all cut perfect umeki, mortise plugs. They used scraps of cedar cut to length and with two or three sharp blows from a wide chisel they could make a perfectly tapered, dovetailed plug. This was all the

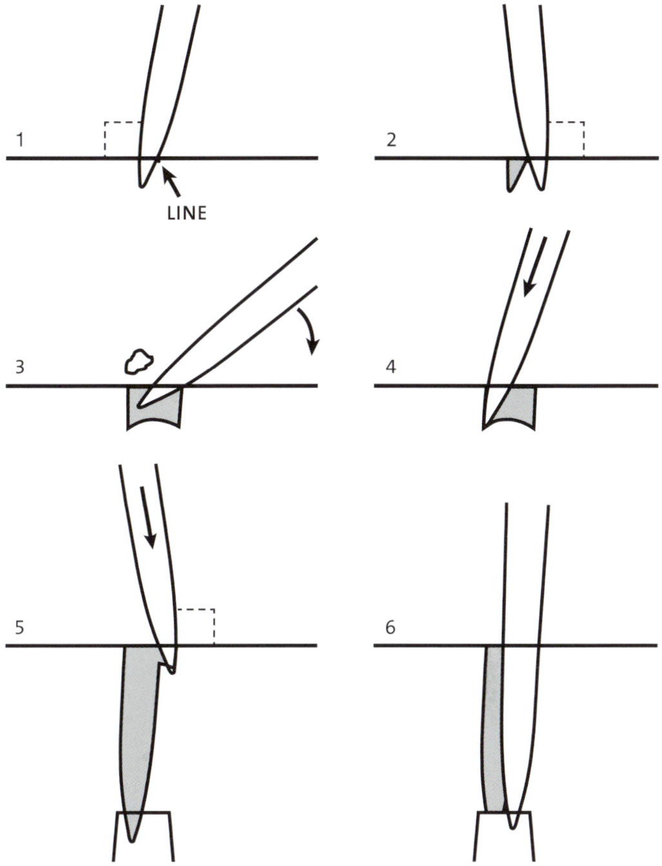

To chisel a nail hole from the plank edge through to the mortise: Set the point of the chisel just to one side of the line (1), tilt so that the outside bevel is at right angles to the plank edge, and make a shallow cut. Place the chisel on the other side of the line leaning the opposite way. Cut again (2) and lever the material out (3). Set the leaning chisel in one side of the hole and drive it (4). The chisel should straighten as it penetrates the plank and the tip emerges from the base of the mortise. Move the chisel to the opposite side of the hole (5) and hammer. It should cut material from the side of the hole (6) and reach the base of the mortise.

After the mortise is cut in the face of the plank, the tsubanomi is used to cut a rectangular hole from the plank edge through to the base of the mortise.

A plug covers a nail mortise in the shimaihagi. Set tight but without glue, the grain orientation of the plug is opposite that of the surrounding planking, ensuring it will swell and remain tight.

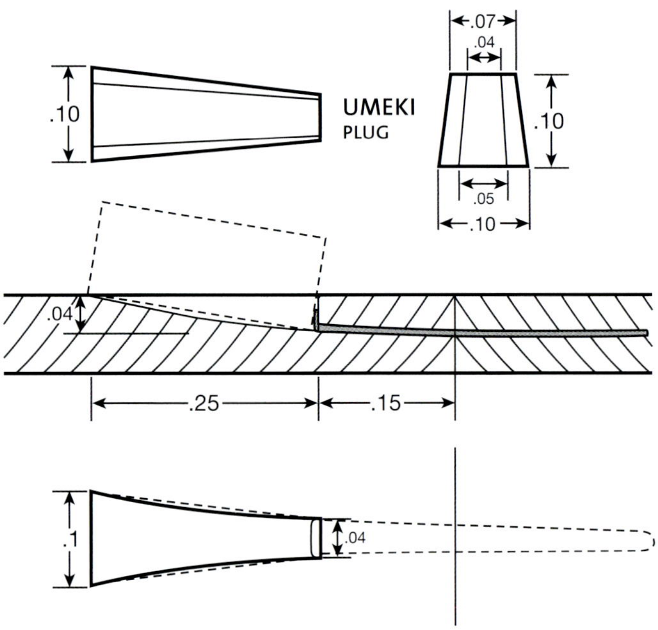

Diagram of Mr. Ando's edge-nailing showing: top, the dimensions of the plug, or umeki; middle, a cross section of the planking with the umeki shown with dotted lines; and bottom, the plan view of the mortise and nail. All dimensions in shaku.

more remarkable because they did not lay out the shape of their mortises; they cut them freehand. I learned early on to make small patterns for a variety of components to keep my work consistent. I struggled to make my first plug fit, but once I had it I kept it as a pattern for all my subsequent plugs. Mr. Fujiwara smiled watching me make these patterns, but it was the only way I could match the consistency of his work.

The plugs are of course driven in with a hammer, and since they enter the mortise at a very shallow angle the forward edge has to be held tightly down with the thumb so

Mr. Ando using his curved tsubanomi to make the final cut of a pilot hole through both planks. The two pieces are held together by a pair of staples, or dogs, a type of clamp used by most boatbuilders.

they get a bite on the dovetailed sides and stay deep in the mortise. None of my teachers put glue in the mortises. The grain of the plugs is at right angles to the grain of the planking, and once immersed the plugs will swell tighter than the surrounding wood.

Mr. Udagawa and I trimmed our plugs flush with his largest chisel, but Mr. Fujiwara and Mr. Ando both used an adze. Only after the plugs were trimmed did we give the planks their final finish with a hand plane.

Clench-Nailing

For the bekabune and chokkibune copper clench nails were used to fasten the rub rails through the top planking (see Chapters 10 and 11 for photos and drawings of clench-nailing these boats). The results were aesthetically remarkable, and made Western clench-nailing seem crude by comparison. We pre-bored tight-fitting holes through the rub rails and planks using tsubanomi. Our copper nails were then driven at right angles to the face of the rub rail. These nails were more than twice as long as the thickness of the two timbers they passed through. We carved shallow mortises directly below where the nails exited, and bent the nails partially down. Before completely bending them, we bent the nail tips ninety degrees. Then the nail was hammered flat into the mortise, with the bent tip burying itself in the end of the mortise.

Mr. Fujiwara trimming plugs with his adze.

The side planks of the chokkibune were also nailed this way at the chine. The nail entered at right angles to the sheer plank, emerged from the inside face of the bottom plank, and then was bent down into a mortise cut in the inside face of the planking. I had some trouble coming up with a precise term in Japanese for this type of planking. Mr. Fujiwara could not think of a specific term for the technique, but Mr. Udagawa eventually settled on *shimetsukeru*, a compound of the verbs *shimeru* (to tie, or to fasten), and *tsukeru* (to attach). Since he came up with this term only after much prompting, it is unlikely the word would be recognized by other Japanese boatbuilders.

Notes

1. One exception is strip-planking, in which narrow strips of wood are used to build a hull. Most boats built this way today tend to be small, such as canoes and kayaks, and the strips are glued to each other. Early strip-planked boats were fastened with nails driven through each strip and into the preceding strips.
2. See Horace H. Underwood, *Korean Boats and Ships*, Yonsei University Press, 1979, p 25. Underwood also references a Japanese scholar who claimed Korean shipwrights were brought to Japan in ancient times to teach shipbuilding.
3. Mr. Osamu Monden runs Studio Umi in Tokyo and he has made many documentary films about southeast Asian maritime traditions (www.umikoubou.co.jp).
4. According to Tetsuhiro Matsui, Yamata Shokai, the other nail source mentioned, has also closed, leaving only a small metal fabricator in Tomonoura, Hiroshima Prefecture, as the last firm in the country making boat nails. However, a competent blacksmith should be able to forge these nails if provided with specifications.
5. Mr. Fujiwara complained that the smaller headed nails were superior in the old days because the head hooked back slightly on itself, which he thought allowed it to bind better in the nail hole. The heads of our nails were at a right angle to their shafts.
6. See Kumi Makino, *Marukobune: The Traditional Sailing Boats in the Lake Biwa Region, Japan* (*Biwako no Dentouteki Mokuzousen no Henyou: Marukobune wo Chuushin ni*), Yuzankaku, 2013.
7. Kasugai also means a clamp, that is, a staple-like tool driven into two pieces of wood to temporarily fasten them together. Though the pronunciation is the same, in written Japanese the characters are different for kasugai as a clamp or staple. In England these tools are called cramps; in America, dogs.
8. Although the origins of the word huundu are unknown, it might be derived from *fudou*, a measuring weight whose shape it resembles.

Mr. Fujiwara doing suriawase on planks braced to low horses by props wedged to the ceiling. Visible directly underneath him is a wedge that adjusts the seam opening so the saw does not bind. It is important to cut evenly through the seam, as evidenced by the consistent amount of sawdust alongside it.

5
Fitting Planks

Because Japanese boats are built without caulking, some of the most important techniques of the craft are those ensuring the planks and other parts come together with a watertight fit. Foremost among these is a technique variously called *suriawase, surinoko,* or *tooshinoko*. Suriawase is a compound of the verbs *suru*, meaning "to rub" or "to polish," and *awaseru*, "to fit" or "to join together." As a compound verb it can also mean "to lap" (as in metal polishing) or "to reconcile." The *noko* of surinoko and tooshinoko means "saw," as in the word for handsaw, *nokogiri*. I have heard the term surinoko used primarily by boatbuilders in western Japan. My teacher in Aomori, in the far north near Hokkaido, used the term tooshinoko (which he pronounced *toosunoko*), and, like many of the boatbuilding terms he used, it is probably specific to that region. *Toosu* means "to force through" or "to pierce," and becomes tooshinoko when combined with the noun.

The basic principle of the technique will be familiar to woodworkers in the West. To create a tight fit between two pieces of wood a saw is run through the joint. The saw cuts a parallel-sided channel, or kerf. After each pass of the saw, the two pieces of wood are moved closer together. With each successive pass the high points of the mating edges are cut away and the joint becomes a progressively better fit.

In Western woodworking this technique is used far less often, almost regarded as a trick in fitting. Among Japanese boatbuilders, however, it is highly refined, employed regularly, and among the most time-consuming and important skills for the apprentice to master. My teachers and I used saws to fit the boards making up the keel, to fit the joints connecting the stem and transom to the keel, to fit the plank seams, and to fit the planks at the transom and the stem. In short, every seam requiring a watertight fit was prepared by making multiple passes with a series of special saws. In addition, much of the joinery used in construction relied on variations of this sawing technique to get tight fits.

Preparation

In most cases the seams of the keel plank (if the keel is made up of more than one board) are fitted first, with the work done on the shop floor. My teachers did not make any special effort when rough sawing to make the edges to be joined absolutely straight. Most readers would assume that when joining two planks one would cut the first plank, carefully plane the edge straight, then do the same with the mating edge of the second plank. In Tokyo, Mr. Fujiwara cut one edge of his material to his inkline using his circular saw, and then placed the cut plank on top of the other stock to trace his second cut line. I noticed during the course of our project some of our longer seams had a slight curve, but this method of fitting planks works regardless, even along a curved edge.

Mr. Fujiwara was not particularly concerned with avoiding knots when laying out the plank seams.[1] Loose knots throughout the boat were chiseled out and filled with square plugs, but when a hard knot was exposed in a seam, we would stand the plank on edge and cut a series of parallel kerfs about 1/8th inch deep in the knot on the face of the edge. This weakened the hard material so it would not bind when rubbing the seam with the saw blade.

To square the edges, Mr. Fujiwara set the planks on edge, and we planed square the two sawn edges we were about to fit. We worked fairly quickly at this, moving down the plank edges planing and checking our work with a square, but we made no attempt to join (straighten) the edge. With the edges squared we prepared for our edge-nailing by laying out our nail locations, cutting mortises for the nail heads, and piloting the nail holes.

The planks were placed flat, side-by-side, on very low horses, with the side intended to face the water turned upward. Each horse, essentially a beam laid across the shop floor, had a notch in the middle to allow the saw blade to pass through, and the seam to be worked on was aligned above these gaps. The planks were braced solidly to the beams overhead with very stout props, about two inches square in section, but were not anchored so tightly that the planks could not be adjusted by tapping their outside edges with a hammer.

Mr. Fujiwara believed the tip of the saw protruding from beneath the planks would be liable to whipsaw just a bit, creating a slightly wider opening on the underside of the seam. In effect, we would not be cutting a perfectly uniform kerf, but a very slight inverted V-shape, which meant the plank edges would not meet square. For this reason he took an additional small step I did not see my other teachers do: he slipped a very thin shim under the planks on the horses on either side of the seam.[2] These shims lifted the edges of the planks less than one millimeter where they met, which he believed compensated for any whipsaw effect.

Sawing

In fitting a seam by suriawase, the initial pass is necessarily the roughest. This pass cuts through the high spots where the edges may meet, and the boatbuilder uses a standard sawing motion to aggressively remove material. As he proceeds, the kerfing process begins to even out the seam. After the first pass, the boatbuilder closes the seam just a bit: too much and the saw will bind on the next pass; too little and the overall process will be slowed. We used a metal hammer to tap the outer edges of one plank, and used our caulking irons sometimes to pry them open. These adjustments have to be learned by experience, but by far the most difficult part of suriawase is the sawing method itself.

As the fit of the planks improves, the technique changes from an angled sawing motion—in which the teeth are pulled back and forth through the seam—to one in which the saw is moved parallel to the face of the planks. Holding the saw steady at about a forty-five degree angle to the work, the saw is moved forward and back in the seam rather than up and down through it; thus the same teeth stay in contact with the seam. Perhaps the best description of this action is closer to the definition of *suru* as "to rub."

Boatbuilders believe rubbing the saw parallel to the plank face is essential because the teeth of the saw leave tiny grooves in the wood. Grooves left by a normal sawing motion cross the plank edges diagonally from one face to the other (what will be the inside and outside of the hull), and thus can channel water through the seam. For a proper fit, the saw teeth must move horizontally with the plank edges so the grooves remain parallel to the plank faces. This feels very unnatural; it is surprising how ingrained the "normal" sawing motion is, and how quickly the body rebels against any deviation. Suriawase is one technique in boatbuilding where an experienced woodworker is at a disadvantage, as I am sure a novice could more easily adjust to it.

When first practicing suriawase, I would sometimes unconsciously revert to an angled sawing motion and ruin a nearly completed joint. Or I might rub the saw the length of a seam properly, only to withdraw it with a sawing motion at the end, again, ruining the joint. My teachers told me the saw's tapered end was designed both so the saw can be more easily inserted into a seam, but also to facilitate removal. The proper action after completing a pass is to raise the saw very slowly while rubbing the seam until just the small tip is still inserted. Then, reaching down and grasping the tip, remove it from the seam by *pushing the saw away* from you in order to minimize scratching across the joint.

The suriawase process consists of multiple passes with either two or three different saws, each with successively smaller teeth and making a finer cut. We tried to saw using roughly the middle of the blade in the kerf, sometimes dropping the saw below a forty-five degree angle, when necessary, to cut through tight spots. We worked a seam in both directions, several times, before changing to a finer saw. Mr.

The author preparing a seam on a plank. Sawing bent over at the waist is hard, tiring work, and progressing backwards one has to carefully withdraw the saw before taking up a new position on the other side of the props.

Fujiwara told me one reason we changed directions was because it was necessary to slowly raise the saw when passing the horses, and he felt approaching from either direction reconciled any unevenness in our work.

Mr. Fujiwara cautioned me not to create a dam of sawdust as I worked. The saw tends to bind in these dams he said, forcing the boatbuilder to revert to a back-and-forth sawing method to clear the obstruction and, as a result, the edges at this spot will need more rubbing. The goal, ultimately, is to move along the edge rubbing the seam as evenly as possible. Mr. Fujiwara tried to get three good passes rubbing with each of two types of saws. He always reversed direction on his final pass with each saw.

When working, we stood astride the planks, bent over so our backs were nearly parallel to the floor. We grasped the saw handle with both hands, like a baseball bat, and moved the saw using only our arms, while our upper bodies remained frozen. From where our feet were planted we could rub no more than perhaps three feet of a seam before having to stop and, stepping backwards, reposition ourselves. Often the kerf was tight enough so I could support the saw handle with my fingertips while I stepped back. I developed a bad habit of letting go of the saw, thinking the seam was tight enough to hold it up. When it fell, it levered the blade out from between the planks and Mr. Fujiwara would correct me, both for mishandling the tools and for ruining that section of the seam.

As we refined the fit of the seams, all my teachers would make only the slightest adjustment of the planks with the hammer; just the barest tap on the outside edge of the plank was sufficient to close the gap the tiny amount needed prior to the next pass. In fact, toward the end of this process Mr. Fujiwara would actually tap the planks closer using just the back of his saw. For all of my teachers preparing the plank seams was a careful, painstaking process. We normally spent half a day rubbing a seam on a twenty to thirty foot plank.

Mr. Fujiwara was, by far, the most stringent of my teachers about proper suriawase. Early on he insisted I remove the planks from their props after each pass so he could inspect my work. The slightest evidence of poor workmanship meant the seam had to be closed tighter on the horses and essentially the work started anew. It took several weeks before he felt he could trust my work without breaking down the setup for periodic inspection, but at no point in the seven months we worked together did he not inspect my final plank edges.

Mr. Fujiwara was always ready to comment on how I could improve my technique often adding, cryptically, that

Unlike conventional Japanese saws, those used for suriawase have blades that taper at the tip. The concave profile of the teeth, best seen in the saw at the bottom, was Mr. Fujiwara's innovation. Part of the tip has broken off the top saw.

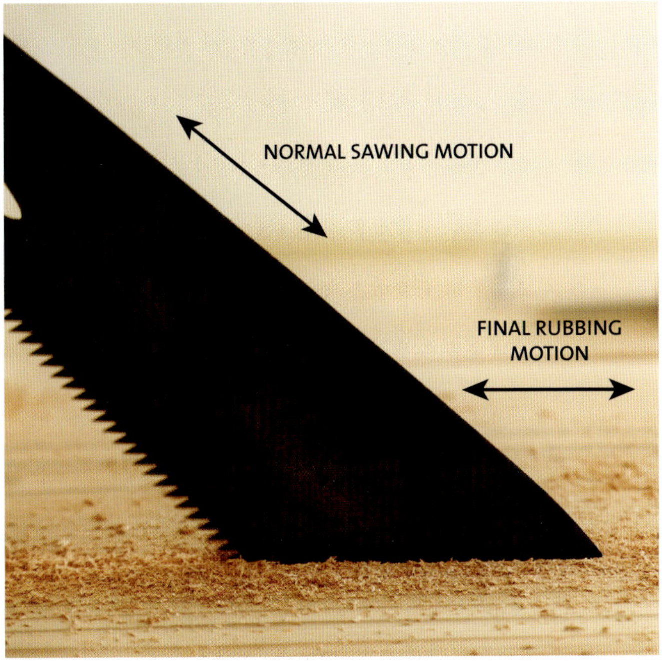

The two types of sawing motion used in suriawase. The angled arrow shows the conventional sawing motion used initially, while the horizontal arrow shows the motion particular to this technique used in final fitting. The saw remains held at an angle but is "rubbed" horizontally. *Photo copyright Kim Sajik.*

Detail of the plank edge after properly completed suriawase. Note how all the striations left by the saw run lengthwise along the plank edge. The rectangular hole is for one of the edge nails.

Japanese-Canadian Boatbuilding

In the mid-1990s I had the opportunity to meet and interview the last remaining Japanese-Canadian boatbuilders of Steveston, British Columbia. Steveston had been the center of the Japanese community in the Vancouver area since the first immigrants arrived, mainly from Wakayama Prefecture, in the early 1900s. Upon arrival, many immigrants worked in the large fish canneries in the area, and later entered the fishing industry and eventually the boatbuilding trade. The Murakami House and Murakami Boatworks, along with the Kishi Family Boatworks, are today preserved by the City of Richmond as part of thc Brittannia Shipyard Heritage Site.[3]

During my research, I met with a half-dozen elderly Japanese-Canadian men who were the last of what was once a flourishing boatbuilding community. At the outset of World War II, all of them were interned by the Canadian government and sent with their families to camps, or scattered among farms from the Okanagan in British Columbia to Alberta to work in agriculture. These families lost everything they had as a result of internment. Furthermore, the Canadian government did not lift the restrictions on Japanese living along the coast until some five years after the war ended. The men I spoke to were among the few who managed to return and reestablish their boat shops.

These men built Western-style draggers and gillnet boats, and while all but one of the men I interviewed had been born in Canada, they used mainly traditional Japanese tools purchased in Vancouver. The boats were carvel (smooth) planked, fastened to steam-bent oak frames. Perhaps the biggest surprise from my conversations with them was learning they used suriawase to fit the planking. As the hulls were planked up each successive plank was spiled (measured), cut to shape, and clamped next to the previous plank. The boatbuilder then carefully ran a saw down the seam, taking special care as the blade passed each frame. After each pass the plank would be tapped tighter to its neighbor and the process would continue until the builder was satisfied with the fit.

I am not aware of any other tradition of carvel boatbuilding using a technique like this. The men also told me they built bulkheads in their boats by edge-nailing them, exactly the same way Japanese boatbuilders edge-nail their planking. Their distinctive trapezoidal plugs can be seen in the bulkheads of these Japanese-Canadian built fishing boats.[4]

The Murakami Shipyard in Steveston, British Columbia, now a historic site administered by the City of Richmond. Before the war Steveston was the center of the Japanese-Canadian community.

Mr. Sakamoto standing in front of a fishing boat he built. He was among a handful of Japanese-Canadian boatbuilders who managed to reestablish his shop in Steveston following his internment.

Fishing boat built by Japanese-Canadians prior to World War II in Steveston. These builders fit the planking of their boats tightly using suriawase, with no caulking. *Photo copyright Robert Critchley.*

we had just this one chance to work together, and I had to master suriawase. In fact, after one particularly strict lesson I wrote the following notes in my journal:

1. Important not to twist the saw.
2. Keep moving with the cut, always stopping the sawing in a different place so as to overlap the points where the saw is removed from the seam.
3. Keep the strokes even, three good passes with each type of saw, always reverse direction on the final pass.
4. Withdraw the saw backwards, pushing away from the body.

Mr. Fujiwara's saws exhibited a peculiar innovation: he preferred their cutting edges to be slightly concave. In fact, boatbuilders' saws are sold with a slightly convex edge, but as Mr. Fujiwara sharpened them he would work this shape out. He believed this shape gave the tip a finer taper (which it did, ever so slightly) and this was useful for inserting and removing the saw.

Fitting the Seams

After all the preparation lavished on the plank seam, it may seem shocking that the next crucial fitting technique for the boatbuilder is to pound both edges with a hammer. Called *kigoroshi*, literally, "wood killing," the purpose is to crush the fibers of the two mating surfaces. Done just before planks are clamped and nailed, the two edges will squeeze against one another when fastened tightly. The joint will become even tighter as the pounded wood fibers rebound from the compression.

Mr. Fujiwara doing kigoroshi one side of the edge while the author follows, pounding the other side. Note the author is using both hands, to help control the angle of the hammer, which is critical. *Photo copyright Tomizo Saito.*

Japanese metal hammers have two faces, one flat and one convex, with the latter used in kigoroshi. The key to this technique is to evenly strike the edge of the planks, using overlapping blows of the hammer, working the middle of the edge only, and *never touching the corners.* This produces a slight concavity and when the planks are clamped together the corners of the edges are like unsupported peaks, and so are crushed against one another by clamping. Any minute gap left in the seam at this point will be filled by the swollen wood fibers.

While Mr. Fujiwara painstakingly taught, observed, and critiqued my suriawase technique, he said very little about kigoroshi other than to caution me from hitting the corners of the plank edge. We stood the planks back on edge, wedged in the notches of our sawhorses. We worked together hammering the planks on opposite sides of the edge and moving one after the other along the length of the plank. To make the proper concavity, we had to angle the hammer blows slightly, something I found difficult. The only instruction I was given was to make sure each hammer blow overlapped the previous one. It seemed like a job Mr. Fujiwara wanted to get over with, and he seemed to hurry his work at the end.

This was in contrast to Mr. Udagawa. In building the seaweed boat he usually demonstrated a facet of the construction two or three times and then left the work for me. Of all the techniques he taught me, kigoroshi was the one he seemed *most* concerned about. Perhaps it was because the planking of this boat was very thin, and therefore the margin for error was so much more critical, but he watched

Detail of plank edge after properly completed kigoroshi. Note the slight concave in the center of the plank, tapering gently upward toward the face of the plank on each side, which remains untouched by the hammer.

Seizo Ando fitting the seam between the garboard and sheer plank. The wedges he used to carefully open the seam are visible in the foreground. It is critical the saw be held at a precise angle. It is very easy for the saw to wander and begin to cut into either plank. *Photo copyright Masaaki Kon.*

me like a hawk while I hammered, cautioning me again and again to be more careful. I would proceed alongside the plank, working one side of the edge, and then come back on the other side of the plank, working the other side of the edge. In essence I created a groove in the plank edge one half at a time. Actually this makes sense, because it is critical that the hammer strike at a specific angle. The difficulty is getting that angle correct and consistent. Trying to pound a groove all in one pass, alternating the angle of the hammer with each swing, would be extremely difficult.

Kigoroshi is ninety percent control and ten percent force. Neither of my teachers actually swung the hammer with much power. It was far more about controlling the angle of the strike and basically letting the hammer fall mainly of its own weight. Japanese cedar is very soft and it doesn't take much force to dent the wood. Mr. Udagawa insisted that no hammer mark be visible. The goal, he explained, was to create a smooth groove, and this meant the blows had to overlap at least by half the width of the hammer head. They also, of course, had to be consistent, at the proper angle, and so on. Weeks later at the launch of our boat, despite his effusive public praise for my work, Mr. Udagawa nevertheless took me aside at one point and told me, in a very serious tone, "You still have to work on your kigoroshi."

Another application of this technique is in making plugs. Mr. Udagawa and Mr. Fujiwara both made square or rectangular plugs for our boats. Mostly these were used to fill knots in the planking that we chiseled out. In both cases I was taught to cut plugs slightly oversize, then pound all four faces with a hammer over an anvil until they fit the mortise tightly. I then pounded them in without glue. Mr. Ando had me make round plugs, again slightly oversized. I hammered them as well but we glued them in place. Mr. Shimojo had me carefully clean out knots in the planking and carve tapered plugs to fit. I did not hammer the plugs but drove them in tight with glue.

Fitting Seams on the Boat

Above I described suriawase as it pertains to parts fabricated off the boat. Fitting the seams for the plank keel, the lower and upper planks (if made up of more than one piece of wood), and piecing together the transom are all done on the shop floor.

Once the actual planking begins, finishing the seams with suriawase has to be done on the boat itself. With the backbone of the boat—the stem, keel, and transom assembly—firmly braced, the lower planks are temporarily propped against the keel; the boatbuilder then does suriawase, working the saw the length of the garboard seam. The saw is now rubbing between the keel and first plank, and over the length of the boat this seam is a long, curving, constantly changing bevel. The greatest danger here is the saw running out of the kerf and cutting into the planking, a mistake both my teachers and I sometimes made.

Mr. Ando holding the blade to support his saw as he uses its tip to fit the plank at the stem rabbet of the shimaihagi. The tapered end of the saw is narrow enough to fit in the seam (which cannot be wedged open) and also to travel down the curved line of the rabbet joint.

Planks were sometimes hung in place and then removed if a large adjustment had to be made. Suriawase was done to get the final fit, and I have never seen or heard of a boatbuilder removing the planks before fastening to do kigoroshi. Probably one reason is that given the beveled edges, it would simply be too hard to do this correctly. Also, none of my teachers ever bothered to pull a plank off to inspect the quality of the seams; when they were satisfied with the fit we left the plank propped in place and began fastening.

Because the seam between the lower plank and the keel lies below the waterline, it receives the most attention. I noted my teacher in Aomori spent four hours on each of the garboard seams, and I was working with him most of that time. He also spent several hours at the stem, using just the tip of his saw, which he held by the handle and the blade, to painstakingly fit the planking into the rabbet. Similarly, I remember Mr. Fujiwara spending hours seated beneath the chine, rubbing the seam between the upper and lower planks.

On smaller boats and in tight spaces, a boatbuilder might work from inside or outside the boat. I have noticed in these situations the process was not quite as painstakingly done as when working on the shop floor. This might be because of the inherent limits of attempting to fit seams in situ before fastening, or because the boatbuilder recognizes that seams above the waterline are not as critical.[5]

Notes

1 For Mr. Fujiwara it was more important to get the maximum amount from our material than to avoid using knots. All of my teachers used their material extremely frugally. The props we used were made from the offcut edges of our planking stock, and in Mr. Fujiwara's case, these were later cut up and served as fuel when we bent our planks over fire. Thrift is an obvious value in the boat shop; all the materials are expensive and Japan's last generation of boatbuilders came of age during an era of extreme privation.

2 Mr. Fujiwara told me, however, these shims were to be used only when working with wide planking. They were unnecessary when preparing the seams of narrow planks.

3 Information on this historic site can be found at: www.richmond.ca

4 I am grateful to Robert Critchley of Sayward Valley, Vancouver Island, British Columbia, for sharing information about the two prewar Japanese-built boats he owns.

5 The first time I watched and studied this method was while building a small seaweed-gathering boat in Urayasu. I marveled at the care we lavished on the seams, thinking any boat built of cedar would swell tight in no time after launching. But my teacher warned me that at launching we would rock the boat from side to side, immersing the chines to check for leaks, and this would be a public display of our skills.

The chokkibune built by Mr. Fujiwara and the author being propelled by the Japanese sculling oar called ro. In urban areas these oars traditionally were not made by boatbuilders but by specialist craftsmen, of whom only a few are still active.

6

Propulsion

The Sculling Oar

My first experience with *ro,* the sculling oar, was in the early 1990s, when renting a small boat on a mountain lake above the city of Nikko. The fleet consisted of about twenty fiberglass dinghies with Western oars and four or five older boats with sculling oars. The owner rebuffed my request for a traditional boat, saying it was not possible for a foreigner to use the Japanese ro, a point he stressed by commenting that he didn't want to be bothered to have to go out on the lake to tow me in. I persisted and finally we struck a deal: I would pay for a full hour's rental if he would just take the first ten minutes and scull the boat back and forth in front of the dock so I could see how it was done. I would then take the boat for just twenty more minutes. After a few false starts I managed to get the boat going and made a lap around the lake. The owner gave me a grudging compliment as I returned his boat.

Like much traditional Japanese technology, the ro is almost certainly a product of ancient China. A number of scholars have placed the invention of the *yuloh,* the Chinese sculling oar, in the Yangtze basin of southeastern China. The late China scholar Joseph Needham identified paintings showing the sculling oar as far back as the Han dynasty (206 BC–220 AD). Scholars have suggested the sculling oar may have come to Japan during one of two migrations of Chinese culture: with the introduction of rice cultivation around 100 BC, or during the Nara period (710–794), when Buddhism arrived.[1]

Today in the heart of Tokyo, a volunteer group teaches the public how to use the ro and the Japanese paddle, or *kai.* A canal park runs through the Koto-ward of Tokyo, near the city's eastern border with the Arakawa River. This part of Tokyo and much of the city were historically criss-crossed by canals. Since World War II the surviving waterways

A man and boy scull a boat in China using the *yuloh*. The boy is assisting by pulling on the rope lanyard rather than the oar itself. Photo taken in 1921 by Eleanor Shaw and Charles Hudson Sayre Merrill. *Photo copyright Louisa Cameron.*

A parade of most of the Wasen Tomo no Kai fleet traveling through a new river park in Koto-ward, Tokyo. Even a single sculler can easily move a large boat fully loaded with passengers. *Photo copyright Atsushi Doi.*

A ro resting on its pin. The block attached to the blade is tapered to match the angle of the ro when in use, and the curvature allows the blade to rotate freely. The hole has to be large enough for the block to swivel over the pin.

The author sculling the chokkibune *Doreen* at her launching in 2003. *Photo copyright Atsushi Doi.*

have been lined with concrete or steel sheet piles, and run as straight as an arrow for miles across the city. Koto-ward, however, turned a half-mile stretch of one canal into a pleasant park, with plantings and walkways along the shore, giving the waterway itself a slightly sinuous run. It terminates at a man-made wetland that has become a haven for birdwatchers on the riverfront of a great metropolis.

In the early 1990s a festival to commemorate the park was organized, and the ward office asked retired boatmen to find traditional boats to lend a historical atmosphere to the celebrations. A few boats were obtained and the festival was a success. Soon after, the boatmen petitioned the ward office for official sponsorship of their newly conceived volunteer group, Wasen Tomo no Kai, best translated as Friends of Traditional Japanese Boats. Since its formation they have operated a fleet of boats, giving free rides twice a week in the canal park and teaching the public traditional boating skills. The chokkibune I built in 2003 with Mr. Fujiwara was donated by the Freeman Foundation to Wasen Tomo no Kai, who reciprocated by christening her *Doreen,* in honor of Mrs. Doreen Freeman.[2]

A common saying among boatmen in Japan is that it takes three months to learn how to use the ro, and three years to master the kai. At first glance it seems the order should be reversed, but the elderly members of Wasen Tomo no Kai quickly dispel that notion when wielding their paddles, some of them over ten feet long, with incredible dexterity. Part of the genius of the ro, on the other hand, is how its design makes it largely self-tending. Resting on a hardwood block tapered to the proper angle, the oar rolls from side to side on a pin extending vertically from the block. The offset handle helps to feather the blade automatically, while a rope attached to the forward end of the handle helps guide the arc of the sculling motion. Once the user gets comfortable, working the ro is not much more complicated than pushing and pulling the handle.

Both my Tokyo teachers depended on ro craftsmen for their sculling oars, and had no idea themselves how to make one. Mr. Fujiwara, with whom I built two boats, heard in the late 1990s that the last ro maker of Tokyo was retiring and, recognizing the potential loss, apprenticed with him. The teacher at the time was in his eighties and the student was in his late sixties. As we discussed the design and construction of ro Mr. Fujiwara described his "apprenticeship" with the older craftsman. Rooting around in a drawer for his drawings he muttered, "These drawings are not very good. He only gave me thirty minutes of his time." Thirty minutes! What he laid out in front of me were two pages of his rough sketches with the principal dimensions of the ro noted. My teacher had been left largely on his own to figure out the intricacies of actually making it.

My late friend Mr. Tomizo Saito, the former captain of Wasen Tomo no Kai, told me that the first four ro Mr. Fujiwara made for the club were considered subpar and were now used only as spares. After these first attempts, Mr. Fujiwara made five more successful ro, one for each of the fleet's boats, and Mr. Saito gave me a chart he had created showing the principal dimensions of all nine, along with their weights. He told me one of the most important dimensions of the ro defined the balance point, which should be twenty to thirty inches aft of the socket. In addition to these dimensions, I also found one published drawing of a ro with a thirteen-foot blade that included more details, such as the thicknesses and widths of the various parts.

Using the ro is a revelation. Since building *Doreen* with Mr. Fujiwara I have sculled her many miles and I can say it takes far less energy to do so than had she been powered with anything like Western oars. She is a heavily built boat, about thirty feet long, yet I can move her fully loaded with passengers with next to no physical strain. Sculling properly requires relaxing and not muscling the ro through its motions. The movement is a leaning forward and backward on the balls of the feet, using the large muscles of the thighs more than the arms and shoulders.

A basic mistake of the beginner is to feather the blade incorrectly and generate lift instead of thrust. The ro will immediately pop off its post and is heavy enough that it will take some effort to set it right again. The rental boat on which I first used a ro had a wire bale looped over the oar at the socket to help hold it in place.

Once underway, the benefits of the Japanese sculling oar become apparent. First, unlike oars that spend half their time in the air on the return stroke, the ro applies almost constant thrust. The only time it does not provide power is at either end of the stroke. The angle of the handle means the user does not have to physically twist the blade; since the handle is not on the centerline of the blade it automatically rotates. Furthermore, the socket for the pin is carefully rounded to aid the rotation. The rope leader is always kept taut, and counteracts the twisting force. The end of the handle when sculling describes an arc limited by the rope. At slow speeds the rower has to concentrate on lifting the handle slightly to keep the rope taut, but once the blade begins to bite, its thrust keeps pressure on the rope. Perhaps the most important feature of the rope is that it resists the thrust being applied by the blade. With Western oars the force of the thrust is borne directly by the rower with the arms and shoulders. With the ro the thrust of the blade acts to lift the handle, a force held in check by the rope. That is a good thing, since the surface area of the ro is far larger than a pair of standard oars, and a lot of thrust is being created.

The only time the ro is ever lifted from the water and feathered is when turning the boat. Then the handle is pushed down, the rope falls slack, and the stern is essentially rowed around. In multi-ro boats the oarsmen do not necessarily have to keep the same cadence; however the side-to-side motion of the rower when sculling at high speed can begin to rock the boat. Because the ro works astern, a boat can be navigated through a waterway only a bit wider than its own hull. The major disadvantage of the ro is that since its long blade can reach three to four feet deep, it cannot be used in shallow waters. Also, unlike oars, ro cannot generate

To maneuver the chokkibune in close quarters the rower uses his paddle. He is using a sculling motion, letting the thrust hold the loom of the paddle against the gunwale.

Whaleboat replica racing in Muroto, Kochi Prefecture. These multi-ro boats, called *sekobune,* were the fast chaser boats in the shore whaling fleets. Today teams In Muroto race them in an annual festival. *Photo copyright Meguru Tada.*

One advantage of the *ro* is that it can be worked by two persons if necessary. Historic photographs show enormous ro wielded by up to three or four people.

Two sockets, a handle, and a pin. The socket on the right is an old style from Mr. Fujiwara's family. While iron pins do exist, they eventually wear out the socket, which is difficult to make. Mr. Fujiwara insisted on wooden pins, since they are much easier to replace than sockets.

The joint between the ro loom and blade was traditionally bound with rope, later with galvanized wire. Today they are often attached with carriage bolts, which allows breaking down the oar for storage onboard.

reverse thrust to move a boat backwards or to slow or stop a boat. In close quarters or shallows, Japanese boatmen rely on the paddle, often using it like a pole.

Making and Using the Sculling Oar

The ro consists of four pieces (see below): the *roshita* (blade); the *ireko* (socket); the *roude* (loom); and the *rozuku* (handle). The handle and loom are attached at an angle with a double-tenoned joint bound with either hemp line or wire. Builders today sometimes use carriage bolts. The joint is also angled slightly so the longitudinal centerline of the blade is slightly different than the centerline of the loom. The most common location for the ro is to the port side of the stern of the boat, and the socket drops onto a small post, called the *rogui,* made of either hard oak or iron. The angle of the loom brings the handle slightly inboard for ease of use. Finally, a rope (*hayao*) is fastened to the bottom of the boat and a loop is thrown over the handle. On larger boats using multiple ro, rogui are mounted on the ends of athwartship beams which cross the boat at the sheer and project over the sides.

The two main types of ro are *tomoro* (stern mounted) and *wakiro* (side mounted). Varieties of Japanese oak are usually used to make ro. In the Tokyo and Osaka region white oak is used for the handle, loom, and socket, while red oak is used for the blade. In northern Japan ro-makers use a wood called *asuza*.[3] There is an advantage to using the heavier woods in the blade as the balance of the ro is critical, and a blade that sinks is advantageous.

The geometry of the ro is critical to its success, and a variety of factors may determine its design; the length of the boat, the height of the rogui off the water, the height of the oarsman, and conditions of use all have to be taken into account. The heavy section of the loom, for instance, acts as a counterweight to the blade, giving the overall ro the proper balance. It is difficult to come up with standard dimensions or proportions for ro since every boatbuilder I have talked to has a different formula. A paper written by two university professors mentions a length ranging from 1.5 to 2.1 meters for the loom and 4.2 to 5.5 meters for the

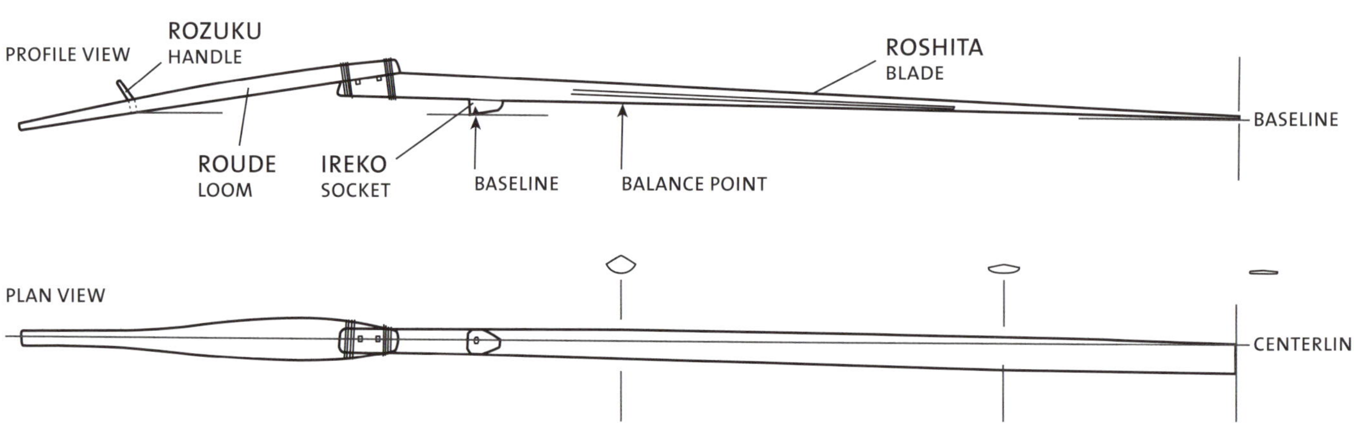

The ro, or sculling oar, used throughout Japan for propelling small craft. While almost certainly a derivation of the Chinese yuloh, it has some unique features distinguishing it from its Chinese forebears.

blade.[4] A boatbuilder on Lake Biwa told me the ratio of distance from the end of the loom to the socket and from the socket to the blade tip should be 5.4 to 10.

When I set out to build my first ro I based my design on the last one built by Mr. Fujiwara, and planned to test it sculling one of the replica whaleboats in the collection of Mystic Seaport Museum.[5] The blade of the ro is usually made of flat grain material to give it strength at its thinnest edges.[6] I used ash, and my blade tapered from 3 1/2 inches at its thickest point, in the area of the socket, to 5/8 inches at the tip. Most ro I have seen have no real foil shape at the tip, which is almost flat. Further up the blade the cross-section develops a peak on its top (the face that generates the thrust) with a rounded bottom. The latter is necessary because at the end of each stroke the blade feathers—or more properly, pivots—rolling almost ninety degrees before the return stroke. This round section decreases turbulence when the blade is feathered.

The loom is quite large and thick, traditionally featuring an elongated teardrop shape. Though it needs to be strong at the connection to the blade, the shape is more for providing mass to counterbalance the weight of the blade aft of the socket. The loom has a perfectly flat bottom and the handle is usually raked strongly forward. The handle is through-tenoned to the loom and Mr. Fujiwara told me the ro maker he talked to said that the distance from the handle to the end of the loom should be the same as the shoulder width of the user.

If there is one critical element in making ro, it would be the angle of the loom to blade connection. The ro is largely self-feathering. While the beginner is inclined to muscle the blade from one stroke to another, in fact all that is required is a push and pull. The ro feathers itself because the handle is offset, so pushing or pulling on the end of the handle causes the blade to rotate on its central axis. The shape of the socket, the rope, and the resistance of the water control the amount of rotation. If the ro were one piece and perfectly straight the user would have to physically twist the blade (like a Western sculling oar), and if the angle between the loom and blade were too great, more force would be spent twisting the blade and less in sweeping it from side to side.[7]

The published drawing I mentioned earlier did not give this angle and I did not know if I could reliably scale it. Luckily, Mr. Fujiwara's teacher had given him this critical piece of information. The angle was derived using a right triangle with two legs of 8.5 sun and 1.3 sun (10 1/8 inches by 1 1/2 inches, respectively). This works out to an angle of about nine degrees. This angle is planed on the top of the blade and the flat bottom of the loom rests on top of it. Originally a pair of floating tenons was used in this connection and the two pieces were bound with two wrappings of hemp rope. More recent ro are wrapped with galvanized wire, and now some ro are fastened with a pair of carriage bolts. I decided on the latter, as I wanted to have the ability to easily break down my ro for onboard storage.

As mentioned earlier, another critical angle is the offset of the loom to bring the handle inboard. Mr. Fujiwara was very particular about this point, and he explained that a string stretched along the centerline of the loom should intersect a point 8 bu inside the corner of the blade's tip. I fastened my loom with a single half-inch carriage bolt and then set the ro upright on a pair of sawhorses. I ran a string from the end of the loom to the point at the port corner at the end of the blade. I then pivoted the loom on the bolt slowly, checking with a square held to a centerline on the bottom of the loom, until the string lined up. Then I drilled for the second bolt and traced where the blade lay against the loom. Taking it apart, I routed about 1/8 inch out of the bottom of the loom for the blade to set in. This was my own innovation as I thought this shoulder would stiffen the connection.

At this point I bolted the blade and loom together and weighed them. Despite following the dimensions my ro tipped the scale at a whopping sixty-six pounds. According to the chart of Fujiwara's nine ro, two of his ro weighed 46.2 pounds and one weighed just 24.2 pounds! Next I checked the balance point, since Mr. Saito had been so insistent this separated a good ro from a bad one. I realized I needed to remove material from the loom to get it right so I took the ro apart and began planing. In the end I got the weight under sixty pounds and the balance point where Mr. Saito had said it should be, between 20 and 30 inches aft of the socket.

The socket is very critical as it not only provides the means, with the pin, to connect the ro to the boat, but its shape also helps the blade feather properly. The bottom surface of the socket is rounded so the ro can smoothly rotate on its axis. The angle of this face in profile should correspond to the angle of the ro resting on the beam when sculling. The shape of the hole receiving the pin has to be oval so the socket can rotate freely over the pin without binding. This includes allowing enough freedom for the ro blade to be lifted out of the water when turning. The face of the socket meeting the blade is perfectly flat, and in that area of the blade the center is left flat as well, or in some cases the blade is mortised slightly to accept the socket. Floating tenons are again used, but in Mr. Fujiwara's case one tenon

The socket is slid on a dovetailed tenon fastened to the bottom of the blade. Another tenon passes through the socket into a mortise in the blade and is wedged tight.

is a dovetail the socket slides on to; a second tenon is then driven through the body of the socket into the blade and the tenon is wedged. The hard corners on the forward and aft faces of the socket are chamfered generously.

The pin is never fastened or glued as it will wear out and need to be replaced. I have seen some iron pins in Japan, but they tended to wear out the socket, which is considerably more work to replace. The beams too, which are often softwood in Japanese boatbuilding, sometimes have a removable insert at the base of the pin since this surface also wears out.

The rope is also very important for the proper use of the ro. I tied off the rope so it kept the end of the loom at about the height of my stomach, which I learned from the members of Wasen Tomo no Kai. When rowing, the rope is looped around the handle and anchored to the bottom of the boat directly below the centerline of the ro, and slightly aft of the handle when the ro is in a neutral position. Running aft it tends to direct a bit of back pressure against the pin, which helps keep the ro in place. The members of Wasen Tomo no Kai insist the rope be led *outboard* of the loom before being looped over the handle. I cannot think what difference this makes, but I have learned that in Japan certain absolutes do not necessarily come with explanations. When I asked I received the expected answer: "Because that's the way it is done."

In keeping with Japanese tradition, my ro has no finish. In fact, until a generation or two ago most Japanese wooden boats were not painted at all, and I cannot remember ever seeing anywhere in Japan a painted or oiled sculling oar or paddle, except for ornamentation on festival boats.

In 2007 as part of the WoodenBoat Show at Mystic Seaport, I was ready to try my ro. First I had to modify the boat. Because whaleboats are double-ended I lashed a beam across

The author using a *ro* on one of Mystic Seaport's whaleboats. The pin is mounted to a beam clamped to the stern deck. *Photo copyright Catherine Wood Brooks.*

the gunwale at the stern and mounted a pin in the beam a few inches outboard of the rail. I stood aft and was able to comfortably scull the whaleboat (normally rowed by six men) with several passengers, around the Mystic River estuary. The biggest disadvantage of my ro was its weight, but given how the ro works this was of little consequence. The only time it mattered was when taking the ro on and off the boat.

I had been taught to let the boat roll slightly when sculling to increase the sweep of the blade and gain more thrust. This has to be done with care, because too much roll and the rocking hull generates turbulence. Keeping the roll in sync with the stroke takes practice. The beginner first needs to understand which way the blade should feather, and the handle makes twisting the ro easy. The only other conscious effort the beginner needs to make is to maintain upward pressure on the handle to keep the rope taut. Pushing down on a pair of oars to lift them out of the water at the end of the stroke is an embedded habit, and an easy mistake to make at first with the ro. If the rope goes slack and a mistake is made feathering, giving the blade a chance to develop lift, the ro pops off its pin. Once the user gets comfortable the overall motion becomes just a push and pull stroke, letting the offset handle rotate the ro, automatically feathering the blade.

For readers interested in building a ro for their own boat, I suggest beginning by sketching a scale profile of the stern of the vessel, with the heights of the pin, the cockpit sole and the waterline. My ro has a loom-to-blade ratio of roughly 1:3 with the aforementioned angle of nine degrees at the joint.

The comfortable working height for the handle is at the navel (so they say in Japan) and assuming one wants at least one-third of the blade in the water, the user should be able to work out the dimensions needed to fit the boat. If length ratios deviate greatly from mine in order for the ro to work properly, one should not be concerned; other boatbuilders and published reports quote widely different ratios from those used by my teacher. Since craftsmen invariably insist their methods are superior to all others, I don't see why the reader can't adopt the same attitude! I believe the angle and the balance point of the ro should be the builder's primary concerns. I also believe softwoods could be used for less expensive prototypes, or even for finished ro.

Over the years Westerners have flirted with Asian sculling oars as auxiliary power on cruising sailboats. Authors and cruising sailors such as Roger Taylor and Lynn and Larry Pardey[8] have experimented extensively with, and written about, both Asian and Western sculling oars. An internet search for the Chinese term yuloh will lead one to much more information.[9] The Pardeys over the years have probably developed the very simplest and easiest big boat sculling setup by essentially giving their sweep oar two functions. In their book they describe mounting an oarlock on one rail in the stern quarter so they can stand and row facing forward while controlling the tiller with one leg. They then use this same oar, passed through an oarlock on the transom, as a sculling oar. Pardey specifically mentions that a bent oar (like the ro) is advantageous for its self-feathering capabilities, and they use a simple freeboard height-to-length ratio of roughly 1:4, or a length such that the oar is about forty degrees to horizontal. In his book he says his wife can easily scull *Taliesin*—29 feet, 6 inches on deck and displacing 17,900 pounds—up to 1.5 knots under calm conditions.

The most radical reinterpretation of the ro is by my friend Mr. Atsushi Doi, a retired pilot for Japan Airlines, who probably spent many hours musing about his design on trans-Pacific flights. He fixated on the drag created when the ro blade turns at the end of each stroke. Mr. Doi believed if the ro's blade was oriented vertically rather than horizontally it would result in less resistance when feathering. The vertical orientation of the blade is, in fact, how Western oars are traditionally used when sculling.[10] Changing the orientation of the blade turns the geometry of the ro on its head. First, the handle's offset now points up rather than down, which limits the scale of Mr. Doi's ro, since in larger sizes the handle becomes too high to operate. The rope also has to be mounted to a tab projecting from the underside of the loom. Undaunted, Mr. Doi has made

Atsushi Doi's ro in use. Note the winglet attached to the end of the blade, designed to twist the blade and reduce vortices at the tip. Mr. Doi is seated in the bow of his boat *May Drums,* which he also designed and built.

over twenty versions, all scaled for small Western-style dinghies like his own boat. He has even tried to improve the efficiency of the blade. Realizing the tip of the blade creates drag vortices (like the wingtips of the early Boeing 747s he captained), he devised a winglet that fits over the end of the blade. It is designed to actually twist the blade as the user sculls to improve the overall efficiency. Mr. Doi claims his ro design results in greater efficiency and speed, and greater self-tending characteristics.

I first met Mr. Doi when he visited our workshop in Tokyo in 2002. He brought along a small model of his ro and enthusiastically showed it to us. Later I asked Mr. Fujiwara what he thought of this "new and improved" ro. He remained silent. Craftsman of Mr. Fujiwara's generation tend to be conservative in the face of radical change, and I suppose what had worked for generations of his family seemed good enough. Mr. Doi, however, was undeterred: he has been granted patents for his new and improved ro in the United States, New Zealand, Australia, England, and Japan.

Mr. Seo at work in his shop in Onomichi, Hiroshima Prefecture. He specializes in making ro and kai, and may be one of only three such craftsmen left today. *Photo copyright Linda Ohama.*

Tourist tub boats in Moto Ogi harbor, Sado Island. The kai passes through a simple rope loop and the user sculls from the bow of the boat, either standing or kneeling.

In one village on Sado Island most of the tub boats are powered by outboard motors. The author was told this was because the fishing grounds were too far from the village to paddle.

Through an article in the *Nikkei Shinbun* newspaper I learned about Mr. Toyoaki Seo, a ro maker on the Inland Sea. In many ways his story typifies not only the difficulties in pinning down hard and fast answers when it comes to Japanese boatbuilding, but also the uncertain future of the entire craft. Mr. Seo stated categorically that he is the last ro craftsman in Japan. This is not quite true, but the number of professional ro makers left nationwide numbers no more than a handful (I know of three) and they are so dispersed today they almost certainly do not know one another. The secrecy I mentioned before does not foster any dissemination of information, let alone networking, and the steady disappearance of craftsmen has furthered this isolation. Mr. Seo's description of how he became a ro maker alludes to this decline:

> After I graduated from high school I started to help my father. I got married, had a baby and became a ro craftsman to feed my family. I never considered letting my sons succeed me, because it is an unstable job. My father never wanted me to succeed him. Now I understand my father's feelings very well.[11]

Mr. Seo says it takes him three days to make a ro by hand, though orders have tapered off.[12] "I suppose young people have never seen or used a ro," he mused. He added, "It will not take more than ten years to become a ro craftsman if one just sticks to it." The reader shouldn't be discouraged by Mr. Seo's time frame. I prefer to take his final words as an admonition to be respectful, and not daunted, by the subtleties of this venerable oar.

The Paddle

The Japanese paddle, *kai,* is typically about four feet long, with a T-handle and a wide blade. White oak seems to be the preferred material for making them.[13] Used with a variety of small boats, they are the primary means of propulsion for the tub boats of Sado Island, where I gained experience making and using them. The paddler holds the kai at the bow and sculls it, pushing water under the boat to propel it forward.

Elsewhere in Japan the kai tends to be longer and narrower, and sometimes are used to pole a boat. In city canals kai were used for moving boats in crowded anchorages. With the loom bearing on the edge of the boat a paddle can be worked in a sculling motion to move a boat sideways. Paddles can also be used like a Western canoe paddle. The length of the kai may be based on the depth of the water or proportional to the user's height. Mr. Fujiwara told me

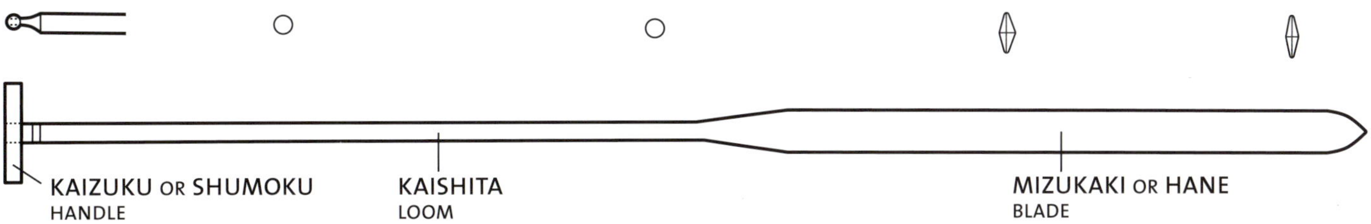

Typical kai, or paddle, used throughout Japan in various sizes. All feature a T-handle with the shaft through-tenoned.

a short kai would be 9.5 shaku (about 9 feet 6 inches) long and used in canals about one-third as deep.

One odd variant of the kai is the *nejikai*, or "twist paddle," which I have heard mentioned by only a few people and seen only on the Noto Peninsula. A boatbuilder there built a small boat he called *chijibune* that used nejikai. The nejikai is a two-piece sculling oar in which the loom, the upper part of the oar, has an odd, rounded hourglass shape. It probably works like the conventional ro but evolved into its present shape from local custom. Unfortunately I did not see it in use and all the chijibune of this region I saw were rotting in the harbors.

Paddle used on Miyoshi River boats in Hiroshima Prefecture. An unusual feature is the attached block, allowing it to be used like a sculling oar.

Multi-Oared Boats

Kaidenma refers to a class of boats propelled by large kai, wielded exactly like a Western oar, with the rowers seated facing aft and grasping the T-handle. In lieu of oarlocks the kai are passed through a rope loop. These days kaidenma are almost always festival boats with many oarsmen, often competing in races. The paddle is much shorter than a Western oar and so the stroke is extremely fast. A racing kaidenma is capable of great speed. In Kushimoto City in Wakayama Prefecture the tradition of racing kaidenma celebrates the fast passage of messages by boat during a clan war hundreds of years ago.

Using the kai like a Western oar is more widespread among working boats in the north. In 2003 I traveled almost the entire coastline of the Tohoku region, and saw some limited use of kaidenma in Akita and Aomori Prefectures. The boat I built with Mr. Ando in Aomori was based on his design from the period before the use of outboard motors, and we made a large paddle, which hung from a rope loop mounted on the after quarter of the boat's rail. Like all kai I have seen in Japan, the T-handle was connected to the loom with a wedged mortise and tenon.

Kaidemna preparing to race in Kushimoto, Wakayama Prefecture. A drummer in the stern beats the cadence. Boats like this can be found participating in annual races throughout Japan. *Photo copyright Yorio Hamaguchi.*

Other Oar Designs

Also in the northern region of Tohoku one can find many boats equipped with a version of the Western oar. Called *kurumagai,* literally "wheeled paddle," they differ from the Western oar in their two-piece construction. The shaft, or loom, has a wide section with a hole bored in it for a thole pin. The blade consists of a second piece of wood fastened to the loom. While small fishing craft in this region are

Launch day for the shimaihagi the author built with Mr. Ando. Each man wields a large kai like an oar, which pass through rope loops and rest on hardwood blocks fastened at the gunwale. The person at the bow rows while the person at the stern sculls and steers.

A pair of kurumagai resting in a fishing boat in Aomori Prefecture. Note the two-piece construction, with the loom (handle, the end closest) fashioned from a narrow plank with a blade attached. Long iron staples reinforce the handle on either side of the holes, which will be mounted on thole pins, one visible on the gunwales.

A fisherman spearing shellfish controls the position of his boat by rowing with the instep of his right foot on the oar. Although the boat design is traditional to the region, it is made of fiberglass by the Yamaha Corporation.

powered by outboard motors, most boats also carry a pair of kurumagai. A now rare type of very small boat called an *isobune* (inshore boat) uses only kurumagai.[14]

In the spring of 2003 while traveling down the Japan Sea coast of Hokkaido south of Sapporo I saw a fleet of small boats; the fishermen were using sight boxes strapped to their heads to see shellfish on the bottom and spear them. What was unusual was that as each man lay over one side of the boat, with a sight box strapped to his head and clutching a spear, the instep of one foot rested on the handle of an oar; in this position they were able to deftly maneuver their boats.

Sails

The use of sails on small craft became obsolete with the advent of outboard motors. The only exceptions today are some tourist fleets, and the sabani of Okinawa. Today sabani are used almost exclusively for racing, and their fully-battened rigs reflect a mainland Asian influence, and have nothing in common with traditional sails elsewhere in Japan.

The traditional small boat sail is rectangular, sometimes quite tall and narrow, flown from a single topyard mounted high on the mast. Headsails, or jibs, are rare, except for a type of drift-net boat called an *utasebune*. These fishing vessels would set their nets and drift sideways with their sails close-hauled. Just two fleets of these boats still exist, and both sail today not to catch fish, but so tourists on chase boats can watch and photograph their dramatic rigs. A small type of utasebune called *hobikisen* sails near the town of Tsukuba on Lake Kasumigaura, northeast of Tokyo.[15] The other fleet is composed of much larger boats with multiple sails that operate out of Ashikita port in Kyushu.

The bekabune I built in Urayasu had mast partners, as these boats traditionally sailed, but we did not make a sailing rig. I interviewed a retired fisherman who sketched out the shape of a bekabune sail: a Western gaff rig set high on an unstayed mast. The Western influence goes back to the late 1800s, as Japan's mercantile fleets began to switch from their traditional coastal sailing ships to more Western-style designs. Photographs of these ships, which flew enormous rectangular sails, often show various headsails and spankers (steering sails), all imported directly from the West.

For a more complete description of the configuration and sailing characteristics of the traditional Japanese sail, see Chapter 14.

Old photograph showing a small sailing vessel, its loosely laced sail panels open. This type of sail was self-reefing, spilling air as the wind increased. *Photo courtesy Dane Owen.*

The fully-battened sails used for racing sabani are controlled by an unusual sheet arrangement that connects to every batten. These boats are notoriously difficult to sail, and many racers depend on outriggers, which are not traditional, to keep them upright. *Photo copyright Hiroyuki Asato.*

Replica utasebune built by Mr. Nobuji Udagawa in Urayasu, demonstrating the drift-net style of fishing. The boat's sails are kept close-hauled and with the nets released to one side, the boat trawls sideways. *Photo copyright Keiju Kurozumi.*

Notes

1 *Science and Civilization in China,* by Joseph Needham, Vol. 4, Part 3, Cambridge University Press, 1971.

2 There is a similar rowing club called Hachi-ro Kai (Eight-oared club) sculling multi-ro boats in Yaizu-city, Shizuoka Prefecture. Many coastal communities maintain and use traditional boats for festivals and rowing events.

3 Japanese red oak (*akagashi*, sometimes *akakashi*) bears no resemblance to American red oak. It is one of Japan's most prized hardwoods, extremely dense and fine-grained with a rich red color. Japanese white oak (*shirakashi*) is similar to American white oak. Asuza is yellow catalpa (*Catalpa ovata*) and also used in Japan for archery bows.

4 "A Study on Ro (Oriental Sweep)," by Zensuke Takusagawa and Isao Yoshioka, *Bulletin of the Faculty of Engineering,* Vol. 25, Yokohama National University, March, 1976.

5 Mystic Seaport, The Museum of America and the Sea, is America's largest maritime museum, located in Mystic, Connecticut. See www.mysticseaport.org

6 A boatbuilder I interviewed in Kyushu in 2007 told me he rived (split lengthwise) Japanese yew into sections to get his blade material, a method he called *mikanwari* (the mikan being the Japanese orange, with the wood split like the sections of the fruit). He also charged more for ro made with wood from the southern face of the tree.

7 An excellent overview of Western sculling techniques, written and illustrated by Sam Manning, was published in *WoodenBoat* magazine, No. 100, June, 1991. Ben Fuller wrote a similar series for *Small Boat Journal,* No. 45 and 46 in 1985 and 1986 (originally published by National Fisherman, Camden, ME).

8 See Roger C. Taylor's *The Elements of Seamanship*, International Marine, 1982; and *Self Sufficient Sailor*, by Lin and Larry Pardey, Pardey Books, 1997.

9 A good discussion of Chinese yuloh with photographs appears in G.R.G. Worcester's classic *The Junks and Sampans of the Yangtze,* Naval Institute Press, 1971. See also Joseph Needham's previously cited *Science and Civilization in China*, Volume 4, Part 3. Various articles on the yuloh and ro have also appeared in the journal of the Amateur Yacht Research Society of the United Kingdom (www.ayrs.org).

[10] Links to photographs and videos of Atsushi Doi's invention can be found at www.amateurboatbuilding.com/articles/howto/sculling_oar/

[11] From the March 27, 2006 edition of the *Nikkei Shimbun* newspaper. I am indebted to Mr. Koichi Saito for translation.

[12] To purchase a ro today is costly. A friend in Tokyo bought a new one in 2004 from a craftsman in northern Japan for $900.

[13] The last time I saw my tub boat teacher he showed me a prototype of a tub boat kai he made of cedar. He told me he thought these could be a good product because he could make them much cheaper than a traditional oak kai, and he thought they would work just as well.

[14] The isobune is a semi-dugout, built of a very thick plank keel, partially hollowed, with single-plank sides fastened to a stem and a very narrow transom.

[15] Information on the history of hobikisen and the current tourist season for these boats can be found at www.city.kasumigaura.ibaraki.jp/hobiki/english/index.html

A volunteer sculls one of Wasen Tomo no Kai's boats on the Arakawa River in Tokyo.

A Shinto priest presides over the launching of a boat built by Mr. Kazuyoshi Fujiwara for Tokyo University.

7
Ceremonies

Shinto is the native religion of Japan and today coexists with Buddhism, which arrived later from mainland Asia. The core belief in Shinto is that *kami*, meaning a deity or spiritual essence, pervades all things. Shinto does not practice congregational worship as Western religions do; adherents instead participate in various rituals invoking the kami to bless and purify objects, activities, and their participants. In addition to their presence in natural objects and topographical features, kami are operative in such diverse phenomena as lightning and wind, and even in promoting fertility. A useful and concise definition is given by Dr. Sokyo Ono in his book *Shinto: The Kami Way* (Tuttle Publishing, 1962). Shinto, he says, is "a mystic sense of nature which plays an important part in leading the mind of man from the mundane to the higher and deeper world of the divine, and in transforming his life into an experience of living with the kami."

Kami represent an ideal, the harmonious integration of the elements of the natural world with mankind and its activities. In Japan today, one can see people leaving offerings at shrines to wish for success in everything from gaining entrance to a university, to finding a spouse, or to having children. When I lived in Urayasu I once walked past a home where a young couple were solemnly watching a Shinto priest bless their new car; on another occasion my wife watched as a ten-year old in his baseball uniform made a hasty offering on his way to a game. One often sees building lots decorated with bamboo stalks, after a Shinto priest has blessed the site for a new house or office building.

A Shinto priest readies his portable altar for a keel-laying ceremony. The vegetables are offerings to the mountain *kami*, while fish is an offering to the sea *kami*.

My personal understanding of Shinto comes mainly from boat-related ceremonies I witnessed or participated in. These are universally Shinto-based, and center primarily on the twin gods of the sea and the mountains. While some boatbuilders invite priests to conduct ceremonies at particular milestones, such as when the backbone of the boat is completed, most take place at launching. Of the five boats I helped build, only the little tub boat was completed without fanfare. My teacher told me he had never heard of a tub boat launched with a ceremony, though he confessed he typically drank with the owner the night of delivery.

A ceremony prior to launching can take place in the forest when the trees are felled. In most cases this is a simple blessing made by the loggers themselves without a priest. In the workshop a ceremony called the *chounadate,* or "blessing of the tools" (*chouna* means "adze") may be performed to bestow good fortune on the tools, craftsmen, and work space. In northern Japan this is also called the *dainose,* from *dai* (workbench) and form of *noseru* (to put on). When the *shiki,* the keel, is laid there may be a ceremony called the *shikizue*. Again, the purpose is to ensure a propitious outcome by blessing the start of a project.

The boat-launching ceremony is typically called *shinsuishiki,* literally, "enter water ceremony," or less commonly, *funeoroshi,* literally, "boat ceremony." The purpose is to ritually purify the boat, as well as its builders and owners. In Hokkaido and other regions of northern Japan the term *daioroshi* is also used for the launching ceremony.[1] Offerings, usually of *mochi* (rice cakes) or fish are presented, usually in pairs. They acknowledge the two most important kami for boatbuilders and fishermen: *yama-no-kami,* the god of the mountains (the origin of the boat's materials), and *umi-no-kami,* the god of the sea. Salt is important for purification, as is sake (rice wine). Beyond that, each launching ceremony reflects local customs and traditions. There may be as many different kinds of launching ceremonies as there are fishing villages. I have even found that elements of a launching ceremony in one village may be considered completely wrong in a village nearby.

Postwar photograph showing Tokyo fishermen celebrating the launch of a new boat built by the author's teacher and his father. One man ritually washes the boat with a bailer while the others pound the floorboards with wooden bats. They all wear the loincloth called *fundoshi,* typical festival garb for men. *Photo copyright Kazuyoshi Fujiwara.*

At a formal ceremony the priest will usually chant, addressing a temporary altar or facing the boat. In my experience these chants are a stylized retelling of the story of the project: why the boat was built and a description of the builders and the new owner. The first ceremony I participated in, at the Urayasu Museum, was somewhat unorthodox because it was not conducted by a Shinto priest. The museum director, the boatbuilder, and I stood alongside our boat while the head fisherman stood in the boat. Facing offerings of sake, rice, dried squid, cabbage, and bananas, he chanted at some length in the low, sonorous tones typical of Buddhist priests. I could only recognize my name and my teacher's name in what the fisherman chanted. Placed above the food was the *gohei,* a wooden wand with strips of white paper folded in a zigzag fashion. It is used in shrines and ceremonies to mark the presence of kami, and is believed to have derived from sacred cloths that were offered as gifts to shrines.

After he finished chanting, the priest made small piles of salt on the boat and invited all three of us to pour a small amount of sake on the salt. He then handed us a flint and steel and we struck sparks on the boat. The ceremony completed, we carried the boat out of the shop and launched it in the museum's lagoon. That evening at a post-launch party I asked one of the younger fishermen what the head fisherman had chanted. He replied, "I didn't understand a word of it."

At the launching of the chokkibune in Tokyo in 2003, a senior boatman climbed aboard and with a paddle slowly spun the boat around in place three times to starboard. Everyone agreed this was an important part of the ceremony, but the custom was so ancient no one knew exactly what it meant, except for a vague notion that the number three was lucky. Mr. Fujiwara had shown me photos of his father launching fishing boats after the War, when the practice was for fishermen to take their new boats up and down the canals while pounding the hulls with large bats. He had no idea what this custom meant, or where it originated. It was entirely the fishermen's idea and he assumed it was for safety, good luck, and a good catch.

A *funadama* from the Inland Sea region, containing a paper figurine, a representation of dice, a roll of five yen coins, and a packet of seeds. Portable shrines like this are placed on boats to protect their owners and bring good luck.

A branch from a sakaki tree and gohei paper strips can be seen resting on the keel plank of this boat at a shikizue, or keel-laying ceremony, in Tokyo.

A utasebune built by Mr. Udagawa flies a selection of flags called tairyo-bata to celebrate its launching in Urayasu. *Photo copyright Keiju Kurozumi.*

Less than two weeks after the launch in Tokyo I was taken by friends a few hours south to the ocean in Chiba Prefecture to meet an elderly boatbuilder in Wada named Mr. Higuchi. I asked what sort of ceremony he remembered for launching new boats. He mentioned that boats were turned three times, and I told him we had done the same thing in Tokyo. When I added that we spun our boat to starboard he interjected, "What? You must turn the boat to port! Tokyo people don't know anything!"

He then wanted to know every detail of our Tokyo launching, but beyond the usual rituals performed by the priest and the turning of the boat I had little more to say. Mr. Higuchi described a series of very quaint local traditions that were a part of boat launchings in his community. His boats all carried a *funadama*, a small shrine, usually placed in the cabin or fastened to a central beam of the boat.[2] His were nothing more than a small block of wood hollowed out and sealed with a little door. Various objects were placed inside as offerings, including some five-yen coins, a pair of dice, rice kernels, a lock of hair (preferably from an old woman), and tiny male and female dolls.[3] All were wrapped in white paper.

Mr. Higuchi stressed that the dice had to be wrapped side-by-side so the ones faced up, the threes faced forward, the fours faced aft, and the sixes faced down. This arrangement is consistent and widespread throughout Japan, and a poem describes the practice. The verse is replete with homophones, as word play is an integral part of Japanese humor. The poem translates:

> One for Heaven,
> Six for Earth,
> Three together for the bow,
> Four together for the rudder,
> Five curved for the sculling oar,
> And two in a pile in the middle.

Placing the maximum number on the bottom is believed to place the "weight" lower, enhancing the stability of the boat. The word play includes "three together" (*miawase*) which also has a romantic meaning of "exchanged glances." "Four together" (*shiawase*) is a homophone for "happiness." "Five curved" (*gossori*) also means "full" as in full of fish.

In Aomori my teacher had a small Shinto shrine mounted high on the wall of the boat shop. It was here and at the bow of the boat that he and I conducted Shinto rituals the day of our launch. We did this alone, with no spectators.

Following the keel-laying ceremony for the chokkibune, we posed for a portrait. Mr. Fujiwara and the author are seated on either side of the Shinto priest. Behind are the senior members of Wasen Tomo no Kai, the club receiving the boat. *Photo copyright Catherine Wood Brooks.*

"Two in a pile" (*ni dossari*) can mean "a heap," as in a pile of fish in the bilge.[4]

Mr. Higuchi continued, saying once these items were sealed inside the funadama, salt was poured on the bow, on the funadama, and on the stern. Next sake was poured on the salt, at all three places in order. The boat was spun three times to port (left) because, he pointed out, a funeral procession makes only right turns.[5]

During the ritual purification of a boat or person, the priest waves the gohei first left, then right, then left again with a dramatic flourish. These motions are made first toward the boat, and then toward the boatbuilders. Sometimes the priest does the same with a branch of the *sakaki* tree (*Cleyera japonica*). Sakaki is an evergreen both sacred to Shinto and a symbol of longevity because when cut it maintains its freshness for a long time.

Once launched, boats are usually paraded, often decorated with flags called *tairyobata,* combining the words for "large, good catch" and "flag." They are custom made and display the names of the vessels as well as messages asking for safe and profitable voyages. The flags are purchased by the boat's owners or his friends, and sometimes by fishermen's unions. The most expensive are hand-painted and can cost as much as eight hundred dollars. Boats fly their tairyobata every New Years as well.[6]

Most boat shops I have worked in displayed some reference to Shinto, whether a sprig of cedar left on the boat for New Years or a small shrine. An elderly boatbuilder in the Gokase River valley in Miyazaki Prefecture demonstrated an interesting integration of Shinto into a craftsman's life. At one point while we were talking about his work he needed to cut a piece of scrap wood to demonstrate a technique. As he stepped up to his bandsaw he paused, bowed his head, and clapped his hands twice, holding them for a moment in prayer. Then he switched on the saw and made the cut. I asked him what he had done and he told me it was his custom to "ask" the power tool to be good to him. He said he performed this the first time he used a power tool in a given month.

The integration of the spiritual into everyday objects and activities through Shinto practices has undoubtedly influenced Japan's myriad customs on a local level. The boatbuilders I have talked with have all, at some point, related a local custom or belief rooted in an interpretation of the natural world. Mr. Hatakeyama, a boatbuilder in Akita Prefecture, told me that many years ago a boatbuilder in his village was asked to interrupt his work to make a coffin. The fishing boat he had been working on, when completed, turned out to be exceptionally profitable for its owner, and so brought increased business to the builder. As a result other boatbuilders began diverting time to coffin making, believing that would enhance the fishing prospects of the boats they were currently building and so increase their value.

On Sado Island my teacher's reputation as a boatbuilder was cemented when an enormous octopus attached itself to the bottom of one of his tub boats upon launching. The local fishermen concluded that all of Mr. Fujii's boats would attract a good catch. This story quickly became legend; in conducting interviews for my first book in 2000, several fisherman solemnly repeated it to me.

Before launching their shimaihagi in Aomori a simple ceremony was performed by Mr. Ando and the author, shown praying before a bowl of salt, two candles, and a bottle of sake. In rural Japan such ceremonies are often conducted without the aid of a Shinto priest. *Photo copyright Kon Masaaki.*

Notes

1 Mr. Masaaki Kon, curator of the Aomori Prefectural Museum of History, clarified these northern boat terms for me.

2 *Funa* means "boat" and *dama* comes from *tamashii*, meaning "soul" or "spirit."

3 The five-yen coin, called the *goen*, is a common offering, since it sounds like the phrase meaning "good destiny." The dolls are made of paper, with the male doll placed behind the female and their arms folded, locking them together.

4 Koji Matano transcribed the original poem from Mr. Takashi Tsuda, an eighty-four year old boatbuilder on Naoshima, Kagawa Prefecture. James Huffman, Koji Matano, and Tsugaru Ryosuke all contributed to my translation and explanation of it.

5 I was not able to find reference to funerals making only right turns. The speaker may have been referring to an obscure or purely local custom.

6 I am indebted to Mr. Tsugaru Ryosuke for precise information about these flags. He is a designer of contemporary tairyobata and his work can be seen at: www.tairyobata.jp

The author and his apprentice, Taka Higuchi, assembling the hull of a tub boat they built on Sado Island. *Photo copyright Noriko Nakayasu.*

8

Apprenticeship

For most Westerners, the existence of an apprentice system in a modern nation seems oddly anachronistic. Formal apprentice programs in the West largely disappeared with the rise of organized vocational schools around the beginning of the twentieth century, although in building trades such as plumbing and electrical work the terms apprentice and journeyman still exist.

The research described in this book took place within the context of the traditional Japanese apprentice system, albeit in an abbreviated form. I worked with each of my five teachers for only the time it took to build one boat: less than two weeks in the case of the tub boat and over four months for the chokkibune. My teachers understood and supported the goals of my research, but were deeply skeptical of what I could learn in such a short time. My experience building boats in America meant nothing to them; in their minds, my previous work had no relevance to their craft. If there was discord between my teachers and me, it centered on how we each perceived my apprenticeship.

At the time of my first trip to Japan I was only vaguely aware of the apprentice system, but through some remarkable circumstances I would come face-to-face with its role in the ancient world of Japanese crafts. The day before I left the country, I followed my guidebook's directions to the Tokyo Kite Museum. This little gem of a collection is located on the fifth floor of a small building in the Nihombashi district of Tokyo.[1] It is a private museum run by an avid kite collector who travels all over the world attending kite festivals. As a high school student I had made kites, and knew a little bit about the traditions of Japanese kites, most of which I had learned from a book written by an American who had studied kite-making in Japan.[2]

The author assists in shaping the stem of a shimaihagi with an axe, while his teacher, Mr. Ando, looks on. *Photo copyright Kon Masaaki.*

The centerpiece of the museum was a large, glass display cabinet filled with a collection of rectangular kites in the classic style of the Edo period. Their simple bamboo frames and rice paper faces were decorated with marvelous paintings. One was of a beautiful woman petting an animal, while another showed the growling face of a samurai confronting a priest. The figures were painted in bold, black outlines, colored with the brightest watercolors.

I had noticed the staff of the museum staring at me, and I assumed that foreigners rarely found their way to this little museum. While I stood in front of the display case a man approached and asked in English if he could offer any help. Recalling the name of a kite-maker and Living National Treasure,[3] I motioned to the display case and asked, "Were these kites made by Teizo Hashimoto?" The man turned and, without a word, walked away.

Japanese manners and protocol can seem so byzantine that foreign visitors sometimes worry that any wrong move or utterance might give offense. I decided it was best just to leave the museum, so I picked up my backpack and headed for the door. I was almost out when the same man, the museum's founder and director it turned out, emerged from his office. He handed me a piece of paper with an address. He said, "Mr. Hashimoto will see you tomorrow at one o'clock."

I suppose the director was as surprised at finding a foreign backpacker who knew of Teizo Hashimoto as I was confused by his reaction to my question. One thing I knew for certain: I had just been handed an amazing opportunity, an experience rivaling any of the stunning temples or shrines I had seen. I quickly arranged for an interpreter and spent the next afternoon, just before my flight home, sitting in a dark studio across from Mr. Hashimoto. He was in his late eighties, very small and lean, almost frail, with a full gray beard. The house was old, on one of the back streets of the Ueno district of Tokyo, and his wife stayed in the kitchen during our entire visit. He very patiently listened to my questions while he painted kite faces, slowly dipping various brushes into bright paints, working with a confident hand throughout our conversation.

Mr. Hashimoto said he had apprenticed with his father, and his kites were in great demand since he had been named a Living National Treasure. He said his biggest regret was the fact that his kites had become so valuable no one flew them anymore. While he was leaning over a painting I asked how long his apprenticeship with his father had lasted. "Ten years," he said.

I must have made some sort of sound, or otherwise indicated my shock at this fact: *ten years to learn to make kites*?

Mr. Hashimoto stopped painting and looked at me silently. Then he plunged one of his largest brushes into his ink pot, moving it around the sides as he removed it, as if to gather all the black ink he could. Holding the handle of the brush, he dropped the head of the brush to the paper, where it landed with a plop at the top of a figure he had previously painted. Just as quickly, with a flick of his wrist, he snapped the brush away.

Thomas Merton wrote, describing the moment when his Zen teacher, Daisetz Suzuki, violated the protocols of a tea ceremony by throwing back his cup in a single, furious gulp. "It was at once as if nothing at all had happened and as if the roof had flown off the building."[4]

I felt the same inner concussion Merton described; something extraordinary had happened and I was just slowly beginning to realize what it was. Above the forehead in Hashimoto's figure the ink left a smooth, opaque black curve, defining the hairline. Along its top edge, chasing the direction Mr. Hashimoto had flicked his brush, the solid black gave way to a comb of ever finer lines, until it seemed as though each individual hair of the paintbrush had painted a single hair on the figure's head. It had taken an instant. The room remained silent. I realized I was holding my breath. As I exhaled Hashimoto broke the silence. "What you just saw," he said quietly, his eyes rising to meet mine, "took ten years."

Mr. Teizo Hashimoto (left), a kite maker and Living National Treasure, at work in his Tokyo studio, and detail of one of his kites (above).

Japanese training in the arts, crafts, and trades is still conducted within a strict, formalized relationship between a master and an apprentice. This relationship is in many ways similar to Buddhist monastic training, demanding of the student absolute loyalty to one's teacher and a total commitment to the process. For Westerners who have studied Japanese martial arts the similarities will be obvious: the ritualized greetings made to the *sensei,* or teacher;[5] the use of demonstration and repetition rather than explanation in the training; the strict and absolute hierarchy which defines all participants; and the students' responsibility to keep the training space clean. The apprentice system is called *toteiseido*, and it is such an integral part of Japanese culture that for most Japanese the suggestion of learning an art or craft in any way but intense study with a single master is nearly unthinkable.[6]

In Japan one sees many examples of how pervasive this culture of teaching remains. During my stay on Iejima apprenticing with the island's boatbuilder, I took many after-work runs with the local junior high school track team. Like teenagers everywhere, they came out to the track in groups of twos and threes, giggling and engaging in innocent horseplay. But once their coach arrived they immediately became serious and focused. First they stood in a circle and bowed to him. After a few words of instruction, the team broke off into groups of sprinters, hurdlers, distance runners, and jumpers. The coach said barely a word during practice, and stood silently on the infield of the track watching. On Fridays the team pulled out rakes and brooms and worked on maintaining the clay track.

The schoolchildren choose just one sport or activity for the entire school year, and my young friends told me they competed in no more than three or four meets. At the close of every workout, they lined up in front of their coach. One student stepped forward and, in a loud voice, thanked the coach for his hard work and pledged on behalf of the team that all its members would do their utmost to train diligently. Then all the athletes shouted their thanks and bowed to their coach in unison.

Except for the cheers, the duties expected of me in the boat shop down the hill from the school were remarkably similar. I was expected to have the shop prepared for the day's work before my teacher arrived; to speak to my teacher only when he addressed me first (break time was for relaxed conversation and longer questions); and to sweep the shop and maintain the tools. By the time I studied in Okinawa these rituals were familiar to me, and my role in the shop was the same with all of my teachers.

A junior high track team on Okinawa bows in unison, greeting their coach at the start of practice.

Today the most formalized apprentice programs in the woodworking professions are run by a handful of temple carpentry guilds, the most famous being the Kyoto Guild of Traditional Master Builders (Kyoto Dentou Kenchiku Gijutsu Kyoukai).[7] Mr. Taka Higuchi, my own tub boat apprentice, worked early in his career for a clay tile roofer in Matsumoto, Japan. It was only the two of them, but it was understood that his first six years constituted his apprenticeship. Later when Taka moved to Sado Island with his family, he found work with a small house construction company. Again, he completed another six-year apprenticeship with this builder before leaving to start his own construction business. His credibility as a qualified carpenter rested on the fact that he had completed this apprenticeship.

I doubt Japanese boatbuilders were ever organized in guilds; they certainly weren't in the modern era. Yet almost every boatbuilder I have met in Japan trained within an apprentice system (the one exception, my Okinawa teacher, was self-taught). Having asked dozens of boatbuilders about their training, the length of the apprenticeship is remarkably consistent: six years. Of course, many men trained with their fathers, and boatbuilding sometimes went back generations within families. My Tokyo teacher was a fourth-generation boatbuilder. Another in Tokyo told me he was an eighth-generation boatbuilder, and was training his son at the time we spoke.

Long apprenticeships raise the obvious question of whether this training is drawn out unnecessarily simply to provide cheap labor for the boatbuilder. But very few craftsmen ever described this system as unduly long or exploitative. They might have chafed at the system, but they accepted it. Only my fourth teacher left his apprenticeship early, after three years, due to low wages and harsh working conditions, but he went on to study with other boatbuilders before establishing a shop.

This last generation of traditional boatbuilders works in near-total isolation from their peers. The market for their boats has dwindled to such an extent that only a scattering of solitary craftsmen remains. During my earliest trips to Japan traveling the coastline looking for boatbuilders, I gave up asking the craftsmen themselves where I might find others. Time and again the boatbuilders answered by putting their index finger to their noses and saying, "*Ichi!*" ("One," meaning, "only me"). In truth, most did have the distinction of being the last boatbuilder in their particular river valley, peninsula, island, or prefecture, but not throughout Japan as they often claimed.

In some cases this isolation is so complete craftsmen think they are the only practitioners of techniques that are actually common among builders throughout the country. Often these men are stunned to learn a technique they are describing to me is familiar to craftsmen elsewhere. I remember one boatbuilder insisting that a dovetail joint he used was a family secret, when in fact I had read a detailed description of how to make the same joint, written by a British furniture maker and published in an American woodworking magazine.

The craftsmen I have interviewed described the early years of their apprenticeships as extremely difficult, both physically and mentally. They came into workshops as teenagers with no skills. The general pattern for the novice apprentice was to begin by performing the most menial duties: keeping the shop clean, fetching tools, and in some cases assisting the master's wife in the kitchen. At the teacher's discretion the apprentice would be allowed to take on an increasing role, first perhaps sharpening the tools. Over time, he would be ordered to do more challenging jobs. Slowly the apprentice would develop into a mature craftsman. To a Westerner, this would appear to happen at a glacial pace. It might be a year or more before an apprentice was even allowed to touch the tools.

Two of my teachers told me when they were building a boat they took no holidays, but worked seven days a week until the project was finished. My Okinawan teacher continued that custom during our project together. The normal vacation for a workman through the 1960s was to take two days off a month; the first and the fifteenth (many public baths in Japan observe the same holiday schedule today). In 2007 I interviewed the last boatbuilder of the Gokase River valley in Kyushu. When I asked him about his days off he told that me he took two. I assumed he meant the first and the fifteenth. I was mistaken. He took off two days *a year*—the Buddhist celebration Obon and New Year's Day.[8]

Mr. Sanshiro Matsui was eighty years old in 1993 when the Lake Biwa Museum commissioned him to build a 62-foot *marukobune*, a type of medium-sized sailing cargo vessel found only on Lake Biwa. Professor Kumi Makino documented the process and in her book describes his apprenticeship, which began in 1923 (see below).

Regarding the educational or teaching aspects of apprenticeship, the process can at times feel like benign neglect. I realized my teachers had no frame of reference for *instructing* a student in the Western sense of the word. They all expected me to learn primarily by observation. The early years of the apprenticeship, which can look like drudgery, are in fact the opportunity for the apprentice to observe the master, and slowly be inculcated with rudimentary skills. Later the apprentice will need only minimal instruction and repetition to master more complex techniques.

The Apprenticeship of Mr. Sanshiro Matsui

Matsui was born the son of a stonemason in 1913. He was skillful as a child, and began his boatbuilding career as an apprentice when he was around ten years old. It was around the time when the traditional boats, particularly marukobune, were in their final heyday. Matsui was not particularly keen on boats at the beginning, and he himself did not intend to become a shipwright. His father, however, wanted him to learn a trade and sent him to one of the boatyards as an apprentice. There were six apprentices in the boatyard.

Life at the boatyard was not easy. They worked daily from six in the morning to six in the evening, with only two days off a month. One day off was spent just washing dirty clothes. Matsui was curious about other handicrafts such as flower arrangement and knitting, and he managed to learn these crafts in his spare time. As an apprentice Matsui was assigned only minor tasks such as repairing nails or softening oakum, and he was not given regular tools until he became sixteen. However, by watching others, he steadily accumulated boatbuilding skills. This is the traditional way of training in Japan. By the time he turned twenty he had become a competent shipwright, and was taken into his master's confidence.

—from *Marukobune: The Traditional Sailing Boats in the Lake Biwa Region*[9]

Only two of my teachers went so far as to specifically demonstrate a technique, and even so they said no more than "watch," and "like this." When invited to try, if I made a mistake they took the tools from me and demonstrated again. This process would be repeated until they were satisfied I could do the work. Deviations from either teacher's techniques were generally unwelcome, even if they yielded the same results. My other three teachers simply worked while I took care of more mundane tasks, and it was entirely up to me to grasp what they were doing and how to do it. When they did assign me a task, I was expected to be able to do it correctly.

Herein lies the fundamental difference between notions of learning, East and West. In the West we view training as the acquisition of a set of skills imparted directly through a close relationship with one's teacher; in Japan, traditional learning is first and foremost about developing the values that lead one to intangible insights. Observation and perseverance are the twin values that enable the Japanese apprentice to successfully develop his or her skills. In Japan the obstacles *are* the teaching tools.

The Westerner may instead view the rigors imposed on the apprentice as obsolete, backward, and counterproductive. And this form of apprenticeship can rightly be criticized for being inefficient, repetitive, and subordinating the student to a slavish obedience to the teacher. At the very least it flies in the face of modern notions that learning should be engaging and rewarding.

My teachers warned me my experience building other types of boats offered nothing, but they were wrong. Had I not known how to use and sharpen the tools, and how wooden boats are built, I would have been completely lost, especially given the short time we had to work together. The basic process of building a Japanese boat was not unfamiliar to me. I was also acquainted with the tools. That said, some methods were surprising, and some techniques and details were completely new.

While my teachers called me their apprentice, my true goals were those of a researcher, and this sometimes conflicted with their expectations. As mentioned, there was almost no discussion in the boatshop. My second teacher was an incredibly voluble and engaging man, but once he had explained what he felt I needed to know, he left the shop and I worked alone. My third teacher invited me to ask him questions, though like all the others he stressed there should be no speaking while working; we talked only during breaks.

There were, however, positive aspects of apprenticeship. I could function as a researcher without fluency in the language. I had depended on an interpreter for two previous long interviews with my first teacher, Mr. Fuji, and when it came time to work with him I was concerned because I spoke only rudimentary Japanese. Ironically, I didn't need any Japanese because Mr. Fuji insisted on working in complete silence and offered no explanations whatsoever. Learning depended entirely on my powers of observation.

Mr. Ando watches the author carefully while he planes the keel plank of the shimaihagi. *Photo copyright Masaaki Kon.*

As my language skills improved I could question my teachers, but often their answers were blunt and reflexive. As mentioned earlier, the last generation of wooden boatbuilders worked in isolation, and had little or no perspective on the larger world of their craft. I might notice some technique that contrasted with the work of other craftsmen I had met, but attempting to explore with my teacher why he did something a particular way often resulted in the answer, "Because that is the way I do it." Any suggestion of an alternate technique almost always elicited the single word: "*Dame!*"

This word (pronounced ***dah** mey*) has a variety of meanings, all expressing the negative with finality. My dictionary defines it as: (1) no good; (2) not serving its purpose; useless; broken; (3) hopeless; wasted; in vain; purposeless; (4) cannot; must not; not allowed. For most of my teachers it was a punctuation mark ending any conversation, signaling unequivocally that there would be no more discussion. When directed at my mistakes, it slammed the door on any explanation or excuse.

I also had to be careful that my questions would not be taken to impugn the extent of my teachers' skill. Many Japanese acquaintances have expressed amazement that, as a foreigner, I was even invited inside a craftsman's shop at all. I am convinced my foreignness was actually a protective shield.

I could overstep the boundaries of etiquette largely because it was taken for granted that I didn't understand proper social norms. There is a widespread belief among Japanese that their culture is inaccessible to non-Japanese, and the need to forgive the mistakes of foreigners reinforces this. I could ask questions and press for answers in a way that probably would have caused a Japanese to be thrown out of the shop.

Furthermore, "why" something is done can be meaningless in the context of Japanese crafts, because only the master possesses an overall understanding of the project. Even skilled workers are not privy to an overview of the work; an apprentice is responsible for a particular task and is expected to focus his or her complete attention on that alone. Having the boss explain the entire process to the apprentice is considered a waste of breath. Skills are mastered in discrete, defined increments, and the totality is too confusing for the beginner. This was generally true in my experiences, and if I were patient, eventually the reason for doing a certain thing became obvious. I learned to resist thinking ahead.

The master's control over the process is inextricably related to the secrecy that is part and parcel of Japanese boatbuilding. Unless all are family members, it is common for the master to order the apprentices out of the workshop while he lays down the crucial dimensions of the boat. The master is the only person who may look at drawings (if they exist) or handle patterns. For the committed apprentice, this is the last hurdle of his or her training. My first teacher told me he began sneaking into the workshop at night with a candle to study the lines his teacher laid out for the boat. He also taught me the Japanese phrase for this thievery: *nusumigeiko.* This word combines the verb *nusumu* (to steal) with the noun *keiko* (lessons).

Mr. Shimojo and the author working on the sabani in Okinawa. *Photo copyright George Kochi.*

When I interview boatbuilders I always ask about "stolen lessons," and all are well aware of the practice. Many laugh at the mention of the phrase and then tell stories about measuring boats when their masters were not present, quizzing customers about designs, or plying their teachers with gifts of sake in exchange for information.

People have asked how I obtained information so easily from boatbuilders notorious for hoarding their secrets. The chief reason is the lack of apprentices, and the realization among the men I call the last generation of boatbuilders that their accumulated knowledge is about to be lost. Time and again I have arrived unannounced at the shop of an elderly boatbuilder, often following the directions of a local fisherman, and within minutes of introducing myself and explaining my work, my host is sharing with me his design ratios and secrets. My desire to document and preserve this craft today resonates powerfully with these men.

The cardinal rule of Japanese apprenticeship I have violated, however, is the fealty of an apprentice to a single teacher. My apprenticeships have taken me to the four corners of Japan: Sado Island in the Sea of Japan; Tokyo Bay; Tohoku in the far north; and Okinawa in the south. At least initially, none of my teachers had the slightest interest in hearing about my work with other craftsmen. My second teacher vehemently insisted that studying with another boatbuilder would just confuse me. Worse still, he and my third teacher had been competitors.

However, my commitment to this research demands I study from as many craftsmen as possible, a process made much easier because I stand outside the culture looking in. Each of my teachers shared with me the craft of a particular boat. These lessons were focused and direct, uncluttered with comparison or context. The broader perspectives I offer in this book are my attempts to integrate what I learned during these apprenticeships, and from my interviews with other boatbuilders.

Notes

1. The Tokyo Kite Museum (Tako no Hakubutsukan) is also the home of the Japan Kite Association. Information in English about both organizations can be found at: www.tako.gr.jp
2. See Tal Streeter, *The Art of the Japanese Kite*, Weatherhill, 1980.
3. Living National Treasure (*ningen-kokuhou*) is a popular term for persons honored by the Japanese government as Preservers of Important Intangible Cultural Properties

for their exceptional skill as artists, performers, or craftspersons.

4 Thomas Merton was an American Trappist monk who studied and wrote about Asian religions. The quote is from his essay "Learning to Live," in *Love and Living*, Farrar, Straus & Giroux, 1979.

5 Boatbuilders are not comfortable with the term *sensei*; instead, my teachers preferred to be called by a variety of terms, including: *shishou*, meaning teacher, or master; *oyakata*, an honorific term for craftsman, artisan, or any superior; and *touryou*, literally a pillar or main support, and by extension used for boss or master craftsman. Other boatbuilders have referred to their former teachers, nostalgically, as *oyaji* (old man, father, boss), a term of endearment used today by elderly Japanese.

6 An excellent essay by an American describing Buddhist monastic training illustrating clearly the cultural underpinnings of this type of learning can be found in G. Victor Sogen Hori's "Teaching and Learning in the Rinzai Zen Monastery" in *The Journal of Japanese Studies* 20:1, 1994.

7 Three excellent books on Japanese carpentry are: Azby Brown's *The Genius of Japanese Carpentry,* Tuttle Publishing, 2014, revised edition; Len Brackett's *Building the Japanese House Today*, Harry Abrams, 2005; and William Coaldrake's *The Way of the Carpenter*, Weatherhill, 1990. Brown is an architect who documented the restoration of a temple, while Brackett worked for several years with temple carpenters in Kyoto. Coaldrake was the first non-Japanese to become a member of the Kyoto Guild of Traditional Master Builders.

8 Obon is a Buddhist holiday for honoring one's ancestors. It is celebrated in July or August depending on the region in Japan.

9 Published in Japanese as *Biwako no Dentouteki Mokuzousen no Henyou: Marukobune wo Chuushin ni*, Yuzankaku, 2013.

Part II
The Boats

Ms. Akiko Yamamoto in her tub boat in 1994, gathering shellfish using a sight box and bamboo spear. Visible inside the boat is a stone counterweight

9

The Taraibune of Sado Island

Taraibune (literally "tub boat") are a unique inshore fishing craft found today only on a remote peninsula of Sado Island in the Sea of Japan. Though they appear anachronistic, taraibune are just one of a widely dispersed collection of bowl-shaped boats found all over the world. Irish and Welsh coracles can still be seen, as can the basket boats of Vietnam and the *putti* of northern India. In North America the Mandan Indians of the Great Plains had a skin craft called a bull boat, and bowl-shaped boats were used on the Tigris and Euphrates rivers as early as the third millennium BC.

Taraibune are examples of traditional Japanese coopering, with some modifications to enhance their use as watercraft. Just before leaving for my first trip to Japan a friend showed me a photograph in a Japanese publication of a woman floating in an enormous barrel. Intrigued, I made a copy and took it with me. While visiting my friend Nobu Hayashi in Hiroshima in 1990 I showed him the photo. He didn't recognize the strange boat but translated the caption, "Sado Island, Ogi Town." Since I had a rail pass and no fixed itinerary I headed for Sado.

Sado Island

Sado lies off the western coast of the main Japanese island of Honshu, and although much smaller than the four main islands of the country, it is the fifth largest. It consists of two parallel mountain ranges separated by a fertile plain connecting two large bays, one at each end, flanked by the mountains. For centuries the inhabitants have made their living primarily from the sea and from farming the meager arable land. The island also has a relatively abundant supply of timber and some of the finest bamboo in Japan.

Like many island communities, Sado is a bastion of a more traditional way of life within a nation arguably the most modern in the world. Archaeological finds show Sado was at least a stopping point for peoples migrating from the mainland of Asia to Japan. In medieval times, as commerce with the mainland waned and the Japanese government closed itself off from the outside world, Sado was considered foreign soil. For several hundred years the people of the island had no contact with the rest of Japan, even though on a clear day Sado's mountain ridges can be seen from the Japanese coast. In fact, its remoteness made it a perfect place to banish criminals or politically troublesome citizens and it was used for this purpose from the eighth to the seventeenth centuries. This quarantine ended with the discovery of gold on Sado about 400 years ago, and the reigning shogun lost no time developing an elaborate gold mining operation—one of the largest in the world—fueled mostly with the labor of prisoners from the mainland and slaves. Thereafter Sado became an important point of trade for coastal ships plying the Sea of Japan.

I arrived on Sado at Ogi, one of the three ports serving the ferryboats from the mainland. I had little expectation I would find the strange little boat depicted in the photograph, but within an hour of wandering the coast I had found tub boats in three fishing villages, overturned and covered with tarps for the winter. There was no activity, and the slate seas breaking on the sharp volcanic coastline told me I was not going to see anyone fishing on this trip. With a light snow falling I began walking back to Ogi. Until that point I had never really taken seriously the idea someone might actually be building these boats. On a whim I decided to ask at a local gas station, where young men and women in bright blue uniforms were putting out banners to greet the day's customers. I walked up to the manager, easily recognizable by his age and spotless white gloves, and with my limited, informal vocabulary asked, "*Taraibune funadaiku wa doko desu ka?*" (Where is a tub-boat builder?)

My question seemed to release the collective enthusiasm of the gas station staff, and for the next thirty minutes I waited while they quizzed each other and made phone calls. Finally one of the staff invited me to get into his pickup truck and before I knew it we were heading northeast along the coast road. After passing several villages we turned into the mountains. After climbing a few miles the truck suddenly stopped and my driver motioned toward an old house and barn set in the bamboo and cedars. The moment I got out he sped off into the snowstorm, giving me a friendly wave. In the barn I found a very old, very small man hunched over a wooden bucket. I had interrupted him as he was trimming the tops of the staves. He was working on the floor, like most Japanese craftsmen, bracing the bucket with his feet. The shop was littered with tools, scraps of cardboard, and old appliances, with a small kerosene stove for heat. He took no notice of me, acting as if tall foreigners walked in out of the snow every day of the week. For about twenty minutes I watched, occasionally asking a simple question, but he worked on, ignoring me. I was getting frustrated with the lack of communication, and looking at the bucket I was beginning to feel there had been a serious misunderstanding, when an elderly woman entered with a baby strapped to her back. She got down on her knees, put her mouth to the man's ear and shouted. As soon as she was finished I too knelt next to the old man and yelled the most provocative thing I could think of, "*Watashi wa Amerika no funadaiku!*" (I am an American boatbuilder!).

Isutaro Ishizuka was a lifelong cooper and one of only two men still building tub boats when I met him in 1990. He passed away before my second visit to Sado Island.

The man's eyes widened and he began a long struggle to get to his feet. Once we were standing he took my hand and began shaking it. I was relieved to have finally made some connection, but I was becoming convinced I had been taken to meet a cooper and not a boatbuilder. I was thinking it would be best to leave, but the man, not yet having relinquished his grip, began leading me to the back of the barn. We passed what were once stables until finally we stood in front of a pile of freshly planed cedar boards. Each was about two feet long and six inches wide. I could see they had been planed to different curvatures, like the staves of a large barrel.

Once we were again seated by the stove the man introduced himself. His name was Isutaro Ishizuka. The woman whom I had assumed was his wife was actually his daughter and the little baby his great granddaughter. He was eighty-four years old and he had been building buckets, barrels, and taraibune for seventy years. Even more astonishing, the pile of wood was for twelve new tub boats. Up until this point I had assumed finding a few examples of derelict boats was as much as I could expect. I never imagined I might find a craftsman still making them.

I spent the rest of the morning watching and photographing Mr. Ishizuka. When I left he waved to me through the frosty panes of the thin sliding door that separated his shop from the snowy day. I hitchhiked back to Ogi and retreated to the small museum in the center of town. This time the sight of a stranger, on an island then almost unknown to foreign tourists (it would take three trips to Sado before I saw another Westerner), elicited a reaction. By the time I stopped to look at the taraibune on exhibit I had several staff members of the museum gathered around me. No one said a word, so I decided to break the polite silence and asked once again, "Where is a tub-boat builder?" At the question everyone scattered back to the museum office, where curators began ordering secretaries to make phone calls. Before the situation could get out of hand I asked, "Ishizuka-san?" (Mr. Ishizuka?). The room fell silent, until one of the curators replied, "Iie, Fujii-san." (No, Mr. Fujii.) I was led to a chair where I sat and pondered the implications of this: There were two men still building tub boats?

The Tub Boat

Relatively little has been written about the history of the taraibune and even less detailing its construction. Apart from government records, the oldest publication discussing these boats is Dr. Shinji Nishimura's *A Study of Ancient Ships of Japan* (Society of Naval Architects, Tokyo, 1931). In one section the author looks beyond the historical into the mythological, searching for the origins of the *kagami-no-fune*, a boat named in one of the foundation myths of Japan. According to this legend a pair of dwarf deities, Ookuninushi no Mikoto and Sukunabikona no Mikoto, are credited with completing the creation of the country. The latter had arrived in Japan from the sea on a kagami-no-fune, landing at Izumo.

Fune means "boat," so Dr. Nishimura's interest focused on the meaning of *kagami*, which primarily means "mirror" but can also refer to a vine or the head of a barrel. One popular assumption has been that the dwarf's boat was a wooden rice bowl and he used a pair of chopsticks for oars. Dr. Nishimura believed kagami referred to a plant and so theorized the dwarf's boat was made of wicker. He referenced the Irish coracle, the bull boat of the Mandan Indians, and the umiaks of Siberia, all of which had frames of bent saplings; it was logical to assume there might have been a Japanese variant.

Dr. Nishimura turned his attention toward the opposite side of Honshu from Tokyo, along the Sea of Japan, an area famous for its wicker work, particularly the production of small baskets. While researching this region Dr. Nishimura came across the taraibune, not made of wicker, but bearing an uncanny resemblance to the mythological boat as he imagined it. In the 1930s when he made this discovery, taraibune were being used along about a hundred miles of the coast and on Sado island.[1]

Small, maneuverable craft like taraibune are perfectly adapted for Sado's rocky coastline, which is dangerous for larger boats. *Photo copyright Toshio Sato.*[2]

A wooden and a fiberglassed taraibune pulled out on the rocks near Shukunegi Village.

A fishermen using a sight box to spot shellfish in the shallows. He has a fishing basket and a selection of spears while his paddle hangs from the rope loop.

Two contemporary publications talk about the history and use of taraibune on Sado Island. *Minami Sado no Gyorou Shuuzoku* (*Fishing Culture of Southern Sado*) was published by the town of Ogi in 1975. It includes a brief treatment of how taraibune are built, as does Mr. Toshio Sato's *Hangiri* (*Half Barrel*), published in 2002. In that book Mr. Sato contends the taraibune fills a need based on a long tradition of inshore fishing known as *isonegi,* and the peculiar geography of Sado Island. In the richest fishing areas of Japan not only is net and line fishing conducted offshore, but also a substantial amount of shellfish and seaweed are gathered by hand or speared from the shallows. Isonegi refers specifically to this inshore fishing or harvesting. In many places this is done by divers, or fishermen wading into the sea, but a small, durable boat like the taraibune is also useful. When an earthquake in 1802 raised the shoreline of the Ogi Peninsula one meter, it created a broad, rocky, shallow foreshore with undersea ravines, a perfect environment for this craft.

Taraibune on Sado are propelled using either paddles (*kai*) or outboard motors (*sengaiki*). Kai are slipped through the rope loop at one end of the boat and sculled facing forward. I have found the easiest way to scull a taraibune is from a standing position with the knees braced against the side of the boat. One then grasps the two ends of the T-handle and swings the blade from side to side, pivoting it so it pushes water under the boat. With practice this motion becomes more of a figure-eight. Anyone with sculling experience should have no trouble moving the boat,

James F. English, Jr., took this photo of the harbor of Sawasaki Village while on Sado Island with the U.S. Army of Occupation in 1946. The Shinto shrine on the left can be found there today. (Inset): Detail of the previous photo, with two taraibune visible leaving harbor, the closer boat with two men in it. The author has never seen two people fishing from a single taraibune. *Photo copyright James F. English, Jr.*

Tub boats in the harbor with a conventional fishing boat in the background. Taraibune were inexpensive, allowing fishing families to have a second watercraft, and so were traditionally used by women. *Photo copyright Toshio Sato.*

although mastery of the kai equal to the fishermen on Sado takes considerably more practice. These hardy folk scull single-handedly in ocean swells while on their knees peering through a sight glass (called a *garasubako*, or "glass-box") and balancing a 25-shaku spear. Most boats also carry a counterweight in the form of a rock or a cement block to balance the boat when the user is working at one end.

For traveling longer distances, Sado fishermen typically scull single-handed from a standing or kneeling position. Outboard motors may be used, but only for getting from the harbor to the fishing grounds and back. Motorized taraibune predominate in one village on the Ogi peninsula where the good fishing is far from the harbor. The motors, either three or five horsepower, are not mounted on the centerline of the boat, but just to one side to avoid obstructing the rope loop aft, which is sometimes used for towing the long fishing equipment. The fishermen do not steer with the motor; rather, they sit or stand facing forward and insert the kai in the forward rope. Holding the blade vertically, they lower it into the water ahead of the boat like a fin and steer by moving it from side to side.

Mr. Sato's book also points out that Sado Island had a rich tradition of coopering. Barrels, buckets, and tubs were important trade items throughout the Sea of Japan, used to store and transport food, night soil, *miso* (bean paste), and sake, and to feed animals. One theory holds that the taraibune developed from the *sakanaoke,* a small bucket used to carry fish.[3] According to others, including my teacher, an animal feed trough somehow floated across a bay to a fishing village, inspiring someone to invent taraibune. Mr. Sato points out these feed troughs were made by cutting barrels in half; the title of his book, *Hangiri (Half Barrel),* is a colloquial name for these boats. In the rest of Japan, where they have been popularized in tourist literature, they are known as taraibune.

Mr. Koichi Fujii

It was just a short taxi ride from Ogi to Hamochi Village, where the driver deposited me outside the workshop of Mr. Koichi Fujii, who would seem to have an unlikely background for a boatbuilder, but hearing his story one cannot help but think building tub boats was his destiny. My first visit I spent just an afternoon with him. With snow swirling outside the flimsy walls of his shop I watched while he finished a lacquered ornamental bucket. Though my Japanese was almost non-existent, Mr. Fujii was a voluble, animated talker. Like Mr. Ishizuka, he seemed completely nonplussed at my arrival. Unlike Mr. Ishizuka, he was a whirlwind, jumping up to grab a tool I had noticed and demonstrating it, gesticulating and miming to get his meaning across. When I finally said goodbye he made it clear he wanted me to come see him again.

I returned to Japan in 1993 and spent three cold, midwinter days huddled with Mr. Fujii and his wife in his Hamochi home, along with an interpreter. My goal was to learn about his life and work. Mr. Fujii was born and raised on Sado. Though Hamochi shares the coastline with nearby Ogi, its fishing industry is subservient to a large and venerable company whose factory dominates the waterfront. The Marudai Miso Company has been fermenting soybeans to make miso paste for hundreds of years.[4] The best miso is fermented in wood. Miso tubs are made of cedar and stand over eight feet tall, their sides held together by enormous

(Left) The author holds a *maebiki oga*, or ripsaw, during his third visit to Hamochi in 1994. By this time Mr. Fujii was the last professional builder of tub boats. *Photo copyright Ms. Kazumi Muraki.* (Above) The fermenting room at the miso factory. Mr. Fujii spent most of his career making replacement bamboo hoops for these enormous cedar tubs built by his father and grandfather.

braided bamboo hoops. Mr. Fujii's grandfather and father worked in the company's cooperage, building the various sizes of tubs needed, and after graduating from an agricultural high school at age seventeen Mr. Fujii went to work with his father. During World War II he served in the Imperial Navy and Air Force. He tended horses at a military stable and later worked as a rigger, where he learned how to splice wire rope. After the War he returned to the cooperage at the miso factory where he worked until his retirement in 1980 at age 56.

At one point Mr. Fujii took us back to the miso company where he had worked and showed us the huge cedar miso tubs he had been responsible for maintaining and repairing. Some were over a hundred years old, and so much of his work had been literally restoring the work of his father and grandfather. Mr. Fujii specialized in making *taketaga*, the braided bamboo hoops that hold the barrels together. While the cedar bottoms and staves are nearly impervious to decay, the bamboo hoops do eventually deteriorate, and replacing them was a small industry. The overall output of the company's cooperage was so great one man did nothing but select and purchase bamboo from local landowners. Sado is famous for the high quality of its *madake* (*Phyllostachus bambusoides*), also called giant timber bamboo, a species that grows to over 65 feet and is still exported today. Another crew did nothing but split and shape the bamboo strips, which were then braided by men like Mr. Fujii.

Although Mr. Fujii was dressed in his work clothes, the staff treated him like royalty. While he was showing us the tubs, three men in dark suits came running into the fermenting room, halted before Mr. Fujii, and bowed deeply. It seemed there were no longer any craftsmen capable of replacing the gigantic braided bamboo hoops on the tubs, and the company had begun to use threaded steel rods in their place. Would Mr. Fujii consider coming back to work to make bamboo hoops, they asked? With a laugh he turned his back on the men and led us out of the factory. Clearly he preferred farming, fishing, and making a few tub boats to returning to the factory cooperage.

Over time I learned more about Mr. Fujii's transition from a cooper to a tub boatbuilder. After leaving the miso company he began to take jobs seasonally, replacing the hoops on tub boats. Usually in the spring he would travel for a few weeks along the coastline, stopping in villages where fishermen would have already harvested timber bamboo for him to use replacing their boat's hoops. Now and then he might also repair wooden buckets.[5] Eventually someone commissioned him to build a tub boat. To learn how he began visiting the workshop of Mr. Tomeikichi Fujii (no relation), widely acknowledged to have been the greatest builder of tub boats in the region. Within a few years both Fujiis were building tub boats, until Tomeikichi Fujii retired in 1975. According to his son, this was in part because the elder craftsman found his prices undercut by his new competitor, Mr. Koichi Fujii.[6]

Mr. Fujii confessed that even after working in the cooperage he did not consider himself capable of building a tarai-

A worker bundles hundreds of strips of split bamboo. Sado Island's timber bamboo is of such high quality that it is harvested, processed, and supplied throughout Japan. *Photo copyright Toshio Sato.*

Mr. Kunitarou Maguchi shown making new hoops for a tub boat in Shiraki village. In the spring Sado's coopers would travel through the fishing villages making replacement hoops for taraibune, which need new hoops every few years if they are used regularly. *Photo copyright Toshio Sato.*

bune. He was thus eager to learn from Tomeikichi Fujii, who had been a senior barrel maker at the factory, and later began building tub boats. In keeping with the traditional spirit of Japanese crafts, the elder Mr. Fujii did not teach per se, but was willing to let the younger man watch him. This is common in Japanese apprenticeships, which value observation and imitation over direct instruction. The process may be slow, but patience and persistence are considered essential prerequisites to mastery of any craft.

However, his teacher would not allow his apprentice watch him draw the lines for the bottom of the boat (the *shiki,* or *ura*) so Mr. Fujii began slipping into the shop at night with a candle to study his master's work. Getting the needed information was even more difficult because the elder Mr. Fujii measured everything with his fingers. Eventually the apprentice was able to painstakingly derive his master's measurements and go into business making tub boats. These hardships must have been behind his boast to me that a cooper works intuitively while a boatbuilder is forced to measure.

Between his retirement from the miso company in 1980 and my apprenticeship in 1996, Mr. Fujii had built over a hundred taraibune. His master had since passed away and with the death of Mr. Ishizuka in 1993, Mr. Fujii was the only man still building them. He built boats for maritime museums in Tokyo and Osaka, and a local tourist company commissioned him to build taraibune capable of holding up to four passengers, as well as a glass-bottomed tub boat. His other innovation was modifying the tub shape to accommodate outboard motors. Today these powered taraibune are

Outboard powered taraibune in Shiraki Village.

A fisherman leaves Shiraki steering his outboard-powered taraibune with his paddle from the bow. Outside of this village, powered taraibune are rare.

found mainly in the village of Shiraki. The fishermen there explained to me that they have day jobs and the best fishing grounds are far from the village; with only an hour or two in the morning to fish they need something faster than the traditional paddle.

The market for tub boats today is mostly elderly fishing families who gather seaweed and *sazae* (turban shell, *Turbo cornutus*), a delicacy that costs up to twenty dollars apiece in the market. As in traditional times, women are the more common users of taraibune, which then as now make a convenient and affordable second family boat. Taraibune without motors are also exempt from government licensing and registration fees. Part of the initial popularity of the boat in the Meiji period was a similar exemption from taxation.

Since the 1940s building taraibune has been only a part-time occupation. The craftsmen who built them were primarily coopers who understood the subtle differences between them and barrels. These men also performed seasonal work replacing bamboo hoops. For this it was necessary to travel along the Ogi coast, staying for up to a week in fishing villages where there was work. Mrs. Fujii told me in 2002, "For my husband it was a retirement job. He didn't have to build boats, but people kept asking him and he knew how to do it." When Mr. Fujii asked me to apprentice with him in 1995 it was literally the last chance to learn this craft from an experienced taraibune builder.

In October of 1996 my wife and I arrived at the Fujii home to begin our short stay, arranged so he and I could build one tub boat together. His enthusiasm was palpable, and while his wife took Catherine to the kitchen he quickly led me to the most formal room in his home, a dark space framed in lacquered *keyaki* (zelkova) wood posts and sliding screens. He sat down at the *irori,* a small open hearth, and began heating water for tea. Once ready he poured two cups. This gesture of hospitality at first entering someone's home is common in Japan, but Mr. Fujii was so glad to see us, and so eager to get started, once the tea was prepared and served he tipped his head back and drank his like it was a shot of whiskey. "There!" he said, jumping to his feet, "Let's get started!" Off we went for a tour of the workshop.

Tools

Mr. Fujii had an impressive tool collection, befitting a lifetime of working with wood. Most he inherited from his father and brother, and he maintained all of the tools he had used while working at Marudai Miso. He owned over a dozen planes and chisels, and a large selection of saws. For shaping the bamboo strips he had a drawknife, called a *sen*.[7] In addition he owned several tools used mainly by house carpenters or temple builders, including axes, an adze, slicks, and *yariganna*, an ancient tool resembling a large Native American crooked knife. He only had a few power tools: an electric drill, a jigsaw, and a circular saw.

Just a fraction of these tools were needed to build taraibune. Mr. Fujii had a plane with a round bottom for shaping the inside curve of the planking. A regular flat-bottomed plane was used to shape the outside curvature and to plane the top edge of the planking after the boat was assembled. A special type of chisel known as a *tsubanomi* (sword-hilt chisel) was used to bore holes for the edge fastenings in the staves and bottom planking.

Mr. Fujii used a special tool called a *yotsuwaku* for splitting the stalks of bamboo. He also had a wide variety of *kumibou*, known in English as fids—wooden tools used for splicing rope—for braiding the bamboo hoops and wedging them onto the boat. A large wooden mallet was used to drive the hoops into place. The hoops are not struck directly with the mallet; a punch is held against the hoop and the mallet strikes the punch. Except for the wooden mallet Mr. Fujii made all the tools for working bamboo using local hardwood.

Finally, Mr. Fujii had a selection of tools and patterns for laying out the lines of the boat bottom, the *shiki*. He never used a tape measure. One tool, a *bunmawashi,* a compass by definition, was actually just a long, narrow piece of wood, the size of a yardstick, with a series of holes in it. We pinned one end to a centerline on our shiki planking and, holding a pencil at the other end, swung an arc to mark out the radii of the bottom of our boat. He had two patterns for shaping

Mr. Fujii's hand tools for making taraibune included fids for braiding bamboo, mallets, punches, planes, marking gauges, patterns, chisels, a drawknife, hatchet, and bamboo splitter.

Drawing on a beam of Mr. Fujii's shop showing a tub boat paddle with dimensions.

Mr. Fujii at his bench, holding a stave with his feet and using his chisel to make a hole for bamboo nails. He is striking the hilt of his chisel to remove it from the wood.

the two radii of planking (side planks and end planks) and a pattern for marking the nail locations. On a beam in his shop he had drawn a paddle labeling all its dimensions. When cutting bamboo for hoops he carried a short, knotted string to measure the circumference of a stalk.

Mr. Fujii worked on the floor of his barn. His workbench was a large block of hardwood with a stop fit in a groove across one end. He would sit at the end of the block on the floor and, depending on the work, sometimes hold the material with his feet. In this position he would plane all the side planking material and make the nail holes. Shaping and braiding the bamboo was also done from a seated position, outside in this case to accommodate the length of the material. Working on the floor is traditional in Japanese crafts, but it can be excruciating for the uninitiated.

Mr. Fujii ordered his lumber locally and stored it under cover at his house for at least one year before using it. He used *sugi*, or Japanese cedar, the same material used in barrels, buckets, and boats, which he purchased flat sawn, which meant only a few planks from the center of the tree would have vertical grain. Mr. Fujii did not waste material in his boats; he trimmed the wood close to the bark edge so his planking had both heartwood as well as the weaker sapwood. In looking at surviving older taraibune, it is obvious a higher quality of wood was previously available. Some older boats are made entirely of knot-free lumber. In his later years Mr. Fujii came to tolerate knots in his material.

Mr. Fujii believed that when using flat-sawn wood the heart side of the hull planking must face the outside, toward the sea. The heart side is more rot resistant, and a survey of the oldest boats built by four different craftsmen showed that all adhered to this rule. Conversely, in barrels and buckets the heartwood faces the inside. However, the principle is the same: the heart side faces the liquid.[8]

All fastenings for the boat are made of bamboo. Mr. Fujii made his own bamboo nails, each approximately 2 sun long and split from small sections of scrap. Because they are used as an edge fastening, both ends are sharpened.

Design

Taraibune fall into two basic categories with regard to shape: round and oval. It has long been believed the first taraibune were round. The oval shape was a logical development because it helps the boat track in a straight line when underway. It is not clear exactly when the transition from round to oval occurred, or who first made oval taraibune. On Sado some people believe all taraibune were round before the 1940s and Tomeikichi Fujii, Mr. Fujii's teacher, was the first to build an oval version. However, the oldest taraibune in the Sadokoku Ogi Folk Museum is oval and is believed to date from the beginning of the Showa Era (about 1926). On Sado the oval taraibune has predominated since at least the 1940s, although photographs show round taraibune also in use on Sado into the 1950s.[9]

The only lines of a taraibune drawn by the builder are on the shiki planks. The shape of the bottom is governed by two overlapping circles with their centers separated by a short distance; their circumferences are then joined by larger arcs to make an oval. Each boatbuilder has his own method and dimensions for this layout. To draw the two smaller circles for the ends of the shiki, Mr. Fujii used a stick with a hole at one end. He would pin the stick to the shiki boards and then, swinging the stick in an arc, draw the circles on the wood. He then used a long string, a helper holding one end, to swing the large arc joining the two circles. Laying out the

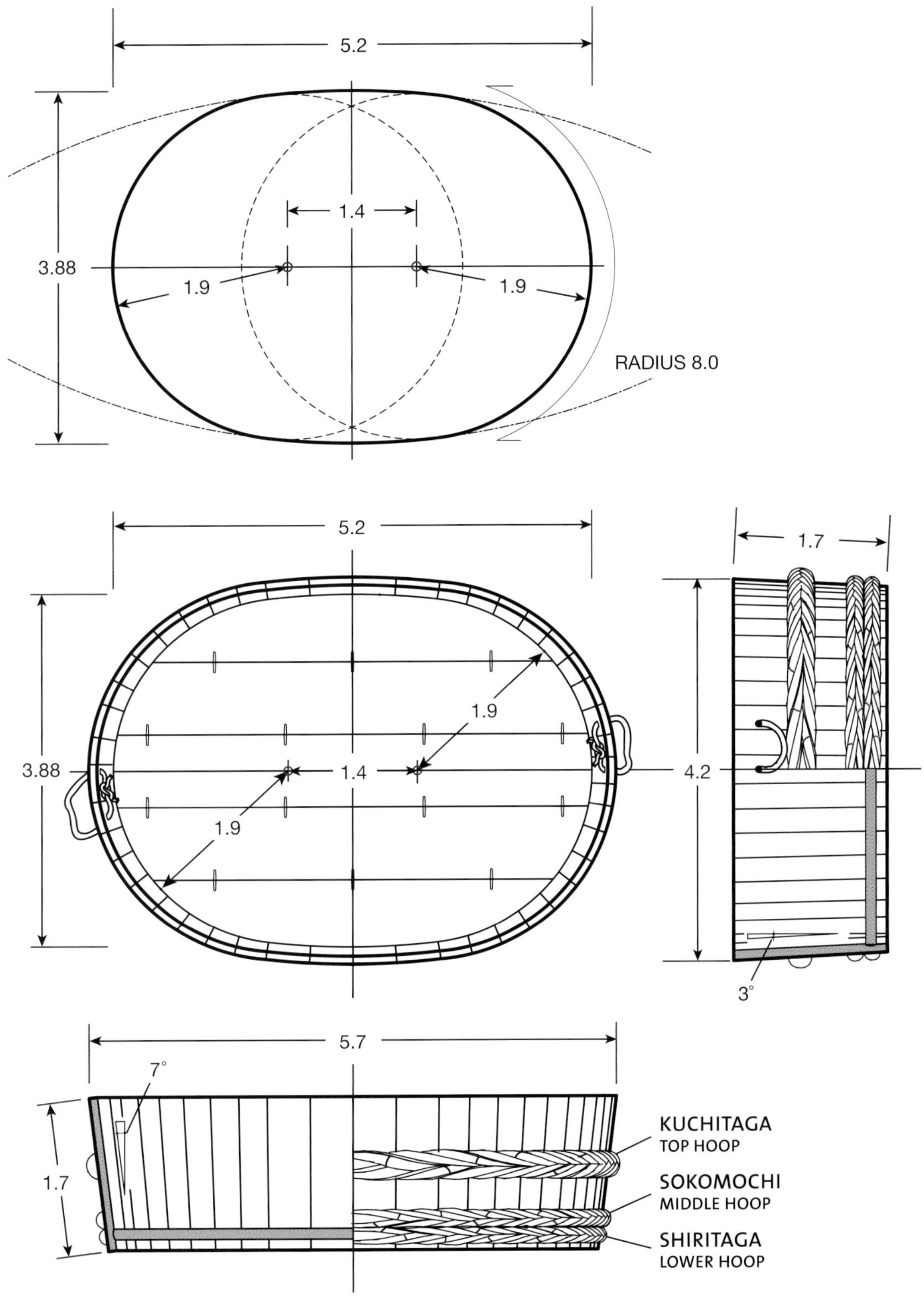

Taraibune dimensions are measured to the inside of the planking. Builders would make boats of slightly different sizes to suit their customers. The author is most familiar with the method used by Koichi Fujii to draw the shape of the shiki. His layout consisted of arcs of two sizes: one for the ends of the boat and one for the sides. Mr. Fujii swung these two arcs so they intersected each other. In measuring taraibune built by other craftsmen, the sides seem more parabolic where the large arc curves to meet the small arc. Probably those craftsmen drew an arc and then bent a batten to join the large arc to the smaller circles. *Tub boat drawings courtesy of the Kodo Cultural Foundation.*

Year built:	2002
Planking thickness:	8 to 9 bu
Bottom thickness:	1.2 sun
Owners:	Niigata Prefectural Museum of History and the Kodo Cultural Foundation

Lines are based on author's research with Koichi Fujii from 1990 to 1996. Dimensions are of the two boats built by the author and Taka Higuchi. Mr. Fujii described these dimensions as ideal for a standard fishing boat. His tourist boats were larger.

bottom was the only measuring involved in building the boat. I never saw Mr. Fujii use a tape measure; his stick and string were set to the dimensions he needed. Later he would measure the circumference of the bamboo we harvested using his knotted string. It reminded me of what he had said about his own teacher measuring only with his fingers.[10]

Another important element of the taraibune shape is the flare of the sides; its oval circumference is larger at the top than at the bottom. This taper is a bit more pronounced at the ends of the boat; the sides flare slightly less. As we shall see during construction, this taper allows the hoops holding the hull together to fetch up tight and is created by making the vertical hull planks slightly wider at the top than the bottom. This difference is created when the edges of the side planks are planed; a bit more material is removed at the bottom edge. Mr. Fujii never measured this amount; it was something he could do naturally, the result of years of practice.

The shiki of some taraibune have a slightly cupped shape. Mr. Fujii believed this feature gave the boats better handling in the water, and that a curved bottom was very important for motor-powered taraibune. This detail is the only real difference between taraibune and Japanese barrels, which have perfectly flat bottoms. In my survey of the oldest remaining taraibune in use on Sado I found both curved and flat-bottomed boats, although it is now hard to accurately determine this feature because older boats may have lost this curve because of the loosening of the hull structure due to age.

According to Mr. Fujii, the ideal length-to-width ratio for the shiki was 5.2 shaku to 4 shaku, although some fishermen specified longer boats to make it easier to carry fishing gear. Customers gave the boatbuilders dimensions when they ordered boats, and Mr. Fujii believed the ideal boat would be as long as its owner's height, and that this was about the largest boat that person could carry. Carrying taraibune was common when boats were grounded by the falling tide, and old photos show them being transported upside down on fishermen's heads. Today fishermen are elderly and mostly women, and most boats are covered with fiberglass, making them far too heavy to carry; these days they are tipped on their sides and rolled. The tourist industry on Sado also uses larger taraibune capable of carrying up to four people.

Bottom

I was awakened at 6 a.m. on the first working day of my apprenticeship by the sounds of Mr. Fujii already at work in the shop outside our window, and I rushed downstairs to join him. Designing the taraibune begins with the layout of the shiki. On the shop floor were the planks for the bottom of our boat, five boards 1.2 sun thick, rough cut and resting on low blocks. These are the widest boards used and in most taraibune they are made from flat-sawn material. The boards were laid lengthwise, edge-to-edge, and Mr. Fujii planed their edges straight for a tight fit. As noted earlier, the heart side of the bottom boards faced down, and once laid out, Fujii drew a centerline perpendicular to the edges. He then drew a large V across the boards with its point where the centerline met the edge; the sides of the V recorded the orientation of the bottom boards.

I watched while Mr. Fujii drew another centerline lengthwise and marked the center points, 1.4 shaku apart,

A fisherman carries a taraibune near Shiraki Village. This is now nearly impossible since most boats have been fiberglassed, increasing their weight, and almost all Sado Island's fishermen are now elderly. *Photo copyright Toshio Sato.*

Mr. Fujii laying out the shape of the bottom, drawing two arcs to scribe the ends of the boat.

The three pieces of the shiki of a taraibune built earlier by Mr. Fujii, prior to assembly. The bamboo nails are arranged in pairs along the edges of the seams. *Photo copyright Toshio Sato.*

for drawing the arcs for the ends of the boat. Pinning his simple compass to the center points and then swinging it in an arc while holding his pencil against the end, he drew two circles of 1.9 shaku radius. In Mr. Fujii's standard-size boat, the outer edges of these two circles are 5.2 shaku apart. The only other fixed measurement he used was the radius of the arcs joining the two end circles. This was always 8 shaku, which made the width of the shiki about 4 shaku.[11]

Later, when the shiki is installed in the hull and the hoops pounded on tight, the bottom boards will be compressed tightly together. If the edges of the bottom boards are beveled correctly the bottom can be forced to cup slightly. Mr. Fujii did this by beveling very slightly the edges where the boards meet. Without removing material from the bottom of the edge, he planed a slight bevel so when the boards are laid together again flat, the edges touch at the bottom and show a gap of a little more than 5 *rin* at the top. Five rin is the smallest useful measurement in the shaku-sun-bu system (see chart, p. 13), corresponding to one-half bu, just over 1.5 mm, or 1/16 inch.

The first bevel allows the bottom boards to cup from side to side. Mr. Fujii also removed a small amount of material at either end of the planks so the shiki would also curve lengthwise. To do this he set the plane on the original bevel and carefully removed material from the ends, being careful to keep the overall bevel a smooth curve. When completed, the boards just touched in the middle at the bottom of each seam and opened gradually a slight amount at the outer edges. This opening should be about 5 rin at the ends of the planks, which means at the ends the top edges will be open a bit more, about 1 bu. Again, these are small amounts; you don't need to remove much material to create a compound curve in the bottom.

The boards are then fastened using small bamboo nails. These are about 2 sun long, 2.5 bu wide, and 1.5 bu thick with a sharpened point at each end. This is the size of Mr. Fujii's tsubanomi, the special chisel used to make holes for nails. Today tsubanomi are extremely hard to find. As an alternate fastening method, one could drill holes and substitute dowels for bamboo nails. The nails for the shiki are located in the plank edges in pairs, spaced along the edges about 1.5 shaku apart. The nail should not fit extremely tight in its hole; it should be the same size as the hole. If they are too tight they prevent the bottom boards from bending into a curve. Of course the depth of the holes must be at least half the length of the nail. With the nails inserted we used a wooden mallet to pound the bottom boards together.

Since the sides of the boat flare slightly, the edge of the shiki must have a slight angle, about seven degrees, and Mr. Fujii used a pattern to guide him as he sawed the edge. He used an electric jigsaw set to the angle and cut just outside the line. Then we stood the shiki up on edge and finished the bevel with a plane. Along the sides of the boat, the flare is closer to three degrees so he flattened the bevel slightly there.

Side Planking

Our first day together I did not do much more than watch Mr. Fujii work, and on the second day he again got to the shop before me. I found him sitting on the floor with his workbench (a large block of wood) next to a pile of stave material. He set each plank on edge on his block and clamped it between his feet. He then leaned forward with his plane in his outstretched arms and drew it back along the edge quickly, a pungent curl of cedar swishing off the blade and falling to the floor. Mr. Fujii didn't say a word when I entered; instead he pointed to a stool sitting in the corner of the shop. I sat down. He had told me earlier of his misgivings about the inadequacy of a training program limited to helping him build a single boat. I couldn't argue with him, especially given the long years typical of craft apprenticeships in Japan. I did point out that since I was a wooden boatbuilder, I knew how to use the tools; a typical apprentice in Japan would know absolutely nothing at the outset of training. Mr. Fujii brushed this off. He granted that I knew how to build Western boats with Western tools, but he wasn't even sure I could use a Japanese plane.

And so he began by having me sit. I watched him from the stool for the entire second day. It did give me a chance to take detailed notes and photographs, though I chafed at the delay in starting work and dispelling his doubts. As the afternoon waned Mr. Fujii jumped to his feet and, pointing to the cedar shavings carpeting the shop floor, said to me, "Clean it up," and walked out of the shop. A few minutes later he looked out of the house as I was about to put the first load of shavings in his burn barrel. "Not there." he said, "they're for the bath." He showed me the small door opening into the clay surround for his iron bathtub. I stuffed the shavings inside, and he lit them. That evening there were hot baths for all.

The planking of the taraibune is of two types: the side planks following the flatter arc (8 shaku radius); and the end planks following the tighter radii of the bow and stern (1.9 shaku radius). In general the planks along the side are much wider than those around the ends. In some of the oldest taraibune I have surveyed the side planking is almost 1 shaku wide, but in general side planks are about half that width. In Mr. Fujii's boats all the side planks were between 5 and 6 sun wide at the sides and 2.5 and 5 sun wide at the ends. The planks were all 1.7 shaku long, and the material was 1 sun thick.

As noted earlier, in order to create the flare each plank must be slightly wider at the top. I never saw Mr. Fujii measure this; when he planed the edges he simply removed a bit more material toward the bottom. For him this meant an extra stroke or two with his plane. Given his experience this was both accurate and far faster than marking the taper on each piece. In contrast, I need to mark the amount of material to remove from the edge to get the right taper. Having built several taraibune since then, I have found the best system for tapering is to make end planks 2 to 3 bu wider at the top (being careful never to exceed 3 bu), and side planks no more than 2 bu wider at the top. The next step is to bevel all the plank edges.

Mr. Fujii had a large collection of patterns, identical to those used by coopers throughout Japan. His included small patterns for various sized buckets, with the largest for taraibune. Each size taraibune has three L-shaped patterns for its curves and bevels. One indicates the bevel around the edge of the shiki. Two others are for the staves: one shows

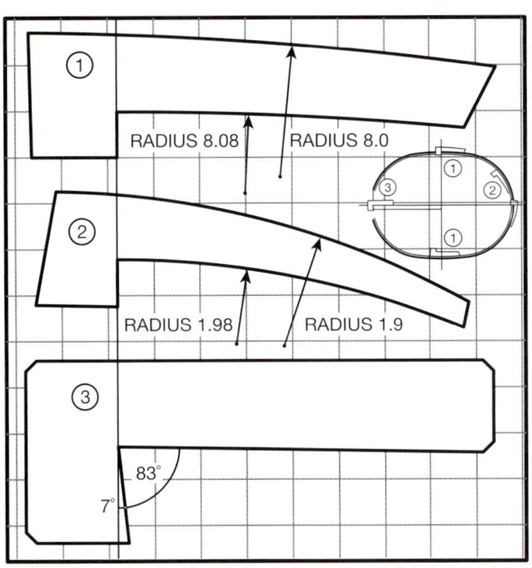

Mr. Fujii used three patterns to build taraibune: the upper two for the shapes of the side and end planking, and the lower one for the bevel of the shiki. Photograph shows the patterns in a different order. Rule marks and grid squares indicate 1 sun.

These patterns are for the boats we built. Patterns for any size boat can be derived from the layout of the arcs. To make the inside edge of the pattern, draw a new arc equal to the layout plus the thickness of the planking.

The angle of the plank edge is the radial line. The outside edge of the pattern is equivalent to the inside face of the planking, which is the same as the original layout.

The taper of the boat sides actually change; the ends flare about seven degrees while the sides flare about three degrees. However, if the shiki curves properly when installed, the angle between the bottom and sides should remain fairly constant. Mr. Fujii used just one pattern, set to seven degrees, to check the bevel of the bottom; in our experience the pressure exerted by the hoops squeezes the bottom and sides together so tightly any discrepancies in this joint disappear.

the shallower curvature of the side planking and the other the tighter radius of the end planking. The bottom of the L-shape of each indicates the bevel of the plank edge.

Mr. Fujii began by planing all the bevels first, carefully stacking the planking when finished so he would not confuse the bottom and the top edges. To create a watertight hull, it is important to remove a bit more material in the middle of the plank edges. When two planks are placed side by side there should be a slight gap, about 5 rin, between them in the middle. Mr. Fujii described this technique as *korosu*, literally "to kill." In Chapter 5 we learned a related term and technique used in conventional Japanese boatbuilding, *kigoroshi,* "killing the wood." This describes how the middle of the edges of planks are pounded with a hammer before being joined. When fastened, the fibers of the edges compress and later swell in the water to make a tight joint. What Mr. Fujii did was similar in principle: by shaping the edges so they touched first at only the top and bottom, when the middle hoop is finally installed and the gaps closed, pressure will be concentrated at the top and bottom of the plank seams. This pressure is most crucial at the bottom, near the taraibune's waterline, where the seam will be tightly compressed. Again, this slight curvature was never measured. Mr. Fujii simply made an extra pass with the plane at the center of the board. He also regularly checked his work with his pattern and by holding planks together up to the light to confirm the correct gap.

My third day in the shop began with Mr. Fujii again ordering me to sit on the stool. I watched him, took notes, photographed, and occasionally cleared the accumulation of sweet-smelling shavings as they piled up around him. Not a word was spoken. I felt a rising sense of anxiety I was never going to get to actually participate in the building of this tub boat, but to be honest, I also wanted to prove to Mr. Fujii I was a competent craftsman capable of this work. Suddenly he jumped to his feet and pointed to the spot where he had been sitting. "Work," he ordered, and I quickly got down on the floor. Finally I had my chance, I thought, but as soon as he handed me the plane he walked out of the shop. I waited a bit, expecting him to watch me, but after a few minutes I realized I had been left alone, so I started in on the pile of rough planks to my left. I worked this way for about forty-five minutes until he returned. He went through my pile of finished planks, putting a few aside and piling most alongside his. Once sorted, he pointed to the pile of rejects and told me to fix them, then disappeared again.

While the length of my apprenticeship was not traditional, the teaching methods were. In a Japanese apprenticeship, patience and observation are essential because little or no direct instruction takes place. My hours seated on the stool were a necessarily truncated equivalent of perhaps years spent sweeping the shop, sharpening tools, and performing other basic labor. But all the while I would have been expected to watch the work and processes taking place around me. With little direct instruction, the onus is entirely on the apprentice to absorb it all. Most importantly, when the day comes to do the work, the apprentice is expected to be completely ready. Luckily I had the tool skills and understood the process, largely through my earlier visits and interviews. That evening my wife told me she had found Mr. Fujii napping when he left me to work alone.

All the work thus far had been done with a flat-bottomed plane. Curving the inner face of the planking required a curve-bottomed plane called a *maruganna*. We worked hollowing the inner faces of the planking to a finished thickness of 8 to 9 bu at the thinnest part, in the middle. Then, switching back to our flat-bottomed plane, we rounded the outside face of the planking. At this point the inside faces do not have to be perfect; after the sides are assembled there is a chance to finish them smooth. But it is important to have the outside faces properly curved at this time. The sides can only be assembled using hoops, first temporary hoops and later the final hoops. With those in place there is no way to work on the outside of the planking. Moreover, the smoother the outside, the more surface area there is for the hoops to grip. Since only friction keeps the hoops on the boat, any bumps and ridges in the planking weaken their hold.

The preparation of the side planking is completed by making holes for the bamboo nails that fasten the planks together. Mr. Fujii used a pattern to draw two lines across each plank edge. The pattern was hooked over the top edge

Mr. Fujii holding a plank pattern to check the curvature of the stave and the bevel of the edge.

(Above) Mr. Fujii's well-worn tsubanomi, used for making nail holes. The hilt is designed to be struck with the hammer to remove the chisel from the work. It is shown here next to a new one, eloquent testimony to a lifetime of service. (Right) This 1980s photo shows finished side planks arranged around the shiki as Mr. Fujii determines their arrangement and the width of the final plank. *Photo copyright Toshio Sato.*

of the plank and had notches 2.5 sun and 1.25 shaku from the top. Using a pencil in the notches we could quickly mark consistent nail locations. Then using a conventional marking gauge we scratched a mark in the middle of the pencil lines. The marking gauge was set to ride on the inside of the planking, and Mr. Fujii had the correct orientation labeled to remind him.

As when fastening the bottom boards, the tsubanomi, or sword-hilt chisel, was used to make the holes. Mr. Fujii had a bamboo cup filled with a rag soaked in camellia oil, and he periodically dipped the point of his chisel into it. This kept the chisel lubricated, making it easier to knock out of the wood. As noted, the bamboo nails do not hold the boat together, rather they help line up the parts and keep the assembly together until the hoops are installed. Since it is crucial for the sides to be smooth, the nail holes must be uniformly positioned. If a hole is off the mark the plank edges will not line up.

Side Assembly

Before assembling the sides of the boat Mr. Fujii first blocked the assembled shiki 1.2 sun off the floor and arranged the side planks that would be required to go around it. Seated in the middle, he held a side plank up and held his finger where one of its edges met the bottom. Then he laid the plank down at that spot and fit the adjacent plank, starting at his last mark. From the original layout of the bottom's curved edge he could tell where side planking and end planking should begin and end, and he made four reference marks showing where planks should line up along the edge of the bottom. As he worked, the arrangement took on the shape of a giant flower blossom, with planks radiating away from the oval shiki like petals and Mr. Fujii seated in the middle like a pistil. When he came back around to his first plank, he made a custom plank to fit the last gap. Since he wanted all the side planks to be at least 2.5 sun wide, he might narrow a wider plank before making his final, shutter plank.[12]

Since the shiki will eventually be pounded down into the hull, the circumference of the side planking has to be just right to ensure a tight fit. Thus it is critical that the bottom be raised 1.2 sun off the ground (Mr. Fujii used scraps from the bottom boards for this) and that the layout of the side planks around it be done precisely. He had a sketch on his workshop wall which he claimed showed the ideal plank count: five wide pieces on either side, sixteen narrow planks at one end and fifteen or sixteen at the other. However, I saw him build boats with different plank counts, and I suspect he was more concerned about using material efficiently than conforming to any standard. Mr. Fujii stressed one point: in laying out the planks, the seams between the side planks should *never* line up with any seams between the bottom planks, as this increased the risk of a leak. As he arranged side planks he made sure a plank crossed each of the bottom seams. Although Mr. Fujii only marked the location of four planks seams around the bottom, I have marked every plank in the subsequent tub boats I have built. When finally installing the shiki these marks help me line up the bottom and sides.

Outside the shop, Mr. Fujii loved poetry, calligraphy, and fishing. There were two poems written on the walls of his barn, one describing the difficulties of raising children and another telling of a marten killing five of his hens. He told us he had recently helped form an ensemble of singers and dancers with other rice farmers. Several evenings, especially

Mr. Fujii's sketch of the ideal number of planks for the sides and ends of a tub boat. Along with his sketch of a paddle, these are the only recorded notations used to guide his work.

Mr. Fujii ready to lay out the planking for the boat built during the author's apprenticeship.

toward the end of our stay, he insisted on taking my wife and me fishing at the Hamochi pier or other spots along the coast. Other evenings we sat after dinner and watched him compose poetry, using a set of calligraphy brushes and ink he kept in a small cabinet next to the table. He even composed a haiku about a particularly beautiful wisteria that stood at the corner of his home, writing the poem in chalk directly on the wall of his house:

In winter, all the leaves fell off, leaving only fruit;
Seeing the fruit swinging in the winter wind,
I wait for spring.[13]

Before assembling the sides of our taraibune, Mr. Fujii took several planks and, holding them on edge, reached for his *sumitsubo*, or ink line. With a simple bamboo brush dipped in the ink well, he wrote on the edges of the planks in graceful characters phrases such as, "Good fishing," "Safety at sea," and "You can't help laughing when you catch a lot of fish." Once we assembled the hull his calligraphy was covered forever. I asked if this was a tradition he learned either from his father or another boatbuilder, and he said no, he had begun doing it himself when he started building tub boats. Furthermore, he never told the boat owners of the messages hidden in their hulls. I have met other boatbuilders in Japan who leave various marks on their boats, only rarely signing their names, but I have never heard of a practice like that of Mr. Fujii.[14]

Mr. Fujii chose a random plank and put its top edge down on the floor, a bit away from the bottom. He inserted the bamboo nails, then took the plank next to it and joined it to the first. Continuing in this way the planks were removed in order and assembled off to one side. Because the planks are put together with the top edge resting on the floor, they leaned in and supported one another, so the assembly stayed together. Once all of the side planks have been put together a temporary hoop, called a *karitaga,* was driven down over the outside of the hull.

The author doing the same work in 2002 at the Niigata Prefectural Museum of History. *Photo copyright Ms. Kyoko Tsuchiya.*

The author assembling a taraibune at the Niigata Prefectural Museum of History in Nagaoka, Japan. *Photo copyright Ms. Kyoko Tsuchiya.*

Cooper shown smoothing the inside faces of barrel staves in a woodblock print by Katsushika Hokusai (1760–1849) from the series "Thirty-six views of Mount Fuji." *Image courtesy of William Pearl.*

The author planing the hull using his own method when building a taraibune for the Kodo Cultural Council on Sado Island in 2002.

Mr. Fujii planing the inside of the hull during the author's apprenticeship in 1996.

The temporary hoop is not braided, but twisted. It is made by taking a long strip of bamboo and wrapping it from the butt end around the side assembly at about the middle. Removing the circle while keeping it at the same circumference, the tail is simply twisted around this loop several times, locking it together. It is then tied tightly with string at all the crossing points of the twist to keep it from loosening when pounded on the boat. Building later boats I found even this arrangement would loosen, so I drill a hole at one of the crossing points and fasten it together with a piece of wire.

The hoop is pounded onto the boat using a wooden mallet and a special punch called a *shimeigi*. This is a block of wood held against the edge of the hoops and struck with a mallet. Mr. Fujii made this and all his tools for working bamboo, including splitters, punches, and fids, out of hardwood. The shimeigi is curved on the inside face to lay nicely against the outside of the planking. It also has a small steel plate screwed to the bottom facing the hoop to prevent it from splitting.

As we drove the hoop on, the side assembly stiffened. It is necessary to get the hoop quite tight, since the next step requires lifting the assembly on its side. If the hoop is not tight enough the side planking can fall apart. Since the temporary hoops must not interfere with the placement of the final hoops, Mr. Fujii sometimes installed two. Because the hull is inverted the first hoop installed is the largest, and it can pass over the smaller of the two temporary hoops. Once one finished hoop is installed one of the temporary hoops can be removed, making way for the second hoop, and so on.

Our next step was to finish planing the inside of the side planking. No matter how carefully one shapes the individual pieces the interior surface will still require smoothing, which is best accomplished by turning the assembly carefully on its side. To maintain the sides in their final oval shape requires two people, and Mr. Fujii's wife would normally help him. Now it was my turn, and while I stood holding and rolling the side assembly on his command, Mr. Fujii sat on the floor, partly inside the hull, and carefully planed all the seams smooth. It was a sublime moment, mimicking exactly a famous woodblock print by Hokusai showing a cooper doing the very same work above. On subsequent tub boats I used cross-braces fastened to the bottom edges of the hull when it was still upside down on the floor. One stick ran lengthwise and the other ran at right angles to the first, each length corresponding to the exact dimensions of the boat. I then screwed the braces into the end grain of the bottom edges of the planking. The braced assembly was rigid enough to allow one person to plane the inside unassisted.

The final step in preparing the side assembly is to put a very shallow groove, about 5 rin deep (roughly 1/8 inch), around the inside of the hull where the shiki will fit. Years earlier Mr. Fujii had talked to me about this technique, describing two Sado Island traditions: one is to have the bottom meet the sides with no dado joint of any kind; the other is to put the slight groove in the side planking which the shiki will drop into. The dado-less method is called *buchikomi* and the grooved method *kirikomi.*[15] To cut this groove he used a small cooper's plane with a sole curved in both directions. Using the groove gives a firmer connection between the shiki and the sides but some people believe this construction is also more susceptible to rot.[16] Mr. Fujii beveled the edges of the bottom to match the flare of the sides, but he did not round the corners of the bottom planks to match the groove.

Joining the Bottom and Sides

Putting the shiki into the side assembly is a task that inevitably requires several tries, and Mr. Fujii and I attempted this a few times before we got it right. The key is careful positioning of the bottom, which has to line up with the reference marks on the sides and be the correct, uniform distance from the bottom edges of the sides. With the planking assembly on its side and balancing the bottom on one edge, Mr. Fujii worked the bottom into the hull, using his feet to push it into position. One must watch the reference marks aligning the side and bottom planks carefully; once the shiki wedges tight it is impossible to rotate it to line things up. Then the only way to make it right is to kick it back out and start over.

Again, building tub boats later I developed a different method: I laid the side assembly right side up and placed several blocks about 3 sun thick on the shop floor inside it. Then I lowered the shiki onto the blocks. At this height the bottom did not quite touch the sides, allowing me to line up carefully my reference marks. With a helper I could then lift the side assembly until the bottom was caught inside it. We then moved the hull to another set of blocks about 1 sun high, the same height as the space I wanted between the bottom and the lower edge of the side planking. By pounding the bottom down until it hit all the blocks I knew it was set to the correct height.

With either method, the bottom should be wedged tightly enough so the boat can be turned upside down to install the permanent hoops, although on our first attempt the shiki dropped out as Mr. Fujii began pounding the first hoop. This happened to me as well on later boats, and I have subsequently learned to screw small temporary blocks inside the boat to support the bottom while the hoops are installed. As far as I know Mr. Fujii never did this.

Mr. Fujii working the shiki into place with his feet. At this point the hull is held together by temporary hoops. *Photo copyright Toshio Sato.*

Making the Hoops

There are two types of bamboo hoops: *karitaga* and *kumitaga,* twisted and braided, respectively. Bamboo hoops are used throughout Japan for all types of traditional wooden buckets and barrels. Most smaller containers use a twisted hoop since the bamboo strips are long enough to circle them several times. In larger vessels such as taraibune, and barrels for sake, beer, and miso, the need for strength necessitates a braided hoop made up of several pieces of bamboo. Braiding allows them to be spliced together. The hoops for taraibune each contain four strips; the hoops on the largest miso barrels contain as many as six or eight.

Taraibune have three hoops and each is slightly different. The top hoop is called the *kuchitaga*. It is generally made of wider strips since it is supposed to be the largest hoop and act like a wave-breaker on the hull. The middle hoop, the *sokomochi,* is considered the most important for holding the hull together. The bottom hoop, called *shiritaga*, is made of narrower bamboo strips and mainly protects the bottom edge of the planking. The twelve bamboo strips prepared for braiding were arranged by size. The four largest were used for the top hoop and the four smallest for the bottom hoop. Since the strips are braided in pairs, we tried to match pairs of the same size.

Mr. Fujii selected his bamboo from the groves around his village. Although he acknowledged even good bamboo was inexpensive, as little as 500 yen (about five dollars) for a 40 to 50 shaku stalk, he complained that good bamboo was getting harder to find. Having never worked with bamboo before, I had to take him at his word, but I regret my language skills were too basic to have a more complex discussion about what constituted the best bamboo. The thirty years he had worked for the miso company, primarily making the enormous hoops for miso barrels, must have given him remarkable insights into this material.

Japanese craftsmen who work with bamboo refer to its size as the circumference of the stalk at eye level; loggers and boatbuilders measure trees the same way. Mr. Fujii believed the best size for making the top two hoops were the tallest stalks measuring no more than 8 sun in circumference at eye level (Mr. Fujii was about 5 shaku tall). For the bottom hoop he preferred 7 sun bamboo. The rings and the sulcus (the groove running lengthwise in bamboo) form the weakest points in the bamboo, so he looked for bamboo with large gaps between rings, in an attempt to minimize the number of weak points. Madake has smaller rings than other species of bamboo, an important consideration given the flexibility needed to braid the material into hoops.

A stand of madake, or timber bamboo. Sado Island has very high quality bamboo and Mr. Fujii looked for the tallest stalks with an 8 sun circumference, measured at eye level.

The dates of hassen (for 1996) recorded by Mr. Fujii on the walls of the workshop. He was adamant about not cutting bamboo during periods proscribed by this calendar.

Mr. Fujii also believed only "male" bamboo should be used in boatbuilding. To determine the sex of the plant he looked at the lowest branch: if it were a single stalk he deemed the plant male; if it forked the plant was female. In fact, bamboo is a monoecious plant, meaning it is both male and female. I have, however, heard an interesting theory supporting Mr. Fujii's rejection of "female" bamboo. The size of the sulcus is determined by the number of branches emerging at each node, therefore bamboo with forked branches will necessarily have a wider sulcus. Single branches, like the kind Mr. Fujii preferred, create a narrow and shallow sulcus. A wider groove is less inclined to flex and more inclined to snap at the weakest point, usually the branch joint on the node. "Female" bamboo is also more likely to split irregularly, especially if the sulcus has multiple grooves. Given the flexibility required to braid the material into hoops, Mr. Fujii's theory makes practical sense despite its botanical shortcomings.[17]

Mr. Fujii relied on the traditional *rokuyou* (literally, "six days") almanac indicating lucky and unlucky days to determine when he could harvest bamboo. He refused to cut bamboo for five days before and after each of six particularly unlucky days called *hassen*, although there were exceptions depending which of twelve Chinese zodiac animals ruled that day.[18] To this day many Japanese loggers, craftsmen, and farmers adhere strictly to this almanac, and JA-Zenchu, the Central Union of Agricultural Cooperatives, still publishes it annually.

Mr. Fujii led me up the steep hillside behind his home to harvest bamboo for our boat. He carried a small saw and a hatchet called a *nata*, the ubiquitous tool of the Japanese farmer. He carefully studied the bamboo and used his knotted string to make measurements. We moved very slowly through the bamboo grove as he carefully and silently studied stalk after stalk. First his cat, and then his wife joined us. Mr. and Mrs. Fujii talked quietly about possible choices. He told me to cut one stalk down and then rejected it once he had a chance to inspect it on the forest floor. Eventually he found three stalks he liked. We cut them down, and I dragged them out of the forest and back to a covered area running the length of the front of his house. Mr. Fujii normally cut, split, and braided his bamboo the same day, since its flexibility is directly related to its moisture content. Since studying with him, however, I have not

The yotsuwaku, used for splitting the bamboo stalk into four pieces. Mr. Fujii made his from two pieces of hardwood; modern versions made of iron are sold commercially.

The bamboo is first split into four pieces. The splitter is driven through the bamboo using the back of the hatchet as a hammer.

always had this luxury, but I have had no problem braiding bamboo harvested even weeks earlier.[19]

Preparing the Bamboo

The first step is to make a split lengthwise along each sulcus. These are the grooves running lengthwise up the stalk, appearing alternately on opposite sides between nodes. Since the sulci compromise the strength of the material, splitting here will place them at the outer edges of the final strips. Mr. Fujii split the bamboo by placing the blade of his nata in each groove and striking the back of it once with a mallet. Once the sulci were split, he made a cut that lined up with the splits at the small end of the stalk, and another cut at right angles to the first one. Opening up the stalk into four quarters, he pushed a cross-shaped wedge called a *yotsuwaku* into the cuts. Using the back of the nata like a hammer, he then drove the wedge through the stalk of bamboo, splitting it into four pieces lengthwise, taking care that the edges of the yotsuwaku bisected the existing splits in the sulcus. Although Mr. Fujii made his own wedges of hardwood, iron versions are available in Japanese hardware stores and home centers.[20]

The second split: Mr. Fujii pushing the quartered bamboo strips past his nata blade, which he holds upright. *Photo copyright Toshio Sato.*

After splitting the bamboo into quarters, the material dividing the sections inside the stalk is removed. Mr. Fujii accomplished this from a seated position, pulling the strips over his thigh and knocking these dividers off with the back of his nata. The work area alongside his house was long enough so he could stay seated in the middle and pull the strips past him. He didn't let me do any of the work shaping the bamboo, except to hand him material as he asked for it.

Front view of the above, Mr. Fujii splitting the quartered bamboo with his nata.

Next, the nata was used to carefully split each quarter in half again, producing a total of eight strips from a single stalk of bamboo. Since the edges of split bamboo are extremely sharp, Mr. Fujii wore an apron made from an inner tube. Remaining seated in the same spot and starting at the small end of each quarter, Mr. Fujii held his nata vertically and pushed the strip quickly through the blade,

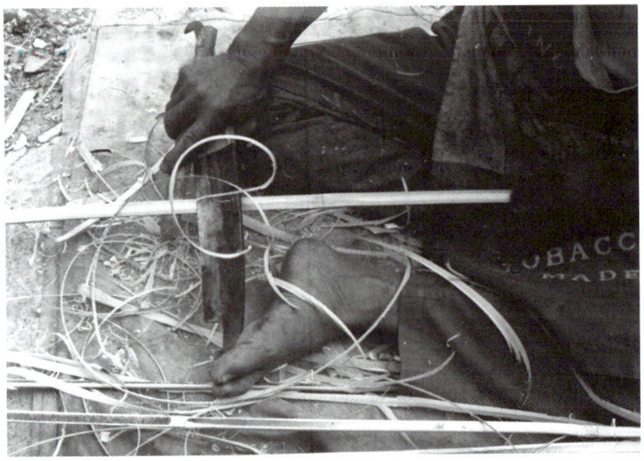

Mr. Fujii was able to do the final shaping of the strips with lightning speed. He held a small piece of bamboo and his drawknife in his right hand, supported by his knee, and pulled the bamboo with his left. The bamboo stick pressed the strip to the blade, while he supported the opposite end of his drawknife with his left foot. *Photo copyright Toshio Sato.*

Mr. Fujii braids hoops seated in a parking lot across the street from his house. Each hoop consists of four forty-foot strips of bamboo.

Mr. Fujii demonstrating how to braid bamboo hoops. *Photo copyright Catherine Wood Brooks.*

twisting the blade as he pulled to control the direction of this split. Although he could push the strips of bamboo at amazing speed, and still split very accurately, this is the most time consuming part of preparing bamboo strips. The blade of the nata is made from a thick piece of tool steel and probably acts more like a wedge than a cutting tool. Today, I sometimes use a Western drawknife with its thinner blade to split bamboo, but it takes experimentation to find the best method.

Each strip has a concave and convex side, so like the cupped cross-section of a measuring tape it will bend in one direction but resists bending in the other. The two edges on the concave side must be trimmed for the bamboo to be flexible. Mr. Fujii wedged his sen (drawknife) against his knee and foot and held a small piece of bamboo as a guide, pulling each strip with the green, outer side facing down. The strips passed under the blade, trimming the two outer corners. The result is a cross section of a rounded diamond shape. The edges of the strips should be blunt; sharp edges will be crushed when the hoop is pounded onto the boat. The strips also taper near what was the top end of the stalk and Mr. Fujii tried to keep this taper gradual and smooth. With very sharp tools and practice the bamboo can be pulled very quickly and still be trimmed consistently. It was good that he did not let me do any of this work, and since he prepared our strips in a matter of minutes, he might have assumed these simple techniques weren't worthy of dwelling on. In reality they take quite a lot of practice to master and what Mr. Fujii could do in minutes later took me hours. In 2002 a student from Sado Island and I experimented with power tools to speed this process. We set up a fence for our electric joiner, and tried running the bamboo strips through it. This produced very uneven results and we gave up. Later, in an interview with one of Mr. Fujii's coworkers at Marudai Miso, we learned that the company once employed a dozen workers who did nothing but prepare bamboo strips. They too had attempted to do this work by machine but abandoned the effort.

Unless the butt ends of the strips are heavily planed, the lower three or four shaku of the bamboo strips are too thick and stiff to braid; therefore a mark should be drawn on the strips about 4 shaku up from the butts. This material will not become part of the hoop but Mr. Fujii always waited until the hoops had been pounded into place on the hull before trimming them off.

Braiding the Hoops

I had seen how fast Mr. Fujii braided hoops on my previous visit and knew it was going to be the most critical part of my training. It was also clear that he was not prepared to explain the process, so in anticipation I had brought a video camera to Sado for my apprenticeship. True to form, Mr. Fujii did not slow his pace for my benefit.

Each hoop is made by first starting a foundation hoop using two strips of bamboo. After marking one strip for the proper size (explained in detail below) Mr. Fujii twisted the two strips and then brought the twisted section around to the base, forming a circle. Now the tails could be braided into this foundation. Mr. Fujii started one hoop for me, dropped it at my feet and then walked away to make the two other hoops. My wife was standing behind me, filming. I sat on the pavement, the beginnings of a hoop on my lap, watching Mr. Fujii in a vain attempt to understand what he was doing. He worked at a breathtaking pace, snapping the forty-foot lengths of bamboo and tucking them into the braid, a giant circle enclosing him tighter as the strips were pushed through. He also wore rubber gloves to protect his hands from the sharp edges of the bamboo strips.

My wife and I puzzled over how to braid and I made some desultory attempts to get it right. Mr. Fujii, meanwhile, had finished one hoop. When he saw me struggling, he jumped to his feet. He took my hoop and turned it in his hands, checking each braid. When he found an error he promptly disassembled the hoop back to the point before I made the mistake, and thrust it back at me. No wiser, Catherine gingerly retrieved the hoop he had finished and we began inspecting it. Between the two of us we managed to get my hoop braided at about the time Mr. Fujii finished his second hoop. As unfamiliar as this teaching process was for me I can say it certainly focused my concentration.[21]

Mr. Fujii made sure I understood the aesthetic aspects of properly made hoops. This was not a frivolous consideration: The hoop most pleasing to the eye would also be the most functional. If the strips and pairs are matched in size and gently taper to their ends, they will lie together neatly in the braid in an unchanging pattern. Uneven strips or an irregular pattern indicate a hoop that will lack friction and loosen. Correctly braided braids are both incredibly strong and very beautiful. The qualities of symmetry, strength, and beauty are interwoven as tightly as the bamboo itself. In the simple truism that applies to any craft: "What looks right is right."

Braiding for Beginners

Although any good amateur woodworker with patience should be able to make all the parts for a tub boat, the preparation and braiding of bamboo hoops is a more difficult undertaking. It is perhaps the rarest skill I learned in Japan, where the number of living coopers is a fraction of the number of boatbuilders. Like many skills, once mastered it seems easy, but at the outset the learning curve is daunting, and Mr. Fujii's teaching methods didn't make it any easier. However, the challenges I faced vividly illustrate the rigors (and necessity) of the long Japanese apprenticeship. For those who understandably will not have this opportunity I offer the following step-by-step description.

The first step in making a hoop is to establish its circumference. This is done by taking one of the first two strips and, starting with the lower (butt) end, wrapping the strip carefully around the boat where the bottom edge of the finished hoop will be positioned. As mentioned earlier, the lower 4 shaku of the strips are probably too stiff to braid, so mark the point where this waste will be cut off later. With the strip held tightly around the boat at the correct height, a mark should be made on the bamboo where it crosses that first mark. This is the circumference of the boat where the hoop will lie. For Mr. Fujii, the lower edge of the upper hoop is about 8 sun above the bottom edge of the planking. The lower edge of the middle hoop is 2.5 sun above the bottom edge of the planking, while the lower edge of the bottom hoop is flush with the bottom edge of the planking.

Beginners should remember that the braid is governed by just a few principles. The green skin of the bamboo should always face outward. No changes should be made in the pattern while braiding. (Conversely, a change observed in the pattern indicates a mistake.) The first two strips of bamboo are tied tightly together at the first of the two marks made when measuring. The work begins by twisting these two strips seven times up to the second mark, then bringing the end around to form a circle with the two marks lining up with each other. Each twist creates a point where one bamboo strip crosses the other. Each crossing should look the same: the strip coming from the left either always crosses over the strip coming from the right, or vice versa, depending on which way the strips were originally twisted. It does not matter which way they are twisted, but the same pattern *must* be repeated throughout the braiding. Like Mr. Fujii, I braid hoops while sitting on the ground with the hoop on its side resting on my left thigh. Looking at the hoop from this perspective the top edge is on the left and the bottom edge is on the right, so the strip coming from the left always crosses over the strip coming from the right. One could twist the hoops in the opposite direction and achieve the opposite effect, but the captions and illustrations here will uniformly reflect this left-over-right orientation.

A further consideration during this first step are the gaps created between the crossing points; these are the openings through which the bamboo will be braided, so it is important that the distance between them remain consistent. When the twisted pieces of bamboo are first brought around into a hoop these crossing points may become bunched together. Early in the process, Mr. Fujii would regularly insert his fid into the braid and, pushing or pulling the tool, would continually adjust the location of the crossing points. These points can be shifted easily at first but as more bamboo is braided the pieces get locked in place by the accumulated friction of the braid. If a very small gap is left at one end of the hoop it will later be impossible to make a space to insert the bamboo. The goal at the outset is to create a foundation hoop that is symmetrical.

Mr. Fujii had a feel for what was needed and would make these adjustments unconsciously. For the beginner I suggest measuring the distance between the two marks (the hoop circumference) before twisting the first two strips. Divide that distance by eight and make a mark on the bamboo to indicate evenly spaced crossing points around the hoop. When the bamboo is twisted seven times (totaling eight twists, since where the bamboo is tied at the butts represents one), there should be a crossing at each mark. If not, use the fid to adjust accordingly. Make sure the green skin of the bamboo is facing outward. The two "tails," what we will call the unbraided ends of the strips, should form a V above the last crossing and the first tie at the butts should be brought around to lie in the base of this V. The two tails are crossed to close the V and tied, holding the butt ends. If the original two marks now line up with each other, the twisted portion forms a hoop the circumference of the hull.

The hull of the taraibune is tapered only slightly. In order for the hoops to seize tightly, it is critical they are of the correct circumference for their position on the boat. Mr. Fujii taught me slight adjustments that must be taken into account for each hoop. I stated earlier the hoop is first formed and the two marks marking the circumference of the hull are aligned. For the upper hoop, the bamboo is slid apart so the marks are moved apart (opened) 1 sun, i.e., making the circumference of the hoop 1 sun larger than the measurement taken from the boat. For the middle hoop these marks should be opened a bit less than 1 sun apart. For the bottom hoop the marks should line up exactly. When braiding begins it is crucial to make sure these two marks remain the proper distance apart for each hoop. These differentials are critical because braiding the four strips together shrinks the diameter of the hoop slightly. The 1 sun enlargement ensures the hoop will remain sized correctly. No adjustment is made to the last (lowest) hoop because it fits tightest on the boat. As we shall see, this hoop is the most difficult to install.

Again, during these initial stages of braiding the bamboo slides along itself readily and adjustment is easy, but at some point the assembly becomes very tight and impossible to adjust. If one then notices the marks have moved, the only recourse is to disassemble the hoop until the adjustment can be made.

The final step in preparation for braiding is to tie all the crossing points so they are firmly fixed on their marks and equally spaced around the hoop. As noted, Mr. Fujii never had to do this. However, I have found tying the crossings helps keep the braid evenly spaced from the outset. Use twine, and when the hoop is complete cut all the ties and pull them out.

I strongly suggest that beginners first practice the four-strand braid with something other than bamboo. Because the bamboo strips are roughly rectangular in cross section, the best material for practicing braiding hoops is flat. Small rope is too flexible and rattan or wood strips may not flexible enough. The plastic strapping used to secure boxes is an excellent substitute. It is cheap, readily available in long lengths and being flat behaves like bamboo strips. Choose the stiffest size available. To get started one needs only four pieces each about ten feet long, which can be braided into a practice hoop about two feet in diameter.

Working in the seated position described, the hoop should rest on one's left thigh, with the long tails running out to one's right. A fid is inserted into the first opening (the opening between the tie at the base of the stalks and the first twist) to create more space for braiding. Taking the left-hand tail first (the one on top), the tail should be pulled back until the tip can be inserted—from outside the hoop to the inside—into the opening formed by the first twist. The full length of the tail should be pushed through this opening until it lies flat against the hoop. The tail will come out of this opening on the inside of the hoop and it is critical that it exit to the right (bottom) side of the hoop. The original opening in the twist now has one tail braided through it from left to right. Now pull back on the right-hand (bottom) tail until you can insert the tip through the same opening just before the left tail. Pull this tail through so it exits to the left (top) side of the hoop and lies flat; then pull out the fid. Mr. Fujii always inserted his bamboo in the opening in front of his fid (the side of the tool facing away from him). A suggestion for the beginner: if the left (top) strand is inserted in front of the fid and the right (bottom) strand inserted behind the fid (the side closest to the user),

Bamboo Hoop Braiding

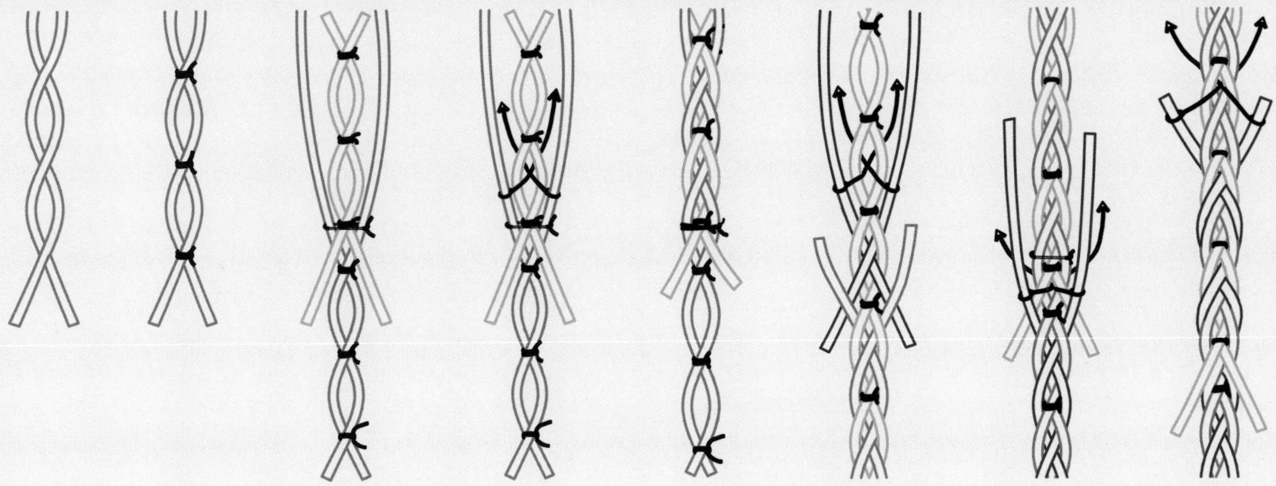

Fig 1 *Fig 2* *Fig 3* *Fig 4* *Fig 5* *Fig 6* *Fig 7* *Fig 8*

Figures 3, 4, 5, 7, and 8 all show the spot where the first strips of bamboo are joined into a hoop. After they overlap to form the foundation hoop (starting in figure 3) the edges of the strips are shown in a slightly darker gray. The edges of the last two strips added to the foundation hoop (starting in figure 6) are darker still.

Make a mark on one strip of bamboo about 4 shaku from the butt end. Measure the circumference of the hoop by wrapping it around the boat where the bottom edge of the hoop will be. Make a second mark where it crosses the first mark.

Top hoop: Circumference is measured about eight sun above the bottom edge of the sides.

Middle hoop: Circumference is measured about 2.5 sun above the bottom edge of the sides.

Bottom hoop: Circumference is measured at the bottom edge of the sides.

Using strips of bamboo of matching widths with the green side facing up, tie two pieces together tightly with twine about 4 shaku above the butt ends.

Pull the strips apart slightly. Begin twisting the two strands by laying the left (top) strip over the right (bottom) strip (**fig. 1**). Continue twisting the two strips seven times until you have a total of eight crossings (seven plus the point where you tied the butts.)

Adjust the crossing points so they divide evenly the space between the upper and lower marks on the bamboo and tie each firmly (**fig. 2**). You should now have eight tied overlaps forming seven openings. The mark near the butt end should be tied but the top mark should not be tied.

Pull the twisted bamboo into a circle with the green side facing out so the free ends (the tails) wrap around the first crossing. Tie this loosely together (**fig. 3**). For each hoop the measurement marks must be adjusted differently:

Top hoop: Slide the bamboo so the marks are 1 sun apart, making the circumference of the hoops slightly larger than measured.

Middle hoop: Slide the bamboo so the marks are a little less than 1 sun apart, making the circumference slightly larger than measured.

Bottom hoop: Keep the marks lined up exactly as measured.

Insert the fid (not shown) into the first opening between the two lower ties to enlarge the opening. Take the left strip of bamboo and insert it into this opening, entering from the outside of the hoop and exiting from the inside (**fig. 4**). Pull all the material through. Take the right strip and pass it through the same opening, making sure it passes under the previous strip, maintaining the left-over-right braid.

Continue braiding these tails through each successive opening until you reach a point halfway around the hoop. Make sure the pattern of the braid remains consistent and the marks measuring the circumference of the hoop have not changed (**fig. 5**).

Insert the butt ends of the next two strips (green side facing out) into the opening ahead of where you stopped braiding. The ends must cross in the opening and the crossing must be oriented in the left-over-right pattern (**fig. 6**).

Begin braiding the new set of tails. When you reach the place where the hoop was first joined together, be sure to braid underneath the butt ends (**fig. 7**).

At this point the hoop has one complete braid all the way around. Continue braiding the remaining material (**fig. 8**). Braid one pair of tails until you reach, but do not pass, the other pair. Then braid the other pair of tails, again without passing the first pair. Braid the two pairs of tails back and forth in this way until the material is all used up.

the correct left-over-right orientation of the strands will always result.

In the West fids are long, slender cones of hardwood made on a lathe, used to open the strands of rope for splicing. Mr. Fujii's fids, called *kumibou,* literally "braiding pole," were roughly rectangular in cross section. He made them of hardwood about 1.5 shaku long, 2 sun wide, and 1 sun thick. They tapered toward one end to a dull chisel-like point and had rounded edges. He would insert the tool into the braid on the flat, and then by twisting it ninety degrees he could open it wider. Twisting the tool gives the user maximum leverage. As the hoop is built and the bamboo strands become increasingly interwoven, the fid becomes absolutely necessary for opening the braid. And take care when the fid is removed because the bamboo will snap shut and can pinch fingers.

Look carefully at the first braid. Where the two tails cross in the opening the tail from the left should lie on top of the tail from the right, matching the pattern set by the original twist. The left tail, after being braided, has emerged and becomes the new right tail, while the right tail is now

(Above) Mr. Fujii finishes a hoop while his wife looks on. Only later would the author come to appreciate just how much she knew about building taraibune. (Right) Mr. Fujii with a pair of finished hoops. He could harvest, split, and braid a set of hoops for a boat in less than a day.

the new left tail. Since the symmetry is important, it helps now to position this crossing in the center of the opening. The braid should not be loose; Mr. Fujii would slap the bamboo with his fid to work it into the braid. You can also insert the tip of the fid ahead or behind the crossing and by pulling or pushing, adjust its location. Keeping the braid tight is also crucial to maintaining the correct circumference. A sloppily braided hoop will bunch the material and wind up being too small.

The second braid is done exactly as the first, feeding the left tail into the next large opening and the right tail into the same opening but once again making sure it passes underneath the left tail. Now is the time to check that the 1 sun differential between the original marks has not changed. Also carefully examine what has been braided, making sure the left strip always crosses over the right strip. The pattern should be totally consistent. The easiest error to make at this point is to cross the tails the wrong way.

Continue braiding until you have reached a point halfway around the hoop, directly opposite where you joined ends to get started. Check the reference marks one last time because by now it should be nearly impossible to slide the bamboo and make adjustments. The next step is to add the two remaining strips of bamboo, brought into the hoop through the next opening in the twist. Taking the butt ends of the strips, feed them backwards from the center of the hoop through the opening until about 3 shaku protrudes. The new strips then need to be aligned in the usual pattern. Where they come through the opening they need to cross one another. The butt of one strip should protrude to the left (top) and its tail should emerge from the hoop on the right (bottom). The other strip should do the opposite. As always, where they cross in the opening, the strip coming from the left (top) should pass over the strip from the right (bottom). Tying these strips where they cross can help keep them sorted.

Abandoning the previous strips for the moment, the new strips are now braided in exactly the same way, continuing on around the hoop toward the starting point. The hoop now has two sets of tails emerging from it as well as two pairs of butts. Mr. Fujii did not trim off the butt ends until after the hoop was installed on the boat. Unfortunately they are hard to work around, especially braiding past them. As you continue working around the hoop with the second pair of strips, you approach the point where you began braiding the first strands. The last braid before overlapping should be inserted in the same opening the original butt ends protrude from. Be sure not to braid over the butt ends; the tails should cross and enter the hoop underneath the butts.

The next challenge for the beginner is overlapping the braid. Up until this point all the braiding has been done through the original twisted strands but now every part of the hoop has a single braid. Since all the original twisted openings now have one crossing in their centers this leaves an elongated diamond-shaped opening on either end. These are the new openings into which the strips will be braided. Since the strips are always braided in pairs, I like to think of adjacent pairs of strips as "neighbors." For instance, if I place my thumbs on the two strips forming the opening I just braided the tails through (underneath the butts) I can use my remaining fingers to hold the two tails out to the left and right. The strips under my thumbs are the neighbors of the tails; they immediately precede the tails I am holding. By following the strips beneath my thumbs I can see where they cross each other in the center of the braid. The crossings form the bottom half of a diamond-shaped opening. The tails in my fingers need to be braided through this opening.

Thought of in this way, the neighboring pairs of strips follow each other around the hoop, and their order never changes. The preceding pair under my thumbs always enters the hoop just ahead of the tails I am braiding. I say to myself while braiding, "Follow the neighbor. Left over right." It requires constant attention, especially because the hoop is now such a confusion of tails and butt ends, but if the principles are followed it all works out. However, even Mr. Fujii made mistakes. In 1995 while demonstrating to me how to make hoops he braided in the wrong opening. As he pulled the strands apart, he said with a laugh, "Even monkeys fall from trees."

All that remains is for the two sets of tails to be braided into the hoop. At this point the pairs of tails are on opposite sides of the hoop. The procedure now is to braid one pair of tails halfway around and up to but never past the other pair. Then switch to the second pair of tails and braid them. Continue working, switching back and forth between the two pairs, until the material has all been braided.

Mr. Fujii had a slightly different method. After braiding one set of tails around and meeting the second set he began to alternate between the two, braiding the rearmost tails over the forward tails, each in turn passing the other. Leapfrogging the two pairs of tails this way he finished braiding the hoop. In my own work I have found it much easier to concentrate on a single pair of tails at a time. With either method the results are the same.

Final Assembly

At this point the hull is upside down, with the shiki inserted about 1.5 sun from the bottom edge of the side planking, and at least one temporary hoop holding the side planks together. Various punches mentioned earlier, fids, and two large wooden mallets are used to install the permanent hoops, with the largest of these, the top hoop when the boat is righted, installed first. Mr. Fujii normally soaked his hoops for a few minutes in the stream running past his house. The hoop is first placed over the boat as far down as it will go. Mr. Fujii ordered me to hold the punch tightly against the side of the boat and pound the hoop in place. He told me to concentrate on hitting the hoop at points where the bamboo strips were larger and stronger, although crushing some of the edges is inevitable. We worked around the boat, forcing the hoop down evenly. Mr. Fujii followed me, sometimes slapping the hoop lightly on its face with the mallet to loosen the weave a little bit. As the hoop got tighter, he abandoned his mallet and picked up a larger punch with a small handle. My job was then to pound with the largest mallet while he guided the punch. He set the cadence with a song. Within a few minutes my shirt was soaked with sweat.

In 1995 I had watched Mr. Fujii's wife swing the mallet for her husband, something I assumed she did because he had back trouble. In fact she later told me she always pounded the hoops for her husband's boats! I was chagrined to learn that this diminutive woman had regularly done work that

An older taraibune in storage still shows a tight seam between the shiki and side planking. Note also the rope loop for the paddle, offset to one side of the boat's centerline.

Mr. Fujii uses a smaller mallet and punch to start the middle hoop. *Photo copyright Toshio Sato.*

Normally called tagashime (hoop punch), these tools for pounding hoops on the boat are called shimeigi on Sado Island. The handle on the upper punch allows one person to hold it while another swings the mallet.

The bottom hoop is sized so tightly it is very difficult to start. Mr. Fujii uses one foot to hold the hoop while trying to advance the fid around the edge using his mallet. *Photo copyright Toshio Sato.*

Mrs. Fujii swinging the large mallet while her husband guides the handled punch. It takes hours to pound the hoops in place.

brought me to near exhaustion, but this was not the last time I would hear stories of boatbuilders' wives taking significant, and often extremely demanding, roles in the shop. She also said her husband's singing attracted visitors to the workshop.[22]

Pounding the hoops is excruciating work. As it nears its proper position a hoop moves just a millimeter each time it is struck. Mr. Fujii brushed water on the hoops to lubricate the sides of the boat and ordered me to keep pounding. The whole process can be summed up as: drive the hoops on as tightly as possible, and then drive them even tighter. The top hoop is in place when its bottom edge is about 8 sun from the upper lip of the hull. Any gap between the planks had now disappeared; the hoop has literally crushed the planks together.

The second hoop is considered the most critical to the integrity of the boat, as it exerts pressure at the waterline and near the junction of the sides and the shiki. Its bottom edge will rest about 2.5 sun from the bottom edge of the planking. It should take the same extreme effort to pound it into place; otherwise it is not tight enough.

The final (bottom) hoop is the most difficult to get on. It doesn't have to be pounded much, but it needs to be stretched to get started on the boat. Since thinner bamboo strips are used in making this hoop, it may stretch slightly as it is wedged on the hull. We used as many as four fids to install this hoop. First, we passed the edge of the hoop over the hull at one end. This was my job now, but on an earlier visit I watched Mr. Fujii work at one end of the hull while holding the hoop in place at the other end with his foot. We inserted fids inside the hoop on either side so their tips just caught the outer edge of the hull. Holding the fid upright, we used the mallet to strike the edge of the fid, advancing it forward. As the fid forces the hoop over the edge of the hull, the hoop can be tapped down onto the hull with the mallet. Little by little, more of the hoop is forced over the hull until the bottom edge of the hoop is flush with the bottom edge of the planking. At this point Mr. Fujii placed his nata carefully against each projecting end of bamboo right where it emerged from the braid and, striking the tool with a sharp blow, he trimmed them off. I always use a small saw to make sure I do not cut any other strands of bamboo.

The next step is to force the shiki more tightly into the hull. We turned the boat over, and made a mark on the side planking inside where the shiki sat. Mr. Fujii then sat

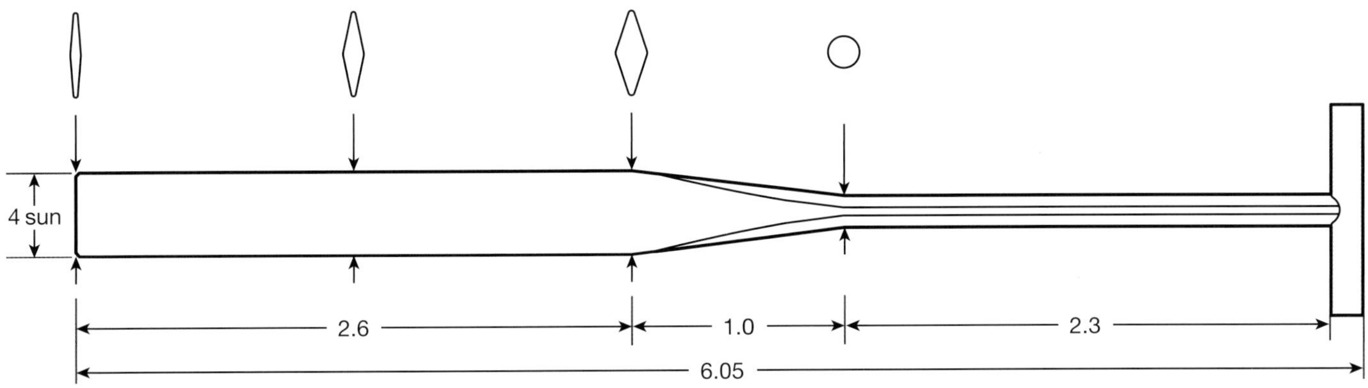

Paddle dimensions shown here, in shaku unless noted, are those used by Mr. Fujii.

inside the boat and with his mallet, pounded between his feet around the edges of the bottom. He watched the gap grow between the marks and the bottom to judge whether it was going down evenly. He kept pounding the bottom down until it was within 1 sun of the edge of the side planking. The shiki acts like a wedge as it is driven into the hull and if forced too far it will begin to push apart the side planking, opening the seams. However, most taraibune (including other boats built by Mr. Fujii) have their bottoms much closer to the edge of the hull. In one of my earlier interviews with him, he said the bottoms, which are cupped now from the squeezing of the side planks, should not be too close to the edge because the side planks are supposed to take the wear when the boats are pulled over rocks and sand.[23]

Now only the final details remained: putting a small bevel on the top edges of the planking and drilling a pair of holes at either end for short loops of rope, about 1 to 1.5 shaku long and tied or knotted on the inside. These ropes serve as carrying handles, but are chiefly used to hold the paddle. The holes (about 2 cm or 6.5 bu) are about 5 sun apart and 2.8 sun below the top edge of the planking. They are not centered on the ends of the boat, but offset slightly to one side. When fishing, the taraibune is paddled with one hand, normally the right. Therefore, one hole of each pair is drilled on the centerline and the other drilled to its right (as viewed from inside the boat).[24]

It had taken us five days to build our tub boat. When it was finished we took a few celebratory photographs. I asked whether tub boats were ever launched with any ceremony and Mr. Fujii said, no, except perhaps a celebratory drink with the owner.

My wife and I had offered to help the Fujiis harvest their rice as a way of thanking them for hosting us, so we stayed another week. The backbreaking effort was relieved, for me, by the satisfaction I felt having finally worked alongside Mr. Fujii building a boat. The Fujiis were absolutely delighted to have our assistance. As other farmers stared, open mouthed, at the two foreigners working in the rice field, Mr. Fujii shouted, "Our friends! Our friends are helping us!" Our last evening in his home, he took out his ink, brushes, and a *shikishi*—a gold-bordered white square of stiff paper—and composed a calligraphic farewell card for us.

The Fujiis epitomized the hard-working lives of so many elderly, rural Japanese who seem inexplicably to continue farming and fishing, despite the protestations of their children. Their labors often seem, at first glance, to border on madness. My wife and I spent the spring of 2003 living in a nearby fishing village and we regularly stopped by to see Mrs. Fujii. On one visit, when she didn't answer the door, we looked in the backyard and found her cutting her lawn *with a pair of scissors.* And yet, while the Fujiis may have worked from dawn until sundown, their pace was always unhurried, almost serene. To this day when my wife and I feel a long list of household tasks bearing down on us we say to each other, "It's time for a Fujii day."

Mr. Fujii's death in 1999 came as a shock, and yet, ironically, it seemed to be a catalyst for an effort to preserve the unique skills he had shared with me. In corresponding with Mrs. Fujii after her husband's death, I agreed to come to Sado and finish his final boat for her. While there in February of 2000, a representative of the Sado-based Kodo Cultural Foundation met with me several times to ask what could be done in the wake of this tragedy. I told him I had enough material for a short manuscript detailing the construction of these boats. I felt that in addition to publishing my manuscript and drawings I should also teach an islander.

In 2002 I returned to Sado to build two more tub boats. This time I had a student, a local carpenter, Mr. Taka Higuchi. We built one tub boat on the mainland as an exhibition at the Niigata Prefectural Museum of History in Nagaoka. On

Mr. Homma demonstrating his method of braiding hoops while standing. The author always saw his teacher do this work sitting down.

Along with Koichi Fujii, boatbuilders Tomeikichi Fujii, Hatsutaro Ishizuka, and Fukuzo Aoki were considered the preminent remaining taraibune craftsmen. Lines and dimensions from a boat in original condition by each of these three other builders are shown for comparison. Also included is a taraibune from the Sadokoku Ogi Folk Museum, possibly the oldest in existence, and a round tub boat from Noto Peninsula.

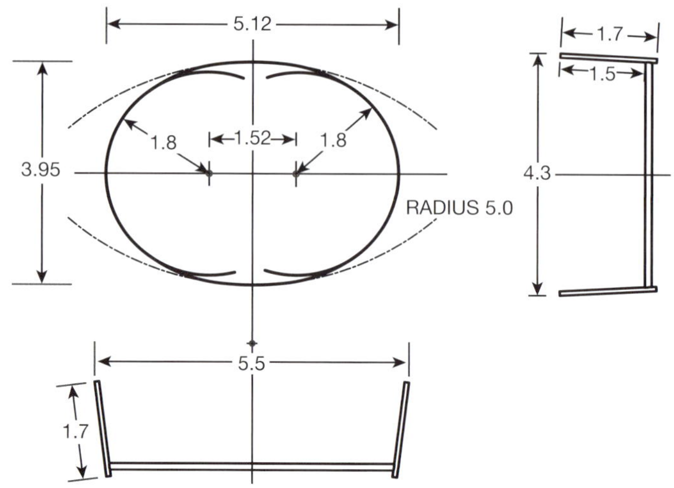

Taraibune built by Tomeikichi Fujii

Year built:	around 1975
Planking thickness:	9.5 bu to 1 sun
Bottom thickness:	1.1 sun
Owner:	privately owned

The bottom is made of flat-sawn material with the sides mostly made of vertical grain, knot-free planks. Flat-sawn side planks usually have the heart side facing out, but not always. Bottom is flat.

Sado we worked in a defunct community building above the harbor of a tiny fishing village on the Ogi Peninsula. Taka and I, along with Mr. Atsushi Sugano, director of the Kodo Cultural Foundation, spent time surveying the tub boats still in use as well as those in private collections and local museums. We also had the opportunity to share our experiences with another craftsman. In 2003 the Kodo Cultural Foundation published the results of my research in *The Tub Boats of Sado Island: A Japanese Craftsman's Methods,* with text in English and Japanese.[25]

The year before, the town of Ogi sponsored a taraibune workshop. Mr. Kanjiro Homma, a bucket maker who had built about six taraibune in the 1960s, taught the class. Five students completed the workshop and each made a taraibune under Mr. Homma's direction. We were extremely fortunate to have him visit us at our workshop on Sado in 2002, where we were able to discuss significant differences between how he and Mr. Fujii built boats, and he demonstrated his methods for preparing bamboo and braiding hoops. Mr. Homma had mainly worked replacing hoops for taraibune in the days when craftsmen would travel the coastline yearly. He also worked with Tomeikichi Fujii, my teacher's teacher, replacing hoops, and is now the last craftsman with first-hand knowledge of this era.

In any folk craft one is likely to find a range of opinions on how something is best done, and it should come as no surprise to find different taraibune builders using different methods. It can be tempting to search for the "right" way, to the exclusion of other methods, but this is misguided. Craftsmen work in a world where customers have special demands, prices and availability of materials change, and new technologies replace old. It is the nature of skilled craftsmen to respond with adjustments and innovations in their techniques. To think otherwise is to not acknowledge their adaptability and creativity.

We were working in the same building Mr. Homma used to teach his workshop, and two of his students' boats were still there. We had asked him to show us his method of braiding hoops, but when he saw our boat the discussion turned to the differences in the shape of the hulls. The overall dimensions of both craftsmen's taraibune were about the same, but Mr. Homma explained that although customers would request a specific length, he believed the beam should be no more than 4 shaku. As noted earlier, Mr. Fujii would connect the curve between the ends of the boat by drawing a radius of 8 shaku. This is a very gentle curve and at first glance the sides of his boats look almost straight. Mr. Homma used a much tighter radius when laying out the sides: 3 shaku, 3 sun, 3 bu, and 5 rin (3.335 shaku). He swung this arc from a perpendicular centerline drawn across the shiki at its widest point, and positioned his compass until the arc created a fair curve with the ends. Mr. Homma's boats also have noticeably more taper in the hull. His planks were about 3 bu wider at

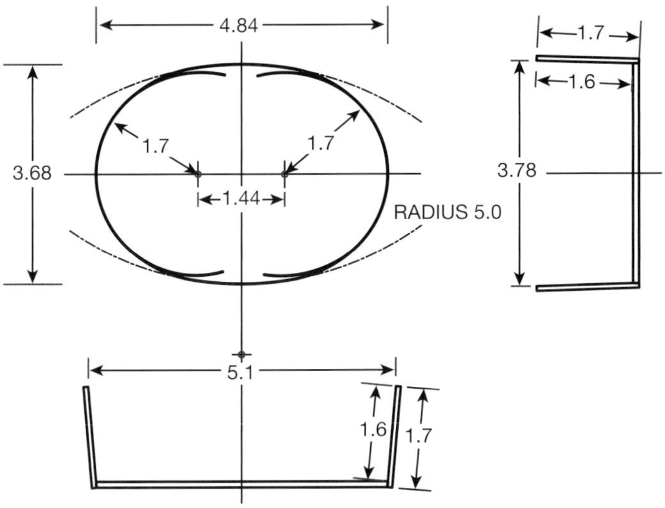

Taraibune built by Hatsutaro Ishizuka

Year built:	1989
Planking thickness:	9 bu to 1 sun
Bottom thickness:	1 sun
Owner:	privately owned

Bottom planking is flat sawn while side planking is mostly vertical grain. All flat-sawn planking is heart side out. All material is knot-free. Bottom has warped with age so it is impossible to determine whether it was originally curved or not.

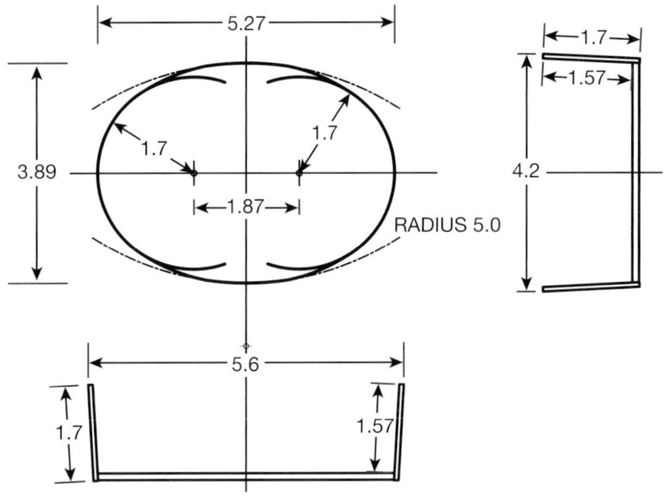

Taraibune built by Fukuzo Aoki

Year built:	around 1970
Planking thickness:	9 bu to 1 sun
Bottom thickness:	1 sun
Owner:	privately owned

Bottom planks are flat sawn while most of the side planks are vertical grain. All flat-sawn planking is heart side out. Some knots in the bottom planking; all the side planking knot-free. Bottom is flat lengthwise but curved from side to side.

the top than the bottom, and he explained that the increased taper let the hoops exert greater pressure.[26]

Mr. Homma told us he looks for 7-sun bamboo for the top two hoops and 6.8-sun bamboo for the bottom hoop, slightly narrower stalks than Mr. Fujii used, and he had never heard of the latter's theory of male and female bamboo. He also obeyed the dates of hassen, explaining that bamboo cut during hassen has more water inside and therefore is more prone to rot or insect infestation. (Mr. Fujii had told me the one time he cut bamboo during hassen he found rot inside.) Mr. Homma said he preferred bamboo cut before hassen, as he believed it tends to be weaker afterward. He also thought it should sit for a few days after cutting, a waiting period he called *shiwami*. If not, he would consider it bamboo that had not set, or *hashiri*.[27] This was at odds with my teacher, who insisted that we harvest the bamboo, then split and braid hoops the same day.

Mr. Homma's methods of splitting and shaping the bamboo were identical to Mr. Fujii's but when he began to braid we were surprised to see him hold the hoop under his arm and work standing up. He also tucked both tails simultaneously in the hoop instead of one at a time as we did. Once he had fed them through the opening and pulled out the slack he would adjust them so they had the proper left-over-right orientation. The greatest difference between his techniques and ours became immediately apparent: he could braid hoops far faster than we could, faster even than Mr. Fujii. Watching Mr. Homma work was a revelation; it had never occurred to us to braid standing up.[28]

Once he had braided the tails back to their starting point Mr. Homma stopped and picked up his drawknife. He trimmed a bit more material off the tails, making them slightly narrower, before continuing to braid. He called this remaining material the "children" and explained if the tails were smaller they would braid more easily and result in a more beautiful hoop. With the hoop braided once around the new openings are much smaller, so reducing the width of the strips makes sense.

Mr. Homma made two final points about installing the hoops. First, he said the side of the hoop where the bamboo strip overlaps on top of the braid (what I called the left when braiding) should face up when the hoop is pounded on the boat. He felt these strips could resist the pounding from the mallet better than the opposite strips, which are tucked under in the braid. Since the hoops are pounded on while the hull is upside down, when finished this side will face down. Following this suggestion also means all three hoops will be installed with the same orientation, a small but visible detail.

Second, he said the top hoop should be padded out by adding a strip of bamboo around the inside.[29] The finished hoops have a cupped cross section and an extra strip is simply

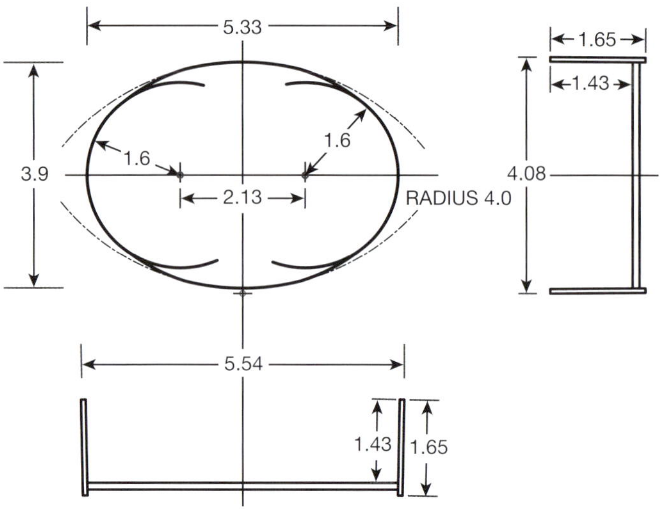

Taraibune from the Sadokoku Ogi Folk Museum, builder unknown

Year built:	1926
Planking thickness:	8 bu
Bottom thickness:	1 sun
Owner:	Sadokoku Ogi Folk Museum

This boat is in poor condition, but very important given its age. All planking is flat-sawn, heart side out, with some knots. It may be the oldest taraibune in existence. Condition of the bottom is too poor to determine whether it was originally curved.

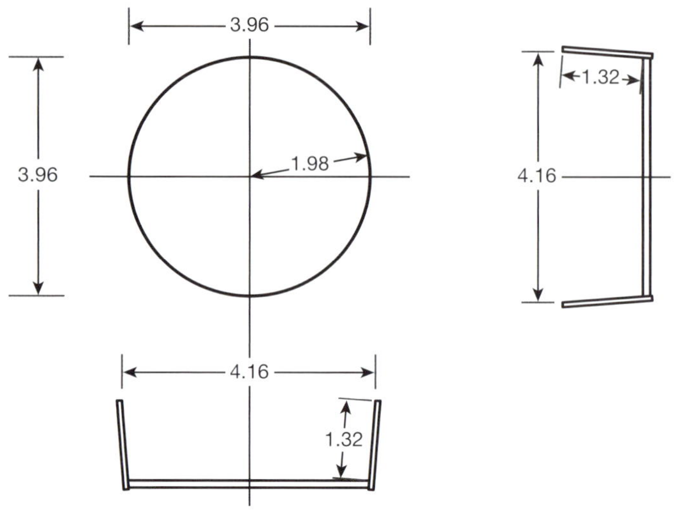

Taraibune from Noto Peninsula, builder unknown

Year built:	unknown
Location:	Found in Nunoura, Uchiura-machi, Ishikawa Prefecture
Owner:	Ishikawa Prefectural Museum of History

The author has not had a chance to examine this round taraibune from the Noto Peninsula, where it is believed only this shape was ever used. Dimensions are courtesy of the curators of the Ishikawa Prefectural Museum of History.

laid inside. One strip of bamboo will circle the hoop about two times and its natural springback will keep it in place inside the concave inner face of the hoop. Normally the pressure created when the hoop is pounded on flattens them; by padding the top hoop it remains convex and improves as a wave-breaker on the hull. In 1995 Mr. Fujii had mentioned that the top hoop should have a fuller shape, and that this was done by adding a strip of bamboo. I had mistakenly assumed at the time he meant braiding more material, but Mr. Homma's explanation clarified this detail.[30]

Further conversations with Mr. Homma illustrated an important divide in the history and development of the taraibune. On Sado there is a very clear distinction made between barrel and bucket makers. The difference is one of scale: Mr. Fujii's background making enormous miso tubs required as many as four men to work together braiding each enormous hoop, while bucket makers like Mr. Homma

(Above) Mr. Fujii with a newly finished taraibune, one of about a hundred he built after retiring from the miso factory cooperage. *Photo copyright Toshio Sato.* (Right) The author and his teacher pose inside the taraibune they built over the course of a week in October, 1996. *Photo copyright Catherine Wood Brooks.*

worked alone on much smaller containers. Both types of craftsmen built taraibune and scholars have suggested that on the Ogi Peninsula the two craft traditions dominated different stretches of coastline. On the north side of the peninsula, called Sotomisaki, these boats are known as hangiri, or "half-barrel." On the south side, Uchimisaki, they are called taraibune, "tub boat."[31]

Fiberglass

In the 1960s the Ogi Fisherman's Cooperative introduced four experimental taraibune made entirely of fiberglass (called FRP in Japan, for "fiber reinforced plastic"). Fiberglass is composed of a loosely woven synthetic cloth saturated with a resin-based glue. Early versions of fiberglass used polyester-based resins but today epoxy-based resins are used. The fiberglass taraibune were made by layering the fiber and resin in a mold. Although they were the same shape as the traditional boats, they were deemed unstable by fishermen and the project was abandoned.

Within a few years, however, the idea of coating the exterior of wooden taraibune with fiberglass took hold. The men who built taraibune did not do this work; companies in Ogi and Akadomari fiberglassed them along with other wooden fishing boats. Fiberglass cloth and resin were applied only to the outside of the hulls, right over the bamboo hoops, and just over the rim inside the side planking; the interiors were left uncoated. Because the resins in fiberglass deteriorate under exposure to the ultraviolet rays of sunlight, fishermen also began to paint their boats.

The new material did not alter the way taraibune were built, but it did eliminate the craftsman's role maintaining the boats. Fiberglass was seen as the cure-all for the problem of hoop replacement as well as the long-term preservation of the boat. "We thought it would make the boats last forever," one fisherman told me. As more and more boats were covered with fiberglass, fewer needed replacement hoops, with consequently less work for the craftsmen able to make them.

The use of fiberglass on taraibune is now almost universal. I am aware of only one working taraibune today not fiberglassed; its hoops are covered in sheet metal and reinforced with wire. Not only taraibune, but most working wooden boats in Japan are now covered with fiberglass.

Fiberglass changed taraibune in other ways too. Fiberglass is heavy, nearly doubling the weight of the boats. Old photos show taraibune being carried by fishermen on their backs. Now too heavy to be carried, they are mechanically pulled out of the water like the conventional boats they share the harbor with. The companies that fiberglass taraibune install wood or plastic runners on the bottoms so they can be dragged across concrete harbor ramps. The total added weight makes the boats nearly impossible for their elderly owners to turn over.

A fiberglassed taraibune near Aikawa Village. In most cases, coating the boats in fiberglass has accelerated their deterioration.

To the author's knowledge, this is the only un-fiberglassed taraibune still being used for fishing. The owner has resorted to using sheet metal and wire to maintain the integrity of the hoops.

The fiberglass exteriors have another adverse effect. Rainwater pooling in the upright boats inevitably seeps into the wood and is trapped by the waterproof coating. The salt content of seawater actually acts as a preservative for wood, but fresh water and exposure to the air encourages the introduction of fungi that cause dry rot.

In 2003 I counted 220 active taraibune on the Ogi Peninsula, including thirty-five boats used in the tourist industry. There are perhaps as few as a dozen taraibune now left in their original condition. These include taraibune in museum collections, and original boats in private hands that

Steadying his tub boat with a paddle, a fisherman near Shukenegi Village uses a sight box to find shellfish. The rack for his spears is unusual; normally these are towed behind the boat.

Yajima Kanko Kanri Kumiai (Yajima Tourist Association) offers taraibune rides led by women in traditional costume. All of these boats were built by Mr. Fujii.

Mr. Fujii built the first taraibune with a glass window in the shiki for the tourist industry.

were put in storage and never fiberglassed. Outside of the Ogi Peninsula I found seven taraibune in Inakujira village near Aikawa, which is across the island from the Ogi Peninsula. Only one of these boats was being used. I also found one taraibune on the beach in Sawata. Over the years I have visited Sado I have seen a clear decline in the numbers of these boats in use and a rise in derelict and rotting taraibune found in the vicinity of the fishing villages.

In one village I found taraibune in which rot in the hull had been scraped away and cement troweled into the gaps. I found two boats actually being used in which all of the rotten wood and bamboo was removed, leaving just the fiberglass shell! In Shiraki village most of the taraibune are turned over or covered. A fisherman there said fiberglassed taraibune will last at least twenty years as long as they are stored properly. Sadly, one owner's experience summed it up: He said his boat was almost thirty years old. It had been fine for the first twenty years but had rotted through in the eight years since he had it fiberglassed.

A Tub Boat Song

Today, Japanese know taraibune only as a quaint relic of the past. They serve as an icon of Sado tourism, appearing on signs, postcards, and souvenirs, including images of the ubiquitous Hello Kitty in a tub boat. Tourist companies in Ogi offer rides in fleets of taraibune large enough to carry four adults, some featuring glass windows in their bottoms. Every August visitors come for the Ogi Festival to watch folk dancing, singing, and taraibune races. Probably none of the tourists who line the wharf waiting for a five-minute ride know that just a few miles away working fishermen are still taking to the water in taraibune at dawn.

Whatever image of taraibune people may have, however, the craft remains useful and popular for residents of the tiny fishing villages of the Ogi Peninsula. The attributes that historically made taraibune attractive remain the same. They are the most affordable boat available, their design is ideal for maneuvering inshore, and they are durable. What has changed is that the craft culture that supplied these traditional boats has almost disappeared. Newer materials have come to replace wood and bamboo, and the substitution of these materials has displaced craftsmen skilled in working them. Japan's postwar economic boom encouraged an exodus from traditional ways of life, leaving the country without a next generation of students to learn the skills of their ancestors.

The men and women who fish are aging as well. Most people engaged in small-scale fisheries on Sado today are in their sixties or older. While a handful of fishermen in taraibune are middle-aged, it is hard to imagine a young man or woman considering these boats as a viable craft for making a living.

Instead the taraibune is a curiosity, fixed in the national imagination partly by a song by Yonekichi Sasaki, popularized seventy years ago. It tells the story of Gosaku, a young fisherman from the mainland village of Kashiwazaki, whose boat sinks off Sado. A fisherman from Ogi rescues Gosaku and takes him to his home on the island, where his daughter Omitsu nurses him back to health. They fall in love and after Gosaku returns home, Omitsu leaves every evening at dusk from Ogi and paddles her taraibune across to the mainland to be with her lover, always returning to Sado before dawn. One night she is tragically lost in a storm. The song concludes:

The love between a young man and woman
floats out to sea.
We can cast our rod between Ogi and Kashiwazaki,
but why can't my love reach to Kashiwazaki?

Over the years the Ogi Tourist Board has attempted to prove the plausibility of this tale. In 1966 three taraibune, paddled by a rotating crew of women, crossed the fifty-three kilometers from Ogi to Kashiwazaki in eighteen hours. In 2007 three more boats, this time paddled by one woman each, attempted to make the crossing in less than twenty-four hours.

The experience of working alongside Mr. Fujii and other craftsmen was as much a window on a nearly vanished world as a lesson in craftsmanship. I would like to think that somehow this endearing boat could survive the modernization that has swept Japan like the waves inundating the reefs of Sado. Workaday craft like fishing boats have long been at the margins of what is considered fit for cultural preservation in Japan. In 2007, however, the Agency of Cultural Affairs (Bunkachou) declared the craft of building taraibune to be an "Important Intangible Folk Cultural Asset." The Sado Board of Education continues to sponsor workshops in tub-boat making taught by Mr. Homma. Even so, rural ways of life in Japan are fast disappearing as young people leave their villages for opportunities in the cities. Poignant and improbable, the song of Gosaku and Omitsu may yet be the elegy for the taraibune.

Notes

1 Dr. Nishimura referred to the Echigo and Echu coasts, now Niigata and Toyama Prefectures.

2 I am indebted to the Sado Board of Education for letting me publish photographs by Mr. Toshio Sato. Most of his black-and-white images here date from the 1980s, before the author met Mr. Fujii.

3 This is the contention of Mr. Hitashi Nakabori of the Sadokoku Ogi Folk Museum, interviewed by the author January, 1995.

4 The Marudai Miso Company was founded in 1898 as the Hamochi Miso Goshi Company. The name was changed to Marudai Miso in 1967. The company was sold in March, 2003 and renamed Sado no Misogura.

5 Itinerant bucket makers were common on Sado, and probably throughout rural Japan. I interviewed the last professional sake barrel maker on the island and he casually mentioned he traveled from brewery to brewery in his work. Later I found out fully half his working life was spent on the road.

6 Interview with Mr. Tomeikichi Fujii's son, Mr. Hasao Fujii, May 4, 2002. At the time of my apprenticeship, Mr. Koichi Fujii told me he was selling tub boats for the equivalent of $1,000 USD.

7 The *sen*, a drawknife, is relatively unknown among traditional Japanese craftsmen, restricted possibly to coopers. Boatbuilders I have talked to are generally not familiar with it.

8 Interviews with Mr. Shigeru Sasaki and Mr. Yoshizo Shirakashi, May 8, 2002. At the time these men were perhaps the last coopers on Sado Island.

9 The curators of the Niigata Prefectural History Museum located a round taraibune (known locally as *fukoke*) from the Noto Peninsula, Ishikawa Prefecture. It was built by a bucket maker from Uchiura around 1960. Apparently oval taraibune were never used on the Noto Peninsula and fishermen stopped using taraibune there altogether in the 1970s.

10 Interview with Mr. Koichi Fujii, January, 1994.

11 When following Mr. Fujii's layout precisely, the shiki is actually slightly narrower than 4 shaku. It could be he was speaking in general terms when he described the ideal ratio.

12 In the West the shutter plank is the last plank fitted to a boat, usually made to fit as tightly as possible.

13 Translated by Mr. Hidemi Yamada.

14 In 2005 I met a sake-barrel maker who told me in his trade it was common to record data on the edges of

staves, such as date built, the name of the builder, and even the wages of the coopers.

15 Mr. Fujii also pointed out that the bottom edges of the planks often wear away from being dragged across rocks. With dado-less boats one can tap the bottom up a bit further to gain some extra working life.

16 Interview with Mr. Hitashi Nakabori of the Sadokoku Ogi Folk Museum, January, 1995.

17 I am indebted to Ms. Pauline Isaachson of Bamboo Specialists Nursery in Auckland, New Zealand, for this insight.

18 The *rokuyou* almanac of lucky and unlucky days is commonly consulted when planning weddings and new business ventures, although I have found no one who interpreted it quite like Mr. Fujii.

19 In 2007 I was invited to meet a sake barrel maker near Osaka. He stored split bamboo sometimes for months, on a damp floor in the dark, and it remained flexible enough to braid into hoops.

20 These tools are called *takewari* in Japanese tool stores and home centers.

21 After returning to the United States I watched my video and practiced braiding long strips of plastic strapping. This way I was eventually able to master braiding hoops.

22 Interview with Mrs. Kiyo Fujii, 2002.

23 Almost all taraibune in use today are covered with fiberglass and so rarely have bottom lips, which would create a problem when applying cloth and epoxy. Mr. Fujii did not fiberglass his boats, and perhaps the companies doing this work sawed off the lips before applying the coating.

24 I have owned a taraibune since 2001 and while I have watched many elderly fisherwomen on Sado paddle one-handed I have yet to develop the strength or skill to master this technique.

25 The book contains a more detailed treatment of the larger history and ethnology of these boats; it is available in Japan at major bookstores, from the Kodo Cultural Foundation (www.kodo.or.jp), and outside Japan directly from the author (douglasbrooksboatbuilding@gmail.com).

26 Interview with Mr. Homma, May 5, 2002. One fisherman who visited our shop immediately recognized Mr. Fujii's design. He called the reduced flare in our hull *ichiwari* (ten percent) and said it was superior. Between boatbuilders and fishermen there is no shortage of opinions on what makes an ideal boat.

27 In Sado dialect the verb *shiwamu* means "pliant" or "supple." *Hashiru* means "to run." The terms refer to seasoned versus freshly cut bamboo.

28 Mr. Toshio Sato later clarified this for me: Mr. Fujii also sometimes worked standing, but at his home workshop he had enough space to braid hoops while sitting on the ground, and that was the only way I saw him work. Also, miso barrel hoops, being far larger, have to be braided while sitting.

29 In 2007 a sake barrel maker in Osaka told me this strip was called a *shimaki,* and he sometimes padded hoops with an insert of wood.

30 Unfortunately I cannot remember whether Mr. Fujii did this with the boat we built together. If he did, I did not notice it because I made no mention of this technique in my notes.

31 The word *giri* for barrel or bucket is Sado dialect only. Mr. Sato's book *Hangiri* offers the most complete ethnology of this region.

An elderly woman returns to Sawasaki harbor.

At the launching ceremony, the senior fisherman of Urayasu offers prayers for the boat while the author, Mr. Udagawa, and the museum director look on. *Photo copyright Kazumi Muraki.*

10

The Bekabune of Urayasu

In the winter of 2000 I returned to Japan. My primary goal was to travel to Sado Island and finish the tub boat that Mr. Fujii was working on when he died. At the outset of the trip I briefly stopped in Tokyo, where Mr. Shunichi Yamamoto, a marine photographer and artist, offered to introduce me to two boatbuilders he knew.[1] He felt that either one or both might be interested in teaching me. Learning how to build tub boats had made me feel more like a cooper than a boatbuilder, and I yearned to study and build a conventional boat. Our first stop was Urayasu, a city just across the Arakawa, a river on Tokyo's eastern border. A new museum was being built there to celebrate the community's rich connection to the bay, particularly the cultivation of *nori,* the seaweed most familiar in the West as a wrap for sushi.

Mr. Yamamoto and I took a taxi to Urayasu's old museum, which had been emptied and converted into a temporary boat shop, with exhibit cases moved to one side and piles of lumber resting on the linoleum floors. The plans for the new facility called for a museum building surrounded by a re-created section of old Urayasu town, complete with water, docks, sidewalks of crushed clamshells, shops, and homes. What we had walked in on was the construction of half a dozen replica boats for the waterfront village. The man building them was Mr. Nobuji Udagawa, one of the last boatbuilders from an era when almost two thousand wooden fishing boats crammed the Sakai River in Urayasu.

If there is one adjective in the Japanese lexicon most closely associated with craftsmen it is *kibishii,* defined as severe, rigid, and intense. Over the years many friends had warned me that even meeting boatbuilders was likely impossible; these men were too aloof and guarded. While my experiences have largely been otherwise, when recalling my first meeting with Mr. Udagawa, the word kibishii comes to mind.

Mr. Udagawa watches and instructs as the author uses a saw to fit the planking on the bekabune, a traditional boat used on Tokyo Bay for harvesting seaweed. *Photo copyright KAZI publications.*

As Mr. Yamamoto and I entered the shop Mr. Udagawa's younger brother Akira greeted us warmly, while the master boatbuilder himself remained crouched alongside an *utasebune.* These boats, over thirty feet long, were the largest fishing craft he had built during his career. Powered by inboard gasoline engines, they also had sailing rigs, which were set close-hauled, since utasebune pulled trawl nets sideways under sail power. Several distinct varieties of utasebune exist, from Kyushu in the south to Lake Kasumigaura north of Tokyo. The Urayasu variety, the only powered boats in the local fishing fleet, also ferried smaller boats out to the fishing grounds.

Mr. Udagawa gave me a perfunctory greeting and, while he stopped working to shake my hand, he took just a moment to show us what he was doing. Usually when I introduce myself to Japanese boatbuilders they are excited to meet a fellow craftsman from America. Most are eager to learn of at least a few of the differences between boatbuilding East and West. Mr. Udagawa, however, gave every indication he was impatient to have us leave. After a very brief visit we exchanged business cards and said goodbye. On the train back to Tokyo, Mr. Yamamoto acknowledged that Mr. Udagawa was a very serious man, but he also insisted that he would be an excellent teacher for me. Given the coolness of his greeting, I was skeptical.

Our next stop was in Koto-ku, located at the eastern edge of Tokyo and home of Wasen Tomo no Kai, or Friends of Traditional Japanese Boats. Made up primarily of retired watermen, this group operates a collection of traditional wooden cargo vessels and other boats in a city canal park. The boats are propelled by *ro,* the traditional sculling oar, and group members delight in giving rides to the public and teaching people how to scull. Under a small canopy where the group had gathered around pots of tea, Mr. Yamamoto introduced me to another boatbuilder, Mr. Kazuyoshi Fujiwara. He sat very quietly while we drank and chatted about boats and my desire to study Japanese boatbuilding. Well into our meeting, he finally stood and said, "Follow me home. I have something to show you." He then grabbed his bicycle and swiftly walked away.

Mr. Yamamoto and I followed, at times breaking into a jog to keep up with Mr. Fujiwara, who stayed ahead of us, his hands holding the handlebars and quickly pushing the bike out of the park and down city sidewalks. He did not look back or say a word to us the entire way home, a distance of about two miles, across Koto-ward and into Sumida-ward. His business card said "Funatomi Boatyard" but when we finally reached his house, a tiny postwar structure with cracked plaster walls surrounded by high-rise apartments, there was no shop or water in sight.

"The shop was next to the house," he said, pointing to a small parking lot, "but it burned down." I asked him where he launched his boats and he pointed to the street. "The river is under there. It's in a pipe now." The street hummed with traffic, and the sound merged with the noise from an elevated freeway a few blocks away. A chain restaurant was across the street. The constant noise made talking outside difficult.

Mr. Fujiwara led us into the entryway of his home where he called to his wife for tea. The outer glass door slid shut roughly but it closed out the noise. To the left was a glass display case filled with exquisite boat models he had made, and to the right were tools, lumber, several sculling oars, and large antiques. There was just enough room for the three of us, and while I expected to sit drinking tea and exchanging pleasantries, Mr. Fujiwara busily pulled out scraps of wood and tools. Just as his wife emerged through the curtain with our tea and cakes, he set two short planks on the floor and, brandishing a handsaw, addressed me. "This is how you make the seams watertight. It is very difficult, but it is the most important thing you must learn in order to understand Japanese boatbuilding."

Mr. Yamamoto and I stayed for two hours, and the entire time Mr. Fujiwara quietly lectured and demonstrated, pulling various tools from wooden chests, always cautioning me how each topic was essential to understanding how to build a boat. He was a natural teacher, and as I sat watching and listening all I could think of was *this is the man who can teach me.* He had apprenticed with his father and worked with him most of his career, and his grandfather had also been a boatbuilder. Mr. Fujiwara had several sons, but by the time they came of age he had stopped building boats. He never had an apprentice.

My trip to Sado to finish my teacher's last boat received news coverage at home, and when I returned to Vermont I was contacted by the Freeman Foundation. The Freeman family has had a long association with Japan and Asia, and has funded various philanthropic and educational projects related to the region. After some negotiations, I was invited by the foundation to put together a research project to allow me to apprentice with a boatbuilder. I sent proposals to Japanese maritime museums, curators, researchers, and every boatbuilder I knew, including Mr. Udagawa and Mr. Fujiwara. Only Mr. Fujiwara and a couple of museums replied. Mr. Fujiwara said he was willing to work with me if we could put a project together. Ultimately, I submitted a proposal to work with two boatbuilders. First, I would study with Mr. Fujiwara and build a traditional boat for the rowing group Wasen Tomo no Kai, which operated under the auspices of the Koto-ward government of Tokyo. Next, in partnership with the Michinoku Traditional Wooden Boat Museum, I would work with Mr. Seizo Ando in Aomori to build a Pacific coast inshore fishing boat.[2]

In early March of 2001, while still waiting to hear the decision of the Freeman Foundation, I received a letter from the director of the newly finished Urayasu Folk History Museum. The museum's grand opening was April first and Mr. Udagawa would be building a *bekabune* in the museum's boat shop as an inaugural demonstration. The director wrote that Mr. Udagawa had specifically requested that I work with him. This was a surprise, since he had never replied to

The boat shop inside the Urayasu Folk History Museum. The structure requires roof framing because boatbuilders must brace props against the ceiling beams to hold parts in place.

The Urayasu Museum's re-created village, with several of Mr. Udagawa's boats in the lagoon. Many of Urayasu's oldest residents gather here, demonstrating the skills of a nearly forgotten way of life.

my letters. The director wanted to know: Did I want to be Mr. Udagawa's apprentice? Furthermore, the opening was in three weeks! My wife Catherine and I discussed the invitation. There was no financial support offered so I would be paying for a plane ticket, lodging, and food. The director told me to plan on staying in Japan for one month to build the boat. The Freeman Foundation research project was still under consideration; no decisions had been made and so there were no guarantees I would get this chance again. The whole proposal was unexpected and seemed impossibly rash. It was Catherine who finally said: "You have to do this."

On April 1, 2001, Mr. Udagawa and I stood side by side among a crowd of onlookers as the museum officially opened. A large golden ball, hung from a trapeze, was mounted above the front door. A ribbon was cut and the ball opened, spewing confetti as fireworks were set off. Once the doors opened Mr. Udagawa and I headed inside, joined by throngs of townspeople. He and I would build the most common type of fishing boat used in Urayasu. Our workshop was on the ground floor of the new museum, and consisted of a plywood floor with a framework of beams overhead, a necessary feature for the various props we would use in lieu of clamps to hold our work in place. We were surrounded by some of the historic boats in the museum's collection as well as display cabinets full of tools, most of them donated by Mr. Udagawa. Just outside our door we could see the waterfront village where his other replica boats were displayed.

Over time, various volunteers and staff pieced together for me the story of how Mr. Udagawa became Japan's first museum boatbuilder. As the museum was being conceived, city officials contacted various exhibit fabricators for replicas of bekabune, but were stunned to learn that a single boat would cost them upwards of $60,000. In desperation they approached Mr. Udagawa. It took repeated meetings and it seems he was no friendlier to them initially than he was to me. In an interview with the magazine *Serai* in July, 2001, he related the final argument used by the museum to convince him to resume building boats, "They told me, 'Your grandchildren don't even know you were a boatbuilder.' They were exactly right. I had never told them about it. After they told me that, I started to feel very sad."

If the pace of Japan's transformation into one of the world's most modern nations seems instantaneous it is because, by any timeline of social evolution, it was. An exhibition of historic photographs of Urayasu was displayed in the museum and on opening day Mr. Keiju Kurozumi, a retired executive and photographer, invited me to tour the exhibit. Large black-and-white photographs documenting everyday life in the fishing village were displayed throughout the upper galleries. The streets alongside the Sakai River were dirt and women and children were wearing simple kimono and wooden sandals. Thatched roofing could be seen in the margins of the photos and the river itself was choked with wooden boats. Out in the channel men rowed or sailed; only the larger vessels were powered by inboard engines. The photos captured the essence of every traditional fishing village and the rituals of this way of life: long hours, hard work, uncertain rewards, and the unforgiving sea. I assumed the photographs were from the early 1900s and asked Mr. Kurozumi if this was the case. He looked back at me with a smile. "I took these photos," he said, "in 1964."

Urayasu

Urayasu means "peaceful bay," an apt name for this community for most of its long history, although like the rest of Japan its modern history has been tumultuous. Urayasu had

Images from 1964 show the Sakai River in central Urayasu crowded with fishing boats. In the foreground a man poles a bekabune. The handle of his clam rake is visible in front of him. *Photo copyright Keiju Kurozumi.*

Bekabune crowd the wharf in Urayasu. Some are configured for gathering seaweed while others are for clamming. Mr. Udagawa built over 300 bekabune during his career. *Photo copyright Keiju Kurozumi.*

always been a fishing village, drawing its sustenance from the broad mudflats of Tokyo Bay. The central village of ancient Urayasu lies along the banks of the Sakaigawa (Sakai River), a small stream branching off the much larger Edogawa (Edo River). These two watercourses spill into Tokyo Bay and the extensive mudflats, along with the combination of fresh and salt waters, once supported clams, seaweed, and fish for the local populace. The central district of Urayasu, now just one of the city's neighborhoods, is known as Nekozane, and is mentioned in documents dating back five hundred years. An earlier salt-making industry was controlled directly by the shogunate, but after its collapse fishing predominated. Sometime before 1867 (the end of the Edo period) Nekozane was officially established as a village.

Today Urayasu is a suburb, more accurately a satellite city, of Tokyo. Only in Nekozane do the streets follow no logical pattern, except to define a cluster of the oldest homes, temples, shrines, and public baths on either side of the tiny Sakaigawa. Outside of Nekozane the streets widen and revert to a perfect grid pattern. Following the Sakaigawa toward the bay, a new concrete and brick riverside walkway emerges, channeling the river in a perfectly straight line. Downstream from Nekozane the large buildings of city government are the first prominent landmarks. These stand at the original, natural shoreline of old Urayasu, but today from this spot Tokyo Bay is nowhere in sight. About a half-mile further down river a concrete seawall rises like a wave, cutting across suburban development, marking the shoreline of the first massive landfill project of the early 1970s. Beyond the wall the buildings are noticeably newer, and closer to the bay construction cranes are busy building high-rise apartments and big-box retail malls. At the current shoreline of Tokyo Bay now sits Urayasu's most famous contemporary industry—Tokyo Disneyland. The Sakai River flows as straight as the boulevards paralleling it, finally entering the bay over two miles from its original mouth.[3]

Motorized fishing boats line the riverbank in Urayasu. Floorboards lie across the gunwales to dry, and some clam rakes can be seen sitting on the boats in the foreground. *Photo copyright Kazuyoshi Kubo.*

The mouth of the Sakai River in 1964, showing fishing boats headed out into Tokyo Bay. In the foreground two bekabune are being towed by an utasebune. Landfill development moved the mouth of the river two miles beyond this spot. *Photo copyright Keiju Kurozumi.*

Urayasu's most famous product was nori, a type of seaweed cultivated on nets strung on poles in the tidal mudflats. Nori production in Urayasu dates back about 250 years, but production greatly expanded around 1900 after overfishing reduced harvests elsewhere. Spores placed on nets in the early fall are ready for harvest in November. For most of its history, nori was gathered by hand by fishermen working from small boats called bekabune. These boats measured about 15 shaku from stem to stern, and their beam, strictly defined by the space between the rows of nori nets, was 3.3 shaku, measured inside the planking.

Most traditional Japanese boats have very thick planking compared to their Western counterparts. Typical construction begins with the bottom, called the *shiki,* with two wide planks on each side. The lowest strake, or side plank, is fastened to a bevel on the edge of the bottom. At the chine (where the two side planks meet) the top strake (of the side planking) tends to overlap the edge of the bottom strake and extend slightly beyond, forming a lip along the joint. Often the top strake is nearly vertical for most of its length. In most boats the planking runs past the transom, forming a well. Fishermen have told me that this well protects the rudder, while boatbuilders point out that running the planking long guarantees that fastenings at the transom will not split the planks. The stems of sea boats are typically rabbeted, while those of river boats are not. The thick planking obviates the need for much internal framing. Bent frames are unknown; sometimes athwartship beams are the only internal framing, while sawn frames are used in other regions.

Bekabune are unusual for two features: their thin planking, and how the planking meets flush at the chine, a feature boatbuilders call *nokke-zukuri.*[4] The resulting smooth hull is necessary because bekabune work between rows of nets where the seaweed grows. To harvest the seaweed, fishermen lift a section of net over a special shelf resting on the boat's rail and then collected the seaweed. A lip at the chine would invariably snag the net, thus the need for a smooth hull. For the same reason boats built specifically for nori harvesting have no rub rails. This light construction is supported by beams and a single pair of sawn frames amidships.

The thin planking may be the key to the *beka* of the boat's name. There are several theories, the most popular being that the name mimics the sound of waves slapping against the thin hull: *peka, peka*. Beka may also be slang for something thin and easily bent.[5] Bekabune came in three versions. The smallest, called *noribeka,* was used strictly for nori harvesting, whereas two slightly larger versions were also used in clamming. The lightest versions of the bekabune were often carried to the fishing grounds on the decks of larger powered boats. They were light enough to be dragged across the mudflats, or even carried on the backs of their owners when the tide ran out. The larger bekabune had railings and even sailing rigs. All three versions had the same beam, standardized by the gap in the rows of seaweed.

Harvested nori is essentially a dark green muck. Once ashore this paste is spread on small wooden frames with woven reed backs and left to dry in the sun. Reminiscent of traditional paper making, the thin sheets of dry nori are peeled off their frames and packaged for sale. The production of nori was pioneered in the nearby Asakusa district of Tokyo hundreds of years ago. To this day the name of Asakusa is to nori what Bordeaux or Champagne is to wine: a legendary synonym for quality. Mr. Udagawa told me in later years that Asakusa nori was in fact from Urayasu. So began a long list of items that he insisted were better in Urayasu than anywhere else: nori, short neck clams, flatfish and, of course, boats.

I did not know exactly what to expect upon my arrival in Urayasu; after all, I had only met Mr. Udagawa once, briefly, and it had seemed a cold exchange. As we began work, however, he bubbled over with enthusiasm. His first concern was that I was living too far from Urayasu, and soon he arranged for me to stay in town at his nephew's house. He also arranged for his son-in-law, who owned a bicycle shop, to loan me a bicycle, and he insisted that I ride home with him every day for lunch. These lunchtime visits strained my beginning Japanese, as his wife interrogated me about every item of food she served, whether I had heard of it, seen it, or eaten it, and Mr. Udagawa lectured me on the superiority of all things Urayasu. His boosterism was indicative of an intense local pride I normally saw only in the countryside.

Contemporary nori cultivation near Toba, Mie Prefecture. Until pollution destroyed Urayasu's fishery, its seaweed, called Asakusa nori, was famous.

It also reinforced the small town origins of his community, and the meteoric change he had witnessed in his lifetime.

Mr. Nobuji Udagawa

Mr. Udagawa grew up in Urayasu, and both his father and grandfather were boatbuilders. He was born in 1929 and his father died when he was fifteen. He apprenticed as a young man in one of the boatbuilding companies supplying the local fishermen. He told me the standard apprenticeship for boatbuilders in Urayasu was six years. Like all crafts, roles in the boatshop were hierarchical, with the master being the only person who understood the overall project. Only the master could lay down the lines of the boat, from formulas that were usually memorized. Younger workers were not allowed to know these dimensions; the master would draw lines on the wood and workers would cut to these lines. Drawings, when they existed, were merely a profile view of the boat drawn on a plank of wood. According to Mr. Udagawa, because of his own perseverance, plus regular gifts of alcohol, his master eventually shared with him the designs of his boats.

In 1954 Mr. Udagawa opened his own shop behind his house on the Sakaigawa. At the time there were six Urayasu *kariya*, the local term for a boatbuilding shop. He employed his two younger brothers and a brother-in-law. In 1955, at the urging of a relative, he bought an electric bandsaw; it was the first power tool in the boatbuilding industry in town. In 1958 he bought a hand-held circular saw, but in that same year a chemical spill upriver severely polluted the fishing grounds. The ongoing pollution had a devastating effect on the fisheries throughout the 1960s. There were protests from the fishermen's union, along with proposals to begin landfill developments to attract new industries. In 1971, the fishermen's union finally sold all their rights to the offshore grounds to developers, and large scale landfill projects began in earnest.

The next year Mr. Udagawa and two other boatbuilders closed their shops. By 1973 the last boatbuilder in Urayasu was out of business. Boats were sold, dismantled for building materials, or burned. The Urayasu Museum shows a film of boats piled as high as houses and set afire. Over the years the Udagawa shop had built fifty larger boats (over thirty feet), and over 300 smaller bekabune. At the height of postwar fishing over 1,800 boats were registered in Urayasu.

Mr. Udagawa then went to work in construction, helping to build the roads and homes now covering the former seaweed beds. He was working for a driving school in 1992 when officials from the Urayasu City Folk Museum called him. He had also owned rice fields, and as Japan prospered and Tokyo grew beyond its boundaries, this land became extremely valuable. Mr. Udagawa told me that his years building boats were a constant financial struggle; the subsequent sale of his real estate allowed him to retire comfortably and build a large house, replacing his original home. His wife was more succinct, "I could hear him hammering, so I knew he was working," she told me, "but there was never any money."

Building the Bekabune

Before we began working, Mr. Udagawa showed me his plan, drawn on a piece of cardboard to 1/10th scale. Since it consisted of only a profile, the half breadth of the keel, and the expanded transom, it was not a complete lines drawing. The remaining dimensions and how the lines were derived were Mr. Udagawa's secrets, which he would reveal in time. He also stressed that he had made slight changes to the designs

Mr. Udagawa's shop on the Sakai River, circa 1970. The boat on the mud in the center of the photograph has been hauled on the ways in front of the shop, which is barely visible. *Photo copyright Kazuyoshi Kubo.*

The keel plank is made up of three planks edge-nailed together before cutting to final shape. It was set up on edge to facilitate nailing.

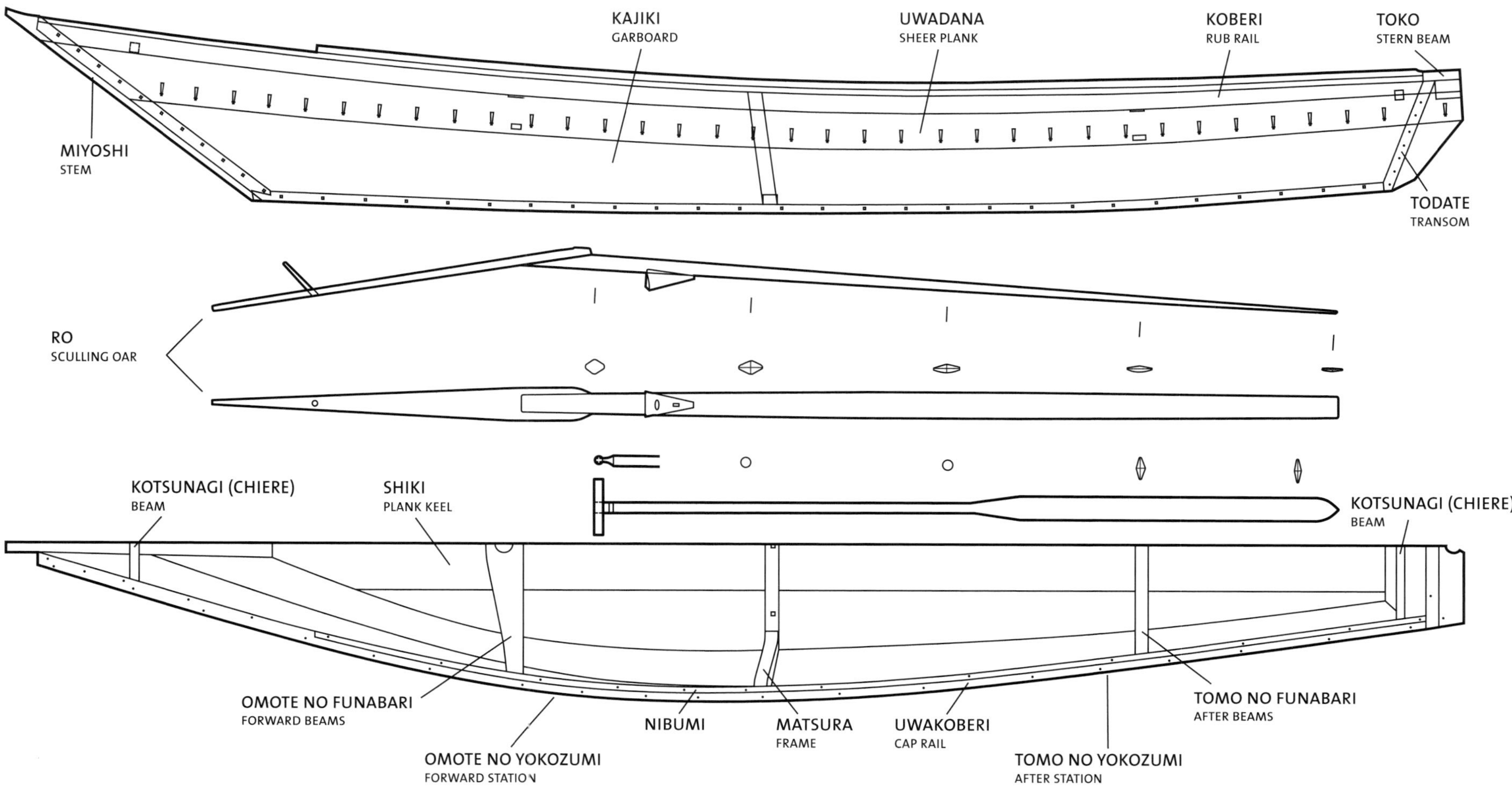

Our bekabune is 15 shaku long with a beam of 3.3 shaku measured the way Urayasu boatbuilders do: taking the length from where the sheer (top edge of the upper plank) meets the back of the stem to sheer at the inside face of the transom. Beam is also measured inside of planking, and is fixed by the space between the rows of nori nets, regardless of boat length. Height is 1.4 shaku measured amidships, although this measurement is not used in construction.

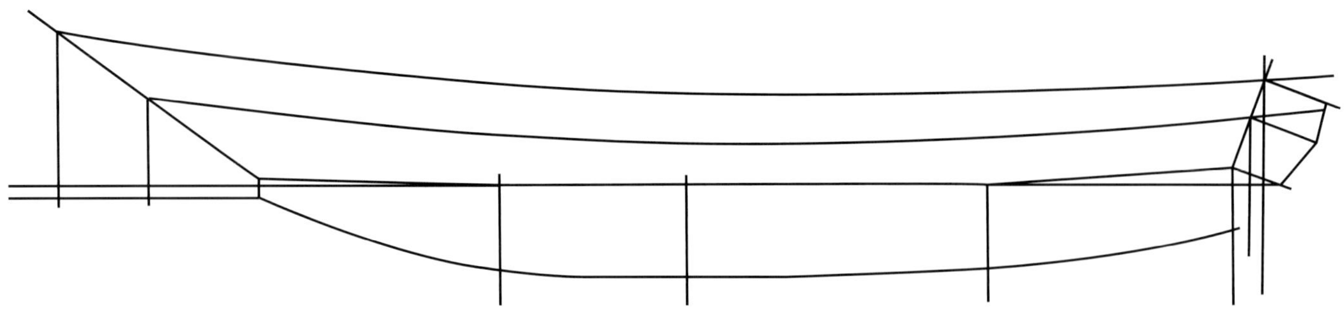

A copy of Mr. Udagawa's 1/10th scale drawing of the bekabune. It shows the profile, half-breadth of the keel plank, and the expanded transom, but lacks a plan view of the chine or sheer. This missing information is typical of Japanese boatbuilders' drawings.

he had learned. For him this was a critical point: he made it clear that every craftsman must be able to call his work unique. This was not idle pride; even though my research was dedicated to documenting precisely how Mr. Udagawa built these boats, he was opposed to the idea I might slavishly replicate his design. This was not about usurping his dimensions; rather, he believed that as a matter of pride a craftsman should make some alterations or improvements to his teacher's work. An innovation, no matter how small, was the final badge of independence from one's master.

Mr. Udagawa was very much the benevolent teacher, laughing at my suggestions that I was stealing his secrets, and also encouraging my future work. He hoped that I would build more bekabune someday, and he taught me an interesting phrase: *ude no mise-dokoro,* which means, "time to show your skill." I told him of the time years before when building a tub boat that Mr. Fujii handed me his plane and walked out, leaving me on my own. He laughed, because he had spent years learning by the same system before striking out on his own. He also acknowledged that people had helped him. His father's sawyer was very good to him, he said, and as brutal as the old apprentice system could be, sometimes a master would give his student some customers when he was just starting out.[6]

Wood

Boats in Urayasu were planked in *sugi,* Japanese cedar, and framed in *kayanoki*, or nutmeg. Cedar and sometimes cypress are used for planking elsewhere in Japan, but nutmeg is used in Urayasu because it grows well in a swampy region of the prefecture. Nutmeg (*Torreya nucifera*) is a bright yellow, dense, pungently aromatic hardwood.

Our first task was to select cedar planks from among a collection that had been drying. The museum had purchased an enormous cedar tree for the project. Of course, Mr. Udagawa had picked it out himself, and was excited about his find, as it was 280 years old and totally free of rot. He had instructed the sawmill to cut the log into three sections: two ten-meter logs from the base and one six-meter log from the top. He would eventually build two utasebune, well over thirty feet long, and five bekabune from this single tree. Boatbuilders have their logs sawn straight through rather than quarter-sawn (the log first quartered lengthwise and each section cut across the grain). Our lumber had not been given a straight edge; the cedar was flitch-sawn, meaning the natural bark edge remained on the planks.

For larger boats Mr. Udagawa preferred a central plank (avoiding the heart) of the tree for the keel plank, using the adjacent planks for the first planks and so on, thus planking the hull symmetrically using material from the center of the tree and working outward. For the bekabune's more fragile, thinner planking he chose material based on quality. He still used planks symmetrically from the log, but he avoided all sapwood and knots. I also noticed that he chose material just large enough to make our planks; there would be as little waste as possible.

The bekabune's keel plank and lower planks had the heart side of the planking to the inside of the boat while the transom and the sheer planks showed the heart to the outside. Mr. Udagawa felt that the keel and first planks should have the more rot resistant wood facing inside where rainwater might collect; any sapwood in these planks would be immersed in salt water, which acts as a preservative. He said we would use the clearest material for the sheer, the topmost plank, called the *uwadana*. "The sheer plank is what you see," he said, "and it has to be the most beautiful."[7]

Mr. Udagawa called his layout of boat lines his *wari*. Other boatbuilders I have interviewed and worked with have called it *wariai*. In English these words mean "proportion," and essentially refer to the beam-to-length ratio. Although boatbuilders may adhere to a particular design, they rely on their wari should they be asked to build a boat of a different size. The beam-to-length ratio is generally between 1:5 and 1:6. If this ratio seems excessively narrow, remember for a given length Japanese boats have planking up to twice as thick as their Western counterparts. Even when fire is used for bending there is still a greater limit on the amount of shape that can be developed. It should also be noted that Mr. Udagawa measured boat length from the hood end of the plank at the sheer to the inside face of the transom, a practice I have found to be widespread.[8]

Building a bekabune begins with the bottom, which is made up of three pieces of cedar joined together. The planks are edge-nailed to one another. The preparation of this joint is one of the most difficult techniques, but the result is a watertight seam that requires no caulking. In the West, planks are joined with seams prepared with a plane. In Urayasu, after cutting to the inkline with a handsaw the planks were brought together on blocks laid on the shop floor.

All sawing and planing of the planking and other parts was done working on blocks cut from beams nine centimeters square. (Our blocking material was all commercial lumber, sold in metric sizes.) Workbenches are completely unknown in traditional boatbuilding and craftsmen use their feet or props to hold their work in place; hence their preference for sock-like shoes and loose-fitting clothing. The greater physicality of working on the floor is not to be taken lightly. At some point Mr. Udagawa noticed my discomfort and one night he built a sawhorse to aid in planing planks. Unfortunately he misjudged my height (he is five feet, two inches, and I am a foot taller) and I had to work with one end of the plank at chin height!

Before preparing the plank seams Mr. Udagawa first laid out the location of the edge nails we would use to hold the planks together. Traditional boats are not fastened with screws; rather boatbuilders use copper nails and flat, hand-wrought steel nails. Occasionally we used a modern wire nail where a small nail was needed.[9]

Building the bekabune required nails of different sizes. Our largest nails, 4 sun long, were used to fasten together the three planks making up the bottom. The nail spacing was 7 sun 5 bu (.75 shaku), and mortises for the nail heads were cut back from the plank edge on the two outer planks. Nails were driven through the two outer planks into the center plank. The sides of the mortises were trapezoidal and the base of the mortise was like a ramp, tapering down from the plank face to half the thickness of the plank. It is here, at the narrow end of the trapezoid, where the nail head was pounded tight. We chiseled the mortises on the outside face of the plank and their sides were slightly undercut. Wooden plugs would later be cut in a dovetail cross section to lock into the mortises.

Once the mortises are cut, a set of special chisels are used to make the nail holes. These chisels, called *tsubanomi*, or "sword-hilt chisels," are now very rare. I have searched in vain to find any toolmakers still producing them, and only the oldest and most experienced tool store vendors have even heard of them. A typical boatbuilder will have at least a dozen in different sizes, some curved to run in through a mortise and reach the adjacent plank. The hilt refers to the poll at the base of the handle. Once the chisel is pounded into the wood it is driven back and out by striking the hilt.

I first learned how fastidious Mr. Udagawa could be regarding these techniques while chiseling these pilot holes. I was using a typical Japanese hammer, which has two heads (one flat face and the other slightly rounded) instead of a Western-style hammer with a head and claw. From simple

(Left) Mr. Udagawa watching his younger brother Akira prepare a plank seam using a handsaw. We used a series of handsaws, each with a finer set of teeth, to fit the seams of the boat. (Above) A pair of tsubanomi and boat nails. Used to cut pilot holes, these chisels come in a variety of sizes for different-sized nails. The nails are made of soft-steel flat stock with the heads offset to one side. The hilt is hit with a hammer to remove the chisel from the work.

habit, after pounding the chisel into the wood I rotated the hammer in my hand to hit the poll and remove it. My motion was consistent with using a Western hammer that had only one head. Mr. Udagawa, who had been talking to visitors, glanced at my technique and leapt over to me, taking the tools from my hands and straddling the plank. "Like this!" he shouted, swinging the hammer down on the chisel and driving it into the plank edge. Then, without rotating the hammer, he let the head drop below the handle and swung it upward, so that the other head struck the poll and drove the chisel back out.

It was a small detail, but of course he was correct; this method was smoother and quicker, and he could drive and remove the tsubanomi in four rapid hammer blows. In addition, rotating the hammer in my wrist, while an ingrained habit, was actually a very clumsy way to strike the chisel upwards. But most importantly I noticed that Mr. Udagawa offered no explanation: his reaction was instantaneous. I had deviated from the way it was done and that was wrong. How I swung a hammer was not an issue of personal preference in his shop. He had his way and he insisted that it also be my way.

With the outer planks set on edge, a hole is chiseled back to the base of the mortises from the centerline of the edge. It is not difficult to chisel and accurately locate the base of the mortise. The hole should be a snug fit, just large enough so the nail can be pushed through by hand. Then pilot holes for each nail are chiseled in the center plank. These holes are slightly smaller and the total length of the pilot hole should be slightly less than the length of the nail. Mr. Udagawa made certain that I checked the depth of my pilot holes often. Too wide or deep and the nail would have no holding power; too shallow and the soft iron nail will bend when driven. When all the pilot holes were chiseled, the planks were temporarily clamped together and a curved chisel was inserted through the mortise to align and clean up the pilot holes.

Fitting the Seams

Now the serious work of preparing the seams began. We laid two planks together, set flat on low blocks, with the nail holes aligned. Props, which Mr. Udagawa called *tsuzu,* were placed against the planks and wedged against the beamwork overhead to hold everything in place. The process of preparing the seam is called *suriawase* (see Chapter 5) and, along with edge nailing of planks, is a technique universal among boatbuilders.[10] The term means to "rub together" or "reconcile," and is accomplished by running two or three different saws, each with a finer set of teeth, through the seam between the planks. While many woodworkers are familiar with running a saw in a joint in order to make it tight, the procedure in Japanese boatbuilding is more complex and takes great skill. The secret lies in the sawing motion. While hard spots may require some initial sawing back and forth through the seam, the final sawing must be done with the blade sawing parallel to the plank face. In other words, the saw edge does not cut up and down at an angle to the stock as usual; instead the blade rubs back and forth in the seam.

Mr. Udagawa believed in sawing the seams in both directions, working the full length of the seam with each pass. After each pass, the planks are tapped closer together and the process is begun again. Once the seam has been cut satisfactorily with the more aggressive saw, we switched to a finer saw. A twelve-foot seam in the bottom of the boat can easily require an hour's work.

I noticed from the start of our project that we were using two brand new saws. Their shiny steel and bright wooden handles contrasted with all of our other tools, which had dark steel blades and wooden bodies and handles stained and polished by years of sweat and use. Mr. Udagawa called the saw with larger teeth *chuume*, and we used this for the initial pass on the seams of the thicker bottom planks. The finish saw he called *koba*, which had finer teeth and the one we used exclusively for the side planking. Late in the project I asked him about these two saws. "Since suriawase is so important for you to learn, I felt I needed new saws to teach you properly. I ordered them from the sawmaker in Sanjo City." I asked him how much they cost. Mr. Udagawa picked up the new saws, one in each hand, saying, "70,000 yen for this one," and, waving the other saw, "80,000 yen for this one." In 2001 this totaled roughly fifteen hundred dollars *for two handsaws*. Needless to say I was stunned at these prices, but I had also visited a few high-end tool stores by then and had seen what the finest hand-made tools cost.

As I tried to master the alien sawing motion Mr. Udagawa occasionally separated the planks to show me the edges. He explained that a standard sawing motion, cutting through the stock at an angle, would leave scratches on the plank edges running from the outside of the boat to the inside, thus creating channels for water. Keeping the saw at a shallow angle and pulling it parallel to the plank face leaves striations that cannot channel water into the hull. I would often concentrate on sawing correctly but then, forgetting this point, withdraw the saw on the pull (the direction Japanese saws cut) and ruin the joint.

Struggling to focus on the correct technique, I wondered why so much care was being lavished on a seam that, even if it

Mr. Udagawa's classic boatbuilder's handsaws, with backs curving to a narrow point to facilitate removal from a seam. The narrower saws are older, having been sharpened repeatedly and lost most of their steel.

With proper suriawase saw scratches run parallel to the plank faces, leaving little chance they can channel water to the inside. The rectangular hole is a chiseled pilot hole for a nail.

did leak, would swell tight within hours. Mr. Udagawa made clear, however, that a boat leaking upon launching would deal a serious blow to the builder's reputation. Caulking, when used at all, was always done from inside the hull, and more often than not was reserved for older boats. Caulking is called *makihada,* and is made from the inner bark of the cypress. Mr. Udagawa warned me that we would be the first to set foot in the boat, and would be expected to rock the boat from side to side, burying the chine under water to publicly check for leaks. All eyes would be looking for the slightest sign of water weeping into the seams.[11]

Mr. Udagawa surprised me with his teaching methods. Unlike Mr. Fujii, who required that I watch him for hours, and then work without spoken instruction, Mr. Udagawa began each process by quickly describing what we were doing. His sentences were short and delivered quickly, almost always punctuated with the sentence-ending *ne?*, meaning "isn't it so?," or "you know what I mean?" Although this is a common conversational device to foster agreement, frankly, he spoke so fast there was no time for a reply. The moment he stopped explaining what he wanted me to do he thrust the tools in my hand and, lips suddenly pursed, motioned for me to get to work. With the nail mortises, for instance, he explained how their sloping sides necessitated a dovetailed plug that would not come out. He chiseled one or two mortises and then handed me the tools, telling me to chisel the third. If he was satisfied, then on I worked. If not, he would demonstrate again; then I was on my own with the rest. This was the process throughout the entire project: describe, demonstrate, correct, and go.

During our first few mornings on the job we were interrupted precisely at ten by a member of the museum staff inviting us to have tea with the director. Although Mr. Udagawa seemed irritated by this disruption, he also accepted the protocols that are a feature of Japanese institutions. We headed for the conference room where we were ushered to our seats beside each other on one side of the conference table, with the director and curators on the other side. One of the ladies in the office always fixed green tea, and the first morning she set the first cup in front of me. The general tension I felt around museum staff had made me aware that they saw me as a special guest, yet I saw myself as the *deshi*, or apprentice, and so I slid the first cup in front of Mr. Udagawa. The second cup was presented to me, then the director was served, and finally the curators.

Nothing much was said at these get-togethers beyond a few pleasantries. The museum staff was generally too nervous to speak with me, and Mr. Udagawa was always eager to get back to work. On the second and third day I was again offered the first cup of tea and again I slid it over to Mr. Udagawa. By the end of our first week the tea routine quietly came to an end.

Killing the Wood

We spent several hours preparing the two seams of the boat's bottom. When the sawing was complete I was surprised to see Mr. Udagawa remove the props, stand the planks on edge and, hammer in hand, begin pounding the edges I had just so carefully prepared. This turned out to be the final step before nailing the planks together; Mr. Udagawa called this *kigoroshi*. Kigoroshi (see Chapter 5) is a variation on Mr. Fujii's technique of planing the plank edges of tub boats, which he called *korosu*, literally, "to kill."[12] We used the convex face of the hammerhead, and it is imperative that the hammer strike only the middle of plank edges, leaving the corners untouched. Mr. Udagawa advanced very slowly, pounding the entire length of the seam with overlapping blows. The goal is to form a shallow valley of compressed fibers between the two corners. When two of these pounded surfaces are clamped together and nailed, the untouched corners compress tightly together and the crushed fibers in the center squeeze back against each other once the boat is in the water.

According to Mr. Udagawa, even this seemingly simple step requires great skill. As crude as it might seem to be hammering our planks, Mr. Udagawa paid more attention to my kigoroshi than perhaps any other task I performed. Weeks later, after we finished, he interrupted his otherwise lavish praise for me by telling me privately I needed more practice at this technique.

Mr. Udagawa had a few large clamps that we used to pull together the keel plank assembly. Making sure the nail holes were lined up, we stood the keel on one edge. While we applied nothing to the edges before assembly, other boatbuilders I have worked with used glue. One in particular uses a two-part urea-formaldehyde resin (similar to Aerolite), but by far the most commonly used glue is a white, polyvinyl acetate sold by the trade name Bondo. Traditionally, some boatbuilders used lacquer in the seams, but lacquer has always been a very expensive material and the advent of cheap glues quickly drove it from the boat shop. Interestingly, all of my teachers said that the use of glue was not for strength, but for ensuring the seams stayed closed. None of them trusted the glue to hold the boat together, but they appreciated how the glued seams would stay shut regardless of seasonal shrinking, keeping dirt out. Any dirt working its way into a seam would eventually compromise the watertight fit.

The nails are slightly bent before insertion to match the subtle curve of the holes. Mr. Udagawa's nailing technique was a complete surprise. With a few firm strikes he drove the nail head down well into its mortise. He then picked up his nail set (a steel punch), placed it against the nail head, and began a rhythmic tapping with the hammer. Mr. Udagawa could "play" his hammer and nail set like a drum, rapping out a complicated syncopation as the hammer and punch drove the nail to the base of the mortise. Between hammer blows he would tap the head with the nail set, and by holding the nail set just off the head the hammer would create a rounder sound. His entire demeanor suddenly changed; he smiled and, looking at me, laughed as the nail came to a halt on his final note. He handed me the tools and urged me to tap out a rhythm as well. The nails must be driven slowly, he explained, so interspersing hard blows with soft and creating a song was integral to the work. I tried imitating him, but Mr. Udagawa was quick to tell me I must develop my own personal rhythm. His brother joined us and took over, driving a few nails with his own rhythms, and the two brothers interacted like a pair of tap dancers, or jazz musicians, strutting away from the work when they had finished and daring the other to match their riffs. Crowds quickly formed in the shop whenever we nailed planks, such was the attraction of the sharp percussion, a sound both mysterious and intoxicating.

Mr. Udagawa called this technique *damashi uchi. Damasu* is the verb "to deceive," and *uchi* means "inside." None of my other teachers nailed in this way although all were familiar with the practice. I had met boatbuilders on Japan's two largest lakes, Biwa and Kasumigaura, who both used this technique. They called it *uguisu no tani watari,* which means "the bush warbler flits across the valley." This bird is notable for building multiple nests and then frantically flying between them to raise multiple broods. When done well, the boatbuilder can create the illusion of an echo tapping the nail, like the warbler's song swelling and receding in volume across a valley.[13]

I remembered what Mrs. Udagawa had said about hearing her husband's nailing and knowing he was working hard. Postwar Japan posed almost unimaginable financial challenges. Making music while nailing was a form of work song, and while it may have been intended to improve technique, the music we made released the tension of our labors and turned our work into a creative, musical game. It was the reward for having cut, planed, and fit a plank properly.

Mr. Udagawa deserved some enjoyment, because he worked like a man possessed. It was disconcerting at first, because there we were, on display in the museum boat shop, with grandmothers and mothers clutching children's hands and watching us, all smiles. It was certainly the most benevolent of settings. We had no deadline, no impatient client waiting for his boat, and no concerns over whether the check would clear. Mr. Udagawa was wonderful with the visitors and loved seeing friends. While I worked on the boat he gesticulated, told stories, and spoke passionately about the old days of Urayasu. When he turned back to the boat, however, to show me the next step, whether it was with a plane, saw, or hammer, it was with an absolute ferocity. He literally threw the tools aside (even those expensive handsaws) to grab the next one. All of his motions were skilled yet frantic.

It dawned on me that he was, in a way, programmed for this. His career as a boatbuilder had been a never-ending struggle to make a living. In a little more than twenty

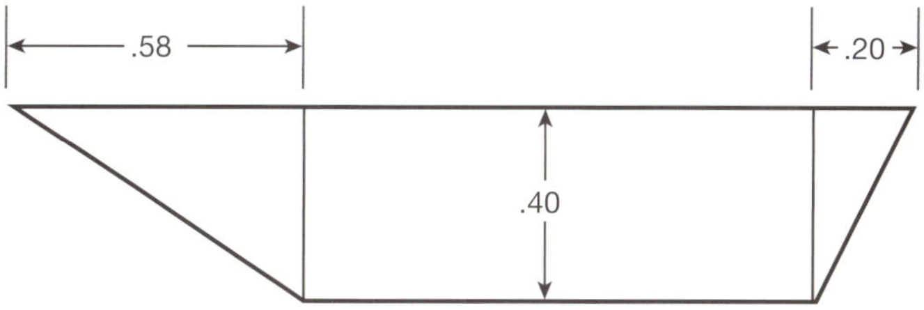

(Left) Plugs for the nail mortises are dovetailed and tapered, with their grain at right angles to the planking so they swell tight and hold in the mortises without glue. (Above) Mr. Udagawa's pattern for the angle of the stem (left), and transom (right), which he made from scrap wood.

years, working with just two or three other men, his shop produced fifty boats in the thirty-foot range, and more than three hundred bekabune and other small boats. That is a prodigious output by any standards, and during half of that period he had exclusively worked with hand tools! Picking up his tools had always been a serious matter, signaling the start of a period of intense concentration, and our working in a museum had not changed that.

We made dovetail-shaped plugs for the nail-head mortises. Mr. Udagawa sawed scrap plank ends and expertly split out dovetailed sections of end grain without measuring. These had a vertical grain and were driven into the mortises with a hammer. Once in the water the plugs swell tight, so require no adhesive. Mr. Udagawa used his adze to trim the plugs flush; it was then my job to plane the keel plank smooth.

Mr. Udagawa used three planes for this job: a scrub plane with an edge slightly convex for quickly removing material, a smoothing plane, and a finish plane. He watched me closely; using only a plane to make a smooth, final finish is a hallmark of Japanese woodworking. Making sure I worked in long strokes, he was only pleased when I could produce full-length, translucent shavings. He propped the bottom up on one edge so we could plane while standing and bent over, rather than squatting on the shop floor. When the bottom was planed completely smooth, the rewards of properly fitting the planks became apparent; the seams were all but invisible.

With the bottom planks joined together Mr. Udagawa could then lay out his stations: three lines drawn athwartships, where he marked all of his measurements for the outer shape of the bottom, as well as the spots where he set the

The finished shiki (bottom) on the floor of the boat shop. To the left is a planing bench Mr. Udagawa set up for the author. To the right is a section of the massive cedar tree that provided the material for several museum boats.

angles of the planks. The corollary in Western boatbuilding would be the mold locations, but whereas in the West these are positioned at regular intervals along the hull, the locations of Mr. Udagawa's stations were one of his secrets.

Setting up the Stations

Mr. Udagawa called his three stations *yokozumi.*[14] Like all traditional boats, bekabune were built without molds, and he used only these three stations for building all of his boats, from the little bekabune (just over 15 shaku long) to the much larger utasebune (well over 30 shaku). The station locations were memorized: the fore and aft stations were 3 shaku aft of the inboard face of the stem and 3 shaku forward of the inboard face of the transom, respectively. The third station marked the location of the greatest beam of the boat: 2.3 shaku aft of the forward station.[15] The keel plank was 12 shaku long measured inside, from the back of the stem to the face of the transom.

Mr. Udagawa had an ingenious method for remembering the half breadths of the keel at his three stations. At his center station (maximum beam) the half breadth inside of the planking was 1.15 shaku, which we marked on the top of the keel plank. To get the forward half breadth he subtracted .08 shaku from this amount, giving a result of 1.07. Then he subtracted 1 sun (.10 shaku) from that amount to calculate the half breadth of the after station, or .97 shaku: the result was the half breadth at the forward station. In essence, he didn't bother to memorize the actual dimensions of the boat; rather, he remembered the maximum half breadth and two numbers to be deducted. Most of the boatbuilders I have met who eschewed drawings generally remembered outright their various secret dimensions. Mr. Udagawa's own method may be unique, or at least rare. Also, while he made basic drawings of his boats he told me he didn't keep any of them.[16]

The backbone setup with one plank installed. Visible in the center of the photograph is Mr. Udagawa's pattern for setting the angle of the plank at two different stations.

Finishing the Backbone

With the keel plank cut to shape it was then firmly fixed by props located at the fore and aft stations. The forward end of the keel was blocked up 1 sun while at the transom it was blocked up by 2 sun. Mr. Udagawa laid out all the dimensions for the transom, again from memory, which we then cut to shape. Most boats have their sheer planks set plumb, but in the bekabune there is a bit of tumblehome aft.[17] Mr. Udagawa set his square along the top of the transom and lined up the outer corner with his mark at the chine. He then marked the inside corner of his square. This reduced the width of the transom at the top by the width of the square on either side. I mention this detail because boatbuilders use the width of the square as a standard small unit in their layout (the legs of squares are 5 bu wide). It is quick, consistent, and leaves one less dimension to memorize.

The angles of the stem and transom were derived by laying out angles at either end of a board 4 sun wide. Mr. Udagawa squared the two ends of the board and measured back .58 shaku from the lower corner on one end and .2 shaku from the other. He then connected the top corners to his marks and we cut along these hypotenuses. By holding the pattern upright on its bottom edge against the keel plank we now had patterns for the angles of the stem and transom. Mr. Udagawa then cut a rabbet across the back of the keel plank for the transom. We beveled the transom to match (checking the angle with our pattern) and planed all surfaces smooth.

Mr. Udagawa braced the transom and, taking his handsaw, laid it flat against the edge he had just planed to fit and rubbed the saw back and forth, with the set in the teeth scratching the faying surface.[18] He did the same to the rabbet

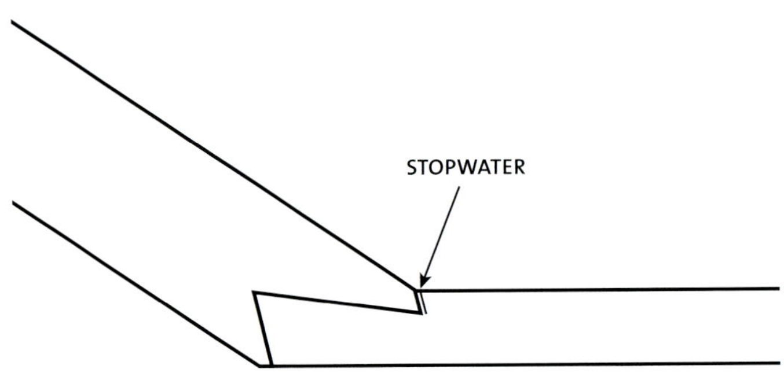

The bite-scarf connection between the stem and bottom. Mr. Udagawa put four strips of newspaper in the back of this joint to act as a stopwater.

joint in the keel plank, rubbing until the saw had roughened the entire surface. Finally, only the faying surface of the transom was hammered before assembly and nailing; Mr. Udagawa did not hammer an end grain portion of any joint. The transom was nailed in with large-headed nails, and just before setting the nails, he used his hammer to bend over the corners of the nail heads so they would grip better.

We made the stem of kayanoki (sometimes simply kaya), or Japanese nutmeg. The stem itself tapered slightly from the base to the top. Mr. Udagawa laid out all the faces and directed me to saw and plane the stem to size. The stem-keel connection joint was a bite scarf.[19] Mr. Udagawa first cut the joint on the forward end of the shiki and then, while holding the stem alongside, traced its shape onto the stem. Once the mating joint was cut on the stem, I held the two pieces together while he ran the saw through the two vertical faces of the joint until we gained a tight fit. The edges of this joint were angled slightly so that the two pieces locked together. Mr. Udagawa placed four small pieces of newspaper in the back of the joint to act as a stopwater. If water did seep through the seam the newspaper would swell tight and close the joint. Bekabune do not have rabbeted stems, which is reflective of most, but not all, river boat construction.[20] Sea boats more often have rabbeted stems to receive the planking.

Mr. Udagawa showed me an interesting technique for setting the stem up perfectly plumb. He fastened one end of his inkline to the center point at the top of the stem, ran the line back, and fastened it to the centerline of the shiki. He then took a turn with the string around the legs of his square and let it hang in midair. Next, he adjusted the string until the corner of the square hung just above the bottom.

The author and Mr. Udagawa fitting the transom. It rested on a rabbet joint cut across the back of the bottom. *Photo copyright Keiju Kurozumi.*

The stem was then ready to be set and Mr. Udagawa pivoted it in its joint until the corner of the square lined up with the keel centerline.

Planking

With the backbone set up it was time to hang the first side planks. Mr. Udagawa measured along the inside face of the stem, from the keel, and from memory marked the heights of the chine and the sheer. He then ripped a second piece of scrap cedar planking 4 sun wide. Once again he cut two angles on either end of the scrap: one with an upper leg of .15 shaku and the other at .21 shaku. After the ends had been trimmed, the plank became the pattern for the angles of the bottom planks at the fore and aft stations, held along the station lines on the bottom.

Mr. Udagawa had one very wide, very thin cedar plank he used for spiling (measuring the shape of a plank), which we propped in place on the boat. Using props from above and below, Mr. Udagawa forced the spiling plank into place, propping it securely and setting the plank angles at our two stations with his pattern. We traced the bottom edge of the keel, and marked the top edge at our chine marks on the stem and transom. Mr. Udagawa had memorized the widths for the plank at the fore and aft stations (.7 shaku and .65 shaku, respectively), and we transferred these marks to the planking stock.

Mr. Udagawa was very specific about the batten he used to lay out and draw the curved edges of our planks. It was 5 bu wide and 7 bu tall (.05 shaku by .07 shaku) and made of clear cedar. At the stern our first plank (the lower of the two side planks, which he called the *kajiki*) extended about 1 shaku past the transom. Later, after we had hung the *uwadana*, the sheer (topmost) planks, we would cut some of this off.[21] Nonetheless, our planking did form a well aft of the transom. Mr. Udagawa made a small chisel cut for reference marks at each of our stations because once I planed the plank smooth all of our ink marks would be gone. He also put a rough planking bevel, which he called the *ne,* on the

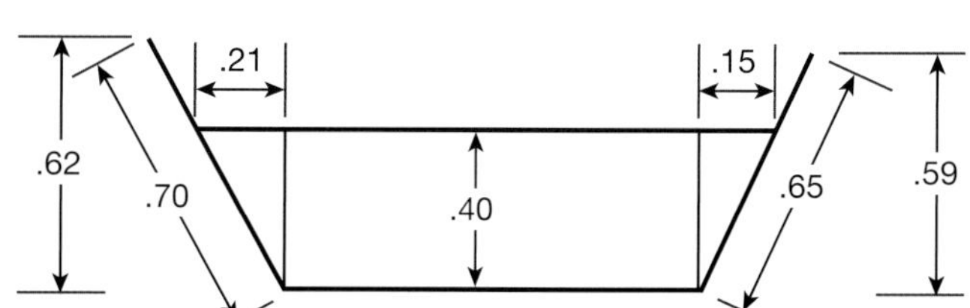

Mr. Udagawa's pattern for the angle of the lower planks, at his forward station (left) and after station (right). The diagonal measurements are for the width of the plank at each station.

The spiling plank propped into place. This was used to measure the shape of the first two planks. Note how the entire assembly is held with props. Japanese boatbuilders use very few, if any, clamps.

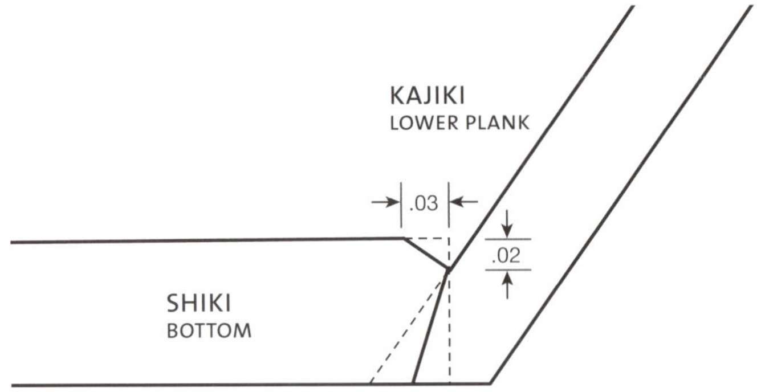

The bevel on the shiki and the lower plank where they meet is determined by taking half the distance between the square edge of the shiki and the angle of the plank. The planking bevel bisects these two lines. The chamfer on the shiki prevents tear-out when running the saw through the seam.

bottom edge of our lower planks. He used no patterns or other measurements to do this, rather worked by feel, calling this *hirameki*, having the knowledge in one's head.[22]

In a Western boat, a dory for example, the inside face of the lowest plank remains flat and the planking bevel is cut entirely on the keel plank. The bevel Mr. Udagawa planed on the keel was actually half of what was needed to mate with the face of the joining planks; we planed a shallow bevel along the base of those planks to match it. Again, my research shows this to be the standard construction method. Although the additional bevel makes getting correct angles even trickier, we had only to plane to a rough fit because we would be making the final fit by suriawase. A joint made with the bevel cut entirely on the keel plank would have made it all but impossible to use this technique, as the saw would have to lie flat against the inside face of the planking.

After I cut out the two lower planks with a handsaw, Mr. Udagawa had me plane them smooth using three planes that we always used to take material from rough to a finished surface.[23] Once planed, our planking was about 7 bu thick. With the planks ready to hang, the final preparation of the keel involved adding a small bevel around the edge. Mr. Udagawa called this the *makihada men*, which literally means "caulking bevel." If this boat ever did require caulking it would be caulked *from the inside*, and cypress bark would be driven in at this bevel. We did eventually caulk some cracked knots in the keel plank.

(Above) Fitting the first plank, Mr. Udagawa carefully runs a saw through the seam between the plank and keel. At this point the plank is held in place entirely by props. Note the wedge in the seam behind him; he can adjust the seam to prevent the saw from binding. (Right) The author doing the same work. Beneath him is a caulking iron used to keep the seam open. *Photo copyright Keiju Kurozumi.*

We finished the backbone assembly after one week of work, and that evening after the museum closed most of the staff and many of Mr. Udagawa's friends gathered in the boatshop for the *shikisueru,* the keel-laying ceremony.[24] Surrounding the boat we listened while an elderly man, whose status was head fisherman, chanted in a song-like manner, essentially telling the story of the project and wishing us well. Then everyone retired to the museum cafe for a lavish dinner. At one point another fisherman stood on a chair and sang songs. Urayasu is known for its peculiar dialect and I couldn't make out a word of the lyrics, but the audience roared with laughter. After the drinking and singing, there was a more serious break while a few museum officials gave short speeches.

As mentioned earlier, the Urayasu Museum opened in 2001, and had actually been quite controversial as a civic project. Nekozane, the former fishing village, had been completely overwhelmed by suburban development from the 1970s onward, and so the vast majority of the population of Urayasu in 2001 had no connection to the former fishing industry. Many citizens wondered why there should be a museum devoted to the history of what was now a tiny, old neighborhood of the city. The citizens of Nekozane, many of them elderly, petitioned for the museum. In the end the museum was approved and during its first week was packed with visitors.[25]

The re-created village next to the museum quickly became the daily gathering place for retired fishermen, who lounged on the dock and in the entrance to the re-created tobacconist's shop. Within days of the museum's opening, they began making nets and other fishing gear and literally brought the exhibit to life.[26] One day I was admiring the large utasebune in the lagoon and asked the fishermen how big it was. "Six shaku," one of the men replied. The boat was at least 30 shaku long so, confused, I asked again. "Six shaku!" another fisherman said impatiently, with a few others grumbling. "It must be over 30 shaku," I protested, and the men's shouts were instantaneous and in unison: "Boats in Urayasu are measured by width!" Urayasu is the only place where I have encountered this practice, and my guess is it derives from the standardized beams of the seaweed boats.

The museum staff was justifiably proud of what they had created, and our keel-laying ceremony was as much a party to reward them as to spotlight our boat. One of the curators stood up to thank Mr. Udagawa and all the volunteers for their hard work. Then he acknowledged me. "We were all very nervous about Mr. Brooks," he said, "but when I saw him pass his tea to his master, I knew he was a good man."

Mr. Udagawa pours sake on the keel of the boat in a ceremony marking the completion of the backbone. The author awaits his turn to make this simple offering. *Photo copyright Keiju Kurozumi.*

At this point I still had not gotten to know museum staff, so I was taken aback, and suddenly realized how closely I had been watched and how significant my small gesture had been. I have mentioned how important persistence and observation are in mastering Japanese crafts; respect and politeness are no less important.

During the dinner Mr. Udagawa told me more about his life and work. He began by telling me that the bekabune we were building was very similar to its earliest form, which was believed to have originated around 1875.[27] The bekabune is actually a fairly well-known type of boat due to the popular 1960 novel *Aobeka Monogatari (Blue Beka Story)* by Shugoro Yamamoto. The author lived in Urayasu for one year, in 1928, and got to know many fishermen, basing his novel on a story involving a man who sees a blue boat on Tokyo Bay, and later buys a bekabune from a man in Urayasu. Actually, Mr. Udagawa had his doubts that the boat in the story was a true bekabune. In a 2001 interview with *Serai* magazine he explained his reasoning, based on his intimate experience within the community.

> In the story there is a scene where children threw stones at the boat. The tenma boats were the same size as beka, they carried fertilizer and smelled bad. That is why kids picked on his boat. In those days people earned their living gathering nori (seaweed), so if you threw stones at a beka people would scold you.

The earliest versions of bekabune were used only for harvesting seaweed, but a slightly larger and more heavily built version appeared in the early 1900s and was used for gathering shellfish as well. We were building an example of the latter type. Mr. Udagawa also stressed to me that every boatbuilder had different *wari,* the term he used for a boatbuilder's system for deriving and remembering dimensions. He worked in the postwar period when marine engines became common and, while the bekabune changed little, the design of larger boats like utasebune had to adapt from pure sailing boats to motorsailers. At the same time the quality of materials changed and wood became more expensive. The pressure to produce boats more efficiently was constant.

Mr. Udagawa and his men took just two days off a month: the first and fifteenth. Otherwise, he worked from eight in the morning until dark.[28] Most of his customers were in Urayasu, where over a thousand bekabune were registered at the height of the postwar fishing industry, along with hundreds of larger fishing boats. He also built boats for the surrounding region, including the Koto-ward of Tokyo, just across the broad Arakawa from Urayasu.

Mr. Udagawa reminded me that his shop had never been profitable; his rice fields had provided needed extra income. It is impossible to compare yen values from more than a half century ago, but a new noribeka, requiring a week to build plus materials, sold for the same amount as a bicycle in 1952.[29] The more heavily built bekabune used for clamming sold for two to two-and-a-half times more.

As we finished our discussion, Mr. Udagawa warned me that given every boatbuilder's unique wari, I could not have more than one teacher. To study with multiple boatbuilders, he said, would be hopelessly confusing. I remained silent, because I knew the Freeman Foundation was considering my proposal to study with Mr. Fujiwara, the boatbuilder I had met in Tokyo. At some point I might have to reveal this, but for the moment I felt it was best to say nothing.

As mentioned earlier, bekabune are the most lightly built traditional Japanese boats, and all the planking is bent cold. (For larger boats Mr. Udagawa pre-bent planking over an open flame.) Props were again used from above and below to hold the planks securely, and soon the hull was surrounded by a forest of them. There was no limit to Mr. Udagawa's ingenuity. He even installed small blocks between props so one could push against the other. This turned the site into an obstacle course for me, and more than once I stepped back and knocked one or two props out of position. The bent planks were like compressed springs, held back by the props, and at one point a lower plank leapt off the setup, knocking Mr. Udagawa over. He complained that the museum shop's plywood floor was too slippery; he preferred the traditional rammed-earth floor of his former shop because the ends of the props could be firmly set in the clay.

About every other day during the project Mr. Udagawa insisted we sharpen all the tools. He sharpened his better handsaws, and he showed me his system for sharpening his planes and chisels. Like Mr. Fujii, he used plenty of water to regularly wash the stones clean. Even more so than my other teachers, he was meticulous about keeping his stones flat, regularly taking them to one of the smooth concrete pillars supporting a walkway over the museum's village. With the stones well soaked he rubbed them vigorously against the concrete until all of the hollows were removed.

Propping one of the planks in place. A rope loop was used at either end, tightened by a twisting a bar running through it. Mr. Udagawa only used clamps when edge-fastening two boards together off the boat.

We carefully chiseled the pilot holes through the face of the planking to fasten to the keel plank. We used the same size nails along the stem, bottom, and transom, 2 sun long and spaced about 4.5 sun apart. Before nailing the bottom plank in place, we ran a series of saws through the joint, with the lower planks securely propped, to get the final fit. Mr. Udagawa used a normal sawing motion mostly at the base of the stem and the forward end of the plank, where the plank angle transitioned rapidly. Over most of the length of the plank he tried to move the saw parallel with the seam, working methodically, as we had earlier prepared the bottom seams. He used two caulking irons, normally set in front and behind where he was working, to force the seam open just enough so that he could saw freely, yet still allow the teeth to cut.

We did not take the planks off to hammer the edges. Once he was satisfied with the fit, we left the planks propped in place and nailed them to the keel. Mr. Udagawa inserted a single wire nail at the stem and transom to hold the top edge of the planks. He then showed me how to very carefully begin making the pilot holes with the tsubanomi. He stressed it was very easy to split the planks at this stage, and one had to carefully size the pilot holes at the stem because kaya is quite hard and the boat nails are relatively soft steel. These nails will not drive through hardwoods; a hole must be chiseled tight enough to give the nail holding power but not so tight that the nail bends over. The chisel point is finer than the nail point, and so we actually piloted the holes a bit deeper into the hardwood than the nail could go. Mr. Udagawa checked my work often, holding a nail against the chisel and wiping a licked finger on the chisel to mark the length of the nail. I took to marking the chisel with a pencil for the rest of the project, erasing and remarking as we switched to different size nails.

We used the spiling plank to obtain the shape of the upper planks, again marking the heights at the stem and transom, while tracing the bottom off the top edge of the lower plank. Mr. Udagawa laid out from memory the width of the sheer at the two stations: 7 sun at the forward station and 6 sun aft. It was only later I noticed these values were exactly 1 sun greater than those for the lower planks. Though he didn't tell me, the deduction of precisely 1 sun at each location is probably yet another strategy he used for memorizing his layout.

Mr. Udagawa cautioned me to cut the planks a little wide of the line on the bottom edges, because I was bound to lose some material when fitting them with suriawase. He also snapped an inkline on the planking stock before I cut them so he could check later for straightness. Sawing can relieve stress in planks, causing longer ones to change shape. Again he emphasized how crucial it was that the sheer planks look beautiful, both in the quality of the wood and their shape on the boat.

Beams

The bekabune has a series of horizontal beams, called *funabari,* that brace the planking, with one beam also serving as the mast partner. All of the beams are tenoned through the top plank, and the tenons are cut and wedged from the outside. Two sets of beams are arranged in pairs, and located at the stations. I chiseled the mortises in the sheer planks to receive the beams, which were cut from kaya.

As mentioned earlier, the planking on the bekabune meets flush, so our nail heads had to be mortised into the sheer planks, then passed down through the plank seam into the lower planks. We first cut the mortises and then, working from the plank edge, piloted a hole back to meet the base of the mortise. Because the planks meet at an angle the nails are curved, and the hole must be slightly off center where it exits the plank edge. Mr. Udagawa did not measure this; having built over three hundred bekabune he could do this work by eye. Threading our nails properly through this thin planking was probably the most difficult part of building bekabune, and so he hovered over me as I chiseled the nail holes. Once the planks were propped on the boat, we drove the curved tsubanomi through the holes and into the plank below.

All work on the boat to this point had been done by hand, but as we were making the beams and frames the museum staff delivered a brand-new, small bandsaw to our shop. After having sawn and planed multiple sixteen-foot planks by hand, it seemed odd to have a power tool arrive at this point. When Mr. Udagawa told me to cut the mast partners to shape on the machine, I suggested that since I had come this far doing everything with hand tools I'd rather continue that way. He rejected the idea instantly, and ordered me to use the bandsaw. I don't know if he was irritated by my frivolity or the inefficiency, but I did as I was told, and the mast partner was the only part of the boat touched by a power tool.

Meanwhile Mr. Udagawa was fashioning a large pine beam, called the *toko,* which ran across the back of the transom and held the rudder stock. He laid out a 1.6 sun diameter hole for the rudder stock and grabbed one of his gouges. The timber was 3 sun thick. He quickly hammered the gouge around his circular line and then began chiseling

The rudder post passes through a hole in the toko, the large beam set across the stern of the boat. Mr. Udagawa cut this in a matter of minutes with a gouge.

The author and Mr. Udagawa fitting the two top planks on their beams. The sheer planks are hung on the boat in a single unit with the beams.

Mr. Udagawa installs a prop at the bow. Bekabune planking is thin enough to be bent without the use of heat. *Photo copyright Keiju Kurozumi.*

furiously at the center, gouging out great chips of cedar and working back toward his line and around the circle. I watched, amazed, has he literally chiseled a hole, his motions so fast that his hands, gouge, and mallet were like a human drill bit. When he was done he asked me for the nutmeg mast partner and he did the same thing, chiseling a perfect hole through the dense, yellow hardwood.

We laid out the location for the nails along the bottom edge of the sheer plank and chiseled the holes and cut the mortises for the nail heads. Only after the sheer planks were fit would we use a curved tsubanomi to finish piloting the holes into the lower planks.

The beams were first inserted between the two sheer planks, and the entire assembly of planks and beams carefully placed on top of the boat. Mr. Udagawa liked to bend the planking in at the bow first and then move aft. We prepared by collecting plenty of props, wedges, and blocking, and we had to stop several times and quickly cut a prop to fit. It took several attempts to get things blocked in place, with Mr. Udagawa again complaining about the plywood floor. We eventually resorted to driving nails into the floor as stops for the bases of our props.

With the sheer planks affixed Mr. Udagawa watched carefully as I sawed the seams. The angle of the seam between the planking bisects the angle of the two planks. He had me work in such a way that I was first sawing with the grain of the two planks, but this wasn't always possible, as the grain direction changes with the sweep of the plank line. I worked slowly and he suggested I hold the saw at a very acute angle to the plank face. He cautioned me not to strain at the saw; it was better to use the caulking iron to open the seam a little bit rather than force the tool. Of course a little sawing motion was fine where the fit was tight, but the final pass had to be a rubbing motion. Mr. Udagawa said that in larger boats he did this with two saws—a rough cut followed by a finish saw—but with the bekabune's thin planking we used just the finish saw. He reminded me again of the launching ceremony when everyone would watch as we dipped first one chine, then the other, in the water to check for leaks.

We bent our nails slightly before fastening, and carefully blocked the planking to absorb the shock of the hammer. It was again time to play a tune with the hammer and nails, but we also felt the hull for any sign a nail might be coming through. The edge fastening method makes repairs to the boats very difficult. Mr. Udagawa said that a plank was never replaced entirely; instead patches are fitted in damaged sections. All around us in the museum were older vessels, many that had been repaired, some by Mr. Udagawa

(Left) Mr. Udagawa sawing the joint between the upper and lower planking. The tenons for the beams, which pass through the hull, are wedged and visible next to him. (Above) The nearly complete bekabune. The mortises for the edge nails fastening the top plank to the bottom are clearly visible above the chine. The hull is still firmly propped in place to prevent the assembly from moving.

himself. All the damaged portions were at the chine, and while one edge of a patch followed the chine the other was a long graceful arc. Because the sawing technique is used in a repair to make a tight fit, the edge must have a radius no tighter than the saw can negotiate.

The bekabune also had two heavy sawn ribs made of kaya, which Mr. Udagawa called *matsura.*[30] They were fitted opposite one another and notched over a single floor timber we clench-nailed to the bottom. I cut away their lower corners to provide a waterway. I spiled their shapes but I was having some trouble planing the faying surfaces to make a tight fit. Mr. Udagawa showed me how to slightly gouge out the center of the face meeting the planking, leaving just the two outer edges touching the planks. This left less wood to plane at the edges to get a final fit. He called this *usotsuku,* which means "to lie."[31] We drove large modern wire nails through the planking to fasten the ribs.

One day as we were finishing the boat the museum director appeared and invited us back to the conference room. The chief curator of the Ota historical museum had come to visit. Ota-ward is a section of Tokyo directly across Tokyo Bay from Urayasu. It was also a famous fishing ground and producer of nori (though several times Mr. Udagawa told me Ota nori was inferior to Urayasu nori). There was also a tradition of bekabune in Ota and a few years earlier the museum had gathered some of the community's last surviving boatbuilders and had them build one. The curator had documented the process, producing an excellent video and book. He presented Mr. Udagawa and me with copies, and complimented us on our project.

Mr. Udagawa initially sat silently, leaving it to the curators to do most of the talking. The visiting curator began by sharing some of the history of Ota-ward, which had many similarities with Urayasu. Both communities saw their fishing grounds covered by huge landfill projects; Haneda airport was built in Ota while the fishing grounds were still active in Urayasu, and later Tokyo Disneyland was built in Urayasu. Among the interesting differences between Ota and Urayasu was that Urayasu fishermen paddled or poled their bekabune stern first, while in Ota they *sailed* their boats stern first. In Ota bekabune the mast step and partners are located aft.

As the conversation drifted into construction methods, Mr. Udagawa forcefully interjected with a list of differences between boatbuilders of the two communities. He said that Ota builders would fasten their boat's ribs to the bottom before planking, whereas we installed ours after the hull was planked. In Ota the builders used *keyaki (Zelkova serrata)* for their hardwood while we used kaya. He also said Ota builders planked from the transom to the stem while we did the opposite.

I felt something simmering in the tone of Mr. Udagawa's voice, but the curator cut him short and continued to describe the end of the fishing era in Ota in the 1960s. He gave us statistics on the hundreds of fishermen who were put out of business when the fishing grounds finally

One of the pair of heavy sawn ribs in the hull. Like the stem and beams, they are made of Japanese nutmeg.

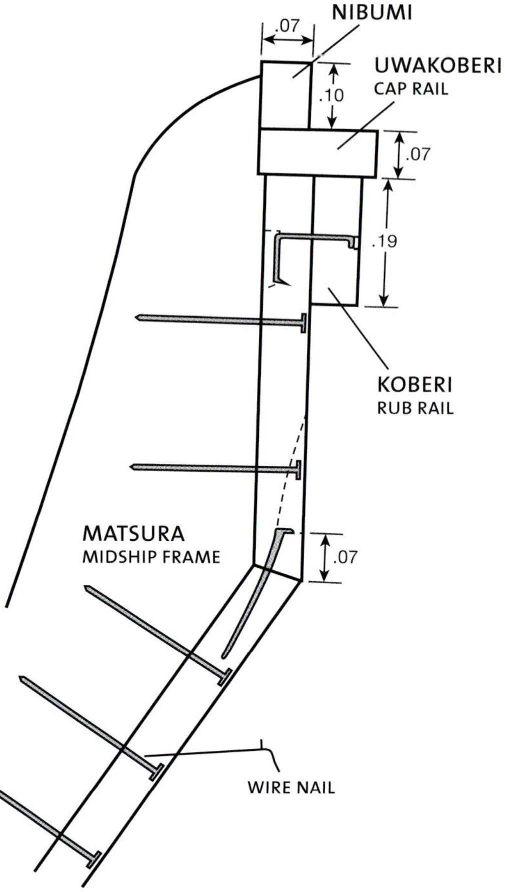

Cross section of the planking at the matsura, or midship frame, showing the construction of the gunwale (koberi, uwakoberi, and nibumi) and the fastenings, including clench nails, edge nails, and wire nails.

An old photo showing bekabune sailing near Ota-ward, across the bay from Urayasu. The boats were similar, but in Ota the fishermen sailed them stern first. *Photo copyright Ota Folk Museum.*

closed. He said Ota's fleet of eight hundred bekabune were either burned or sold to other towns around the bay, including Urayasu. Mr. Udagawa was silent. After the meeting adjourned, as we walked back to the shop he suddenly caught my arm, turning me to face him. Raising a finger he said to me, "No Urayasu fisherman *ever* bought a boat from Ota." That was that and we went back to work.

Gunwales

The smallest and lightest bekabune had no gunwale whatsoever. We were building a larger, heavier version, and the gunwale of our boat consisted of three parts: the *koberi* (rub rail) mounted flat against the top edge of the sheer plank; the *uwakoberi* (cap rail) covering the sheer plank and the rub rail's top edges; and the *nibumi,* a small timber mounted on top of the cap rail. First I planed the top edge of the sheer planks perfectly flat, checking with a straightedge laid across the hull. Mr. Udagawa checked my work carefully, looking for any unfairness (deviations from a smooth, graceful curve) in the lines of the sheer as it swept from bow to stern.

Next we laid out the locations of the nails for the rub rail. These were *doukugi* (literally, copper nail), the only nonsteel fastenings in our boat. The nails were evenly spaced about 7 sun apart, with care being taken to center them on either side of the beam ends. The nails had an offset head like our other boat nails and the shank was also flat rather than round. Our rub rail was made of cedar, the same thickness as the planking, and about 2 sun wide. We did not bend it; instead I sawed it out of our stock with a slight sweep, so there was no edge-setting.

We had to set the koberi slightly high where the sheer planks flared, so there would be material for us to plane the top edge flat to match the planking. While Mr. Udagawa measured this allowance, I took a piece of scrap and made a gauge that would help set this offset automatically. I showed it to Mr. Udagawa, saying this little tool was something I used when building boats in America. He looked surprised, but then quickly realized how it worked. He plucked it from my hand, and with a big smile cried out, "*Subarashii!*" (Wonderful!), then dashed out of the shop to show it to the retired fishermen who were working in the museum village. When he returned he gave it to me and watched me finish setting the rub rail height. He repeated the story of my invention to nearly every museum visitor who happened by the rest of the day.

Mr. Udagawa's encouragement was constant and always enthusiastic. He often served like a docent while I worked. The sight of a tall foreigner building a traditional boat in the museum's shop was bound to draw attention regardless, but Mr. Udagawa was only too happy to tell my story again and again, describing my work with sincerity, but a level of flattery that made me feel a bit uncomfortable. It was all a far cry from our first stiff and formal meeting, and he was in no way the harsh and unforgiving teacher so commonly associated with Japanese crafts. It was impossible not to like Mr. Udagawa and be swept up in his enthusiasm. Yet, for all of his encouragement he was first and foremost serious—about his craft, his community, and my training.

Visitors to the museum were surprised to find me, a foreigner, working alongside Mr. Udagawa. Their comments often carried a tone that, at least initially, I found irritating. There seemed to be a casual assumption that as a non-Japanese I could not possibly use Japanese tools or understand Japanese boatbuilding. Mr. Udagawa vigorously defended my presence whenever he heard these comments, although one day my attempt to refute a statement earned me a stern correction from him.

A visitor was watching me prepare to plane a plank smooth, and she commented that I would not be able to do this because Japanese planes are pulled, rather than pushed. As a foreigner, she said, I could not possibly use these tools. Her certitude made me angry, so without saying a word I spun Mr. Udagawa's plane around and pushed it across the plank. A thin ribbon of wood curled out of the mouth of the plane, leaving a smooth surface in its wake. The woman instantly reversed her opinion. "You *can* push a plane," she exclaimed, surprised yet smiling.

Mr. Udagawa was on me in a flash. "You must never push the plane!" he exclaimed. His eyes were wide with amazement. I am not sure if he was more shocked by my actions or that the plane seemed to work just fine when pushed. No matter. Pushing a plane crossed a line, like twisting the hammer with my wrist, a very fundamental rule and not negotiable. Some innovations were acceptable but some were not, and it was hard for me to know the difference.

Holding a backing block behind the planking we cut holes through the rub rail and along the top of the sheer planks with the tsubanomi. Where it exited the inside of the sheer I chiseled a small, tapered mortise, about one-third the depth of the planking. The copper nails were driven, head facing down, through the koberi and sheer. They were then carefully folded over into the mortise, with the tips just reentering the plank at the base. This is a very tricky process. When bending the nail over it is easy to force the head back out. The first blow must be close to the plank, starting a sharp fold that holds the nail in place. As the shaft is bent down one hammer blow on the tip will turn it down, then the final hammer blows continue to fold the nail. As it enters the mortise a nail set is used to finally drive the nail flat against the wood. It is a very beautiful fastening, giving one the impression the rail and plank are bound, or sewn, together.[32]

The nibumi were sawn to shape, not bent, with two pieces to each side of the boat. Other finishing touches included a simple deck forward and floorboards made of a very hard-wearing wood called *kurosugi* (black cedar). I instinctively reached for the plane and began surfacing the black cedar, but Mr. Udagawa stopped me with a shout: the floorboards would be left rough-sawn to improve footing and besides, he said, black cedar was very hard on tools.

Our boat, like all the replicas in the museum's lagoon, would be unpainted. Mr. Udagawa told me that in the old days new boats were pulled from the water a few months after launch and the bottoms were charred with burning rice straw. The surfaces were also rubbed with ashes. This was a primitive form of anti-fouling, intended to keep barnacles and other marine life from growing on the hull. Even house carpenters sometimes charred exterior siding as a preservation technique before the use of paints and other preservatives.

With the boat basically finished, we awaited the launch that was scheduled for the upcoming Sunday. Mr. Udagawa spent an entire day with me, teaching me his wari (dimensions) for the largest of the boats he built—the utasebune. He took a plank of cedar, and with his square and a ballpoint pen, drew a plank drawing of the boat. Like the bekabune, his drawing was 1/10th scale and showed the profile, the half breadth of the keel plank and the expanded transom. The profile drawing showed the pronounced drop of the sheer and bottom at the bow of the utasebune, something

Toto Mitsumata no zu, (View of Mitsumata in the Eastern Capital), woodblock print by Kuniyoshi Utagawa (1797–1861) showing fishermen charring the bottom of a boat as a preservative. This technique was also used in domestic architecture. *Image courtesy of William Pearl.*

Principal Dimensions for the Utasebune

Beam	Five shaku. Measured inside of planking.
Length	Calculated as beam times 6 (based on Mr. Udagawa's standard ratio for larger boats), so 5 times 6 equals 30 shaku. Measured from back of stem at the sheer to inside face of transom.
Depth	Calculated as beam times .4 plus .12 to .15 sun, so 5 times .4 equals 2 plus .12 to .15, or approximately 2.13 shaku. Measured amidships from top of cap rail to top of shiki.

The lagoon of the Urayasu Museum. The two bekabune in the foreground are paddled by museum volunteers. In the background is an *utasebune*, a motorized boat that pulled nets under sail power. All three replicas were built by Mr. Udagawa.

that can appear quite strange to Western eyes. Mr. Udagawa explained that the drop in the keel was to help the boat track straight, and the dip in the sheer gave the bow less windage; it was therefore less likely to be blown off course. As mentioned, boats in Urayasu were always sized by their beam. In brief, Mr. Udagawa derived the principal dimensions for his utasebune as described in the table at left.

Mr. Udagawa recited all of the other myriad dimensions for the boat, including the scantlings, shape of the transom, and other details, while I scribbled notes as fast as I could. Finally, he said that the advent of gasoline engines required boatbuilders to adjust their traditional dimensions by adding a bit of depth to the keel plank to make up for the added weight. This small sum he called the *mochi.*[33]

For setting his plank angles on larger boats Mr. Udagawa used a straightedge laid against the planking with a plumb bob hanging from it. To set the angles he measured on the horizontal from a point on the straightedge 1 shaku back from the string to the vertical string (the horizontal leg of a right triangle). He memorized just this horizontal dimension for each plank at each station. He didn't bother to use an actual level; he simply held his square horizontal. The dimensions for deriving plank angles in this way he called his *donoma,* and the stick with the plumb bob he called his *hakarigata*, literally, "measurement pattern."[34]

Mr. Udagawa is the only boatbuilder I know who never saved his plank drawings. He drew one for the bekabune on a sheet of white cardboard the day we started working and, had I not asked him for it, he would have discarded it. He specifically told me he also always destroyed the patterns he made for the angles of the stem, transom, and planking, making a new set for each boat. He told me earlier he had developed his own plank angles, so these patterns represented the heart of his methods. These were secrets Mr. Udagawa had guarded as jealously as his master had guarded his.

After our day discussing the wari for the utasebune he was happy to give me the drawing. I asked him about several other types of boats he built during his career and wondered if we could go over their wari, but he waved me off, saying the bekabune and utasebune were his most significant boats. Besides, he finally admitted sheepishly, he had forgotten the dimensions for the other boats.

Given the volume of what one would have to remember I could understand why Mr. Udagawa could only recall some of his boats. It also made me appreciate once again how hard it must have been for him to learn in a system where the teachers neither speak to the students nor share the most crucial information. "My teacher wouldn't show me the drawings or explain any of the layouts," he told me, "so I would come to the shop early and look at his drawings and take notes. It still wasn't enough for me to understand." Luckily another foreman liked Mr. Udagawa. "He recognized my persistence," he said, "and I gave him a lot of sake."

We did not make a sculling oar or paddle for our boat (see Chapter 6). In Urayasu these were traditionally made by a different craftsman. The *ro,* or sculling oar used by bekabune was the smallest made, with a blade about eight feet long. The waters around Urayasu were shallow enough so most fishermen poled their boats with paddles, called *kai.* A fisherman would have kai in several lengths depending on where he planned to fish. Although our bekabune had a mast step we did not build a sailing rig or rudder. Old photographs show bekabune flying a tiny gaff-headed sail, obviously a Western rig.[35]

Launching

Our launching ceremony was officiated by the most senior retired fisherman of the village. I have witnessed several of these ceremonies, and although most are conducted by Shinto priests, owners and boatbuilders sometimes lead them. They all reflect local customs, and the ceremony in Urayasu was unique because of the combination of Shinto and Buddhist rituals. The fisherman held Buddhist prayer beads, and chanted before a Shinto display of *gohei,* white paper strips symbolizing purity. The deck was covered with fresh fruit, vegetables, and dried squid. Among the two hundred or so spectators many had brought bottles of sake as gifts. After long, sonorous chants, the head fisherman opened a bottle and poured a small amount of sake on piles of salt placed on one of the beams. The museum director, Mr. Udagawa, and I were invited to do the same.

The fisherman then took a flint and a piece of steel and struck sparks inside the boat. He handed the tools to Mr. Udagawa, who did the same. Finally, I was asked to strike sparks. This interesting custom is called *kiribi,* and seems to come from Buddhist legends that striking sparks on the back of a person ensures their safety on a journey. At the time Mr. Udagawa told me this was a local custom. He may have meant it was local in boat launchings, because a generation or two ago it was a relatively common practice, or at least well known.[36] This completed our ceremony in the workshop, and we then carried the bekabune outside to the museum's lagoon where, bearing the flags of the United States and Japan, a cadre of former fishermen slid it into the water.

As promised, Mr. Udagawa invited me into the boat with him to check for leaks. Two fishermen knelt on the shore with bailers, one at either end of the boat. Their job, on Mr. Udagawa's signal, was to soak the boat as a final purification, inside and out, at the end of the celebration. Mr. Udagawa squatted facing me and tipped the starboard side of the boat. "See?" he cried. There were no leaks. Then we moved to the port side, burying the chine underwater. Small trickles of water began to weep into the hull. A look of horror came over Mr. Udagawa's face. Out of concern for my reputation, he told me to get out of the boat immediately so it could be wetted down as quickly as possible. He

The bekabune is launched in the museum lagoon, carrying the flags of the United States and Japan, in front of a crowd of onlookers. *Photo copyright Kazumi Muraki.*

jumped to shore. I lingered, inspecting the spots where an errant stroke of my saw or poorly aimed hammer might have left a tiny gap. Mr. Udagawa was frantically calling for me to join him. The two fishermen on their hands and knees at the edge of the water anxiously waited for the order to soak the boat. Before I stepped out I took a bailer and scooped up the water that had accumulated. To salvage my reputation I tipped it overboard and joked to the crowd, "*Sake dake desu*" (It's only sake).

Later that evening, after our celebrations were over, Mr. Udagawa and I walked along the Sakai River to his home. I told him about my proposal to an American foundation for funds to work with more boatbuilders, including Mr. Fujiwara in Tokyo. Mr. Udagawa once more insisted this was bound to confuse me, and that I should have one teacher only. I tried to argue that my research required studying as many different traditions as possible, and it pained me to see him hurt, this man who had been so incredibly generous to me.

As we passed the few wooden boats moored in the river, I decided to change the subject, and asked if he had built them. He said he had, and he even pointed out a bekabune, derelict and sunken, resting under a bridge. We came upon a long, narrow boat, relatively new, sitting at its mooring under a green cover. I had admired this boat for weeks while walking along the riverbank. Thinking that it might cheer him, I told him what a fine boat it was and asked if he had built it.

"No, that's a Fujiwara boat." My heart sank, and I simply did not know what else to say. Mr. Udagawa rested his elbows on the railing of the walkway and we stared at the boat in silence. At this point I was certain that anything I might add would just make the situation worse, but I felt terrible leaving Urayasu with this hanging between us. It seemed unthinkable to come back to Japan and work just a few miles away with a man who had been one of his competitors. After a long pause, Mr. Udagawa backed away from the railing and we resumed our walk. Finally he said, without looking at me, "It's a good boat." The tension seemed to ebb a little bit.

A year later my wife and I were living in Urayasu while I worked with Mr. Fujiwara. On weekends I would stop by the museum where Mr. Udagawa was building another utasebune. This time he had several apprentices, all younger men who had joined the Urayasu Shipbuilding Preservation Association, an organization he founded. One day I was in the museum galleries and I heard a familiar rhythm. The syncopated tapping filled the building, and I moved, like so many other visitors, toward the sound. Children ran past me, desperate to find the source of a music they had never heard before. The nailing stopped before I reached the shop, but then another sound rose, softer, growing like a wave. I stepped into the back of the crowd as Mr. Udagawa paused briefly and grinned, acknowledging the applause, then turned back to work, not yet finished with his encore.

Several years later I was sitting on a tatami floor with Mr. Udagawa, in the formal room of his house, talking about boats, boatbuilding, and the Urayasu he remembered. He showed me some old photographs of himself in his workshop. He looked very young, wearing white shorts and a white tank top, his arms glistening with sweat. A single light bulb hung from a wire over his head. Otherwise the shop was a dark cave of scrap wood, tools, and planking. We talked about the six public baths still surrounding his home in Nekozane. "In the winter you would come home from the bath and snap the ice off your towel!" he said with a laugh.

It was always hard to know where Mr. Udagawa's enthusiasm pushed him to exaggerate. He loved reminiscing, and these conversations always seemed to conclude with enthusiastic endorsements of anything made, grown, or harvested in Urayasu. He suddenly broke his reverie and became serious. He told me he was a *kado ga aru hito,* or "a square-cornered person," in other words, blunt, direct, and completely honest.[37] "As a craftsman I cannot abide a dishonest situation." He looked at me, his eyes narrowing, and asked, "Do you remember when we first met?"

At that moment I could not recall the day years earlier when we were introduced at the museum's first temporary boatshop, when Mr. Udagawa barely acknowledged my presence. He snapped at me again, "I thought you were some ass from abroad." I was shocked at his bluntness. Then he added, "I said to myself, '*Doko no uma no hone?*'" He laughed and his fierceness suddenly evaporated. I had to ask him what this phrase meant.

"It means 'Where is this horse bone from?'" He went on. "Urayasu was a small village and any strangers were regarded with suspicion. People naturally talked very harshly about them. But you wrote to me after you left, and you sent me documents and explained what you were trying to do. So slowly my attitude toward you changed."[38]

The man I studied with and knew so well seemed to me the furthest thing from cold and off-putting. He was the most enthusiastic booster of my research, and whenever we were together he proudly introduced me as his finest apprentice. I felt embarrassed by the praise, which he always delivered with the same enthusiasm he expressed describing Urayasu nori. The struggles he had endured to learn and practice his craft had not hardened him in the least, and I often remember with a smile how he was both serious but warm, generous yet uncompromising. "It is good to finally tell you this," he finished, "Now we can understand each other."

Notes

1 Shunichi Yamamoto is a prolific artist, writer and photographer with a particular interest in traditional boats. His work can be seen at yamamotoshunichi.com

2 The Michinoku Traditional Wooden Boat Museum (Michinoku Hoppo Gyosen Hakubutsukan) is located in Aomori City, Aomori Prefecture. Its collection comprises some three hundred boats, mostly from the Tohoku region, by far Japan's largest single collection of traditional boats.

3 The first land reclamation project in Urayasu was undertaken in 1958. By 1981 the area of Urayasu had been increased by more than fourfold through landfill.

4 *Nokkeru* means to put one thing on top of the other; *zukkuri* means technique. The chine is any corner or knuckle created where two planks meet. In most Japanese boats the top plank overlaps the lower plank, but the bekabune is unusual because the upper and lower planks meet with flush edges.

5 There are boats in other regions referred to as beka and other names for seaweed boats, including *noribune* and *noritoribune*.

6 The apprentice system is called *toteiseido,* and sending customers to a former apprentice is known as *norenwake*, literally "splitting the *noren*," the curtain that bears the name of the shop.

7 He blushed, laughing, when describing a beautiful boat as *komata no kireagatta onna,* which means "the short steps of a beautiful woman." He also described a boat's pleasing contours as *yanagigoshi*, like the "narrow waist of the willow tree."

8 Because of this habit most boatbuilders have no precise idea of the overall length of their boats.

9 At this writing I know of only one firm, located near Hiroshima, still making boat nails, although a competent blacksmith should have no problem fashioning them. For this 2001 project our nails were made by a blacksmith at a Yokohama firm. He was in his early eighties at the time and has since passed away; the company has no plans to continue supplying traditional fastenings.

10 While the technique is universally known, boatbuilders have various names for it, including *surinoko* and *tooshinoko*; however the most common term is suriawase. One boatbuilder in Ishikawa Prefecture called it *aiba,* a derivative of the verb *aibiau,* which means "to come to a mutual agreement."

11 Years earlier, a boatbuilder had told me that Western boats must be inferior to Japanese boats, because he had heard that every seam in brand new boats required caulking. He added, "And how are you supposed to caulk a boat from the outside when you are at sea and it is leaking?"

12 Kigoroshi is a compound word combining *ki* (wood) and *korosu* (to kill).

13 The famous chirping floors of Nijo Castle in Kyoto, designed to warn of approaching assassins, are called *uguisubari*, loosely translated "nightingale floors." Mr. Austin Moore, Ms. Minako Tagami, and Ms. Miho Udagawa helped clarify this definition.

14 Mr. Udagawa is the only boatbuilder I have met to use this term, which combines *yoko* (athwartship) with *sumi* (ink). The more common word for station among boatbuilders is *toubun*.

15 I have found almost all boatbuilders use a system consistent with Mr. Udagawa's for the location of the three stations: fore and aft stations measured as he did, equidistant from the back of the stem and the inside face of the transom, with the third station located at the maximum beam.

16 In my experience, Mr. Udagawa's practice was unique. I have found that those boatbuilders who made drawings did keep them and in many cases still possessed drawings made by their fathers and grandfathers. Unfortunately these drawings are almost universally incomplete, requiring the original builder to fully interpret them.

17 Tumblehome is where the top of a boat's hull angles inward. This is called *kaeru,* a verb meaning "to return" or "to come home." In a 2003 interview he mentioned that when a top plank angles out (called flare in the West) it is called *hiraki*, specifically the distance beyond vertical.

18 Faying surfaces are the faces touching each other when joining two pieces of wood.

19 Also called a *kamatsugite,* or "sickle joint," as the shape of the parts is reminiscent of the shape of a sickle.

20 I saw rabbeted stems on the *ayubune,* the most common wooden fishing boat on the Yoshino River in Tokushima Prefecture.

21 Literally, *kajiki* means "added shiki" and *uwadana* means "upper shelf."

22 Hirameki is defined as "insight;" more commonly craftsmen say they work *kan de,* or "by intuition."

23 He called these three planes *arashiko* (rough), *chuushiko* (smoothing), and *shiage* (finish).

24 The local pronunciation for this in Urayasu was *shikizue.*

25 When it was being planned it was estimated the museum would have 30,000 visitors a year. In fact, the museum had that many visitors *in the first month.* An enormous success, the museum hosted 300,000 visitors in its first three years.

26 While Japan has many excellent historic house museums, "living history" museums are very rare.

27 An 1830 document refers to a *hekabune* as a small boat used for fishing in the Haneda section of Tokyo Bay. It is thought the phrase *hekaheka* means "easily bent."

28 Some businesses still operate on this schedule. When my wife and I lived in Nekozane in 2002 the local public baths were closed on the first and the fifteenth.

29 The Urayasu Museum calculated the cost of a new bekabune was also equivalent to the average starting monthly salary of a college graduate.

30 Normally boatbuilders refer to sawn frames as *abara,* or *rokkotsu,* which is the same word for the rib in one's body. The origin of Mr. Udagawa's term is unknown.

31 This is lying in a more lighthearted sense, like fibbing.

32 Clench-nailing is common in traditional Western boatbuilding, but is a more complex technique in Japan. Mr. Udagawa did not have a specific term for clench nailing and, after struggling to come up with one, finally settled on the verb *shimetsukeru.*

33 Perhaps from the verb *mochiageru,* which means "to lift," or "uplift."

34 Both of these terms may be unique to Mr. Udagawa. A boatbuilder in Gifu told me this tool for setting planks was called the *sagefuri,* the Japanese term for plumb bob, while my teacher in Tokyo told me he had no name for it.

35 The traditional sail consists of long panels hanging vertically from a horizontal yard. See Chapter 6 on propulsion for a more detailed description.

36 I did not get a full explanation of this custom until I read Alice Gordenker's article on kiribi in the December 16, 2010 issue of the *Japan Times* online. Gordenker writes that kiribi kits are still sold in some parts of Tokyo, primarily in religious supply shops. A link to a fascinating video showing this practice can be found at the bottom of this article: www.japantimes.co.jp/text/ek20101216wh.html

37 In contrast, a *maru ga aru hito* is a "round" person, or one who tries to please everyone.

38 The bone of a long dead animal is also useless, so a better translation might be, "Who is this good-for-nothing?"

The author cutting out a plank. No power tools were used in preparing the planking, which the author cut to shape and planed entirely by hand. *Photo copyright Keiju Kurozumi.*

Our replica chokkibune under construction in 2002. These boats served as water taxis negotiating the myriad canals and rivers of Edo-period Tokyo.

11

The Edo-period Chokkibune

My attempt to put together a research proposal for the Freeman Foundation was hampered by a limited response from potential partners in Japan. Despite sending proposals to dozens of museums and boatbuilders I received just a handful of replies, and most were not encouraging. Museums either did not know of any local boatbuilders or felt they did not have the facilities to host a boatbuilding project. One letter, written in pencil, came from Mr. Kazuyoshi Fujiwara, the boatbuilder I had met in 2000 at the Tokyo rowing club Wasen Tomo no Kai and who had brought me home to his workshop. He wrote that he spoke with Tokyo's Koto-ward government and proposed that they host us in a temporary workshop on the front lawn of the ward office. The boat we would build could be donated to the club for their rowing events. Mr. Fujiwara assured me he could draft a budget detailing materials, a workshop, and his labor for teaching me.[1]

He proposed building a *chokkibune* from the Edo period.[2] These boats are romanticized in Japanese novels as a type of water taxi for transporting samurai to the pleasure quarters. *Chokki* means "tusk of a boar" and refers to the sharply raked stem, which combined with a long, narrow hull gives this boat its speed. Mr. Fujiwara said he had Meiji-period photographs of chokkibune and he was confident he could design one for us to build.

The Freeman Foundation sent me to Japan in December of 2000 to meet with potential partners for the project. After meetings at a maritime museum in Aomori, my wife and I traveled south to Tokyo. Once there, I was taken again to Wasen Tomo no Kai, this time by an assistant to the mayor of Koto-ward. After the visit we went back to the ward office to meet with various officials in several different

Mr. Kazuyoshi Fujiwara working on the chokkibune.

departments. We discussed where a temporary workshop would be erected. Koto-ward took this project extremely seriously and committed a significant amount of logistical support. After these meetings, my wife and I, along with Mr. Fujiwara, were ushered into the mayor's office for obligatory introductions, photographs, and an interview for the Koto-ward newsletter. The mayor explained at length how important the canal system had been historically in this part of Tokyo, when the city was criss-crossed by an extensive network of waterways. Essentially, the chokkibune is to Tokyo what the gondola is to Venice.

The major river bordering Koto-ward is the Sumidagawa, and in 1698 the Eitaibashi bridge was built across its mouth. This prevented large sailing vessels from entering, but ushered in an era of small boat traffic. Records indicate up to seven thousand small boats registered in Edo, and contemporary reports talk about traffic jams on the canals rivaling what occur on Tokyo's freeways today. In addition to chokkibune, other prevalent boats were small, flat-bottomed barges (*kodenmasen*) and lighters (*nitaribune*).

At our meeting with the mayor, Mr. Fujiwara sat listening silently. He had come to the meeting wearing an old hand-made jacket, embroidered with an elaborate and beautiful pattern on the back. It was made in the early 1900s and displayed the Fujiwara family crest. His grandfather and father had worn it for special occasions such as boat launchings; he was proud to be able to wear it this day and glad he could build another boat. When the mayor invited him to say something, he began to talk quietly about the history of his family, with its several generations of boatbuilders. I sensed that protocol dictated very short remarks in the mayor's presence, but Mr. Fujiwara spoke for quite a long time. Everyone listened patiently, and it became clear that our understanding his family's role in the boatbuilding traditions was important to him, and he wasn't stopping until we heard about it. As soon as he finished the various city officials jumped to their feet, all present bowed to each other, and the meeting was over.

Just before we left for home I was able to attend the New Year's blessing of the fleet for Wasen Tomo no Kai. Mr. Fujiwara was given the honor of pouring sake on all the boats, which were decorated with sprigs of pine and offerings of rice cakes. I expressed to Mr. Fujiwara my fervent hope we could work together.

Return to Urayasu

A few months later I received word the Freeman Foundation had approved my final proposal, which included building a chokkibune with Mr. Fujiwara in Tokyo as well as building an inshore fishing boat with Mr. Seizo Ando in Aomori Prefecture (see Chapter 12). Koto-ward would be the institutional sponsor of the Tokyo project, and the Michinoku Traditional Wooden Boat Museum would sponsor the second apprenticeship. After a summer session studying Japanese at Middlebury College, I would start working with my new teacher in early September of 2002.

Because Mr. Udagawa and Mr. Fujiwara had once been competitors, it was with some trepidation I contacted my former teacher to confirm my new project. Not only was Mr. Udagawa enthusiastic, he insisted my wife and I live in his neighborhood in Urayasu, just across the Arakawa River from Koto-ku. He wrote to say he had already spoken to a friend who owned an old apartment building. It had just eight units on two floors, which were empty except for one end unit she had converted into an art studio. The price was ridiculously inexpensive for Tokyo, just $250 a month, but it came with a small catch: there was no bath.

The building was constructed in the early 1970s in Nekozane, the historic center of Urayasu, at a time when most working-class homes did not have baths. People bathed in the local *sentou,* or public bath, six of which were still operating in the neighborhood. The day we arrived our landlady, Mrs. Kumagawa, somewhat nervously showed us our obsolete accommodations. In contrast, Mr. Udagawa was enthusiastic. He brushed aside any mention of inconvenience and explained that we needed to try each sentou in turn because all six had different water temperatures. Since I wasn't due to start working with Mr. Fujiwara for a week, I was able to help my wife with settling in: shopping for bedding, cooking utensils, and dinnerware, setting up accounts with

Mr. Fujiwara pours sake on the boats of Wasen Tomo no Kai, a Koto-ward rowing club, as part of a New Year's celebration.

utilities, and registering with city hall. Each evening we took our towels, fresh clothes, and toiletries and tried a different sentou. They were busiest in the early evenings, and we were joined on the narrow streets by elderly residents heading to and from their baths.

We enthusiastically settled on the sentou closest to our apartment, just a few blocks away from our landlady's large, modern house and across a bridge over the Sakai River. Our fellow sentou users were mostly older people who almost certainly had baths in their homes but still enjoyed the ritual of meeting friends and neighbors at the sentou.

The layout of sentou is uniform throughout Japan: In the entryway are small lockers for storing your shoes. From there two doors open to changing rooms and baths, one for men and one for women. In our sentou my wife and I would step through our respective entrances and come face-to-face again at a raised desk where Mrs. Hosegawa, the elderly owner, would take our money (about $1.30). Behind her a low wall separated the men's and women's side with Mrs. Hosegawa's dais giving her a complete view of both. She would give us each a low bow and we would enter our changing areas, which ended with a glass door into the bathing area.

At first the regular customers were a bit surprised by our presence. On the men's side rarely did anyone ever speak to me, but over the low wall separating the men from the women I could hear the loud greetings my wife received every time she appeared. The only small drama on my side of the bath was discovering which of the men were *yakuza*, Japanese gangsters. On a fairly regular basis one or two men would reveal full body tattoos, the unmistakable sign of membership in the criminal underworld. I mentioned these patrons to Mr. Udagawa when he came to our apartment and asked how we were settling in. His local boosterism remained true-to-form. "Those are Urayasu yakuza," he said, "They won't hurt you." Far from being an inconvenience, bathing at sentou is one of our most cherished memories of our year in Japan.

At the start of my first workday, I arrived early at the grounds in front of the Koto-ward office. For several weeks Mr. Fujiwara and Mr. Tomizo Saito, one of the founders of Wasen Tomo no Kai, had been setting up our temporary workshop. The building was a small, prefabricated structure and the two men had added a plywood floor and wooden uprights supporting overhead beams. Our planking, which had been milled from a single massive cedar tree from Ibaraki Prefecture, sat stacked and tarped just outside the shop. Mr. Saito pulled up in his small white van with Mr. Fujiwara. We bowed to each other and then Mr. Fujiwara explained that I was to arrive at the shop before him each morning, open the door, and bring down the tools, which we stored in tool boxes placed on the overhead beams. I would also start boiling water in an electric pot for instant coffee. At the end of each day it was my job to sweep the shop, take all garbage to the dumpster alongside the city offices, clean his ashtray, and put all the tools away.

My first job, Mr. Fujiwara explained, was to make myself a toolbox, using his as a pattern. Carpenters' toolboxes are very simple in Japan: a low rectangular box with a top that slides in place. When I finished he began dividing his tools. He had daubed the planes, chisels, and hammers I would use with bright orange paint. As we worked, I mentioned that in the West the toolbox was often very elaborate, with dovetailed joints, sliding drawers, and even decorative carvings. An elaborate box was one way a carpenter demonstrated his skills. Mr. Fujiwara did not see the point; to him, materials were too precious to be wasted on building something as frivolous as a fancy toolbox.

Mr. Kazuyoshi Fujiwara

Our first day also included an interview with a local newspaper. Mr. Fujiwara talked about his family, and about learning boatbuilding by working with his father. He remembered watching the launching of large wooden barges before the War. For most of his career he and his father worked together. After apprenticing with his father from ages sixteen to twenty-two, the two men, along with four helpers, built about two hundred boats between 1945 and 1970. These boats were about 35 to 42 shaku long. They didn't acquire their first power tools—a hand held planer and circular saw—until 1959. He told me the shop never

Launch day in the early 1950s. Mr. Fujiwara at age twenty-eight sits in the bow (far left) next to his father and his father's master. In the background are the wood-drying sheds of the Kiba district, home to Tokyo's wood wholesalers for hundreds of years. *Photo copyright Kazuyoshi Fujiwara.*

owned a bandsaw. The market for wooden boats, including net fishing boats called *toamibune*, but also some smaller cargo vessels called *nitaribune* and *tenmasen*, dried up in the 1970s. There was some repair work, but he was finally forced to close his boat shop and work in residential construction until his retirement. He had finished a small wooden boat for a museum in 2001, his first in almost thirty years, and now he and I would be building the chokkibune together.

I was surprised by some of Mr. Fujiwara's answers to the interviewer's questions. When asked about teaching me, a foreigner, he said that ten years earlier an American college student had asked to study with him, but he had declined. Then he added, "In order to learn one has to make mistakes. It will be very hard for Mr. Brooks to learn because I do not make mistakes." I was sitting right next to him and I am sure he noticed the look of amazement on my face. The interviewer seemed enormously impressed by this statement, and took it at face value, but I thought it was preposterous. There was no way we were going to build a thirty-foot boat over the course of months and not make mistakes. But one of the lessons I had begun to learn working with Japanese craftsmen was the great pride they took from their work. Men like Mr. Udagawa and Mr. Fujiwara did not betray the slightest doubt about their abilities and, in conversation at least, were each quick to point out that their traditions, their boats, and their methods were the very best. A fancy toolbox was unnecessary, because a master craftsman had no need to advertise his superiority; he knew he was Number One.

After the interviewer departed Mr. Fujiwara took a piece of wood and drew a picture of an airplane dropping bombs on a house. He labeled it simply "B-29." It was a reference to the firebombing of Tokyo during World War II, in particular the infamous raid on the night of March 9–10, 1944, that killed over one hundred thousand people and was centered on the waterfront of Koto and Chuo wards. He told me that night he and his father loaded wheelbarrows, primarily with boatbuilding tools, and the family walked out of the city and into the countryside. They lost everything else in the raid, including all of his grandfather's plank drawings. The small house he currently lived in, with its tiny rooms and cracked plastered walls, was the home they had rebuilt after the War.

I didn't know what to say, except finally, that I was sorry. Mr. Fujiwara surprised me by laughing and telling me it was all right. Then I asked him why he didn't agree to teach the college student who had approached him years earlier? He became serious and, looking straight at me, said, "Because he didn't give me a good enough reason."

I took it as a warning, frankly. Mr. Fujiwara had never had an apprentice. His four sons had come of age at a time when wooden boatbuilding was a dying craft, and he himself was forced out of boatbuilding and into construction work. Furthermore, by the 1980s Japan offered endless possibilities for education and careers. While he was realistic enough to understand his sons could not continue building boats, he was also intensely proud of the depth of his knowledge, which he told me represented all that his father and his grandfather knew. It was no frivolous thing to be passing along this level of expertise.

The importance of Fujiwara family traditions was symbolized by the copper pinwheel we would use to mark our boat. Called a *kazeguruma,* it had always been mounted on the bows of Fujiwara-built boats. He showed me a historic photograph of one of their boats in Tokyo Bay that displayed the pinwheel. Mr. Fujiwara did not know why his grandfather had chosen a pinwheel for the family mark, but that did not diminish the significance and obligations of this tradition.

Mr. Fujiwara explained that in the shop we would work together in complete silence. I was to wait until morning or afternoon break or lunchtime before asking questions, although if I were afraid of making a mistake I could interrupt him for clarification. Otherwise he would give me rudimentary instructions but mostly teach via demonstration. It was my responsibility to observe and to learn, and this was sacrosanct. Because our workshop was situated on a major thoroughfare there was often a crowd of onlookers. Early on an American living in Tokyo stopped by at the end of the day and while I swept up we chatted. Mr. Fujiwara said nothing, but the next morning he posted hand-made signs at the shop entrance and on the windows: "Do not talk to the boatbuilders."

As our first day ended I retrieved a gift for Mr. Fujiwara. Unlike my other teachers, he had shown some interest in my work at home. I decided rather than give him the usual gift of alcohol or food, I would give him a Western woodworking tool. I brought him a very nice century-old Stanley smoothing plane. It was completely different than a Japanese plane, all metal with knurled adjusting knobs and carefully machined parts. I assumed he would be fascinated by it, or at least appreciate the differences embodied in a woodworking tool from another culture. Instead, the instant I presented it, I sensed his hesitation. Giving a gift to one's teacher was required by protocol, but as soon as I offered the plane, the look on his face made me wish I could somehow take it back. His discomfort was palpable, but finally he gave me a sharp, short bow, put the plane in his bag and said goodbye.

As I closed up the shop and rode the subway home I could have kicked myself for wanting to give him something special. I should have stuck to the more usual gift of a bottle of sake or whiskey. On top of this, there was also some tension because Mr. Fujiwara knew I had studied with Mr. Udagawa the year before, and now I was living in Mr. Udagawa's neighborhood. Within the Japanese craft world, having multiple teachers is unthinkable. Perhaps I had relied too heavily on my status as a non-Japanese, which had always been an advantage in conducting my research as it served to exempt me from these rules. It would be months before the subject of the plane came up again, and it took several bottles of sake just to start the conversation.

Our lumber supply, milled from a cedar and a cypress log into planks of 28 feet. Material of this size and quality is still readily available in Japan.

The forward part of the bottom laid out, with the seam visible between the two asymmetrically arranged planks. The sapwood faces the outside of the boat where seawater will preserve it.

Building the Chokkibune

The next day we began building the boat. Our lumber came from the same forests Mr. Fujiwara had become familiar with building boats with his father. A log of *hinoki,* or cypress, would be used for our stem, transom, sheer planks, and gunwales. Our logs had been flitch-sawn and our bottom plank would be composed of two pieces taken from either side of the heart of the log. Instead of bending the keel plank, we would be cutting a joint aft, with the aft end slanting upward to the transom. Mr. Fujiwara called the forward end of the bottom the *shiki* and the aft end the *tomojiki.*

Mr. Fujiwara explained that whether a boat is used in fresh or saltwater, the heart side of the wood planking should face the inside of the boat. He said for freshwater boats there should be no sapwood used if possible, since it is prone to rot. Some sapwood can be visible on the outside of ocean-going boats, since the saltwater environment acts as a preservative. He added that we would tolerate some sapwood on our plank edges (in order to get the most width from our planking stock) but we would try to keep it shallow enough so our edge nails passed only through the more durable heartwood.

Mr. Fujiwara used a historic photograph of a chokkibune, in conjunction with his family's boatbuilding ratios, to design our boat. He drew the lines 1/10th scale on a plank of wood and the drawing was complete; there were no missing lines or secrets. All of my other teachers accepted and maintained the secrecy endemic to the craft. But Mr. Fujiwara was at least a third-generation boatbuilder who had apprenticed with his father to carry on the family business; there was no reason for one generation to hide anything from the next. While he was well aware of how other craftsmen struggled to learn from secretive masters, he found the notion of secrecy quaint.[3]

Mr. Fujiwara established two stations on his plank drawing and scaled off our offsets at these two points. We pinned our batten with small nails at the offsets Mr. Fujiwara had scaled from the two stations on his drawing, and the forward and aft ends. Our chokkibune was a one-off project, but he explained for boats he built over and over he developed additional offsets, such as the chord of the curve off a straight line driven between two points. When we laid out the tomojiki he demonstrated this. We drew straight lines from the corner of the transom, which was 1 shaku wide, to the corner of the tomojiki joint, which was 1.8 shaku wide. We made marks on our straight lines 1.5 shaku aft of the joint and 1 shaku forward of the transom and squared outboard 1.8 sun and 1 sun, respectively. Next we sprang our

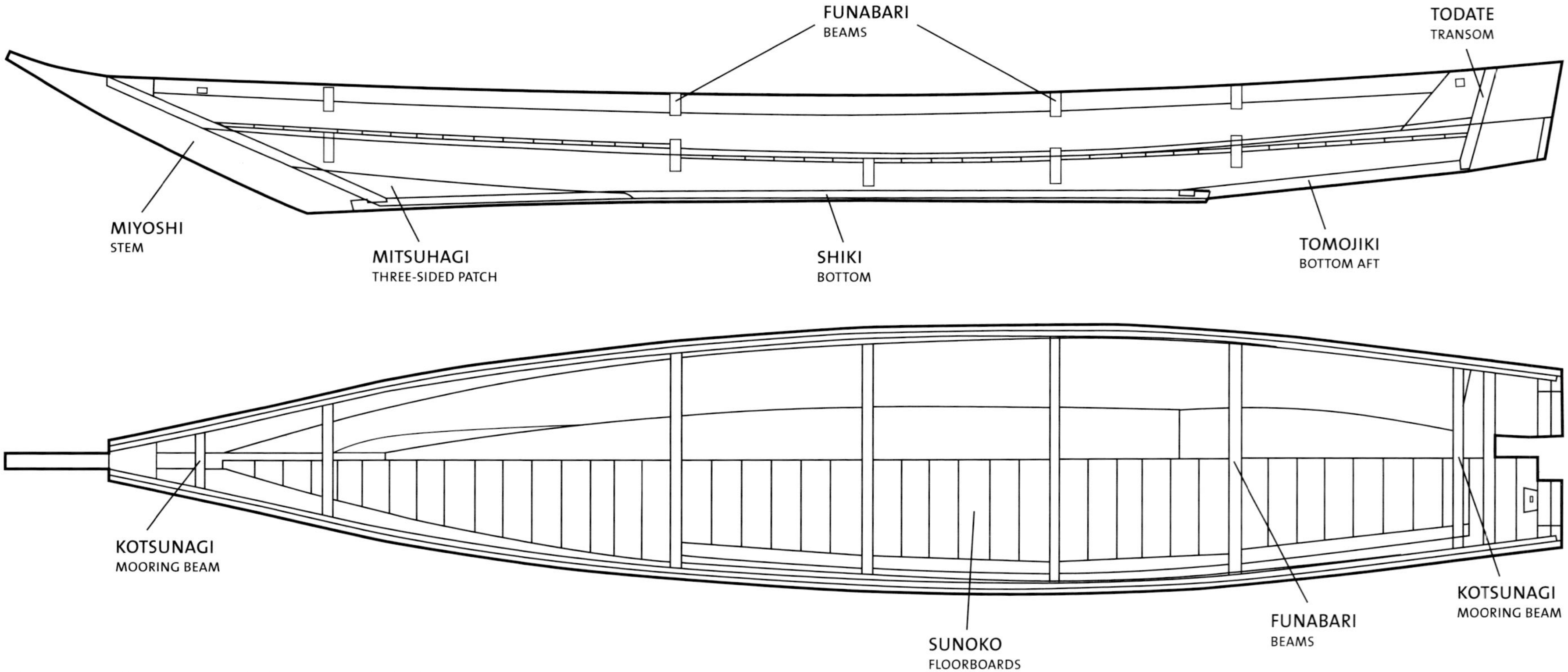

Plan and profile views show the long, narrow hull of the chokkibune. The wider, thicker planking of most Japanese boats limits the amount of bend possible, so at 29 shaku long and 5 shaku wide, the chokkibune has a length-to-beam ratio of almost 6:1. The extreme rake of the stem gives the hull a very fine entry and high speed, important for the chokkibune's role as a water taxi in the rivers and canals of the capital city during the Edo period, old Tokyo's counterpart to the gondola of Venice.

batten along these four points. Mr. Fujiwara had scaled all these dimensions from his 1/10th scale drawing.

Our batten for laying down these lines was made from a clear piece of cedar and measured 5 bu by 7 bu, and we always used it standing on the narrower edge. The batten was placed to the outboard side of our points, but Mr. Fujiwara drew the line on the outside of that, increasing the width of our bottom plank on each side by the width of the batten. He said this added material would make up for what was lost fitting the first plank to the bottom using the fitting technique called *suriawase* (see Chapter 5).

The lengthwise joint in the cedar plank keel was not centered. They were cut from two flitches taken from either side of the center of the log, and were 2 sun thick by 28 shaku long. Similarly the transom, which was made of three planks of hinoki 2 sun thick, was cut on a taper parallel to the bark edges of the log. Mr. Fujiwara cut away all the sapwood in the hinoki. By reversing the direction of the center piece we maintained parallel edges top and bottom.

The edge nails for both the bottom and transom were laid out along the joints about 8 sun apart, sometimes adjusted to avoid knots. In the keel all the nails entered through the narrower plank, and all the mortises were to the outside of the planking and transom. Mr. Fujiwara insisted that I cut the nail mortises with a curved bottom, matching the curve of the nails we would use. They were cut just under half the depth of the planking. He could chisel them by eye, but as soon as he had demonstrated one for me I quickly made a pattern of their shape. I did this throughout the project, patterning various mortises that he could cut consistently without any layout. He never objected to my reliance on these patterns, which I used to compensate for my lack of experience.

True to his rule, we had been working in nearly complete silence every day, except for one phrase Mr. Fujiwara used over and over. A dozen times a day he would motion for me to come and watch what he was doing, while muttering, "*Kou iu fuu ni.*" I had no idea what it meant and was reluctant to ask, since I was under enough stress trying to imitate his techniques correctly. I later found out it means simply, "Like this." Mr. Fujiwara would eventually take time to discuss our work in more detail, but this almost always occurred outside of work hours.

Mr. Fujiwara had a nice technique for cutting the mortises, which he insisted have the sides sloping away in a dovetail shape. He told me to cut the sides with a wide chisel, always with the bevel of the chisel facing the inside of the mortise and the chisel held vertically. The bevel forces the edge of the chisel to undercut the side just slightly, automatically creating a dovetail-shaped cross section. Later, we cut our plugs, which Mr. Fujiwara called *umeki,* with a matching taper and angled sides, and they locked in the mortise without glue. In cleaning out the base of these mortises, Mr. Fujiwara did not like me pushing the chisel (like a paring tool), or worse, hitting it with the palm of my hand. He insisted, just as Mr. Udagawa had, that I always strike the chisel with a mallet.

Now that we were using chisels Mr. Fujiwara took time out to teach me how to properly sharpen our edge tools. He had a set of natural waterstones, as well as one brand-new diamond stone. He didn't like the new stone at all, so we never used it. Some of his stones were less than a quarter-inch thick and cracked all the way through, but he had glued the broken pieces to a base block of wood so they could still be used. He told me I should take exactly thirty strokes on the bevel of the blade and then seven strokes flattening the back. After two or three sharpenings like this I was to move to a finer stone. He had about three different grits of stone and the last one, a lovely yellow natural stone, was for the final honing.

My teacher was a hawk-like observer of everything going on in the shop, and more than once he told me he had an excellent memory. He interrupted one of my earliest sharpening sessions to point out I had failed to take thirty strokes on the bevel as he had instructed. From then on I kept a silent count as I sharpened, knowing that even while working he was probably watching and counting as well.

Fitting the Seams

We set up the parts for the bottom and transom for suriawase. As we worked, Mr. Fujiwara stressed I had to master this technique, and I made no reference to having been previously taught it by Mr. Udagawa. Mr. Fujiwara was well aware of what I would have learned building the bekabune in Urayasu, but at this stage he taught me as if my prior boatbuilding had never happened. Neither of us had yet mentioned any of my earlier Japanese work.

Our planks rested on beams running across the shop floor and we braced them from overhead. Some details insisted on by Mr. Fujiwara, however, differed from the suriawase of my other teachers. First, we sawed our planks with the mortise side facing up, and Mr. Fujiwara placed a wooden shim on our blocks on either side of the kerf, lifting the two plank edges not more than an eighth of an inch. He explained that the blade can whipsaw on the underside of the plank, opening up the bottom of the kerf. The shims

(Left) Before setting up our planks on the shop floor Mr. Fujiwara made a series of kerfs in the knots along the plank edges in order to weaken them. During suriawase the knots then sawed as easily as the surrounding wood. (Above) Mr. Fujiwara and the author fitting the first plank to the bottom using handsaws. Note the wedges used to keep the seam open enough to prevent the saws from binding. The black on the planks in the foreground is the remnants of bending the planks over an open fire. This charred material was planed off later. *Photo copyright Tomizo Saito.*

compensate for this. He also believed nailing tends to pull one face tighter together, leading to a cupped plank. With proper sawing, the edges will be just slightly out of square, cupping the planks in the other direction. The result is perfectly flat planks.[4]

These were *very* subtle variations. Mr. Fujiwara concentrated just as carefully on the proper sawing motion to fit planks. He stressed that ideally one should rub the joint with the teeth of the center of the saw blade. Passing each beam, however, required raising the blade and cutting with the teeth at the tip. "This is why we reverse direction," he pointed out, "because it lets us use the middle teeth at these spots when working in the opposite direction." It was all about equalizing the rubbing action as best we could over the length of the seam. He also instructed me to create a very even line of sawdust as I rubbed the joint. There should not be any excessive sawing in one spot, particularly in the final passes.

We had two grades of saw for this work: a rough-cut saw with large teeth and a smaller-toothed saw for our final passes. Normally boatbuilders' saws have a pronounced convex edge, but Mr. Fujiwara had over years of sharpening intentionally changed the shape of his edges to concave. He said this created a narrower tip in his saws, which facilitated inserting and removing it from the seam. Over time and after repeated sharpening the edges of saws tend to get flatter, and some very old saws can develop a concave profile to the teeth, but Mr. Fujiwara is the only boatbuilder I know who intentionally sharpened his saw specifically to get this shape. He hired a *metate*, a professional saw sharpener, to come and gather all our saws for fine tuning.

Killing the Wood

Once Mr. Fujiwara was satisfied the seam was ready, we set the planks up on edge and pounded their centers, a technique called *kigoroshi,* literally "wood killing" (see Chapter 5). His technique was the same as that of Mr. Udagawa: using overlapping hammer blows with a round-faced hammer and avoiding the corners of the edges. The planking of the chokkibune was much thicker than the bekabune, and we worked together, pounding down either side of the edge. He did not stress the importance of this step nearly as much as Mr. Udagawa had.

However, Mr. Fujiwara included one final step: with the edges pounded and the plank still clamped upright he laid one of his saws on its side so the line of teeth lay along the plank edge. Holding the blade flat he quickly rubbed the edge, moving along the length of the seam. He told me it was to even out the scratches left by the rubbing motion of the saw. Though none of my other teachers took this step I have subsequently seen references to it being done by other boatbuilders.

As we prepared to nail our planks together for the shiki and tomojiki, Mr. Fujiwara took out an old boat nail and pointed out how the nail had been hammered to shape, the shank's width tapering over its entire length. The new nail, in contrast, was cut from steel stock and the shank only tapered on its lower half. He said this made for a poorer nail because the taper gives the nail holding strength, acting like a wedge driven into the hole. Our pilot holes would be tapered, and so the straight section of the shank would have less holding power. Our new nails, however, were galvanized, so they would have more rust resistance than the older, uncoated nails.

The finished transom, nailed and glued together.

Workers move rollers underneath a large tenmasen, an unpowered cargo barge built by Mr. Fujiwara's father. *Photo copyright Kazuyoshi Fujiwara.*

The same boat after launch. Mr. Fujiwara's father is the fifth man from the right. Mr. Fujiwara himself, age ten, is sitting at the far left. *Photo copyright Kazuyoshi Fujiwara.*

It was my job to bend our nails to the proper curve, and Mr. Fujiwara did not hesitate to reject any he didn't like. The curve is critical, since they need to follow the pilot hole precisely. We laid the nails against a nail set on the shop floor and I hammered the shanks to get the proper curve.

Throughout the project Mr. Fujiwara used a glue I had not seen before in Japan. It was composed of a white powder he kept tightly sealed in a plastic bag and mixed with water to form a thick paste. This we spread on one side of a joint and painted the other with a mild acid. I did not recognize the Japanese brand name and he did not know what the glue was made of, but it was probably a urea-formaldehyde glue using formic acid as a catalyst.[5] Like my other teachers, Mr. Fujiwara did not trust this glue to actually hold the boat together—we nailed all the parts—but he believed that the glue prevented seams from opening over time. He said he began using glue in the 1970s (near the end of his career); prior to that time he and his father put nothing in the seams.[6] In older boats, he said, sunlight can dry the wood and seams will open. Dirt working its way into open seams created leaks and fostered rot.

The two planks were nailed together while set up vertically and clamped with some large bar clamps. We just drove the nails home, and I decided to take the opportunity to ask Mr. Fujiwara if he didn't hammer with a musical rhythm the way Mr. Udagawa had. It was the first time I had mentioned my former teacher, other than telling Mr. Fujiwara we were living in the same neighborhood. He smiled and said he knew about this kind of nailing, but he didn't do it and considered the practice frivolous.

With the bottom assembled, Mr. Fujiwara cut a rabbet across the back of the tomojiki for the transom. He called this joint an *ukejiri,* combining the terms for a protruding lip or shelf (*uke*) and an end (*shiri*). He used a different term for a rabbet cut with the grain such as a stem rabbet: *kakikomi.*[7]

From the start of our project the public relations department of Koto-ward office was busy arranging interviews with radio, television, and newspapers. During the first few weeks we were interrupted several times by camera crews or reporters. Since Mr. Fujiwara and I conversed very little, I was able to learn much about his background listening to him being interviewed. He talked about his father, with whom he apprenticed, and how his father built huge wooden barges before World War II that carried goods into the canals and rivers of Tokyo from ships in the harbor. He said they took off only the 15th and 30th of each month and generally worked over eight hours a day.

In response to these interviews, Mr. Saito scanned and printed what few photographs Mr. Fujiwara had from this era. The scale of the wooden barges his father made was immense. I asked him about the scantlings—the dimensions of the timbers— of some of these vessels and he said planking could sometimes be 4 sun thick. I asked him if they fit such thick planking using suriawase and he said they did, and sometimes it was necessary to tie a rope to the handle of the saw blade so two men could pull it! He also showed me how a rag could be looped around the blade of the plane and tied to the user's forward wrist to gain more power when planing.

Beveling the edge of the shiki I made a mistake, cutting the bevel on the tomojiki right to the end where we would make the scarf joint. Mr. Fujiwara stopped me, saying this transition was critical and we had to wait until the bottom was completely assembled before fairing the bevel between the two pieces. I apologized for my mistake, but, as he glued a piece back on as a repair, he told me he had made precisely the same mistake forty-six years earlier.

These bevels on the bottom were not cut with complete precision. Mr. Fujiwara had two patterns to guide us, but he knew suriawase would make the fit precise. We also cut a small chamfer on the top edge of the shiki and the inner edge of the transom. This bevel was to relieve the corners so they wouldn't break out when we sawed through the joints to fit parts.

Mr. Fujiwara using an adze to bevel the bottom, which he later finished with a plane. He had two patterns to guide him; one can be seen hooked over the edge of the bottom.

Once the bottom was beveled we propped it in place on two large wooden blocks. Mr. Fujiwara called his props *tsuzu;* he and Mr. Udagawa are the only boatbuilders I have met who used this term. This was the final setup and the backbone would remain propped until the boat was completed. One prop forward of the blocking pushed the forward end of the bottom down 1.2 sun. Several of Mr. Udagawa's larger boats also featured this drop in the keel forward. In Urayasu, the sheer also followed this line, something that looks strange in the West, where a boat's sheer usually has a graceful curve sweeping upward.[8] The drop in the keel, Mr. Fujiwara explained, acted as a forward rudder and helped the boat track in a straight line. This makes sense because most traditional boats like the chokkibune do not have any sort of vertical keel timber to resist sideways movement.

The two parts of the bottom were joined with a scarf Mr. Fujiwara called a *kamatsugite.* The edges of the scarf are angled and a pair of keyaki wedges in the center of the joint locks the timbers in place. Although he did a careful layout of these joints, he cut the angles by eye. In the tomojiki, which is almost 2 shaku wide, the edge of the joint is peaked in the middle, so two long wedges enter from either side and overlap in the center.

The Stem

The *miyoshi,* or stem, was cut from a clear piece of hinoki. To connect it to the shiki, Mr. Fujiwara cut another bite scarf in the forward end of the shiki. To set the angle of the stem he stretched a string touching the two main props at a point 2.2 shaku above the bottom. He then marked a point on the back of the stem 5.88 shaku up from where the back of the stem meets the shiki in the kama joint. We stretched the string tight on our two points and propped the stem until the 5.88 shaku mark was at the same height as the string.

Once the miyoshi joint was cut and fit we covered all the faying surfaces (the faces of wood that meet each other in the joint) of the two wedges with glue and drove them tightly into the joint. There was no additional fastening of any kind at the stem-bottom connection, but the miyoshi remained firmly propped and braced overhead until nearly the end of the project. At first I thought the glue was simply to keep the wedges from moving, but in retrospect glued wedges would act like a stopwater, keeping water from working through the joint into the hull.

The kama joint in the shiki (bottom). Kama means sickle, and the joint resembles the blade of this tool, which curls back on itself. The edges of the bottom were left square here to aid in the layout and fairing of the bevel between the two pieces.

The kama joint connecting the miyoshi to the shiki. This is the most complex joinery seen in boatbuilding, and again Mr. Fujiwara cut the angles by eye.

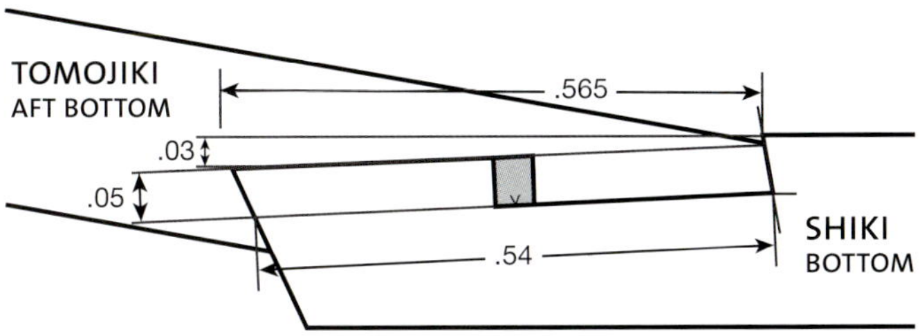

Cross section of the kama joint. The back of the shiki is tapered 3 bu before layout, allowing the joint in the tomojiki to be a bit thicker for strength. Mr. Fujiwara had no specific dimensions for the angles, which he cut by eye. The shaded rectangle is the tapered wedge used to lock the joint.

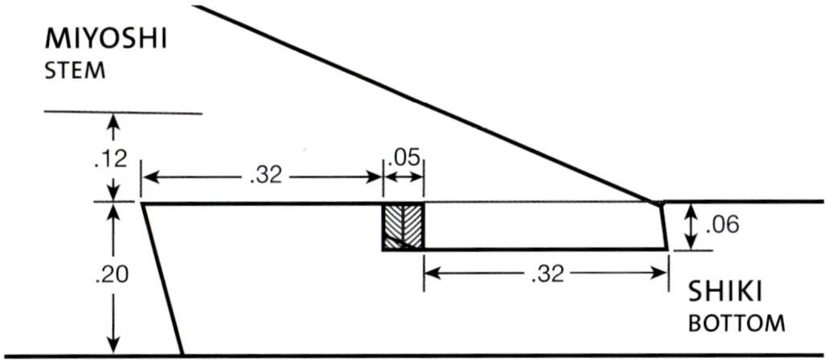

Cross section of the kama joint. The two hardwood wedges in the center are glued and driven tight to lock the joint. The .12-shaku dimension is the amount the shiki is pushed down forward.

One morning upon his arrival to the shop Mr. Fujiwara looked at me and announced, *"Brooks-san, hansei."* I scrambled for my dictionary and found the definitions: "reflection, introspection, reconsideration." The term has become popular in corporate Japan to denote the reevaluation of a project, to determine how successful it was. In keeping with the high value placed on cooperation in Japanese society, hansei invites individuals, or members of a team, to pause, reflect, and find some way a project might be improved.

The first morning Mr. Fujiwara used the term was to announce a clarification of something he had been trying to teach me the day before. He and I both understood my learning was unnaturally compressed within the span of this single project, so just as I felt pressure to learn and succeed I knew he was also trying to teach me as much as he could.

From that day on, morning hansei sessions became a near-daily ritual. I would have the coffee warming and the tools prepared by the time Mr. Saito drove up in his little white van with Mr. Fujiwara, who would walk quietly into the shop. Once he had finished arranging his bag and putting on his work shoes he would look at me and announce, *"Brooks-san, hansei."* I would instantly respond with *"Hai!"* (Yes!), and stand attentively awaiting his words. Then he would clarify a point from our work the day before or make a general point about boatbuilding.

Our morning hansei-hai routine made us both smile, with me awaiting the single word from him that would trigger my response, and Mr. Fujiwara, unable to contain a sly smile as he approached the shop, maintaining the suspense as long as possible. Beyond the introduction, however, these discussions were never frivolous or wandering but always to the point and about the task at hand.

On one such occasion Mr. Fujiwara paused to sketch out three ways used by boatbuilders to create a joint or bend in the bottom. Besides making a kamatsugite (scarf) as we did, some boatbuilders make the entire bottom out of a full-length board. This requires bending it at a single point, like a fold. One boatbuilder told me he poured hot water on the keel and bent it over a pipe. A variant method involves cutting a dovetail across the bottom of the joint 1/3rd the thickness of the plank, and kerfing the plank 1/3rd the depth directly above. The plank can be slowly bent at the joint using boiling water, continually kerfing the top

The backbone setup, with pairs of braces holding the assembly at the two stations and one prop forward pushing the bow down slightly.

as it closes. When the keel is fully bent a dovetail wedge is inserted across the underside to lock the joint (see Chapter 12). Mr. Fujiwara made it clear that of the three methods ours was superior, and added that any boatbuilder who used another method was an inferior craftsman.

I mentioned to Mr. Fujiwara that the small fishing boats of Sado Island had a kama joint at the forward end of the bottom plank as well as aft. In their case, the forward end of the bottom also canted up slightly. He immediately insisted that I was wrong; no boats in Japan were built this way. A month later my wife and I took a short vacation to Sado and I photographed several of these boats showing this construction detail. Later I showed the photos to Mr. Fujiwara who stared intently at them. After he was finished he handed them back to me without a word, and we returned to work. He was the most inscrutable person I have ever met; I could not tell if he felt insulted by being contradicted or was curious about the revelation, but I realized I needed to temper my own impulses to share everything I knew.

Mr. Fujiwara had spent his entire life in Tokyo. Like Mr. Udagawa, he never learned to drive and had traveled very little elsewhere in Japan. Yet he was absolutely certain about any fact concerning boatbuilding traditions throughout the country. At the same time, he was my only teacher who took any real interest in my boatbuilding in the United States. I brought to Japan a small scrapbook of photographs of my boats and he pored over them at break time, and eventually asked me if he could borrow the album. He had so many questions about one of my largest projects that I wrote the naval architect in California and had him mail Mr. Fujiwara a set of drawings.[9] For several days at every break he would unroll the drawings and study them, occasionally asking me a question.

His certainty about his own boatbuilding culture was not surprising. In my initial travels looking for boatbuilders, I quickly discovered the worst source of information on the location of other craftsmen were the boatbuilders themselves. When I asked any craftsman if he knew of others building boats the answer was invariably, "I am the only one." I finally gave up asking after hearing this answer from at least a dozen men. In many cases when pressed, I discovered they were not just claiming to be the only boatbuilder in the region, but in all of Japan! The sort of networking via magazines, boat shows, and the internet so familiar in the West is still largely unknown in Japan. I can think of just a single boatbuilder who actually led me to another craftsman, and in his case he had to sheepishly admit his fellow boatbuilder worked just down the street.

In preparation for spiling the shape of the first planks, which Mr. Fujiwara called the *kajiki*, we joined three sheets of plywood together, nailing plywood butt blocks between sheets. Mr. Fujiwara took scraps and cut patterns for the plank angle at our two stations. We set the spiling plank, which he called a *kataita*, propped at these angles. He marked on the batten and keel plank the nail locations, spaced 5 sun apart, and his stations. He also traced the edge of the transom and stem on the spiling plank.

At one point we edge-set the spiling plank pretty significantly, contorting it to meet the edge of the keel, which I knew would throw off its accuracy. Mr. Fujiwara didn't seem to care or notice. It was also so wide and unwieldy that it did not come close to meeting the stem-keel connection along its entire length. He used his square like a tick stick and marked offsets on the batten for the plank edge. I realized our batten would give us only an approximation of the plank shape.

The kajiki is made of three pieces of wood, the joints first fitted on the shop floor with suriawase and then edge-nailed together. Mr. Fujiwara used two patterns for the bevel on the plank to shape the edge of the bottom. On any boat

The spiling plank, made of plywood, propped in place. Patterns defining the angle of the kajiki are placed at the stations.

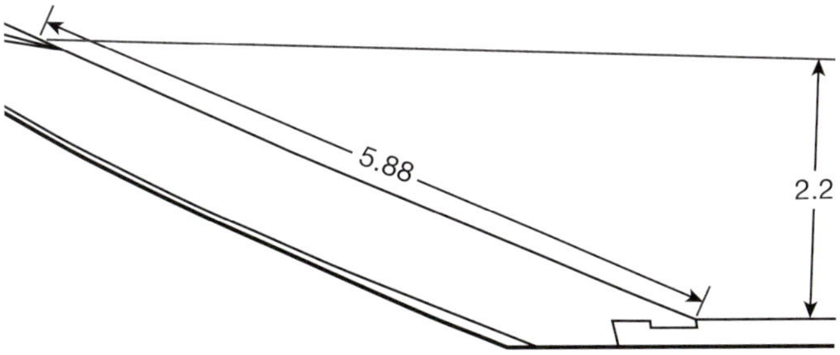

The angle of the stem is derived by stretching a string touching points on the two main props 2.2 shaku up from the bottom. The string is carried forward to a point 5.88 shaku up the back of the stem.

this is a constantly changing bevel, but he just patterned the angles at the two stations and we beveled the bottom working between the stations by eye. Later we would fit this seam with a saw.

On most Western boats the inside face of the plank would remain flat, with the entire bevel cut on the edge of the keel. This is not true in Japanese boats. Though there are no doubt exceptions, Japanese boatbuilders bevel both faces: the edge of the keel and where the face of the plank meets it. The importance of this becomes clear when you consider the need to run a saw through the seam to make it fit. A slight bevel on the plank allows the handle of the saw to stand clear of the plank face so the boatbuilder can work the saw in the seam.

The forward, bottom corner of the kajiki was made of a small triangular piece of wood, added to our planking

View underneath the plank showing how we shaped the bevel of the mitsuhagi, which rests on a block beveled at the same angle.

The author fitting the seam of the mitsuhagi. The mortises for the edge nails are visible to the right. Mr. Fujiwara felt an even line of sawdust indicated proper execution of this technique. *Photo copyright Tomizo Saito.*

Mr. Fujiwara and the author pounding the plank edges. This takes a good deal of control, as evidenced by the author holding the hammer with both hands. *Photo copyright Tomizo Saito.*

material at a slight bevel to create a bit of flare in the bottom planks forward. Mr. Fujiwara called this piece the *mitsuhagi,* or "three-sided patch," and it made fitting the first planks at the stem and keel easier. Interestingly, the two pieces were not symmetrical port and starboard; once again, he was more concerned with using material efficiently. He made a beveled block to hold this piece at the proper angle while we fit the seams with a saw on the shop floor.

Keel-Laying Ceremony

With the backbone of the chokkibune in place and before we hung the first planks, we paused in the project to conduct the *shikizue,* or keel-laying ceremony. A local Shinto priest set up a temporary altar in the shop, piled high with ritual offerings of vegetables, fish, and fruit. These items were both gifts to the spirits and representative of the natural world, the spiritual center of Shintoism. The priest conducted a Shinto purification ritual *(oharai),* tossing rice and squares of white paper to symbolically purify the boat. Participants were invited to place on the altar a small sprig of *sakaki,* an evergreen (*Cleyera japonica),* then bow and clap twice.

Mr. Fuiwara's tsubanomi, or sword-hilt chisels. Note the curved chisels, used to do the final cutting of pilot holes once the planking is propped in place.

The first two planks ready to hang on the boat. Note the mitsuhagi forward, which are not quite the same size. At the far end of the planks, one can see the curve of the bottom edges created by the tomojiki. This creates a unique problem fairing the edge of the bottom. *Photo copyright Tomizo Saito.*

The ceremony was very solemn and attended by only a few people involved in the project. The priest gave us a small wooden tablet, intended to protect us and our surroundings, which we kept in the shop. There were no celebrations at the end of the ceremony; several of us posed for a formal photograph with the priest, who then packed up his belongings. We went back to work.

With the backbone complete we were now ready to begin planking. We sprang a thin batten around the edge of the bottom and marked the nail locations on the batten. We then laid the batten on our planks and transferred the marks of the nail locations. Using the tsubanomi we made the pilot holes in the bottom and also cut shallow mortises in the outside of the plank for the nail heads. With the planks propped in place we used the curved tsubanomi to run through both timbers, making sure the pilot holes in the plank and bottom lined up.

Mr. Fujiwara had one last step before fastening our first two planks. The tomojiki, or aft end of the bottom, forms an inclined plane as it rises up to the transom. This creates some complications because its outer edges have to follow a fair curve with the forward section of the planking. Since he was scaling dimensions from just a 1/10th scale drawing he realized the potential for error transferring these measurements to the full-size boat. To double-check these lines he used a lofting technique he called *nawanosumi.* Lofting is a term well known to boatbuilders in the West, and refers to the process of drawing the lines of vessels full size on the mold loft floor in order to check the accuracy of measurements, and derive shapes for patterns. Nawanosumi, from the words for rope (*nawa*) and ink (*sumi*), is based on the same principles, deriving construction details by laying down lines full size and measuring angles and dimensions.[10]

Using the string from his inkline, Mr. Fujiwara struck a straight base line connecting the two points where his station lines met the lower edge of the plank. The line ran out through the ends and he marked these points, which corresponded with points on the stem and transom. He then measured the chord of the two curves of the inner edge of the plank defined by the station points. He compared these offsets to the shape of the bottom plank to confirm the plank would fit. This method, shown in the bottom drawing of the plank at upper right, was a check of our spiling, which he did not trust.

Nawanosumi is a very tricky process and it took me some time to understand it. Mr. Fujiwara was willing to halt our work and spend a good part of the afternoon going over the technique with me in order to make sure I understood it. Had it not been for my experience lofting boats in the West I would never have grasped it. As we finished, he told me the technique of nawanosumi developed in Japan about 150 years ago. I mentioned this date coincided with contact with the West but he insisted it was a purely Japanese invention. Even as difficult as it was to grasp he added that some masters would snap random lines on their drawings in order to confuse apprentices and prevent them from learning these secrets.

While teaching me nawanosumi Mr. Fujiwara looked at me and asked, "Did Mr. Udagawa show you this?" I told him the bekabune had a simple plank bottom bent slightly at the stern and we did not use this technique. His face betrayed absolutely no emotion, but his question opened a touchy line of inquiry. It was the first time he had directly mentioned my former teacher. But it opened that door, and at key points going forward he would ask me if Mr. Udagawa had taught me the same lesson, or whether he built his boats the same way. I always gave the most perfunctory answers possible, and he gave no indication how they affected him.

Meanwhile, in Urayasu Mr. Udagawa was a regular visitor to our apartment. He was still building boats at the Urayasu Museum and on weekends I would stop by to check on his progress. He always greeted me enthusiastically and asked how the Koto-ku project was going. I usually didn't say much, for fear of accidentally inferring some comparison between him and Mr. Fujiwara. Mr. Udagawa was always extremely positive, and had long ago stopped telling me how a craftsman should have just one teacher. Instead, he seemed to have completely embraced the idea of my building a boat with Mr. Fujiwara. Finally one Saturday he said, "I am planning on visiting your workshop."

Mr. Tomizo Saito was one of the founders of Wasen Tomo no Kai and volunteered daily for us in the boatshop. He drove Mr. Fujiwara to work and back home every day. I was referred to as *deshi* (apprentice) and the good-natured Mr. Saito liked to call himself *deshi no deshi* (the apprentice's apprentice). There are various terms for one's master, but Mr. Fujiwara preferred *touryou,* which means head carpenter, or foreman. The Monday after Mr. Udagawa's announcement I took Mr. Saito aside and told him of Mr. Udagawa's intentions. He knew the boatbuilder well, since in his eagerness to learn traditional boatbuilding he was a regular visitor to Mr. Udagawa's shop at the museum, and he also knew to tread a fine line between the two craftsmen. His eyes went wide with astonishment when he heard of Mr. Udagawa's plan.

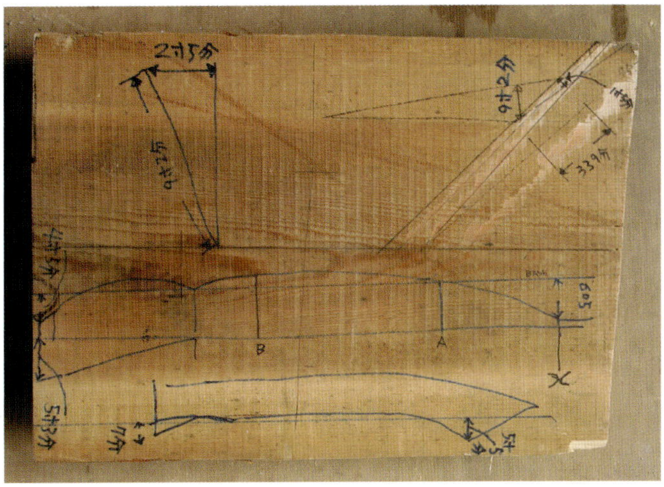

Sketches and lofting based on nawanosumi. At the bottom is the lower plank shape, with its curved bottom edge and the secondary curve aft (to the left) where it must fit against the tomojiki. In the middle is a plan view of the keel. Upper right is the lofting of the plank's lower edge aft, drawn full-size in section view, showing the chord of the curve (.339 shaku).

Mr. Fujiwara and the author chiseling nail holes in the first two planks. *Photo copyright Tomizo Saito.*

Beginning the fire-bending process for the kajiki. The offcuts from our planking stock provided the fuel.

He looked in Mr. Fujiwara's direction but it took him several moments before he could say anything. "Unbelievable!" is what he finally managed to get out.

At break the two of us sat down with Mr. Fujiwara and told him. As always, he was as imperturbable as a sphinx, receiving the news in complete silence. I turned to Mr. Saito. His eyebrows were arched and he was straining to read Mr. Fujiwara's face. Mr. Fujiwara snuffed out his cigarette and we went back to work. Barely a word was spoken the rest of the day.

Bending the Planks

The first two planks required pre-bending, and for this we had to set up a staging outside the shop for *yakimage,* or "fire bending," from *yaki*, to cook or to heat, and *mage* from the verb *mageru,* to bend. I had read about this technique, which is used throughout Asia, but this would be my first time to try it. In the West wood is steamed, and while this is very effective one has to work extremely fast. As soon as planks or ribs come out of the steambox they have to be bent quickly onto forms or directly on the boat; they remain pliable only while they are hot. Yakimage is a slow process, heating the wood with an open flame and slowly increasing the bend over several hours. The disadvantage is that you have to estimate the amount of bend required, since you are working off the boat. Mr. Fujiwara made a short spiling batten and tried to estimate the amount of curve the plank needed at the bow. He didn't feel comfortable with this and finally he drew a straight baseline on his plank drawing and scaled the offset of the curve.

Normally yakimage is done in the shop, next to the boat, utilizing the overhead beams for all the props required to bend the planking. Because we didn't have the space in our shop, we used pipe staging to essentially build a box framework. Mr. Fujiwara brought tall sawhorses to put our planks on and we fastened short planks to the overhead pipes to provide a stable surface for our props.

We also had to consider the amount of twist the planks required. The two planks transition from about a forty-five degree angle amidships to vertical at the stem. The offcuts and scraps left over from our planking stock provided the fuel for our fire. My job was to use the hose we ran to the site to keep the underside of the planks wet, but they became scorched nevertheless. In order to get the planks hot enough to bend, charring the surface seems unavoidable. We spent most of the afternoon feeding the fire, wetting the planks, and periodically leaning on the planks ends and inserting longer props.

Despite his attempts to get accurate measurements for the amount of curve, in the end Mr. Fujiwara just bent the planks to a point where they looked right. He pointed out that we had used nearly all the scrap wood created up to this point for the fire, and thus Japanese-style boatbuilding was very ecological, resulting in little or no waste of material. He concluded that this style of efficient boatbuilding would be valuable in other parts of the world.

The planks were left overnight to cool and were ready the next day to be fastened to the boat. We propped them first amidships, where Mr. Fujiwara ran a saw through the seam until he was satisfied with the fit. We also checked the plank angle using an interesting tool I had seen on the day I met Mr. Udagawa a few years earlier. Although it is well known to boatbuilders, who call it simply a *sagefuri* (plumb bob), Mr. Udagawa called his a *hakarigahata*, while

Mr. Saito, on the right, adjusts a prop trying to get twist in the rub rails, while Mr. Fujiwara checks the amount of curve by measuring off a straight line running down the plank.

Mr. Fujiwara uses a plumb bob and a stick to set the plank angles. For any angle all he has to remember is a horizontal measurement from the string to the 1-shaku mark on the stick.

Mr. Fuijiwara could think of no specific name for the tool. It consisted of a straight piece of wood about 2 shaku long with a mark 1 shaku back from the end. A string tied to the middle dropped through a kerf at the end of the stick, where a nail hanging from the end of the string acted like a plumb bob. Mr. Fujiwara held the stick against the inside of the plank and measured horizontally from the string back to the 1-shaku mark. At our forward station this offset was 7.75 sun; at the after station it was 8.5 sun. Angles were never described in degrees.

A Visitor

The evening before his visit Mr. Udagawa stopped by our apartment to say he would be coming by our workshop the next day. He was in a very serious mood, unlike his usual visits, and I asked him if he had ever met Mr. Fujiwara. He told me he wasn't sure; if he did it was many, many years ago when they were both building boats, sometimes competing for the same customers. Mr. Fujiwara had told me the same thing.

He didn't specify a time, and it was afternoon when he finally showed up, driven to our shop by a friend. Mr. Fujiwara was working at the back of the shop. I put down my tools and rose to greet Mr. Udagawa. He and I stood at the front of the shop and talked about the chokkibune. Mr. Udagawa said he thought the boat looked great. I kept glancing at Mr. Fujiwara, but he kept his head down and continued working. I was becoming concerned both because I had stopped working and had been told before that conversations during work hours were not allowed. I then thought that since Mr. Udagawa had been my teacher perhaps it was up to me to make a formal introduction, so I began to move toward the back of the shop, with him following. As we approached Mr. Fujiwara, however, he headed for the front of the shop, walking down the opposite side of the boat, never glancing at us. They had passed within feet of each other (the entire shop wasn't more than 500 square feet) without acknowledging one another! Mr. Udagawa and I now found ourselves at the stern of the boat, with Mr. Fujiwara now at the bow, and we paused and talked a little longer.

Mr. Udagawa had been in the shop several minutes at least, and my nervousness was finally overcome by the absurdity of the situation. Mr. Saito was looking on helplessly. I finally stepped toward the bow calling Mr. Fujiwara's name. He looked up, as if surprised. "Mr. Udagawa is here," I said, and stepped back. They moved toward each other and Mr. Udagawa, in keeping with his energy and enthusiasm, gave a short, sharp bow, like the snapping of a folding knife. Mr. Fujiwara removed his baseball cap and bowed slowly in return, more like a bough dipping in a breeze. Mr. Saito and I were staring alternately at the two of them and at each other, rolling our eyes as if to say, "What happens next?" Their conversation was strained at first, but then Mr. Udagawa asked a specific question about our boat and Mr. Fujiwara led him to one of his drawings. Within moments they were deep in conversation.

Talking about boats broke the ice and Mr. Saito and I realized the two men were going to be fine together. Mr. Udagawa didn't stay very long, but before he left Mr. Fujiwara asked him a question. "Saito-san showed me a photo

Mr. Fujiwara, left, discussing one of his plank drawings with Mr. Udagawa.

The planks were first fastened in the center; then the seam was finished by nailing outward fore and aft.

of your most recent boat at the museum, and I noticed you used large-headed copper tacks." Mr. Udagawa replied, "I couldn't get any proper ones so I had to use tacks from a drum maker." Then he said goodbye and was gone. Mr. Fujiwara said nothing about the visit the remainder of the day.

The next day when he arrived at the shop, Mr. Fujiwara pulled a large coffee jar from his bag filled with several pounds of copper boatbuilding tacks. He told me he had a source for these hard-to-find fastenings. He handed them to me, saying, "Please give these to Mr. Udagawa."

The planking blocked at the stern.

Detail of the plank fastened at the bow, with the scarf joint for the stem visible. Note the crack extending from the upper nail. It is easy for the curved nails to exert downward pressure on the fragile plank edges, so they are driven slowly, sometimes straightened with a tap from the hammer. Later this seam will be covered with copper plating.

Lower Plank Widths	
Up the aft face of the stem	3.36 shaku
Station A	1.31 shaku
Station B	1.5 shaku
Transom	1.455 shaku

Attaching the Planking

The kajiki were propped against the backbone assembly, and we checked the angle with our patterns at the two stations. We drove four nails amidships into the keel and then began to work fore and aft, propping the planks in place, fitting a section of seam with the saw, and nailing. One nail split the planking because the curve of the nail extended too close to the head, which puts downward pressure on the plank as the nail is driven home. The nails are close to the plank edge so the wood is less supported and fragile. To avoid splits we watched the nail carefully on the final blows with the hammer, and hit the nail to straighten it if it seemed too curved. In one case Mr. Fujiwara decided the nail had to be removed. He pierced the plank from the inside, driving his tsubanomi through until the tip came out against the nail head. Using the chisel like a punch he drove the nail out enough to grab the head with his nail puller.

At the stern we had another problem. The two planks required a great deal of edge-setting to lie fair to the transom. Earlier Mr. Fujiwara had beveled the transom by quickly sighting along the planking, aiming his square in line with the plank as best he could, and tracing the resultant bevel against the transom's edge. Rather than trim the planks to fit better, we edge-set them, which required stout props pushing them tight against the transom.

Ultimately, the poor fit at the transom and elsewhere was not a problem, because suriawase can remove a great deal of material relatively quickly and resolve the fit. Based on my experience in the West I would have measured things more carefully and planed parts to fit much closer. What Mr. Fujiwara did was just the opposite. Scribing and measuring were done very quickly, then time was taken getting the connection right at assembly. In the end, suriawase creates a completely watertight fit so it is hard to argue against this technique given the final results. However, at one point while fitting a seam with his saw, Mr. Fujiwara mused, "All in all, Japanese boatbuilding is really quite primitive."

The sheer planks, called the *uwadana,* are nearly vertical over their entire length, requiring us to cut the top edge of the lower planks and put an extreme bevel on them where the sheer planks joined them. Mr. Fujiwara cut this edge quickly, since he knew he would be adjusting it later when it was beveled. First he marked offsets for the width of the lower planks at each station. He scaled plank widths from his drawing at the stem, stations A and B, and transom.

Working from inside the boat Mr. Fujiwara fastened his inkline to the hood end of the plank (the forwardmost tip) at the stem and stretched the string aft, past point A and fastened the line to B. Leaning back and sighting the string on point A, he marked some intermediate points. Next he shifted the line from point A to the transom, sighted the line on B and marked more points. It was a fairly crude process, but he was trying to mark a fair line with only four reference points, offsets he had scaled from a 1/10th drawing. Had I been building a similar-sized Western boat my plans would have had ten or more offsets, which I would have faired precisely beforehand on the full-size lofting.

Aft Mr. Fujiwara used a batten to connect his marks, but forward, where the planking curved to the stem, he used a fascinating technique to draw a fair line. He pinned his inkline to the forward point at the stem and stretched it to another point about 5 shaku aft on the inside face of the plank. In the center, the line stood proud of the curved plank by several inches. He had a mark for the plank edge in front of him centered between the points where his string touched. He grabbed the taut line at the center and, moving it quickly in a circle, he "threw" the line while snapping it. Amazingly the string hit his mark, and laid down a fair, curved line between his three points.

Inklines and chalklines are by design intended to draw perfectly straight lines, so using one to draw a curve was a revelation bordering on a magic trick. Mr. Fujiwara invited me to try and I simply couldn't do it. I was never able to hit the mark with the string and I never had the right tension on it to lay down a clear line. Mr. Fuiwara was at a loss to explain how he did it. He simply knew how to do it, but did not know how to teach me. He let me try a few more times and then just shrugged at my failure and we went on with our work. Once the line was drawn, we rough-cut the top bevel on the planks by precariously balancing a circular saw on the plank edge and making a vertical cut, then fairing the bevel with a hand plane.

My failure to master the inkline technique was instructive. Even though one would consider this skill important, Mr. Fujiwara elected not to waste any time elucidating it for me. At one time or another I encountered moments like this with all of my teachers. If I were stymied by some calculation or technique my teachers would pause momentarily to review, but if I didn't get it right away we quickly moved on. This is not an indictment of the teacher; it is the failure of the student.

This may seem odd to the reader, an abrogation of responsibility on the part of Mr. Fujiwara, but in fact it is in keeping with the apprentice tradition. In the West we view making sure the student attains mastery over the subject as the teacher's responsibility. Here it was the reverse. All the responsibility for learning was on my shoulders. If I could not master a technique it had nothing whatsoever to do with Mr. Fujiwara. He knew the technique, he had demonstrated it, and that was the end of his responsibilities. Any additional practice I needed I could do on my own time. This system puts all the onus on the student, but it also gives the student the freedom to experiment, to find creative solutions. Depending on the situation, it can also apply a tremendous amount of pressure. This too is important, since it reinforces the need to remain observant and focused on every detail of what is happening in the shop. In all my apprenticeships I was initially told to sweep the shop and fetch the tools, but the first time I was told to use the tools the pressure to succeed was palpable. The stress of expectations is a superb motivator.

We put our wide, plywood spiling plank on the hull to mark the nail locations on the bottom plank for transferring to the sheer plank's edge. When we were done Mr. Fujiwara paused to sit down with me and explain the ratios he used to design our boat. Handed down through his family he called these *wariai* (*wari* means proportion). He explained the wari he used for our chokkibune would work for any size boat of this type, as well as toamibune and nitaribune. Tenmasen, he pointed out, have a different wariai.[11]

There were two values for the boat's wariai: one governed the dimensions at our two stations while the third determined a dimension for the transom. It is a ratio of beam-to-sheer height at the stations and beam-to-beam between the after station and the transom. In the case of the chokkibune the wariai were 4 and 6.5. They worked as shown here, with all dimensions in shaku measured at inside of planking.

Chokkibune Calculations and Measurements

At the two stations:	
4.48	beam at chine
+ .14	total amount of flare at sheer
4.62	beam at sheer
x 4	wariai
1.848	height of sheer from inside of bottom plank
For the transom:	
4.8	beam at sheer at after station
x 6.5	wariai
3.12	beam at top of transom

Note how the decimal point is moved one digit to the left to get the real dimension in shaku. One could also just place the decimal in front of the wariai value to calculate, but Mr. Fujiwara did not do this. The system is also predicated on the builder having a length-to-beam ratio for various sized boats as a starting point. Later, when I measured the finished boat I found the figure for the beam at the Station B was significantly different from the value we used to calculate the transom beam. This was the result of adjusting the planking and sawing seams to fit.

This sort of discrepancy is quite natural, especially when one considers Japanese boats are not built on forms or molds the way Western boats are. Consequently there is a great deal of latitude when building to adjust plank angles, widths, and so on. The builder is also struggling with much thicker and wider planking that can only bend so far. Mr. Fujiwara called his craft primitive, but that flies in the face of the level of skill required. As we have seen, Japanese boatbuilding is improvisational, and the boatbuilder free to make last-minute adjustments.

Beams

Like the bekabune, the hull of the chokkibune is stiffened by pairs of horizontal beams crossing the hull. The beams are through-tenoned into the sheer planks, with the tenons wedged from the outside. The tenons were straight-cut and this meant the corresponding mortises were cut at angles through the planking. Amidships this was straightforward, because the planks crossed the beams at nearly a right angle, but forward, where the planks narrowed and flared outward, it became more complicated, requiring compound angles. All beams were in pairs, with the lower beams very wide, dropping below the sheer planks and bearing against most of the lower planks. They are almost like floor timbers, but don't quite touch the keel.

Mr. Fujiwara fitting the forward beam into its mortise in the sheer plank. All the beams were carefully mortised into the planking.

We inserted the beams in the top planks and then assembled them on the boat as a single unit. The planks had to be bent to nearly their final location before the forward beam's tenons could be inserted into the angled mortises. The lower beams are also nailed through the outside face of the lower plank with our large-headed nails. The tenons of the top beam are covered by the rub rail, while the lower tenons are covered with *douban,* or copper plates.

Sheer Planks

Our sheer planks were hinoki, a wood Mr. Fujiwara said was more beautiful but not any stronger than cedar. He said the butt end of the tree should be oriented toward the bow in this plank. I wish I had pressed him more for his reasoning for this. The natural flare of the trunk at the base would actually have been better oriented to the stern, because all the sweep in this plank was aft. His reasoning may have been about strength rather than shape, because my teacher in Okinawa also insisted the butt end of our material be oriented toward the bow; his reasoning was it better absorbed the force of the bow striking waves. Another reason, my own theory, is that orienting the butt end toward the bow provides clearer, knot-free material where the plank is making the greatest bend.

Mr. Fujiwara surprised me one Monday by saying he had visited the Urayasu Museum over the weekend. He did not see Mr. Udagawa but he saw his boatshop inside the museum, along with the older boats in the collection and Mr. Udagawa's replica boats in the museum's lagoon. He commented on the older boats, specifically the repairs that had been made to their hulls. Two years earlier Mr. Udagawa had pointed out these same repairs, telling me they were his work. Since boats typically have just two wide strakes per side, planks are not replaced in their entirety when a hull needs repair. Instead a patch is installed, set into the planking after the damage has been cut away. These patches are called *nukiita* and are almond-shaped. The unique shape conforms to the tightest curve that can be cut with a boatbuilding saw, since the patches are fitted using suriawase. Once fit, the nukiita are edge-nailed to the surrounding planking.

Stories from the past became a common topic during breaks in the boatshop. Mr. Fujiwara had a keen sense of history, and like Mr. Udagawa had lived through both the devastation of the War and the city's reconstruction and meteoric growth. Both men chose lifestyles more in keeping with prewar Japan than the present day. Mr. Fujiwara's tiny, two-story wood-frame house sat next to a gravel parking lot where his boat shop used to stand. Like the lines on his face, the plaster walls were crazed with cracks, and he enjoyed pointing out to me which fissures had been caused by which major earthquakes. Surrounding the house on all sides were gleaming apartment towers.

Often at break times Mr. Fujiwara would talk about history and offer obscure points related to boatbuilding. One day I was showing him a book of historic boat photos I had found at a Tokyo museum. In a shot from the early Meiji period he casually pointed out that one of the boats bore his family mark on the bow. Often during conversations about the past he used extremely obscure terminology. Mr. Saito had a portable electronic dictionary and I had an antique dictionary, and we would both scramble to look up terms while Mr. Fujiwara talked. In almost every case Mr. Saito admitted defeat: his modern dictionary had no citation, while the word would appear in my dictionary. The triumph of my old, dog-eared paper dictionary pleased Mr. Fujiwara immensely, and he always smiled while I read a definition and showed it to Mr. Saito.

One term neither of us could locate at the time was a word Mr. Fujiwara used for "gangplank." He explained the cargo barges and lighters that carried goods on the canals used long gangplanks. Often the canals were so choked with watercraft that gangplanks were laid from boat-to-boat and finally to shore. He called these *aibiaimashyo,* which he said derived from the verb "to make way for one another." Although we searched diligently for a reference to the term, we were unable to find one, a fact that also seemed to please Mr. Fujiwara. I imagined he felt he was the last living Japanese with knowledge of this term.[12]

Quite a bit of "bench work" went into preparing the sheer planks, but in a Japanese workshop it is all done on the floor. Nail mortises for the nails were cut and our sheer planks had to be through-mortised for each of the beams. All the mortising was done while the plank was still rough sawn. The final finish was done with hand planes, but Mr. Fujiwara took particular care with these planks. Like Mr. Udagawa, he recognized that the sheer planks are the most visible, and he believed they deserved greater attention for finishing. We blocked them high in the center and held down their ends to our floor beams with props. The curve allowed us to set our planes for a very fine cut, thereby yielding the smoothest finish possible. He also stressed at this point we had to sharpen our planes perfectly, and during the planing he regularly sent

Close-up of (left) a mortise with a copper clench nail used to fasten the sheer to the lower plank, and (right) a mortise for the iron nails used to fasten the plank to the stem.

(Above) The uwadana were planed entirely by hand, and Mr. Fujiwara insisted we stop often to sharpen our tools. (Below) The plank assembly on the boat.

When propping the sheer planks, Mr. Fujiwara worked slowly bending the planking in at the stem. The planks were fitted and nailed amidships first.

Mr. Fujiwara fitting the plank seam. He would work from either inside or outside the boat, whichever he felt was more comfortable.

(Above left) A copper nail is driven through the outside planking and exits from the top of a mortise on the inside of the bottom plank. (Above right) A bit of cypress bark for caulking is stuffed under the nail, and the tip is bent over a nail set. (Right) The tip of the nail is pounded down into the base of the mortise, completing the clenching.

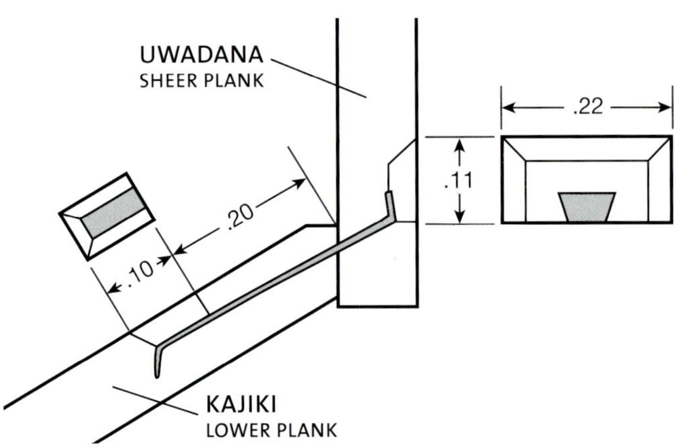

Cross section showing the copper clench nail at the chine. Mortises, beveled on three sides, are cut for the head as well as the tip of the nail. The flat base of the outside mortise is later covered with copper plating. The tip of the nail is clenched into the base of the inside mortise.

me back to the sharpening stones—far more often than I would have in my own shop.

With the planks hung on the beams the whole assembly was placed on the boat. The beams amidships were wedged securely; like the bottom planks, the top planks would be fitted and fastened first at the middle, working out toward the bow and stern.

The sheer planks are fastened with long copper clench nails passing down into the lower plank and emerging at the top of a shallow mortise. Before driving these nails Mr. Fujiwara had me hammer them against an anvil to make them stiffer, a crude form of tempering. Once set in the mortise, the shaft of the nail was first bent back slightly and then, hammering over our nail set we turned the tip, which was hammered into the planking on the inside.

The same issue of the nails stressing the plank became apparent as we moved closer to the bow. The angle of the nails becomes increasingly steeper, and in some cases we ground the heads of the nails down to fit their mortises. Mr. Fujiwara finally decided to not fasten the forward two nail holes along the chine.

The two smallest beams in the boat, called *kotsunagi,* are for tying lines to and have no structural use. Mr. Fujiwara cut them both at a slight taper and we chiseled holes accordingly. We pounded them through the two planks until they fetched up tight and then sawed them off flush with the outside of the hull.

Next we worked on the *koberi*. Also made of hinoki, we set up outside and pre-bent them using fire. They are also fastened with copper clench nails, and on the outside face we carved a double line of mortises for the nail heads. But Mr. Fujiwara's supply of these copper nails was limited, so we alternated nail locations. From the outside the koberi looks traditional, with copper covers in every mortise, but inside the boat the line of clench nails form a wave pattern.

Caulking

We glued and nailed parts of the boat we assembled on the shop floor, but we did not put any glue in the seams between planks. Mr. Fujiwara caulked parts of the seam between the bottom and lower planks he considered problematic. His caulking material, called *makihada,* is made from the inner bark of the cypress tree, thin strands of which are woven into a loose rope. He said that he could only buy it in large quantities and that the material was now extremely expensive, having cost him 70,000 yen.[13]

Because makihada is a very dry, fragile material, we gingerly used our caulking irons and hammer to tap strands of it into the seam. We worked from inside the boat, in keeping with tradition. Unlike the cotton caulking used in the West, which can be driven extremely hard if necessary, makihada is so fragile it will break up into dust if worked too aggressively. Of all the materials used in boatbuilding today this must be among the most obscure.[14]

It had been two months since we started building the chokkibune, and we worked right through Christmas. Mr. Fujiwara had never mentioned the approaching New Year's holiday, one of the most important in the Japanese calendar, but then he invited my wife and I to come to his home and help make *mochi,* a traditional New Year's activity. This thick, sticky dish is made from cooked rice, pounded with a distinctive long-handled mallet in a giant wooden pestle made from a tree trunk.[15] The Saturday we arrived at his house he had an enormous iron cauldron sitting on a wood fire boiling rice. Smoke and steam filled the cold, clear air and soon we set to work pounding rice. Passersby literally stopped in their tracks at the sight of our activity, but Mr. Fujiwara and his wife weren't the least bit flustered. After all, they had been doing this every New Year's day for their entire lives.

Copper

For the remainder of the project I spent most of my time installing copper plating. In urban areas copper was commonly used on boats. It was decorative but also functional, since the copper improved the watertight integrity of some seams and covered the heads of fastenings; it was replaced after a decade or so exposed to the elements. Mr. Fujiwara told me the reason one doesn't see copper used on boats in rural areas was cost.

Strands of makihada caulking draped over a beam. Made from the inner bark of the cypress tree, this material is used like cotton caulking in the West, except it is always driven from inside the boat.

A strip of copper covers the seam between the sheer plank and the rub rail. The strips are peaked slightly when dropped in the groove, then pounded so the two outer edges tuck tightly into the kerf sawn on either side.

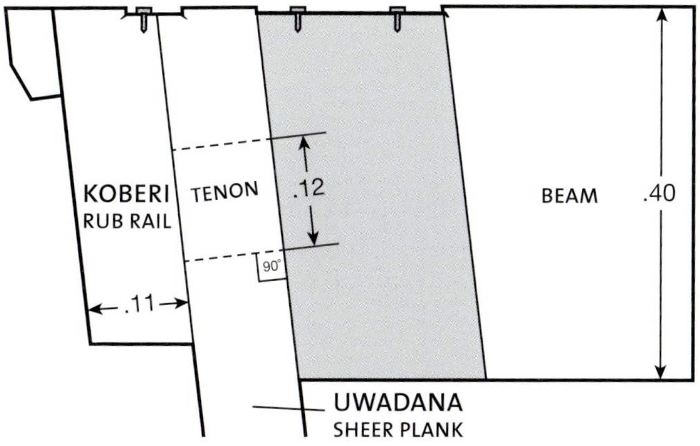

Cross section at the gunwale showing the upper beam and tenon through the uwadana, koberi, and rub rail. The shaded portion is the copper sheet wrapping the beam-to-uwadana connections.

The author coppering the stem rabbet. Visible is the kazeguruma, or pinwheel, symbol of the Fujiwara family of boatbuilders. *Photo copyright Tomizo Saito.*

(Top left) The tenon of a beam where it emerges on the outside of the hull. It is wedged and the surrounding area mortised for copper cladding. (Left) Beam end covered in copper. The geometric pattern drawn on the copper is decorative and distributes the fastenings in a symmetrical pattern.

Mr. Fujiwara's bailer, a design passed down from his father and modified slightly by him.

Boats appear in many of the woodblock prints illustrating traditional Japan and these watercraft often feature striking patterns of dark, geometric figures set against their wooden hulls. No doubt the artists of the day were intrigued by this technique, and there is nothing analogous to it in the Western boatbuilding tradition. In the West we try to hide fastenings with putty and paint, or wooden plugs; in Japan the need to cover nails creates an aesthetic highlight.

Mr. Fujiwara showed me how to cut shallow mortises around beam ends and along seams for the copper cladding. I used a caulking iron to make a kerf where the edges of the copper could be tucked. Like flashing a roof, the copper is laid from the bottom up, so water runs off the boat. I used a pen and drew a grid and diagonals on every piece of copper. The copper was nailed with the same tiny tacks he had presented to Mr. Udagawa, each evenly spaced at the intersections of the grid.

Copper plate has to be cut very carefully to size, just enough to fill the kerf. The pieces are bent slightly and then worked flat using hardwood punches called *meuchi*. Mr. Fujiwara had made these in several sizes and shapes.

We also coppered the end grain of the planking at the stern, around the beams where they penetrated the inside of the hull, the stem rabbet, and even across a seam in the transom. Mr. Fujiwara mentioned small cracks could be caulked and then coppered as a repair. We did not put any bedding compound under the copper, something I would have been inclined to do. He was amused by my description of traditional bedding compounds used in the West, such as combinations of beeswax and pine tar. It was difficult enough describing the ingredients, the former being rare and expensive in Japan and the latter almost unknown.[16]

I calculated later it took over 4,000 tacks to fasten all the copper inside and outside the boat. Mr. Fujiwara did not have to point out to me this was apprentice work, and I made no complaints.

The Craftsman's Nature

Mr. Fujiwara returned to the subject of apprenticeship. He insisted one must not simply learn from one's master, imitating his work, but must innovate, going beyond his teachings to create something new and unique. Mr. Udagawa had stressed the same point, arguing that one could not call himself a craftsman until he had emerged from the shadow of his teacher. To illustrate this, Mr. Fujiwara showed me his bailer (*akatori*). It was an exquisite piece of work, with a through-tenoned handle and small copper reinforcing plates.

"Do you see this edge?" he asked me, pointing to the beveled forward rim of the bailer. "This is my father's bailer design, and maybe my grandfather's." He went on, "Do you see this slight curve to the forward edge?" I had to look closely because it was extremely subtle, a very slight convex edge. "I realized the curve would put pressure on the rim of the bailer as it was pushed along the bottom of the boat." Describing this almost imperceptible detail he finished, "This was my idea."

One had to consciously study his bailer, sighting carefully down its lip, to see what Mr. Fujiwara was talking about, yet he went on to tell me it was precisely this kind of innovation that defined a craftsman. He put this in terms of self-respect, telling me no real craftsman would be satisfied simply imitating his master's work. I explained my goals as a researcher were not to break new ground with my techniques but record faithfully my teachers' methods. Like Mr. Udagawa, he could not accept this; if I was serious about learning I had to also be thinking of my own pride. At first glance it was an odd paradox: both seemed to want a slavish devotion to their methods while we were working together but each expressed the hope I would eventually take my own skills beyond theirs.

An apprentice does not question anything the master says or does. When we attached the rub rail on the chokkibune, Mr. Fujiwara adopted the same slow, laborious method of laying out the location as had Mr. Udagawa. I made the identical time-saving gauge I had used with Mr. Udagawa and showed it to Mr. Fujiwara. He looked the gauge over and understood instantly how it worked. But instead of celebrating my invention, he walked to the front of the shop, put my gauge in his bag, and ordered me back to work. We spent the last few hours of the day working in complete silence and he said barely a word as he left for home.

The next day I went back to work where I had left off. After about an hour Mr. Fujiwara suddenly appeared beside me, my gauge in his hand. "You can finish the job with your little tool," he said. I never mentioned it again and there was no need to discuss it further. His actions made it clear to me my ideas about building the boat were not altogether welcome, yet he wasn't entirely averse to them. The Japanese apprentice probably would have never made the suggestion; deference to one's teacher would have trumped all other considerations. This exchange does show, however, a sophisticated level of communication taking place between two men ostensibly not speaking to one another.

At the stern we installed two wide boards of hinoki covering the aft ends of the sheer planks. Mr. Fujiwara called these *kurukoberi.* Given the sweep of the sheer, in many Japanese boats the grain of the planking begins to run nearly diagonally across the planks at their aft end. This short grain makes the upper corner of these planks vulnerable to splitting or breaking. Though not found on all boats, it is seen enough that I believe the kurukoberi is intended to strengthen this part of the planking by adding a second layer of material with the grain running fore and aft. Our kurukoberi was decorated by a series of rectangular mortises that framed the edges and filled the centers. Like our nail mortises, these were shallow and filled with copper plate. They were entirely decorative, however. In many other types of boats the leading edge of the kurukoberi is carved or otherwise decorated with motifs. The *shimaihagi* (see Chapter 12) represents the pinnacle of this sort of decoration.

Mr. Fujiwara also worked on the *toko,* the large beam spanning the stern of the boat. It was made of pine, he explained, because it sometimes had holes to accept a rudder post, and one of the two parts must be softer than the other. Rudder posts are made of hard oak, so a toko would periodically be replaced as it wore out in service. Mortised into the toko was the *rogui,* the small wooden post our sculling oar would pivot on. The rogui had a tapered shaft and could be hammered out when it wore out. Another softwood pad at the base of the rogui, called the *okiza,* was also replaceable.[17] The top face of the okiza needs to be sloped to match the hardwood block on the sculling oar.

Later, the looped rope holding the sculling oar would be draped over the handle and passed through a hole in the floorboards. Through-bolted onto the bottom would be a hardwood cleat, called the *neko,* with the rope passing through the cleat and around a T-shaped wooden fitting. The cleat and fitting create enough friction to keep the rope from slipping, while allowing the length to be easily adjusted for the sculler's height. Mr. Fujiwara made the fitting from two pieces of keyaki, octagonal in section, which he tenoned together. He called it a *shumoku*, and the joinery was the same as the T-handle of a paddle.[18]

I did not make the ro, the sculling oar, for the chokkibune. Mr. Fujiwara had been making them for the fleet of Wasen Tomo no Kai for several years and had one the proper size for our boat. According to him, the handle of the oar should be at waist level in operation and 6 shaku of the blade should be in the water. The distance from the handle to the forward tip should be equal to the shoulder width of the rower. He told me the angle between the handle and blade should be eleven degrees and most importantly, the balance point of the ro should be 2 shaku down the blade from the pivot point (see Chapter 6).[19]

As we approached the completion of our chokkibune, Mr. Fujiwara brought up my upcoming departure for northern Japan to build another boat. Like Mr. Udagawa, he was

The toko, showing the rogui, or hardwood post the sculling oar pivots on. The pad, called the okiza, is made of pine and periodically replaced when it wears out from the use of the oar.

The cleat and fitting bolted through the bottom of the boat, called the neko and shumoku, respectively, which allow the rower to easily adjust the length of the rope controlling the sculling oar.

adamant that the experience would be more confusing than edifying. He was quite clear about what he thought of boats built outside of Tokyo. "They don't know how to build boats in Aomori," he told me emphatically, "You can't learn anything from a boatbuilder there." I listened, neither agreeing nor disagreeing, but when he was finished I asked him if he had ever traveled to Tohoku (as the entire region of northern Japan is known). He said he hadn't. I asked him if he had ever *seen* a boat from Tohoku. Again, no.

I have remarked on the intense pride of many of the craftsmen I met and worked with. Exchanges like this one seem, at face value, to be small-minded and unfair. Boatbuilders, particularly this last generation, worked in near-complete isolation from one another as the craft rapidly faded through the latter half of the twentieth century. If one boatbuilder did know another, in all likelihood he was a competitor. Beyond that, however, it simply was not relevant to one's life or work to pay attention. These craftsmen are rooted in their particular locales, building local boat types tailored to their customers. The parochialism of the craft, as well as its secrecy, gave them no reason to have an interest in the larger tradition.

It has been hard to reconcile my teachers' deep generosity and kindness with what may appear to be an inappropriate sense of superiority. I have been cautious about criticizing them because of the real danger of a cultural bias in interpreting them. But one thing I do know: my teachers are connected to a much deeper tradition than I am. It is not uncommon to meet boatbuilders or other craftspeople who can trace their lineages in the trade through perhaps three generations. The very first boatbuilder I met in Japan, in 1990, told me he was the eighth generation of his family to build boats. Perhaps a sense of self, steeped in tradition and forged in isolation, naturally develops an attitude of superiority. Boatbuilders who claimed to be "the only one" may have in fact meant, "I'm the only one worth talking to."

The craftsman also occupies a particular niche in society. While almost no Japanese today embark on a multi-year craft apprenticeships, craftspeople are still held in high esteem. After all, these are the people who did pass through the crucible of arduous training. Every Japanese is well aware of the traditional method of this instruction, one based on rote training, low wages, and slavish devotion to one's teacher. The ethic of the craftsman is one of uncompromising dedication to the work, and supreme confidence in oneself.

Before we finished the boat a small delegation of the senior members of Wasen Tomo no Kai visited our workshop. With planning underway for our launching ceremony, they said they had a very serious matter to discuss. They explained, facing me, that all the boats in their fleet were named after birds, but they were aware of a Western tradition of giving boats female names. I had no idea where this was going, and I couldn't understand why they weren't talking directly to Mr. Fujiwara.

"We would like to name the boat after your wife, Catherine." I looked at Mr. Fujiwara, who nodded his agreement. Catherine had been a welcome visitor to our shop. I thanked them for the kind offer, but thinking of our silent partner in this project, the Freeman Foundation, I proposed another idea. The principal of the family foundation, Houghton Freeman, had lived in Tokyo with his family for twenty-five years and I thought if anyone should have the honor of the boat's name it should be them. "Mr. Freeman has a wife." I said, "I suggest you name the boat after her." I then wrote her name in the Japanese phonetic syllabary, while everyone looked on intently. After making sure they understood exactly how to pronounce it, it was decided. The chokkibune had a name: *Doreen*. Everyone, Catherine included, was pleased.

Launching

The public relations office of Koto-ward worked hard to make our launching ceremony a major event for the city, and several hundred people were on hand, including multiple television, radio, and newspaper outlets. A crane truck came to our worksite and loaded the boat, then deposited it in the canal at Wasen Tomo no Kai's boathouse. A tent was erected, and by the time my wife and I arrived the Shinto priest had set up his portable shrine. Catherine and I were ushered to a line of chairs adjacent to the shrine where we were seated next to Mr. Fujiwara and the Deputy Mayor. The members of Wasen Tomo no Kai were standing, crowded under a tent to our right. They wore their jackets with the crest of the rowing group, while Mr. Fujiwara wore his ancient coat bearing his family crest.

In front of us the crowd was thickly packed on the walkway next to the canal. The same priest who conducted our keel-laying ceremony officiated, first blessing the altar and then ritually blessing the boat and the boatbuilders. The Deputy Mayor then gave a speech, followed by Mr. Fujiwara, and then me. The final part of the ceremony was an open invitation for individuals to step forward and say a prayer at the shrine. It was understood this was limited to those of us who were seated and for one or two senior members of Wasen Tomo no Kai. In the order of our seating arrangements first Mr. Fujiwara prayed, followed by me, my wife, and the Deputy Mayor.

After Mr. Saito and another member of Wasen Tomo no Kai offered prayers, I thought the ceremony had ended when Catherine suddenly squeezed my hand. Mr. Udagawa burst from the crowd. I had not noticed him before, such was the crush of people, and he is a small man. But he always moved with a vigor and speed that seem to enlarge his presence, and suddenly there he was, standing at the altar, his head bowed. My wife and I couldn't take our eyes off him, and I pictured Mr. Saito shaking his head in amazement. Mr. Udagawa's clap was like a gunshot, which was followed by his usual quick, efficient bow; then he turned toward Mr. Fujiwara and bowed again. Mr. Fujiwara rocked forward, bowing from his seat, his eyes widening slightly in a look of amazement. It was a powerful gesture of respect that a moment before I would have thought unimaginable. As Mr.

Mr. Fujiwara on launch day, wearing a hand-embroidered jacket bearing the Fujiwara family crest.

In the foreground a Shinto priest conducts the launching ceremony at a temporary alter, while seated behind are Mr. Fujiwara, the author, the author's wife, and the Deputy Mayor of Koto ward, Tokyo. *Photo copyright Keiju Kurozumi.*

Udagawa disappeared again into the crowd, I glanced to the right at my wife, whose eyes were filling with tears. I looked left at Mr. Fujiwara, his face again as impassive as ever, hands on his knees, his eyes cast down toward the ground.

Mr. Saito had the honor of being the first aboard the chokkibune after the ceremony. With a long, narrow paddle he moved the boat into the center of the canal and gracefully spun her to starboard, making three complete circles for good luck.

Just before my wife and I left Tokyo we had a dinner party with Mr. and Mrs. Fujiwara, and Mr. and Mrs. Saito. We shared reminiscences and jokes and I indulged in too much sake and beer, as did Mr. Fujiwara. We were both good and drunk. Mr. Fujiwara wished us well on our upcoming circuitous drive north. We had leased a van and

The chokkibune upon launching, January, 2003 in Koto-ward, Tokyo.

were planning on driving long stretches of the coast to look for more boatbuilders, before finally arriving in Aomori for my next apprenticeship. For once, Mr. Fujiwara had nothing critical to say about working with my next teacher. He even intimated he might visit us there. The relief brought on by the successful completion of our project and the alcohol combined to erase all the reserve I normally felt around him. The evening had been one of almost nonstop laughter and I was in a jovial, almost giddy, mood. Suddenly I remembered the gift I had given him our first day in the workshop. "Fujiwara-san," I blurted, "what did you ever do with that plane I gave you?" Still grinning, I added, "I figured you threw it into the Sumida River on your way home that day."

Mr. Fujiwara's reverie evaporated, and I knew I had made a mistake, but I still could not imagine how my gift would have offended him. With a pained look he said, "I didn't understand it," which was enough to make things clear. Once again I was reminded of our roles—master and apprentice—and the responsibilities on both sides of that relationship. What mattered was knowing what to do, and what not to do.

Mr. Fujiwara's face settled into that old, serious look and he changed the subject. "Do you remember how you answered when I called your name?" he asked, his eyes now staring intently into mine. It took me a moment to recall that I would immediately say, "Hai!" (Yes!) and await his next word.

"Why did you answer me that way?" he asked. I didn't have an immediate response. Sometimes I said it just for fun, turning his shout of *Hansei!* into an amusing routine with my *Hai!* However, I also said it out of respect, a desire to behave in the most appropriate manner for an apprentice: obedient, attentive, and observant. Yet I couldn't immediately frame an answer encompassing the several reasons; I probably looked as though I didn't understand his question. Finally, I turned the question around. "Why do you ask?"

His inscrutable face gave way, betraying a struggle with an unresolved mystery. With his eyes still fixed on mine he finally said, "That's exactly how I responded to my father."

Notes

1 Koto-ku is one of twenty-three wards (*ku*) of metropolitan Tokyo. These wards are semi-autonomous and refer to themselves as cities within Tokyo, and the ward offices (*kuyakusho*) are more like city halls. Koto-ku has a population of just under 500,000 people.

2 Edo is the old name for Tokyo, and the Edo period encompasses the reign of the Tokugawa shoguns from that city between 1603 and 1868.

3 In urban Japan, oars and paddles were not made by boatbuilders, but by craftsmen who specialized in them. Late

in his career Mr. Fujiwara tried to learn how to make Japanese sculling oars from the last surviving maker in Tokyo, and was finally exposed to this culture of craft secrecy. "He gave me only a half an hour of his time, and seemed reluctant to talk," Mr, Fuji told me, exasperated.

4 One obvious solution to this problem would be alternating the nails on the inside and outside, but I have never seen this done on a boat in Japan. The *sabani* (see Chapter 13) does use fastenings inside and out, but these are not boat nails.

5 In the West this type of glue is made by a British company and sold under the trade name Aerolite.

6 Prior to the use of glue some boatbuilders put lacquer (*urushi*) between plank seams.

7 Mr. Fujiwara is the only builder I have met who used this term. I have heard rabbet joints called *enuchi* and *sanehagi* by other boatbuilders.

8 The sheer is the top edge of the top plank, a very visible line on a boat's hull. The top plank is also called the sheer plank or sheer strake.

9 Tri-Coastal Marine of Richmond, California designed a replica Lake Champlain sail ferry we launched in 2002, just two weeks before starting work with Mr. Fujiwara in Tokyo. Information on this boat can be found at my website and at tricoastal.com.

10 Lofting takes its name from the mold loft, an open space in a shipyard where this work took place. When lofting is used for building Western-style boats in Japan it is called *genzu*, from the word for "original drawing."

11 *Tenmasen*, for Mr. Fujiwara, are canal cargo boats, although the term *tenmasen* is widely used to describe many types of small workboats.

12 Much later I was able to find reference to the verb *aibiau,* which means to yield or to make way. Mr. Fujiwara's term was another verb form, but I discovered that a derivative is *aiban,* or gangplank. More common words for gangplank are *michiita, ayumiita,* and *watariita. Michi* is a route or road, *ayumi* means stepping or walking, and *watari* can mean a bridge. The ending *ita* means plank.

13 Roughly $700 US.

14 Perhaps in deference to the fragility of this material, a boatbuilder on Lake Biwa made his own caulking irons out of bamboo. He believed a living thing must only be struck by another living thing.

15 A boatbuilder once told me he also made *ofuro,* or wooden bathtubs, and he caulked the seams of his tubs with *mochi.*

16 As mentioned earlier, the closest thing boatbuilders used for a bedding compound was lacquer, which was sometimes put between planks before fastening. It was always prohibitively expensive, and boatbuilders long ago substituted modern glues for lacquer.

17 *Oku* means to put or to place, while *za* means seat.

18 A *shumoku* is a wooden mallet used for striking a bell, which this fitting resembles, and also the name for the T-handle of the kai, or paddle.

19 Mr. Fujiwara derived angles using two dimensions of a right triangle. While he told me the oar should have an eleven degree angle, in fact the layout of his triangle results in about nine degrees.

A dugout bottom of an *isobune*. The scalloping of the adze work is visible. Mr. Ando spent his apprenticeship shaping these boat bottoms working long hours for nearly no pay.

12

The Shimaihagi of Aomori

In the summer of 2003 my wife and I arrived in Shiranuka Village in Aomori Prefecture. We had come so that I could build the final boat of my Freeman Foundation-sponsored year in Japan with the last boatbuilder of the region, Mr. Seizo Ando. We planned to build a *shimaihagi* (literally, "four planks put together"), a type of fishing boat commonly used throughout coastal Aomori Prefecture. The local sponsoring partner of our project was the Michinoku Traditional Wooden Boat Museum and then consulting curator Mr. Masaaki Kon.

The completed Shimaihagi upon launching in Aomori City.

North to Shiranuka

Aomori is the northernmost prefecture of the main island of Honshu. On a clear day one can see Hokkaido in the distance from its northern shores. This region is known as Tohoku, and except for a 1994 visit to a dugout builder in Shiohama, Oga City, in neighboring Akita Prefecture, I had never been to this part of the country. Before arriving in Shiranuka, my wife and I drove our rental van up the west coast of Honshu along the Japan Sea. We crossed by ferry over to Hokkaido and explored the southern end of the island before returning to Honshu and traveling down the Pacific coast to Shiranuka.

Shiranuka is one of several villages forming the larger town of Higashidori-mura. It lies on the Pacific Ocean along the eastern edge of the Shimokita Peninsula. The peninsula is often referred to locally as masakari (broadaxe) because of its shape. A long, narrow band of land runs up its eastern edge, with Aomori Bay on one side and the Pacific Ocean on the other. Most of this eastern edge is beach, with a few rocky headlands. Shimaihagi boats were once commonly used along this shoreline for inshore fishing and for gathering seaweed and shellfish. Even today one can find villages with rows of old *funagoya* (boathouses) along the beach. In all likelihood an old shimaihagi can be found inside.

The purpose of our extended road trip was to travel along the coast in search of boatbuilders. Those I had met while traveling north along the Sea of Japan told me they used no plans whatsoever, and I was curious to see if this approach was universal.[1] The boats in this northern region varied dramatically: on the Akita coast we found semi-dugouts called *hatahatabune,* named after the sailfin sandfish (*hatahata*) they were used for catching. These boats looked barely different from dugout canoes; they were long and narrow, built of thick wooden bottoms and plank sides. Further north I again met the man I had come to see in 1994. To my knowledge he is the only living boatbuilder who made true dugout canoes commercially.[2]

View of Shiranuka Village, Aomori, from the headlands overlooking the harbor. In the distance is the controversial Rokkasho nuclear reprocessing facility, which has kept this community more prosperous than other parts of rural Japan. *Photo copyright Toshikatsu Hanabe.*

An isobune, or kakkobune, the smallest fishing boat of the region. These can still be found in the fishing villages in Aomori but few are in use.

Still further north, in Aomori and Hokkaido, I found several small boat types with carved timber bottoms and plank sides, although these reflected much more elegant design and construction than the hatahatabune. Even more interesting were the carvings that began to appear on the fishing boats. In some cases they were simple renderings of a sea bird, usually carved at the stern, or a stylized *kanji* (Chinese character) at the bow. Once we reached the Shimokita Peninsula, however, boats featured elaborately carved and painted boards at their sterns, along with geometric motifs along the rails, stems, and sterns. As luck would have it, the boatbuilding traditions of Shiranuka reflected the most ornate carving in the entire region.

Mr. Seizo Ando

I had never met nor spoken with Mr. Ando prior to my arrival in Shiranuka. All arrangements for this apprenticeship had been negotiated by Mr. Kon, the leading scholar of the region's fishing boats and curator of the Aomori Prefectural Museum of History in Aomori City. Mr. Ando had built his last boat twenty-two years before this project, and never had the opportunity to teach anyone.

The Andos lived in a large modern home right on the main coastal road running through town. His boat shop next door was a much older building. Also living in the house were his wife and her elderly mother, plus a son and his wife with their two small children. We regularly interacted with all of the family members except for Mrs. Ando's mother, who we would see sitting in a window or occasionally taking a walk in the neighborhood.

The Andos ran a seasonal fish-processing business located in a small factory beside their home. Mr. Ando had built an apartment inside the factory for our use. It was a kind gesture, and although at first the fish smell was almost overpowering, amazingly within a few days neither of us seemed to notice it.

Mr. Ando was born in Tomari Village, next to Shiranuka, the two towns separated by a steep, rocky headland. Shimaihagi boats were unknown in his childhood village, but fishermen in both villages used a smaller boat called an *isobune* (sometimes *kakkobune*) for gathering seaweed and shellfish close to shore. *Iso* means "inshore" and these gorgeous little boats are semi-dugouts, with carved bottoms and plank sides. There seems to be no agreement on the derivation of the term *kakko*, a local term I heard used elsewhere in Tohoku. Possible interpretations include a variation on *kako*, meaning "sailor" or "seaman." A boatbuilder in Miyagi to the south told me it meant "to put together," perhaps related to *kakou suru*, "to manufacture." Mr. Ando said it meant "a beautiful shape."[3]

Although his father was a fisherman Mr. Ando did not follow his father to the sea. Instead, he apprenticed at age fifteen for three years with a local boatbuilder in Tomari named Katsuburo Aikasu. His boss, whom he referred to using the honorific *oyakata,* built large squid boats as well as the smaller isobune. The boatshop employed five men and Mr. Ando's apprenticeship consisted of shaping the bottoms of isobune, which were carved from thick planks, with an adze and plane. His other tasks included the classic work of the *deshi* (apprentice): sharpening tools and cleaning the shop. The workday began at five a.m. and ended at seven p.m. with a one-hour lunch break. When I asked how much he was paid he angrily replied, "*Tadabataraki!*" which means, literally, "Free work!" He insisted his master never taught him anything and that he left his apprenticeship early because of the miserable conditions. "I researched until I understood, and taught myself," he said.

At age twenty-three Mr. Ando moved to Shiranuka, where an older man named Unomazou Kawabata was building shimaihagi. Mr. Ando was able to determine the dimensions of shimaihagi from other boats in the village, and he also talked with the fishermen to learn their thoughts on how these boats could be improved. He watched boats being built in Mutsu, a larger city over the coastal hills from Shiranuka on Ominato Bay. Using this information Mr. Ando developed a design for his shimaihagi. The greatest change he made during his career was redesigning the stern so the boats could carry outboard motors (*sengaiki*).[4]

The "four planks" from which the name shimaihagi derives do not include the bottom (keel) plank, which Mr. Ando called the *shiki*. Another Aomori boat found at the end of the Shimokita Peninsula is called a *rokumaihagi*, or "six planks together," and is made of three planks on each side of the plank keel. In both these boats the planks overlap, which Mr. Ando called *wakizuke*.[5] Alternate methods used locally are called *kadotsubushi*, in which a timber acts like a chine log, carved to shape, forming the corner between the bottom and side planks; and *mudamahagi*, in which the bottom plank is carved from an extremely thick board, with planks added to it to form the boat's sides. The small isobune are examples of mudamahagi construction.

Mr. Ando built about one hundred isobune and shimaihagi in Shiranuka; he worked alone when building these smaller boats. During his early thirties he built ten *ika-tsuri-bune*, larger boats weighing up to ten tons for catching squid, *ika*. These boats were built using a Western plank-on-frame method, and ran from 35 to 60 shaku long. When building squid boats he hired four workers to assist him. The boats were too large for his shop so they worked on the beach, taking about three months to complete each one. Mr. Ando noted that when he was building a boat he worked seven days a week until it was completed; during his most active boatbuilding years he probably took off just fifteen days a year. Another boatbuilder from this region told me he sometimes worked as a fisherman in between boatbuilding projects, and local boatbuilders would alternate between working together on large projects and working independently. In this very rural region many people alternated between fishing, farming, and other work.[6]

Not long after our arrival in Shiranuka I found an old shimaihagi sitting just behind the breakwater in a crumbling boathouse. The roof of the building had caved in, filling the boat with asphalt shingles, yet it was still in remarkably good shape. I asked Mr. Ando if it was one of his boats but he said it had been built by Mr. Kawabata. One day a local man, Toshikatsu Hanabe, stopped by our shop. It turned out the boat I had found had belonged to his father. Mr. Hanabe was one of only two people in the village who spoke English, and he quickly became our best friend in Shiranuka.

(Above) A shimaihagi built by Unomazou Kawabata, the local boatbuilder whose work Mr. Ando studied. (Right) Mr. Ando standing in front of one of the squid boats he built. He hired helpers only when building these larger boats.

Mr. Hanabe's Recollections of His Father's Shimaihagi

The construction of shimaihagi flourished in the 1960s. My father and his older brother helped the boatbuilder build our boat fifty-five years ago [1954]. *They cut down the tree and prepared the log and brought it to the boatbuilder's shop. At that time the residents of Shiranuka village earned almost all of their income from either farming or fishing. The biggest earnings were from cuttlefish, taken from the end of summer through winter. That was followed by abalone gathering in winter, then trout fishing in the spring, and seaweed* [kelp] *and sea urchin collecting. The shimaihagi were used for gathering all kinds of fish and especially for kelp gathering in the summer months, when there was fine weather for drying the catch.*

The kelp fishing used to begin at seven in the morning and usually ended by one in the afternoon. At daybreak we gathered at the boathouse and pushed the boat to the sea. Four people rowed. No one talked. We all knew what to do and it was hard work. I was one of the starboard rowers and it generally took an hour to reach the kelp grounds. We gathered kelp only in calm weather so it was generally sunny and hot.

The Fisherman's Association assigned a stretch of beach to fishermen for drying, and we tried to find kelp beds close by, usually in about ten meters of water. My father's site was north of the Oipe district, the site of the electric power plant now. When we arrived at the kelp beds we dropped an anchor. A siren signaled when we could start fishing and at the sound all the fisherman's poles went into the water. We had sight boxes (a wooden box with a glass bottom) to see the kelp, and our poles had a twisted iron rod on the ends that we twisted into the kelp. We pulled the kelp straight up and once it broke the surface we laid the poles down and hauled the catch into the boat. By spinning the pole we could release the kelp and continue fishing.

My role was to control the ship. Even at anchor the boat moved and I listened for instructions. One man held the sight glass in his teeth and using his hands told me where to maneuver the boat. Another man might be holding the sight glass in his mouth while spearing the kelp. Sometimes fishermen yelled different instructions at me. I was just a young boy, but I saw how competitive each fisherman was. There was a rivalry among these men, each one trying to catch more than the other, like hawks or lions in a fight with nature to secure a living. I realized then how harsh was the life of a fisherman.[7]

A large fiberglass boat in the foreground surrounded by small isobune, Shiranuku, circa 1960. These boats were used to harvest the sea's bounty in a variety of ways: gathering seaweed, diving for abalone, and spearing sea urchins. *Photo copyright Toshikatsu Hanabe.*

He eventually wrote down his recollections of his father's boat, nicely describing how these boats were used when he was growing up, and the interconnected roles of farmer and fisherman (excerpt above).

Mr. Ando told me that the first fiberglass boats appeared in Shiranuka in the 1970s; they were about four tons, and ten meters long. A few years later a fiberglass version of the small isobune appeared, built by the Yamaha Corporation and made with extraordinary attention to detail. The isobune is a relatively primitive boat, so to see it constructed of modern synthetic materials is jarring; however, the popularity of this type of boat in the local fishing fleet presumably made it profitable for mass production.[8] Mr. Ando said that no manufacturer had developed a fiberglass shimaihagi. Although he was busy building small boats right up to the end, Mr. Ando retired from boatbuilding in 1981, building his last shimaihagi for himself. He then moved to Tokyo and worked in a large factory for fourteen years before returning to Shiranuka at age sixty-two.

Throughout our previous seven months in Tokyo, whenever we mentioned that we would be living in Aomori our friends reacted with horror. "You will never understand them!" was the warning. The Aomori dialect is considered by some to be the most impenetrable of the country's many regional forms of Japanese. Hearing native speakers tell us even they could not understand the language made my wife and I increasingly nervous. One Tokyo native insisted he once went on a business trip to Aomori and rode in a taxi for an hour. "The driver spoke non-stop and I did not understand a single word he said to me."

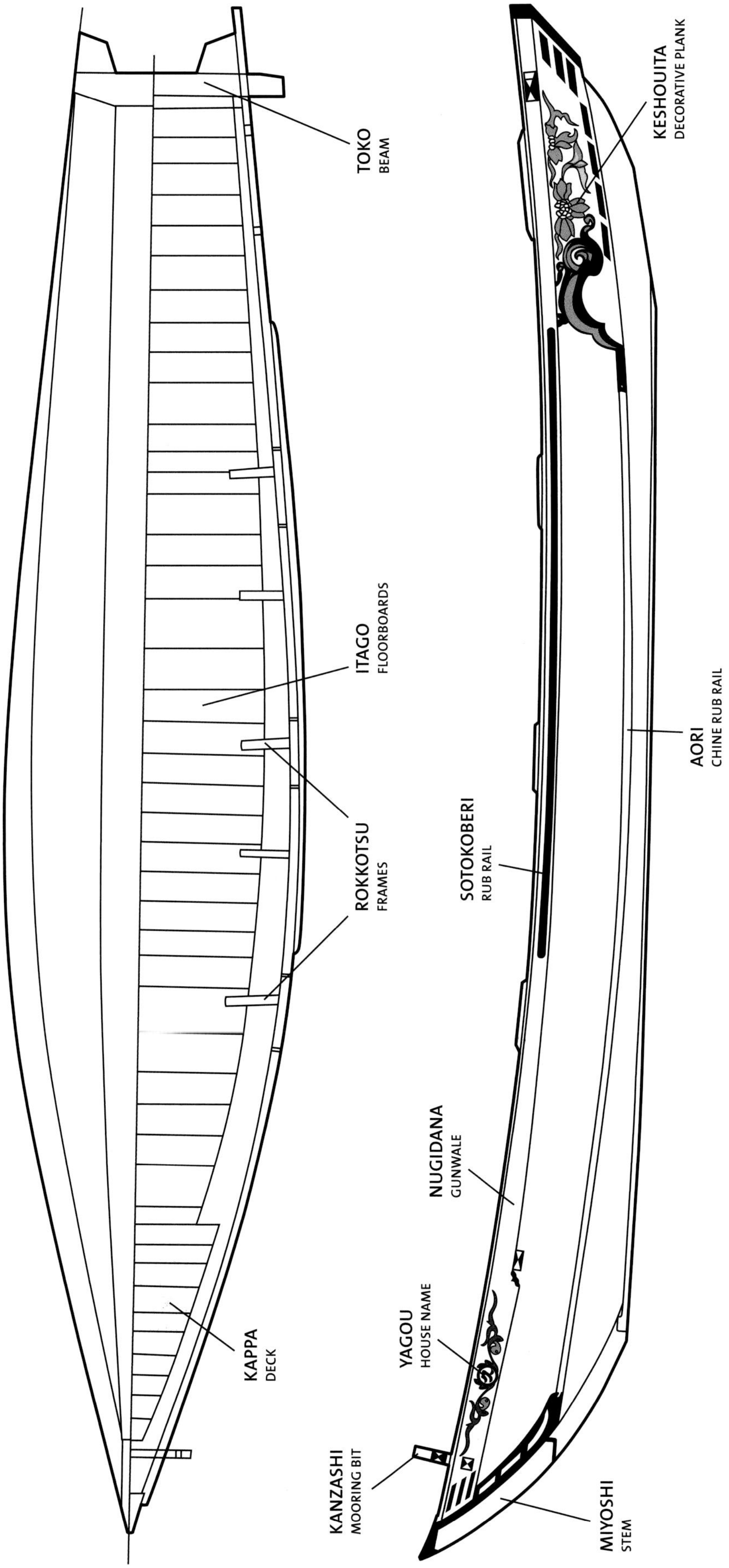

The shimaihagi measures just over 27 shaku in length with a beam of 6 shaku, giving her a length-to-beam ratio of 4.5:1. Shimaihagi were rowed by fisherman using large paddles, though later outboard motors became common. The most obvious feature of the shimaihagi is the decorative carving believed to protect the boat's owner and to ensure a good catch. The yagou, or house name, is the centerpiece of the carving at the bow, while various motifs important to Shintoism and Buddhism decorate the planking at the stern.

In fact, we had very little trouble communicating during our stay in Shiranuka. There are actually three major dialects in Aomori: Tsugaru-ben in the west; Shimokita-ben on the peninsula; and Nambu-ben in the south. We were living on the border between Shimokita-ben and Nambu-ben. Mr. Ando did use terms I had never heard before, but I discovered I could usually find these words in my oldest dictionary, published in 1896.[9] A bigger problem was that his pronunciation was often at odds with standard Japanese. He pronounced shimaihagi as "shimeipagi," and his village of Shiranuka he called "Suranuka." He also pronounced several consonants in a non-standard way. Except perhaps for the very elderly, all Japanese can speak a standard dialect with ease. After a few weeks I became used to his pronunciation, though there were times when older fisherman visited the shop and everyone present would revert to a thick local dialect; except for the odd word, I would be lost.

The night before we started building the boat we hosted two American friends on a break from their studies in Tokyo, graduate students in Japanese at Yale University and the University of Chicago. I had met them both at language school at Middlebury College. Joe Hankins had dazzled the faculty there with his command of *keigo,* the most polite form of the language. At the end of their visit, Joe came by the shop and expressed to Mr. Ando his deepest gratitude for their hospitality, using all of the appropriate honorifics. Mr. Ando did not say a word, but just looked up at Joe with his mouth slightly open. As soon as Joe walked out of the boatshop, Mr. Ando turned to me and said, "Your friend is funny. I didn't understand a word he said."

Wood

The shimaihagi's planking was made of cedar. The frames were a variety of cypress called *hiba* (*Thujopsis dolabrata*, also *Hiba arborvitae*)[10] and the carved planks at the stern, called *keshouita*, were made of a Japanese white bark magnolia called *hoonoki* (*Magnolia hypoleuca,* or *Magnolia obovata*). The curved beam near the bow used as a bitt for tying lines was made of *kuwa* (mulberry, *Broussonetia papyrifera*). Several other types of wood were used for specific parts of the boat, including *enju* (Japanese pagoda tree, *Sophora japonica*), *nara* (oak, *Quercus serrata*), *itaya* (painted maple, *Acer mono*), and *kuri* (chestnut, *Castanea crenata*).

Mr. Ando personally chose the cedar tree used to plank our boat. He selected a tree with a circumference of 8 shaku, and he estimated the volume of the log to be twenty koku (each 10 cubic shaku).[11] He instructed the sawmill (*seizaisho*) to cut two thick planks from the middle of the log, with the cut between them along the centerline of the heart. This yielded material for two bottoms and transoms. The remaining planks were used symmetrically in the boat. Working out from the center of the log, the next planks cut on either side of the center were used for the top planks; the next two planks on either side were used for the bottom planks. The remaining material used in the boat, including hoonoki and hiba, came from wood Mr. Ando had stored in his shop since he built his last boat.

Mr. Ando calculated the costs (in 2003) for procuring the cedar were roughly: $2,000 for the actual tree; $700 for the bulldozer to cut and pull the felled tree from the forest; $800 for the services of the sawmill; and $300 to truck the material to his shop. He also estimated he spent $500 on new tools for the project.

Tools

Mr. Ando had the normal complement of woodworking tools, including axes, hammers, nail punches, planes, saws, chisels, and sharpening stones. Of course he also had the two tools unique to boatbuilders: special saws for fitting plank edges and *tsubanomi* chisels for making nail holes. The only power tools he used were a circular saw, a power plane, a drill, and a bandsaw (which he called either *obinoko* or *bando*). Mr. Ando bought his first power tool, a power plane, in 1965. This is quite amazing when one considers he and other local boatbuilders at the time were building fishing boats as large as ten tons, using only hand tools!

Mr. Ando used the traditional inkpot and bamboo brush for measuring and marking. He had a square (that he sometimes called *kani*) and I had a modern shaku tape measure. For longer measurements Mr. Ando used a 6-shaku stick marked off in 1-shaku intervals he called a *jougi*.

In lieu of drawings Mr. Ando used various wooden patterns. These patterns were the closest thing he had to drawings; they were well made and well worn, as he had used them over his entire career. They included patterns for the shape of the curved stem and the angles of the bottom planks. He had memorized most of the dimensions of the boat, although the two main props he used to hold the bottom in place had been marked long ago with various heights for parts of the boat. He is the only boatbuilder I have met who recorded design information on props.

Since Mr. Ando had retired from boatbuilding over twenty years ago, one of our most important patterns was his own boat: the last shimaihagi he had built, twenty-two years earlier (1981). He kept it for his own use, in his boathouse near the beach. Early in the project, as he was laying out some dimensions, he paused, silently, before saying, "I forgot." He told me to get my tape measure and we drove to the boathouse. As he called out measurements taken from the boat there, I wrote them down. This happened several times before we finished.

Stem

In his shop Mr. Ando actually had a finished shimaihagi stem that he made over twenty years ago, but it had split at the base. Because the stem is curved at its base, he selected a piece of cedar with a natural curve to it. He traced it using his pattern, trying to match the curve in the wood grain to the curve of the stem. He then used the back edge of the pattern to trace the line of the stem rabbet.[12] The stem pattern was marked with the heights where both planks would end in the stem rabbet, and he also transferred these marks to the finished stem.

On this first day Mr. Ando primarily used his axe to rough-shape the stem. I was surprised to see how confidently he could cut to his line, generally within 1 bu (1/8 inch), before reaching for his plane to finish the job. Throughout the project Mr. Ando relied on his axe to do much of the initial work in shaping parts of the boat. It was always an impressive display, especially considering he had not built any boats for over twenty years. Other boatbuilders I have worked with relied more on the adze for rough work, only occasionally using an axe. Mr. Ando's word for the axe may have also been my first introduction to the Aomori dialect. He is the only craftsman I have met who uses the term *masakari*. Every other craftsman I know calls this tool an *ono*.[13]

Mr. Ando used his circular saw to cut the depth of the rabbet before reaching for his axe to clean out this joint. He left plenty of material at either end of the stem. A joint still had to be cut at the bottom of the stem for the connection with the plank keel. A brace was nailed to the extra material at the top of the stem. This in turn was nailed to the overhead beams of the shop. The brace held the stem in place until the hull was completely planked.

While Mr. Ando was shaping the stem he ordered me to the back of the shop where I was given some sandpaper and shown a pile of rusting tools. For the most part the shop had remained undisturbed for over twenty years, and with the ocean breaking on the beach about a hundred yards away, the salt air had given everything a thick brown coating of rust. I spent the better part of my first three days cleaning all the tools, occasionally interrupted by other requests.

Bottom

The material used for the bottom was a long piece of rough-sawn cedar, 2.1 sun thick. Mr. Ando oriented the plank with the heart side of the wood facing the inside of the boat. He first planed the plank smooth with a power plane and then laid it flat so he could draw its shape for cutting. He snapped a centerline the length of the plank with his inkline. From a mark a few sun back from the bow end (leaving material for the stem-keel scarf joint), he measured back 21.5 shaku and drew a line at right angles across the centerline. He used his measuring stick, which was 6 shaku long and marked with 1-shaku increments. These two marks represented the back of the stem and the inside face of the transom. At the bow

Mr. Ando using his axe to rough out the stem. Despite being away from boatbuilding for over twenty years he could cut to within one-eighth inch of his line.

Mr. Ando added 5.25 sun forward of his line; this material would be cut for the joint between the stem and keel. Starting from the back of the stem, he made marks at 4.5 shaku and 6 shaku. He measured forward from the transom line and made marks at 3.5 shaku and 6 shaku; he then measured aft another 4.25 shaku from the 6 shaku point and made a mark. These five points were his stations for the shape of the bottom.

The first points inboard of the stem and transom were the locations of joints where the bottom would be partially cut and bent. At all five stations Mr. Ando laid out from memory the widths of the bottom from the centerline. He connected these points using a batten measuring 9 bu by 9 bu in cross section, and he rough-cut the bottom to shape using the circular saw. Mr. Ando used several battens, all made of cedar. I mention this because, given how few points he used to draw the shape of planks, it would be essential to use a batten of the same size and wood species in order to replicate the curves he made. Unlike all of my other teachers (and Western practice), who bent their battens *around* nails, his battens had several well-used nail holes right through their centers for fastening them to the work.

Finally, Mr. Ando marked the midpoint between the two 6-shaku marks. He called these three points *toubun* and all the subsequent dimensions for the planking between the stem and transom would be laid out at these three locations. My teacher in Tokyo had also used the term toubun, but interestingly my teacher in Chiba had called these marks *yokozumi*, specifically, *omoteyokozumi* for the forward layout and *tomoyokozumi* for the aft layout. A researcher from Hakodate would later visit and tell us these points were called *kanaba* in Hokkaido, and that boatbuilders there referred to *omotekanaba* (forward station) and *tomokanaba* (aft station), as well as a center point called *mannakakanaba* (middle station).[14]

Mr. Ando then set the bottom plank on blocks on its side edge and, using the axe followed by the plane, he cut the two bevels on the shiki's edges. He planed the planking bevel by eye and the angle remained constant for the entire length of the bottom. The lower plank would lie against the bevel. Then he chamfered the top corner of the plank keel. This smaller, secondary bevel allows the builder to more easily work the saw through the joint when fitting the planking to the keel.

Before setting the bottom in place Mr. Ando turned it over and on the bottom face cut the joints creating the breaks at the forward and aft ends. These joints were identical tapered grooves running across the bottom of the plank and cut to a depth of 1 sun. When they were finished and the plank was turned over and blocked in place, they were 8 bu wide at the top and 4 bu wide at the bottom. On the port side the joints tapered to 4 bu wide at the top and 1 bu wide at the bottom.

The next step was to begin assembling the backbone of the boat: the transom, bottom, and stem. Large, square blocks of wood were placed under the bottom just inside the two joints. Stout poles were wedged on top of the shiki and against the overhead beams of the shop. I have heard boat-

The author and Mr. Ando setting up two stout props to hold the shiki in place. These were not removed until the boat was completely planked up. *Photo copyright Masaaki Kon.*

builders call these poles *tsuzu* (Tokyo and Urayasu) and *hari* (Gifu), but Mr. Ando had a very direct name: *tsukaibou*, literally, "use pole."

The reliance on props is just one of the major differences between Western and Japanese boatbuilding. Western boatbuilders rely much more on clamps (Mr. Ando called these *manriki*) to hold parts of the boat together, and boatbuilders in the West like to say one can never own enough of them. The use of wooden props is both ingenious and maddening. In the later stages of building a boat the workshop can become an obstacle course of poles braced against the ceiling and the floor. This setup reflects another nearly universal feature of traditional Japanese boatbuilding: almost all boats are built right side up. In the West, particularly in America, there is no standard adhered to, and even very large boats are sometimes built upside down.

Both of the main props holding the bottom in place were also marked with the heights of the sheer at the stem (3.25 shaku), the top of the transom (1.93 shaku), and the sheer at the center station (1.5 shaku). The force of the main props was so great that the bottom, over two inches thick, still bent down slightly between them. We checked the amount of this curve and found it to be 7 bu. Mr. Ando said this curve should only be about 3 bu, but rather than easing off on the prop from above he placed a small prop under the middle of the shiki to raise it slightly. The original wooden ceiling beams had been augmented by steel I-beams, and it was against these that we braced the boat.

Mr. Ando cut the joints on the bottom plank to accept the stem and the transom. At the bow this joint is called a *kama*, because the way the joint hooks the two pieces together resembles the rice farmer's sickle of the same name. After he cut the joints he clamped the base of the stem alongside. Then he pinned his inkline string to the stem height marked on the aft prop and aligned it with the same mark on the forward prop. Holding the end of the string near the top end of the rabbet joint on the stem, he pivoted the stem on the clamp so the string aligned with both marks on the props. This gave him the proper height and angle of the stem, and with the stem propped in place he traced the shape of the joint onto the side.

Mr. Ando then removed the stem and cut the matching half of the stem joint. Once both halves of the joint were roughed out he clamped them together and used the prop again to hold the stem upright. He then inserted his saw into the joint and carefully sawed through the seams, gradually removing material from both pieces. With each pass of the saw the fit of the joint improved.

While the stem assembly was still clamped together Mr. Ando went to work on the joints in the bottom where it would be bent. He had previously sawn grooves across the bottom face of the plank keel; now he made sawcuts directly above these grooves to a depth of 6 bu. As he worked, a teapot of water was heating in one corner of the work-

Taken later in the project, this photograph shows the marks on the main prop indicating the heights of the sheer, transom, and planking.

The *kama* joint between the bottom and stem. Two tapered, hardwood wedges passing through the center of the joint hold it together. The hole aft is for a stopwater, a Western technique not usually seen in traditional Japanese boatbuilding.

shop. When it was ready, he poured the boiling water over the two joints. The hot water would soften the remaining wood in the center of the plank (5 bu thick) and allow it to bend without breaking. As the wood was heated we placed props under either end of the plank keel, forcing the ends up. As the ends bent, the saw cuts closed tight. Mr. Ando would resaw the closed cuts, opening the kerf and allowing the plank ends to be raised a little bit more. He called this method *kirimage,* literally, "cut bending."

Each saw kerf only allows the plank to bend a little at a time, but given the danger of breaking the plank, working slowly was prudent. Mr. Ando continually applied pots of boiling water on the joints, making sure that each time he sawed through the kerf he did not go deeper than his original cut. When the forward end of the plank had been raised by 2 sun he stopped. The stern end was raised 4.2 sun using the same procedure.

The joint made to bend the shiki at the bow. The dovetail groove cut in the bottom is filled with a wedge, forcing the saw kerf made above it to close.

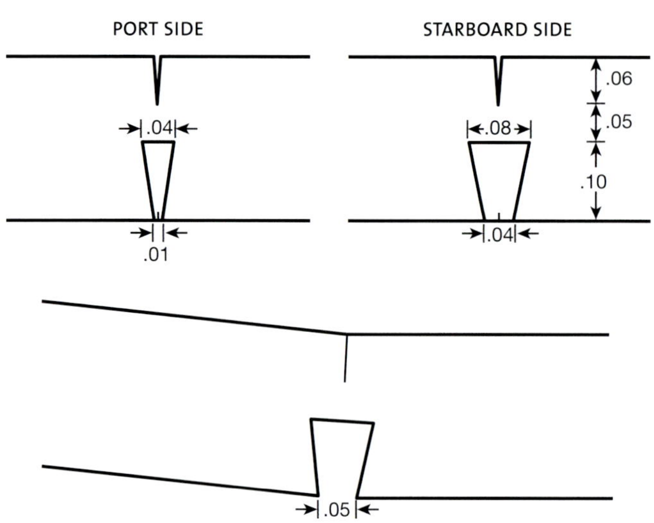

Profile view of the bottom showing the layout of the tapered dovetail cut across it in preparation for bending (top drawings, port and starboard). Once bent (bottom drawing) a tapered wedge is cut to fit the dovetail, which has widened during the bending process.

As a result of the bending, the original grooves cut underneath had opened wider and would need to be filled with special tapered wedges. Mr. Ando re-measured the size of the grooves and cut cypress wedges to fit their new shape. Before inserting the wedges, however, he laid them on the shop floor and hit their two angled faces of with his hammer. By compressing the fibers of the wood the wedges would expand inside the joint and ensure a tight fit. This, of course, is a variation on the technique called *kigoroshi,* literally, "wood killing" (see Chapter 5) and is a common practice among boatbuilders. A critical part of this technique is making the wedge slightly oversized, so that after it has been compressed it still will fit snugly into the joint. Mr. Ando also lubricated the wedges with motor oil.[15]

With the bottom now bent and solidly wedged, Mr. Ando made the final fit of the stem joint. When he was satisfied with the fit he covered the joint's surfaces using a white glue with the brand name Bondo, which he later used in the seams of our planking. He said he used lacquer when building boats long ago but it had always been one of the most expensive materials.[16] He was using Bondo for the first time on our shimaihagi.

Two small tapered wedges of hiba were driven in from opposite sides to hold the stem joint together. Mr. Ando used the same kigoroshi technique on them, and they too were lubricated with motor oil. He later drilled and fastened a vertical bolt through this joint. This was a modern addition on his part, as the vast majority of traditional boats do not supplement this type of joinery with mechanical fastenings. A narrow board was then used to brace the top of the stem to one of the overhead beams of the shop.

With the stem completely fastened, Mr. Ando inserted a dowel into a 4-bu diameter hole drilled horizontally across the back corner of the joint. In English this is called a stopwater, after its purpose—to stop any water from leaking in through the joint. Mr. Ando called it *akadomesen*, and made it out of hiba using his axe and plane, compressing the sides of the dowel with his hammer before driving it into the hole. Western boatbuilders make these dowels out of a softwood such as cedar, so that the plug will swell faster than the wood around it.[17] They also place their stopwaters in a slightly different location—where the joint in the keel and the rabbet intersect—to stop water leaking through both seams. Mr. Ando told me his boss had taught him this technique. The only other boatbuilder I knew to do anything similar was my teacher from Urayasu, who put four sheets of newspaper in the aft vertical face of this joint.[18]

Transom

Mr. Ando cut the transom to shape using dimensions from memory. He left extra material on the sides because he would later bevel these edges to match the angle of the planking. The transom is narrower at the top than at the corner where the two side planks meet. This shape, called tumblehome, is not uncommon; Mr. Ando called it *uchikaburi* while I have also heard it called *kaeru*, meaning "to return home."[19]

Mr. Ando laid out the tumblehome in precisely the same manner Mr. Udagawa did in Urayasu: he squared down from the top edge of the transom and lined up the outside edge of his square with the corner where the two planks meet at the chine. He drew a mark on the inside edge of the square at the top edge of both sides of the transom. Because the legs of the squares are 5 bu wide this created an automatic deduction of 1 sun overall. Like all the boatbuilders I have worked with, he used the width of the square in this way to layout tapers and angles throughout the boatbuilding process. The method is quick and consistent, and frees the boatbuilder from memorizing numerous dimensions.

Mr. Ando cut a right-angle rabbet joint at the end of the plank keel. Because the transom leans back, he beveled the base of the transom to create a matching right angle to fit the joint. He employed an interesting and widely used technique to precisely set the angle of the transom. He first made a mark precisely 1 shaku down from the top of the transom on the outside. Then he pinned the string from his inkline to the top of the transom and hitched the string around the handle so it would hang below the mark like a plumb bob. Once the string was steady he measured horizontally from the string to the mark. He adjusted the transom until the horizontal measurement was 6 sun, and then I nailed a brace into the plank keel, temporarily holding it until the planking was completed.

Mr. Ando ran his saw through the two faces of the joint connecting the transom until the fit was right, made three nail holes and mortises, and nailed the transom into the plank keel.

Lower Planks

Mr. Ando called the first pair of planks on either side of the bottom *shitadana* (bottom shelf). This was the first time I had heard this term, as my teachers in Tokyo and Urayasu, along with most boatbuilders I have interviewed, called this plank the *kajiki*. Before setting the lower plank in place Mr. Ando marked the edge of the bottom with the locations of all the nails. The nail holes were evenly spaced about 6.5 sun apart, although toward the bow the spacing narrowed to about 5 sun. He made sure the nails were placed so that the joints in the bottom lay evenly in the middle of the 6.5-sun spacing. Some nail locations had to be slightly adjusted to avoid knots and no nail was closer than 2 sun to the stem or transom.

The rough-sawn material for the planking was 9 bu thick and Mr. Ando laid one edge against the plank keel, placed props underneath, and held the plank in place with a large, temporary staple. Sometimes called "dogs" in English and generally known as *kasugai* in Japanese, he called them *tsukami*. They were homemade fastenings forged out of rough metal rod, 3 bu thick, with bent corners and square points forged at their ends. The legs of the dogs are spread apart slightly, so that as they are driven into the wood they pull the two pieces together. Props from the ceiling were used to

The rabbet joint across the end of the shiki for the transom.

Mr. Ando fitting the transom in a rabbet cut across the end of the keel plank by running a saw through the joint. Even a joint as straightforward as this is sawn in order to create a better fit.

Patterns used to set the angle of the lower planks. Dating from the early 1960s, only Mr. Ando knew which boats they were used for.

Rough beveling the planking with an axe. Sometimes Mr. Ando held the axe blade with both hands and pushed it across the work. *Photo copyright Masaaki Kon.*

adjust the angle of the plank. More props held the plank up tight against the transom, but Mr. Ando had to clamp a bar across the plank at the stern and then put a prop under it in order to give the plank enough twist. It was impossible to twist the plank so that it lay alongside the stem; that would have required a twist of nearly ninety degrees. Instead, Mr. Ando twisted it about one-third of the way and nailed a thin piece of plywood 4 sun wide to the forward end of the plank. He roughly cut a curve in the end of this plywood piece to fit the stem rabbet, and then bent the forward end of the plywood to fit it into the rabbet. He called this short spiling plank a *zuchigata*, unlike my other teachers, who called it a *kataita*, a "pattern plank."

Mr. Ando used other patterns to set the angles of the lower plank at the middle of the boat. He had made these many years earlier and they consisted of two narrow pieces of wood cleated together to form the proper angles. One leg of the pattern lay against the bottom while the other lay against the first plank. They were labeled with the date (in this case May 3, 1962), Mr. Ando's name, and boat dimensions. There were only two patterns, one for the forward station and the other for the middle and aft stations. As he checked the angle of the lower plank I adjusted the props. The labels on these patterns had meaning only for Mr. Ando; they would be useless to anyone else.[20]

With the lower plank fixed in place at the proper angle Mr. Ando transferred the marks he had made for the nail locations on the bottom to the edge of the plank. The plank material still had the rough edge from the sawmill, so in order to trace the shape of the shiki onto the lower edge of the plank he had to determine how much wood to remove at the edge of the plank. The dimension Mr. Ando used had to be larger than any gaps between the plank and the edge of the plank keel. He also wanted to avoid any bad wood at the plank edge. In this case a measurement of 1.3 sun was adequate, and he used his square to make a series of marks along the plank this distance from the beveled edge of the plank keel. He also carefully measured distances from the points along the stem rabbet to reference points he made on the spiling plank. Finally, he traced the location of the transom directly onto the planking stock.

At this point Mr. Ando had all the information he needed to draw the entire bottom edge of the lower plank—along the stem rabbet, the edge of the bottom, and the transom. With the plank laid flat, he transferred his reference points from the spiling plank to the plank itself. By connecting these points he drew the curve where the forward end of the plank met the rabbet. He also laid his stem pattern on the planking stock in order to help draw this curve. Mr. Ando used his batten to connect all the points he had measured from the edge of the bottom and, using his circular saw, he cut to this line. Now that the plank had a square edge he placed his plank angle patterns back on the bottom and recorded the angle between the pattern and the edge of the bottom where the lower plank would lie with a bevel gauge, a tool he called a *jiyuugane*. He recorded this angle at the three station marks and the transom mark.

With the angles transferred to the plank at these points he used his axe and plane to bevel the plank edge, including along the stem. Mr. Ando swung the axe using very short strokes, but he occasionally held the blade with both hands and pushed it. The final step in beveling the plank was removing the sharp edge left along the bottom. He planed this small chamfer by eye.

Next Mr. Ando laid out the top edge of the plank. He had the dimensions memorized for the width of the plank at each station: 1.35 shaku wide at the forward and middle stations, and 1.15 shaku wide at the aft station. He measured and marked these locations along with the widths at the transom and the height at the stem rabbet. He drew a straight line from the forward hood end to his mark at the first station. Midway along this line he made a mark 1.8 sun further out. Mr. Ando then bent his batten on these six points, but before drawing the line at the very aft end of the plank past the transom he sprung the batten out (wider) by 1 sun. He specifically called this his secret, which I understood as an innovation of his own and not something he had learned from another boatbuilder. The effect on the boat would be to make the top edge of the lower plank flare out a bit at the stern. The top edge of the plank was then cut.

With one lower plank cut to shape, Mr. Ando laid it on the other piece of planking stock and traced out the shape on the other plank. I noticed later that the grain orientation of the two planks was different: on one the heart side of the wood faced inside the boat while on the opposite plank it faced outside. I also noticed that Mr. Ando had oriented the grain of the bottom so the heart side of the wood faced the inside of the boat.

Up to this point we had been working with rough-sawn planking. It was now time to plane the faces of the plank smooth. In order not to lose the nail locations that were marked in ink, Mr. Ando took a small chisel and made a mark at each nail to a depth of about 1 bu, so that these marks would remain after the plank was planed. He first stacked the two planks flat on the low beams on the shop floor. He used a hand-held electric plane, turning them over together to plane their outside faces first. I finished them with a hand plane. He then reversed the planks and planed the two inside faces. We removed just enough material on the faces of the planks with the electric plane to eliminate the marks made by the sawmill. The hand plane removed paper-thin shavings to obtain the final finish.

Woodworkers take particular pride in their skills with a plane, and frequently sharpen the blade. Mr. Ando insisted I sharpen my plane as soon as I finished each plank face. As his apprentice, I also did almost all of Mr. Ando's sharpening. In every account of Japanese apprenticeships I have read, this seems standard; after keeping the shop clean the apprentice's first duty is learning how to sharpen the tools. There were times when Mr. Ando and I would be working in a relay; just as I handed him a freshly sharpened tool he would be ready to have me sharpen the tool he had been using.

The only other preparation for the shiki and the planking was drilling out any problematic knots in the wood. Mr. Ando knew from experience that large knots could loosen from the surrounding wood and create leaks. He didn't chisel and fit square plugs like my earlier teachers. He had three drill bits for plug diameters: 4 bu, 8 bu, and 1 sun. He also had a selection of homemade dowels left in his shop for twenty years that were slightly thicker than the drills. He proceeded to drill out the knots, carefully checking both sides of the plank to follow the angle of the knot. He used the kigoroshi technique, laying the dowels on a block of wood and rolling them while pounding their sides before driving them hard into the holes. He used no glue and said there was no need to orient the grain of the dowel in any particular way. Once

The author planing a plank while Mr. Ando adjusts a hand plane. All this work was done on low blocks laid on the shop's concrete floor; there were no workbenches. *Photo copyright Masaaki Kon.*

inserted, he cut off the excess and planed the plugs smooth to the surface of the plank. A few days later Mr. Ando had me cover these plugs with a puddle of white glue.

Two places in the shiki had splits and signs of rot, so Mr. Ando chiseled out two mortises to remove all the decayed material. He then cut two pieces of cedar to size and pounded their edges before inserting them with glue. These too were planed flush. With the backbone of the boat now complete, Mr. Ando conducted a very short, private keel-laying ceremony. He placed two small candles on the center of the shiki along with a small dish of salt and two small glasses. He poured a bit of sake directly on the keel and filled the two glasses. The salt was for purification and the sake was a gift to the *kami,* or spirits. After a moment of quiet prayer he picked up the glasses and handed one to me. We drank the sake so it wouldn't go to waste.[21]

The author steadies a plank while Mr. Ando chisels a nail hole. He works from the inside face of the bevel to the outside of the plank. *Photo copyright Masaaki Kon.*

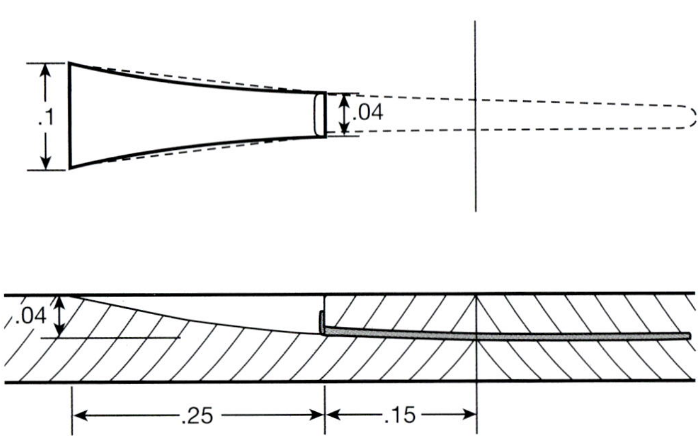

Mr. Ando's layout for edge-nailing. One slight difference between his technique and those of my other teachers was his preference for cutting slightly convex edges for the mortise, leaving the bottom edges of the mortise straight. The mortise has a half-dovetail shape in cross section, and the plugs are driven in without glue.

Making Nail Holes

As mentioned earlier, nail holes are not made with a drill but with a special chisel called a *tsubanomi.* It is a two-step process: a hole is made in the lower plank, and once that plank is propped back into place another chisel is sent through the plank hole to pilot the edge of the keel (see Chapter 4). Because the lower plank angle changes throughout the length of the boat, standing nearly vertical at the stem to running almost flat amidships, the initial holes must be carefully chiseled at the correct angles. Mr. Ando drove the tsubanomi from the face of the bevel toward the outboard face of the plank (opposite the direction the nail is driven), starting from a mark on the inside face of the bevel 4 bu from the top edge. He wanted the nail holes amidship to emerge at a point 1.5 sun up from the edge.

We did most of this work with the plank set up on edge. Boatbuilders often work with the planks set up this way, setting the bottom edge into a pair of U-shaped hardwood blocks placed on the floor (Mr. Ando called these *hasamu*). The plank is thinner than the cutout in the block, and a wedge driven into this gap to hold the plank upright.

Sending the tsubanomi through the plank at the right point is simply a matter of practice. Mr. Ando also rocked the tsubanomi slightly while driving it through the plank in order to create a larger hole matching the size of the nail shank. He would frequently dip the end of the tsubanomi in oil so it would drive through the wood more easily. He changed the angle slightly toward the bow so the chisel would emerge a bit closer to the plank edge. One must chisel the hole just right: too loose and it won't be watertight; too tight and one risks splitting the plank with the nail. We checked this by pushing the nail by hand through the hole in the lower plank. In the bottom plank the hole should be a tight fit, but not *too* tight. Furthermore, if the pilot hole is too shallow the nail may bend, too deep and the nail will not hold. In general, the depth of the hole made by the tsubanomi in both pieces of wood is about 85 percent of the nail length.

A small mortise was required where each nail hole exited the plank face. Mr. Ando used a chisel 1 sun wide to make this mortise, which was triangular in cross section and just 3 bu deep. He did not make any mortises in the area along the stem because, as he explained, when we bent the plank there would be a danger of it splitting at these points. These mortises were cut later after pre-bending the first planks.

Bending the Planks

We would again use the Asian technique of bending the planks with fire (see also Chapter 11). In Japan, the ideal material for boatbuilding is wood that has been air-dried for one year, and thus retains a significant amount of moisture. This moisture is critical to the bending process, because it is not simply heat that makes the wood pliable. The cellular structure of air-dried wood is still flexible and the moisture within the wood transfers the heat quickly. When done properly, the heated fibers stretch on the outside of the bend, and compress on the inside of the bend without fracturing. In addition, certain species of wood bend better than others. Both of Japan's traditional boatbuilding woods, cedar and cypress, have good bending properties.

Mr. Ando set up a horizontal beam 2.5 shaku above the shop floor and near the shop doors for good ventilation. The two lower planks we had just finished were laid on top of this beam with their bottom edges facing each other. Mr. Ando raised the outer edges by slipping a small piece of wood 5 bu thick between the planks and the beam. These blocks actually twisted the planks in the opposite direction Mr. Ando would be bending them, thus increasing the amount of overall twist. He clamped strong wooden timbers at the forward edges of the planks. They were then through-bolted in pairs like scissors, overhanging at one end and held with rope at the other. Mr. Ando called these bars *nejiribou*, or "twist bars." They gave us a place to brace our props for bending and also spread the load, since the outermost corners of the planks would be too fragile to push against. Two narrow scrap boards were placed under them at the top edge of the planks to keep them from scarring the wood.

Props were placed under the inside edges of the bending bars to hold them level with the beam. We would twist the planks by pushing against the long ends of these bars, forcing the tips of the planks down toward the floor. Before we began Mr. Ando checked old photographs of his shop to compare our setup with the way he had done it years before. Once he confirmed we had it correct it was time to apply heat.

Mr. Ando used charcoal for fuel and placed it in two half-sections of a steel barrel on the shop floor directly underneath the planks. Once the fire was hot he began pouring boiling water on top of the planks. As soon as he had soaked the planks he used his props on the end of the bending bars to force the corners of each plank down. He repeated this about five times, adjusting the props to increase the twist, all the while continuing to soak them with boiling water. He gauged the amount of twist by eye. To achieve the desired amount of bend took over two hours. He splashed water on the underside of the planks a few times as a precaution to ensure the heat from the charcoal fire did not char them.

In Tokyo, Mr. Fujiwara and I had been forced to do our plank bending outside due to the smoke from our wood fire. Mr. Fujiwara also took careful measurements of the curvature as we bent the planks, and in this way he knew when to stop. For Mr. Ando it was all done by intuition. His use of charcoal also allowed for more control of the heat and less smoke.

Mortise for the nail head in the bottom plank, showing the rectangular pilot hole for the nail shank. These mortises would later be filled with putty.

The bending process. Bars spread the load across the entire width of the plank. The twist is achieved by propping the bars against the shop ceiling. The process is slow, taking several hours. *Photo copyright Masaaki Kon.*

The two planks remained propped in place until the next morning, and when released sprang back just slightly. Mr. Ando then cut the remaining mortises for the nail holes at the stem. We hung one of the planks on the boat, again using the dogs and props to hold the plank in place against the stem, bottom, and transom. With the end of the plank now curved up to the stem Mr. Ando could see it was too long and he pressed it against the rabbet, marked it, and used the stem pattern to draw a new curve. He then transferred the same curve to the other plank still lying on the shop floor. We took the one plank off the boat, re-cut the curve on both planks, and re-planed the bevels.

Both planks were then propped in place on the boat. Mr. Ando used a single dog at the stem to hold the two ends together; he later replaced this with a clamp. At the stern he clamped bending bars around the two plank ends just behind the transom and with props under the ends of the bars he was able to twist the planks to match the angle of the transom. He then looped rope around the aft ends of the planks. He inserted a stick in the center of the loop and began twisting the rope, pulling the two planks tight against the transom. I never thought to ask Mr. Ando if he had a name for this method of clamping; Western boatbuilders call it a "Spanish windlass."

With both planks now in place Mr. Ando rechecked the angles of the planks at the stations using his patterns, moving the props as necessary to adjust them. At this point I noticed the fit between the plank and the bottom was generally good, except in the area between the stem and the forward station. There the two bevels did not match and there was a wide gap underneath. This would not be a problem, however, as the next technique Mr. Ando used would make the plank fit perfectly.

Fitting the Seams

Mr. Ando did not call the saw fitting technique *suriawase* or *surinoko* (see Chapter 5), rather *toosunoko, toosu* meaning "to pierce."[22] He had two of the special saws for this; the larger he called *oonoko* and the smaller he called *konoko,* or "big saw" and "little saw." He initially took the large-toothed saw and inserted it into the seam between the lower plank and the plank keel. He began sawing through this seam, moving down the length of the boat.

Despite my previous training Mr. Ando insisted on doing almost all this work himself. Of all my apprenticeships the shimaihagi was the boat on which I did the least amount of direct work. This is not to say I wasn't busy; I was constantly on call to set props, tighten clamps, carry materials, and to fetch and sharpen tools. As in all of my projects I was also writing notes, making sketches, taking photographs, and shooting videos. If Mr. Ando did ninety percent of the direct work on the boat I did ninety percent of the tool sharpening (and all of the cleaning); in all of my other apprenticeships my teachers sharpened their own tools and left me to sharpen mine.

The only other person active in the workshop was Mrs. Ando, who brought in a tray of food and tea every morning and afternoon. She sometimes stopped in at the end of the day and if she found me cleaning she immediately began to help. If Mrs. Ando was busy she would send her daughter-in-law with our food and tea. Mr. Ando's son worked as a local house carpenter and while he occasionally looked in

Mr. Ando beginning to fit the first plank with his saw. Note the props holding the plank from above, below, and to the side.

on our work I noticed he never actually stepped inside the shop.

The shop space was clearly Mr. Ando's territory, and the only people who seemed to feel comfortable there were his wife, his little granddaughter and her friends, and the boatbuilder's old customers and their wives. The children came in giggling after school and the retired fishermen would stand or squat, smoking cigarettes and watching us work. One elderly woman told me she enjoyed hearing the sounds of boatbuilding again in the neighborhood. The shop's large, open door faced directly onto the main road, and often vehicles would slow down or stop to see our boat taking shape.

A few businesses from larger towns nearby would send trucks laden with goods to sell in Shiranuka. The drivers would broadcast long, sonorous advertisements for their wares through loudspeakers mounted on the truck roofs, a traditional way of marketing to remote villages. Twice a week a truck from a vegetable store would descend the hill toward the shop at about walking speed, driven by an old man singing over and over in the most bored tone imaginable, "*Hana wa go-hyaku en*" (Flowers, five hundred yen).

One day I decided to videotape this ritual, which is fast disappearing even in rural Japan, and I stepped outside the shop to film the vendor's slow progress toward me. I was swinging the camera as he passed, but he stopped broadcasting abreast of the shop and looked at me. With his mouth still to the microphone, he stared at me and asked, "Did I see you on television last night?" I nodded. We had a short conversation about the project, his half of which was broadcast throughout the neighborhood.

Beyond the sawing itself, the way the planks are propped is crucial to toosunoko. If the planks are pinched too tightly together the saw can bind in the seam. Mr. Ando cut chamfers on the edges of the plank keel, transom, and bottom plank to make it easier to insert the saw. It is also important to carefully gauge the angle of the seam; the saw can begin to wander and easily cut into the corner of the plank or keel. Mr. Ando used oak wedges to hold the joint open just the right distance. As he sawed down a seam he moved the wedges ahead of his work. Once he had completed a pass he would tap the planks very lightly to close the gap and start again.

Mr. Ando initially used the standard up-and-down sawing motion in the seam. Because the saw cuts most effectively this way he moved very quickly down the seam at the start, and the gaps I saw earlier disappeared after he had made just a few passes over the length of the boat. He did

Two local women were daily visitors to our shop, which was right on the main street through town.

Working and retired fishermen, many of them Mr. Ando's former customers, were frequent visitors to the shop. Here a crowd watches Mr. Ando carve the rub rail.

Fitting the first planks, with Mr. Ando working the fit in the back of the stem rabbet. *Photo copyright Catherine Wood Brooks.*

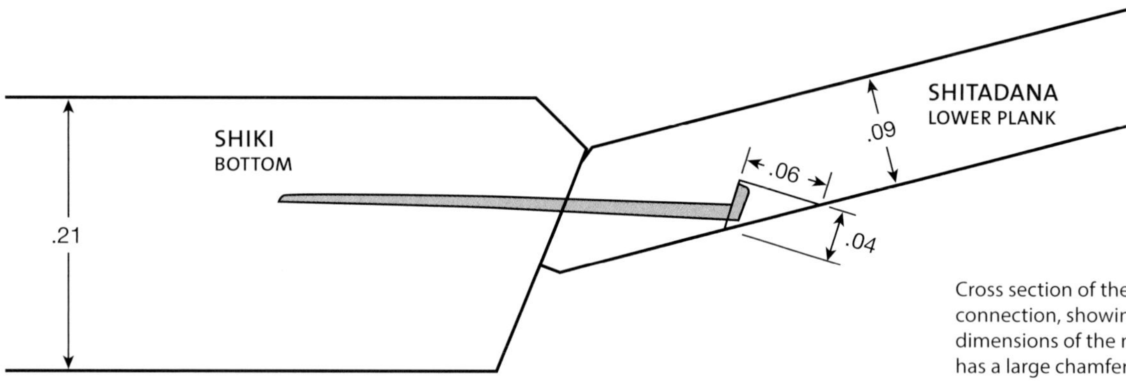

Cross section of the bottom and lower plank connection, showing the plank bevel and the dimensions of the nail mortise. The bottom has a large chamfer along the outer edge.

most of the work with his large saw. It was only on the final pass that he used the small-toothed saw, with a forward-and-back motion. He also did toosunoko along the stem rabbet. He did all this work from inside the boat, except when fitting the outside seam of the stem rabbet, where he used just the tip of his smaller saw to rub the seam around the curve. Where the boatbuilder positions himself is really a matter of comfort; toosunoko can be done from either outside or inside the boat.[23]

At one point I was helping to saw the seam for the first plank and noticed my saw had wandered out of the seam and cut into the plank keel. I pointed out my error to Mr. Ando, knowing that mistakes were not tolerated. More than once my working on the boat ended abruptly when he saw something he wasn't satisfied with. At these times, the mood in the shop would go dark, visitors might leave, and we would work in silence for the next hour or more.

When Mr. Ando finished with the seam, he took out some of the props at the stern and we let the plank ends drop away from the transom. He needed to plane the proper angle on the transom where the lower plank met it. This he did by eye, looking down the blade of his square while holding it against the bottom edge of the transom. Once he had lined up his square with the slope of the plank he marked the angle. He then raised this mark on the back of the transom by 2 bu and planed the bevel to this line. He told me this puts a bit more slope in the rise of the plank aft. He noted that older shimaihagi always had this extra slope because it improved their speed when rowing.

After the introduction of the outboard motor, the shimaihagi underwent several changes. The greatest impact motors had on the boat design was in the stern; the transom had to be strengthened to mount the motor, and the bottom planking aft had to be flatter so that the stern would not squat at high speed.

Fastening the Planks

Mr. Ando fitted and completely nailed one of the lower planks before fitting and nailing the other. He began by carefully pulling the stern props, opening a small space in the seam. He spread some of his Bondo glue on a board and applied it to the seam with a small piece of bamboo with a sharpened point, a tool he called a *hira*. He worked the entire length of the seam, carefully loosening a section of the plank and applying glue. He also put glue where the plank would meet the transom, but none in the stem rabbet.

Mr. Ando began nailing the lower plank to the bottom from a point near the forward station, moving toward the stem. He would insert his tsubanomi in the plank's nail hole and then hammer it into the plank keel. He used 3.5-sun nails but did not drive the tsubanomi quite that far. The heads of these nails were bent at ninety degrees to the shaft and all the nails along the lower plank were oriented with the heads pointing up. As before, he often dipped the point of his tsubanomi in oil while he worked, and he oiled every nail. He also used a prop with a wedge under the plank edge at each nail, moving it as he worked. Because of the angle of the bevel, the plank would tend to pull down as the nail was set. The prop supported the plank edge so it didn't move. He initially drove the nails with just his hammer but in order to set the heads in the mortise the final blows were struck using the hammer and a nail set.

Mr. Ando used shorter nails, 2.5 sun, along the stem and for the very last nail at the top of the stem rabbet he used a modern wire nail.[24] All of the remaining nails aft were 4 sun. Up to this point all the nails had been straight, but as he moved back to his starting point and began to nail aft he put a slight curve in each nail before driving it. He did this by laying the nail on the shop floor so it rested on the end of the head and the tip. A single tap from his hammer, about 1 sun below the head, put a slight bend in the shaft. Because the nails enter the bottom at a slight angle there is a danger they can come through the top face. The curve is meant to keep the nail from doing this. Sometimes, as the nail head approaches the plank, the bend in the shaft is too great and will act like a wedge, splitting it at the nail hole. Mr. Ando would hit these nails from below to straighten them out, and then finish hammering them in.

Moving aft, Mr. Ando worked in sections, first skipping five nail spaces and putting in one nail; he then set the remaining four nails in the space. He worked like this until the plank was nailed all the way to the transom. At the stern he drilled two holes for each side, straight down through the forward face of the transom and at right angles to the planking; he then bolted the planks to the transom, the heads to the outside of the planking, the nuts against the inside face of the transom. Like the joint at the stem, the use of bolts to fasten the lower planks to the transom is a modern innovation. In traditional boats this connection would have been nailed.

After fastening both planks, Mr. Ando again checked the angles at his stations. He also laid his measuring stick across the tops of the two planks, at right angles to the centerline of the boat. He put his level on top and checked to see if the two plank edges were at the same height. He repeated his secret of adding 1 sun to the width of the planks at the aft ends. With the two planks now fastened it was obvious how this extra material gave the lower planks a little bit of flare.

Mr. Ando adjusted his props where necessary to make sure everything was even (although the planks were nailed he was still able to adjust their outer edges a bit). He used his axe and plane to put a bevel on the outside edge of the lower plank where the top plank would meet it. This bevel was roughly vertical except for forward of the first station where he angled it toward the inside. Mr. Ando didn't measure or lay this out in any way; he shaped it by eye. When these bevels were finished he made a very tiny chamfer on the top corner of the edge of the planks; this was to make it easier to insert the saw later when fitting the top planks. He also noticed that the hood ends of the two planks were uneven at the stem; using his chisel, he cut material off the higher one to make them match.

Before we finished for the day Mr. Ando found some squared pieces of hiba in his shop and using his axe made small plugs with four-sided points. These roughly matched the holes left by the dogs and Mr. Ando had me use them to fill the holes. I hammered them in the holes (with no glue) and sawed them flush.

Top Planks

Mr. Ando called the top planks (known as sheer planks in the West) *uwadana,* which means "upper shelf." The planking stock was rough-sawn cedar varying between 9 bu and 1 sun thick, measuring 28 shaku long and 2.5 shaku wide at the butt (widest) end. Mr. Ando began laying out the nail spacing by marking the edges of the lower planks. He used the transom as a starting point, first making a mark for nails 3.5 sun to either side. He then marked nail locations every 7 sun, narrowing the spacing to 6 to 6.5 sun from the forward station to the bow. As before he adjusted spacing to avoid knots in the lower planks and he kept his last nail 3 sun away from the stem. He used his tsubanomi to make a hole at all these nail locations, driving it straight into the plank, parallel to their faces, and square to the edges.

Mr. Ando checks the level of the two planks. His angle pattern is visible at his feet and the bolts fastening the planks to the transom are visible behind him.

Chiseling the pilot holes in the plank edges. Mr. Ando cut them all in line with the face of the plank.

The sheer planks were oriented so that the butt ends were at the stern of the boat. We lifted the first top plank alongside the boat and Mr. Ando set props underneath its lower edge. He used a dog to fasten the top of the plank to the top of the transom, and a clamp to hold the plank at the stem. The planks stood nearly vertical over their entire length.

At this point the planks still needed to be twisted in along the bottom edge to meet the transom and the stem. Mr. Ando first hung his inkline from the top edge in order to set the plank angle. Using the same method he employed in setting the transom, he measured horizontally across the gap from the hanging line to a point 1 shaku below where the string was fastened. He wanted the distance to be 2.2 sun at the forward station; at the aft station the slope was supposed to be 9 bu, or almost vertical.

He then went back to the transom and the stem, pushing the bottom of the plank in at each place and rechecking the angles at the stations. It was a slow process. He explained that he did not want to simply set the angle by propping the top edge from the ceiling (which would be much easier, and how he had adjusted the edges of the bottom planks); instead, he said, it was better to manipulate the plank only along the edges where it met other timbers: the transom, lower planking, and stem. Similar to Western boatbuilders avoiding edge-setting, he was trying to get the plank to lie in the most natural curve possible at the angles he wanted.

When he was satisfied with how the plank hung, Mr. Ando transferred the nail location from the lower plank to the upper plank and traced along the top edge of the lower plank, the back of the stem, and both sides of the transom. He called his method of tracing and the plank he used *jikigata*.[25] I noticed this plank had the heart side of the wood facing the outside and I gingerly asked Mr. Ando about this practice, and why the grain orientation of the lower planks did not match each other. He said that although a boatbuilder should use the heart side out if possible, he did not believe that it was absolutely necessary.[26]

Once again the widths of the top plank were marked from memory. Before removing the plank from the boat to cut it to shape Mr. Ando marked the location of his stations and transom on the bottom edge of the plank. On the inside face of the transom he measured up the transom's centerline 1.84 shaku. He then squared over from that point to the top plank and made a mark. He also marked two additional points on the bottom edge of the plank: one 4.4 shaku forward of the forward station, and one where the plank met the base of the stem. He laid one leg of his square on his traced line at each point and marked several heights (see table at left) squaring off his line at each point. These marks represented the distance from the bottom to the top edge of the upper plank.

The rough sheer plank stock, still with its bark edges, propped in place so its final shape can be traced. Mr. Ando had offsets memorized for the width of the plank at each station.

Mr. Ando transferring nail locations from the bottom to the top plank.

Distance from Bottom to Top Edge of Upper Plank	
Base of stem	1.55 shaku
4.4 shaku forward of first station	1.5 shaku
Forward station	1.45 shaku
Middle station	1.4 shaku
Aft station	1.35 shaku
Height at inside of transom	1.84 shaku (measured up centerline of transom) height squared over to plank

Next Mr. Ando used his inkline to strike a straight line on the plank from the height at the aft station through the height at the transom and extending several shaku aft. The distance between the station point and the transom point was 7.13 shaku. At the center between these points—which he did not measure, but determined by eye—he made a mark 1 sun below the line. At a point 1.5 shaku aft of the transom point—measured—he made a mark 1 sun above the line.

The batten Mr. Ando used to connect all these points measured 7 bu by 9 bu. It was a different batten than the one he had used earlier, but I neglected to ask the reason for the change. He laid the batten on the flat (the 9 bu face) and bent it around nails set temporarily at all his marks. Where he had traced the back of the stem he added 1.2 sun to the line to account for the depth of the rabbet and he used the back edge of his stem pattern again to help draw this curve. He also added to the line he traced off the lower plank. Because this was traced from the top edge of the plank, he needed to add the equivalent of the face of the lower plank bevel.

Once Mr. Ando had these points marked, it was clear that the plank needed more material at the forward and aft top edges in order to accommodate the sweep. From scrap material he cut two long triangular-shaped pieces to add to the planks. He sawed straight edges on the top plank where these pieces would be attached. Working on beams laid on the shop floor, he brought the pieces together and braced them in place from overhead. He used toosunoko to fit the seams tightly. These small pieces were edge-nailed to the main body of the planks. In this case, however, he cut a long mortise half the depth of the plank. He used his tsubanomi, working from the plank edge, to make a nail hole to meet this mortise.

Mr. Ando then lined the pieces up, inserted a curved tsubanomi into the mortise and through the nail hole, and hammered it into the adjacent plank. He glued this seam before nailing the pieces on with small-headed nails. He cut the sides of the mortise to slope away; therefore his plugs, made of hiba, had angled sides. Once driven into place they wedged into the mortise like a dovetail. One important detail: Mr. Ando nailed these pieces to the upper planks so the nail heads and plugs were on the inside of the boat.

The planks were then cut to their final shape, and Mr. Ando planed a pair of bevels on the forward edges for the stem rabbet. These bevels he measured, but he also beveled the edge of the forward end of the plank where it would meet the lower plank back to about the forward station. The

Using the stem pattern to draw the forward edge of the top plank. This pattern was decades old. Note the triangular piece of wood edge-fastened to the plank to make up for the sweep in the sheer.

Adding material to the aft end of the sheer plank. Note the location of the transom marked on the plank.

Plug for a nail mortise. The two sides angle like a dovetail so no glue is required to hold them in place.

The nailed batten ready to mark the top edge. Note how the nails pass through the batten, a technique I had never seen.

Fitting the top plank.

Working in tight quarters near the bow. My teachers have told me that a nice, even line of sawdust indicates proper toosunoko technique. *Photo copyright Masaaki Kon.*

rest of the plank retained its square-cut (right angle) edge. Even though he had recorded the nail locations on the plank when it was hanging on the boat, he still took a batten and tacked it to the edge of the lower plank. He marked the nail locations on this batten and then used it to lay out nail locations on the top plank, marking these with a chisel.

Starting at the corner of the plank where it met the base of the stem, Mr. Ando used his tsubanomi to make the nail holes. He rocked the tsubanomi back and forth slightly as he hammered it to widen each hole a little. The plank was laid across beams on the shop floor, outside facing down, and he chiseled the first holes at a very steep angle. As he moved aft the angle gradually moved upward, approaching forty-five degrees at the first station and nearly ninety degrees at the center station. Remarkably, he adjusted these angles by eye, without taking measurements or using any pattern.

When the first plank was completed he placed it on the planking stock and traced the shape of the other plank. It was finished in the same manner as the first, adding pieces at either end to increase the width, beveling the edges, and making the nail holes. When both planks were finished Mr. Ando laid them back to back, their inside faces together, and laid them on the beams. Just as with the lower planks, he first planed their faces with a hand-held electric plane, and I finished them with a hand plane. Once the planks were planed smooth he chiseled the nail head mortises at each nail hole. These were the same shape as the mortises he cut in the lower plank.

In preparation for hanging the planks on the boat, Mr. Ando nailed a small piece of wood to the top edges at the forward end of each plank. These blocks were meant to prevent the props, dogs, or clamps from scarring the edge of the planks. We stacked blocks of wood to support the aft end of the planks and once again used dogs to fasten the planks to the top of the transom; dogs and a clamp were used at the stem. With the ends fastened in this way, he installed props horizontally, braced between the side walls of the shop and lower edge of the plank. He checked the height of the plank, and installed a vertical prop to the shop ceiling to push the plank down to its proper height. Once this was set he placed a prop under the plank to lock it in place. Using his inkline like a plumb bob he then rechecked the plank angles at the two stations. At the forward station the horizontal measurement from the line to the plank was about 2.25 sun; aft it was .9 sun.

Mr. Ando used toosunoko to fit the planks. He sawed briefly from inside the boat for the stem rabbet and then took his smallest saw and rubbed down the rabbet seam from the outside. Except for the brief work at the stem he did toosunoko standing outside the boat on a staging plank, always working from above the seam.

Mr. Ando marked the wall where the props were set. With the two top planks blocked in place he drove one nail amidships to fasten the top plank to the bottom plank. We then removed some of the horizontal props so he could move the plank away enough to put glue on the seam. His prior wall marks allowed him to set the props back in their original locations. Because there was still a lot of pressure holding the plank on the boat, he had to use his oak wedges to open the seam. He spread the glue from amidships forward and then replaced the props in this section.

Mr. Ando then nailed the stem, using six of the smallest nails (2.5 sun). Starting at the forward end, he switched to longer nails (3.7 sun), to fasten into the lower plank. His used a leapfrog pattern as he worked aft, skipping one nail and then coming back to the spot he skipped, then skipping another nail, and so on.

Mr. Ando had used props on the lower plank to support the plank edge while he nailed. He did not do this with the upper plank; instead he drove his caulking iron (*yatoko*), a small wood-handled tool with a flat metal blade, into the inside face of the plank right at the bevel on the lower plank. I held the handle of the caulking iron so he could drive the nails without the upper plank dropping.[27]

Mr. Ando had a habit of shouting *"Umai!"* when he finished a task, an adjective meaning skillful, or expert, and he always sang out this self-praise with gusto. He was remarkably skilled, and when I was feeling charitable it struck me as amusing; however, when I felt under his heel it could be grating. The day we nailed the planking was not a good one for me. While I struggled to support the planks with the caulking iron, I took a bit of pleasure in loudly pointing out to him when some of the nail points came out through the face of the planking: *"Machigaimashita!"* (You made a mistake!). He would put his tools down and peer under the boat to see where the nail came through. After this kind of exchange we would work in silence for an hour or so.

These mistakes had to be corrected by pulling out the nails and resetting them. Mr. Ando used the same technique all my teachers used to remove a nail. He first placed the tip of his tsubanomi on the nail end and, using the chisel like a nail set, drove it back out slightly. Once he had enough room, he placed the nail set against the head and drove the nail back a bit further. When the head of the nail was backed out, he used a large dog to hook it and pulled it the rest of the way out by hammering the other end of the dog.[28]

Using just the tip of his saw, Mr. Ando rubs the seam in the stem rabbet.

Props still holding the plank were carefully backed off so glue could be spread in the seam just prior to nailing.

Once all of the mistakes were corrected and the top plank had been completely fastened, I counted thirty-eight nails per side in the seam between the top and bottom planks. At the transom Mr. Ando used a special square-pointed chisel I had never seen before called a *kiritsubanomi* (from *kiritsukeru,* "to cut at") to make the initial hole in the plank. He used a regular tsubanomi to finish the hole, and placed three nails in the transom for each plank.

Special Features

Kanuki was Mr. Ando's name for the two small beams, one near the transom and the other by the bow, used for tying lines to the boat.[29] To make these he split a piece of hiba with his axe and planed the aft beam with a very slight taper over its length. He then used a large drill to make holes opposite each other in the two top planks. With a narrow saw he cut the openings square and oiled the inside surfaces. With the boat propped against the sidewall, he then hammered the beams through, starting from the starboard side, crossing the boat, and into the opening on the port side. The tapered shape of the aft beam jammed tight and Mr. Ando cut off the excess flush with the outside face of both planks. The forward kanuki was not tapered and extended through the planking on either side of the hull by about 4.5 sun.

The next step was to finish off the stern of the boat. One of the most evocative names used by Mr. Ando for parts of the shimaihagi was the *fundoshi*, for the decorative plank installed behind the transom. Fundoshi are the traditional, plain-white loincloths, sometimes worn by festival participants, taiko drummers and, with a more decorative flair, by sumo wrestlers. The boat's fundoshi is a panel angled back from the transom and features a carving dedicated to the owner of the boat.

Mr. Ando carving the fundoshi with a single character taken from the name of the boat's eventual owner.

The fundoshi with the character for *ku*, the last syllable of Michinoku, the name of the museum that received the shimaihagi boat from the Freeman Foundation.

To finish the stern Mr. Ando first sawed the ends of the top planks off at an angle and then rounded the inside corners of the bottom planks, adding a layer of wood to the tops of the inside corners in order to strengthen them. The fundoshi angled away from the back of the transom and would be easily visible from behind the boat. He described it as "*tokuchou ga aru*," a "special feature" of this type of boat. He also said that the fundoshi was entirely decorative, with no practical use. It was the first of many carvings he would add to our boat. Though ultimately a working boat, these traditional and beautiful carvings would transform it into a work of folk art.

The fundoshi begins at a point 6.5 sun below the top edge of the transom and angles out to a point 8.4 sun from the base of the transom. A bottom piece runs from the end of the bottom to the base of the fundoshi to close off this space. Mr. Ando took thin pieces of cedar and initially fit the fundoshi by nailing it through the side planks with wire nails. The piece closing the bottom was beveled on the sides to fit against the bottom planks and nailed at the forward and aft edges with wire nails.

A thin board that Mr. Ando had cut into a fan shape was nailed on top of the fundoshi. This was to be carved with a *yagou*, a shop or trade name. He explained that the name represented the owner of the boat, not the boatbuilder. The boatbuilder's "signature" was the particular style of carving that he would add later.

Mr. Ando decided that the yagou for the boat would be the character *ku*. The Freeman Foundation was donating the boat to the Michinoku Traditional Wooden Boat Museum, and it was customary to choose for the yagou a single phonetic sound from the name of the owner, in this case the final syllable of Michinoku. He felt this kanji was the most interesting and aesthetically pleasing of the four kana comprising Mi-chi-no-ku. His own yagou, which he had carved into the shimaihagi he had built for himself, was *marusei*, the kanji for *sei* (from his given name Seizo) enclosed by a circle, *maru*.[30]

Mr. Ando called this small piece of wood the *keshou-ita* and he carved the yagou with a selection of gouges (*marunomi*) and carving chisels (*choukokunomi*).[31] He later carved the same yagou in the rub rails mounted on the

Mr. Ando did most of the decorative carving on the boat, but he left the painting for his apprentice. *Photo copyright Catherine Wood Brooks.*

gunwale. His carving style was very straightforward. After sketching the yagou in pencil on the wood he carved the outlines; he then used his gouge to cut between the borders and give the carving texture and depth. When he was finished I painted the carving black and we nailed it to the face of the fundoshi. This carving style obviously has a long tradition in this region, as it can be seen on boats throughout Aomori and southern Hokkaido.

Deck

Mr. Ando called the foredeck the *kappa,* the same term used in Urayasu and other places, although the dictionary pronunciation is *kanpan*. A hiba beam located about 4 shaku aft of the stem supported the deck. Mr. Ando installed the beam the same way he installed the kanuki, first using his electric drill to make a series of holes through the top planks and then cutting a rectangular hole with a saw. The forward walls of these openings were cut square to the face of the planking, and Mr. Ando notched the forward face of the beam to match these cuts. With the beam inserted through the openings he moved it forward to engage the notches in the planking, and then used a pair of wedges on either side to lock the beam in place. The ends of the beam protruded about 1 sun beyond the outside face of the top plank.

The decking itself was cedar and ran fore-and-aft. Mr. Ando used toosunoko to fit the side deck planks against the top planks and put glue on the edges before putting the deck in place. He toenailed the deck to the stem and beam with short wire nails (2 sun), and used longer wire nails (3 sun) to nail from outside the planking into the deck edges. Later, he enclosed the area beneath the deck by adding a cedar door, making hinges for the door out of pieces of a woven cloth belt.

Installing the Framing

The boats I built in Urayasu and Tokyo were framed with horizontal beams running across the hull called *funabari*. The old coastal trading ships such as the *bezaisen* and *kitamaesen* were framed the same way. This practice is widespread throughout the southern parts of Japan, including Honshu, Shikoku, and Kyushu. As one travels north, however, the framing of traditional small boats begins to change. In Tohoku most boats are framed with large, sawn timbers cut from natural crooks, a piece of wood taken from a plank cut from the curve at the base of the tree. Although there are several names for boat frames, including *abara, rokuzai*, and *matsura*, Mr. Ando taught me a new term: *rokkotsu*.

Natural crooks have become increasingly hard to acquire, and I have met boatbuilders who are now forced to build frames out of several pieces. Fortunately, Mr. Ando had some beautiful slabs of hiba stored in the attic of his shop that had been cut before he retired from boatbuilding. They were rough sawn and 1.5 sun thick, with a grain that swept in a sharp curve. We dusted them off and put them to use.

In preparation for fitting the frames we visited Mr. Ando's boathouse again to measure the exact locations of the frames in his previous boat. The first frame (aft) was located 7 shaku forward of the top edge of the inside face of the transom. Working forward from this frame, each set of frames was evenly spaced 4.5 shaku apart.

Each frame was essentially L-shaped, and Mr. Ando had a pair of rough patterns hinged with a bolt so that he could adjust their shape to the hull. He used these patterns to scribe the rough shape of the frames. Once cut, he tacked each frame in place and used a homemade tool—a small piece of wood holding a bamboo pen—to scribe the frame more precisely to the shape of the hull. He scribed all the edges of the frames, cut the outer line on the bandsaw, and beveled to the inner line with his axe. The final step was smoothing these surfaces with the hand plane. To make fitting the frames a little bit easier he used a round-bottomed plane to hollow out a little bit of the face that lay against the planking, the exact technique Mr. Udagawa had taught me in Urayasu.

Mr. Ando's hinged patterns for spiling frame shapes.

The frames rough cut and installed for final scribing and fitting.

Homemade tool for scribing, hinged so it can be opened to different widths, with a nib of bamboo to dip in ink.

The frames were installed in pairs, with the lowest legs overlapping and lying alongside each other at the plank keel. Each pair of frames was slightly canted, so that a line drawn between the centers of the frame tops would line up with the seam between the overlapping legs of the frame at the keel. When finished, the frames were 3 sun wide at the plank keel, 4 sun wide crossing the lower plank, and tapered to 3 sun wide at the gunwale.

The shimaihagi also had two more floor timbers that only spanned the bottom and lower plank. Mr. Ando cut notches in the frames at the seam between the lower and upper plank. These notches were used later to hold the beams supporting the floorboards. He also cut limber holes where the frames pass over the seam between the bottom and the lower plank.[32] Using a narrow-bladed saw he did a bit of toosunoko to finish fitting the frames, and when they were ready we through-bolted them. The heads of the bolts were on the outside of the hull: two bolts in each frame through the plank keel, one bolt through the lower plank, and two bolts through the top plank (the uppermost bolt would be installed later). Inside the hull, the nuts were countersunk into the tops of the frames. We wrapped a small length of caulking around the shoulder of each bolt head in order to make sure the holes remained watertight. Mr. Ando told me to tighten the nuts until the heads were pulled into the cedar planking flush with the surface.

Gunwale

The railing of the shimaihagi consists of three pieces: the *nugidana*, which lies on the outside of the plank; the *sotokoberi*, or rub rail, which is fastened to the face of the nugidana to protect it; and the *uwakoberi,* or cap rail, which lies on top, covering the edges of the upper plank and nugidana. I suspect the term nugidana combines *nuki*, a normally horizontal wooden brace used in house carpentry, with *dana*, meaning "shelf." Previously I had heard this part called the *koberi*.

Mr. Ando used his pattern to lay out two yagou in the nugidana near the bow, this time surrounded by the leaves of a flowering plant. He said this motif was the tree peony and came from China.[33] Since he had executed all but the most rudimentary work on the boat up to this point, it came as a surprise when he said I would carve the two yagou at the bow.

To fasten the nugidana Mr. Ando drove small, traditional boat nails from the outside and through the top plank. Earlier he had cut square mortises to receive the heads of these nails, which lay just under the surface of the nugidana when he was finished. On the inside of the boat he bent the nails over and pounded the points back into the plank. Both my Tokyo and Urayasu teachers had also used clench nails, but theirs were made of copper, which are much softer and easier to bend.

While Mr. Ando worked on the gunwale I took out some large sheets of paper and began tracing some of his patterns. I had copied the plank angle patterns earlier and I now laid down his stem pattern and began tracing it out. Ando saw me and suddenly exploded. "You can't use my pattern for your drawing!" he shouted. I was taken aback by his outburst. He was quick-tempered at all times, but he had never shown this level of anger, and I had been taking notes, making sketches, and photographing the project for weeks. It was my daily routine, and filled the time between chores.

I reminded him that the entire project was predicated on my documenting his techniques. It made no difference. He was suddenly furious, insisting I put his stem pattern away. I tried explaining to him my intent to take this information home to America and make a drawing of his boat.

"That's fine," he barked, which took me by surprise.

I added, "and then I'll give a copy to the Michinoku Museum," where the foundation had agreed to donate the finished boat.

"No!" Ando yelled. "That's bad!"

This made no sense. I explained the situation again. Once home in America I would finish scale drawings of the boat and patterns. This was fine, he repeated. Then I would share this research with the museum in Aomori. At that point he again erupted. Frustrated into silence, I finally decided to use the term familiar to all craftsmen in Japan.

"*Nusumigeiko desu ka?*" I asked, "Am I stealing your secrets?"

"Yes." he said, emphatically, "That's it!"

He went on, finally explaining that, "It's okay if you tell my secrets in America," he said, "but you can't tell them locally." Suddenly I got it. Mr. Ando imagined that somehow, someone in this region might begin building shimaihagi, or even worse, building his version of these boats. In reality, the era of these boats ended thirty years earlier— he had seen that with his own eyes—but the possibility of fostering competition locally, or aiding someone in the region to appropriate his design, he still saw as a visceral threat. It reminded me of the day many years earlier, when I was first shown incomplete drawings by a boatbuilder, and he too had refused to reveal his secrets to me, despite the fact he was the last boatbuilder of his region.

"Your measurements are okay," Mr. Ando finally said in what felt like a concession, "but you can't trace my patterns." He then immediately put me to work making the rub rails. Ironically, going forward it seemed as though he couldn't keep me busy enough actually working on the boat.

The rub rails were made of half-round hiba; I shaped them from square stock first with an axe and then a plane. They were just over 13 shaku long and we fastened them to the nugidana in the center of the boat where it was widest. The cap rails were also hiba (.65 sun by 1.8 sun). We began by nailing these at the stem, then working aft and slowly bending them around the rail of the boat. We could not complete the fastening of the cap rail until the hauling beam (*toko*) had been installed. Once the toko was complete the cap rail was fastened over it, covering the rail all the way aft.

We worked side-by-side for the rest of the day. Mr. Ando did not give me any chance to reach for my notebook. After our afternoon break he showed me exactly how he derived the shape of the stem pattern I had tried to trace—the widths at the top and bottom and the crown of the inner and outer faces. I recorded it all dutifully, and when Mr. Ando told me to clean up and left the shop at the end of the day, I laid his pattern on my paper again and quickly traced its shape. Like generations of apprentices before me, I had become a stealer of secrets.

Mooring Bits and Forward Beams

Because the Japanese haul their small fishing craft out of the water stern first daily, a strong beam is found on almost all wooden boats for attaching tow ropes or wires. This is the *toko;* it is also used to attach nets when fishing, and in some boats it has a hole for the rudder stock. The ends of the toko typically overhang the sides of the boat, creating bitts for hauling.

The toko on the shimaihagi was made of a piece of hiba measuring 2 sun by 5 sun. The forward face of the toko lay against the back of the transom. Mr. Ando cut a groove 5 bu deep around three sides of the bottom of the toko so it notched over the planking and the nugidana. Because the top of the toko would be flush with the top of the transom and the planking, it would be necessary to notch out the top plank and nugidana to receive it. He cut this joint for an extremely tight fit. After placing props under the boat to support it, he applied Bondo before using a mallet to pound the toko down into the joint. He used three wire nails along the transom to fasten the toko and two large wire nails down either side, straight into the edge of the planking.

At the chines we installed half-round pieces of wood Mr. Ando called *aori*. These would protect the hull at the corner where the planks met. I have not seen rub rails at the chine on other types of boats except in the Tohoku region. The aori were made of cedar and Mr. Ando instructed me to shape them from leftover planking stock using the axe and plane. The aori ran from the stem all the way aft to the keshouita and Mr. Ando fastened them with modern wire nails.[34]

At the bow a small beam called the *kuwanugi* is installed, named after the Japanese mulberry (*kuwa*) it is made from. Although not much more than a curved branch of the tree, it has powerful significance for the shimaihagi. It is mounted on top of the rail directly above the forward kanuki and let in to small notches cut into the top of these gunwale. It is then through-bolted to the kanuki. After squaring its sides Mr. Ando cut through mortises in the beam at each end for two small vertical posts. He called these *kanzashi*, a term for women's ornamental hair pins. Their tops were faceted and he gave me instructions later for painting them bright colors. These pins are commonly used, but the beam itself had special meaning for Mr. Ando. I idly asked why he used mulberry and he replied, "Mulberry protects the boat from lightning." I smiled, assuming he was repeating a bit of folklore that no one really believed. He read my mind because he raised his voice, looked me straight in the eye and slowly repeated, "*I said they protect the boat from lightning!*"[35]

Decorative Carved Planks

One of the most fascinating aspects of building the shimaihagi was watching Mr. Ando carve two large planks decorating the stern of the boat. As related previously, when my wife and I drove north into the Tohoku region we noticed that the fishing boats increasingly featured carved decorations, and Shiranuka, our destination, was the apogee of this tradition. Although I am sure he did not realize it, Mr. Ando may be the last boatbuilder with direct knowledge of this custom.

Nothing in my work, in the West or in Japan, prepared me for a process both artistic and spiritual. The tenor of the shop seemed to shift while Mr. Ando carved the two large planks of hoonoki; they would be nailed to the hull once decorated. He sat on a low pile of lumber with the planks in his lap. He said nothing at all and rarely looked up while he worked. I moved as quietly as possible, cleaning the shavings from around him as they piled up, and taking pictures. Decorative work on this scale for a fishing boat might seem frivolous, pretentious, or extravagant, but the solemnity with which Ando worked convinced me he was channeling something very ancient and elemental.

The carvings on boats in this region have particular significance. Mr. Ando's patterns were large sheets of very thin paper on which he had drawn his designs years ago. He laid the patterns on the wood and began to run his pencil over the design. The lines on the paper were worn from repeated use and a very faint pencil line transferred through the paper to the wood. He removed the paper pattern and,

The stern showing the toko, a large beam used to haul small boats stern-first out of the sea.

When painted, mooring bits called kanzashi are an elegant detail on these fishing boats.

Carving detail showing the tree peony.

Geometric designs and other motifs of the carved keshouita.

working directly on the planks, completed sketching the outlines in pencil.

Mr. Ando first used his carving chisel and gouges to cut the outline and scallop out the designs. Despite the simplicity and speed of this carving style, it still took him more than two full days to carve both keshouita, a considerable commitment of his time considering these planks have no structural function in the boat.

The central motifs of the carving were two blossoms of the tree peony, surrounded by leaves. The forward edge of the keshouita displayed a very stylized shape, almost like a wave, with a yellow peony blossom emerging from the center. The carving was bordered by geometric shapes along the bottom and back edge.

Mr. Ando instructed me to carve similar geometric shapes on a small keshouita framing the forward edge of the top plank at the bow and bordering his yagou. Because he had earlier stressed that only he would be carving I asked him to go over exactly what he wanted me to do; making a carving mistake was not something I looked forward to. There was something about his explanation that didn't make sense, so I asked him to explain it again. He did, and this time what he told me to do was slightly different than his original instructions. He was on his way out of the shop to run some errands when I asked him again for clarification. Again his instructions changed! I repeated what he wanted. Ando grunted. I repeated it again. I then spent the afternoon carving the two yagou and when he returned Mr. Ando looked at my work and said nothing. This was the only actual carving I did.

Over the course of the summer I asked local fisherman about the origins of these carvings. Several told me that local boats were highly decorated due to the influence of the Ainu, the indigenous people of Japan and Sakhalin (Russia).

The author carving the yagou, or house name, for the shimaihagi. *Photo copyright Catherine Wood Brooks.*

Today most Japanese of Ainu descent are concentrated in Hokkaido. They have a very distinct culture and have long been victims of racial prejudice. I was therefore surprised to hear people acknowledge Ainu influences in a craft that would otherwise be considered strictly Japanese. If true, these carved planks represent a remarkable intersection of these two cultures.[36]

Peonies are strongly associated with China and Chinese Buddhism. The ancient Chinese capital of Luoyang, where Buddhism was established in China, is called the City of Peonies and still holds an annual peony festival in late spring. The flower is seen to have a mandala-like form, and also signifies honor and prosperity, while the root, flower, and leaves all have medicinal uses. The peony motif can be found throughout Japan both at Buddhist temples and Shinto shrines, and has a strong regional significance, because it formed the family crest of the Tsugaru feudal lords of Aomori, known as the Hirosaki-han.

Ceremonies related to boatbuilding and fishing are generally Shinto based, and the gods of the mountain and the sea are the two preeminent deities invoked. The tree peony may symbolize the mountain forests, which are the basis for other boatbuilding ceremonies such as the tool ceremony and the keel-laying ceremony (see Chapter 7). Because the meaning of keshouita has a feminine connotation, it might also be an inference to the female guardian spirit of ships (*funadama*). In any event these carvings represent a form of folk art not seen elsewhere in traditional boats.[37]

Late in our stay my wife and I took an evening walk along the beachfront and found the carved board from a boat on a pile of firewood, stacked along the back wall of a house. Because it was obviously going to be burned, we stood there in the dark debating what to do. To us it was a treasure worth saving, but we didn't know the people who lived in the home and obviously did not want to resort to theft. For the next few evenings we kept walking past the house trying to decide how to save this carving. We were slowly becoming desperate, imagining each night that it might be thrown in the stove. My wife finally forced me to the door, saying, "You're the one who speaks Japanese," and I reluctantly and sheepishly asked the man living there if I could have the carved plank off his firewood pile. He seemed very perplexed, but when I referred to it as a piece of art he laughed and told us he was happy to have us take it. The plank got packed in our van and eventually shipped home to Vermont, with other treasures of our year.

As I traveled around this region during the summer of 2005 I saw similar carvings on boats, but by far the high point of decorative carving was on the shimaihagi boats of the Shiranuka area. The other common small boats of this region, the isobune, also have carvings, but these are primarily limited to a house name and often a small representation of a sea bird. While I was carving, Mr. Ando stressed that the keshouita was his signature, and cautioned that should I ever build a shimaihagi myself it was essential that I not copy his carving style, but develop one of my own. We painted all of the boat's carvings, as well as the beam ends and the mooring bitts, with a set of artists' acrylics in black, red, green, and yellow.[38]

I cannot overemphasize how important these motifs were to Mr. Ando. The total time spent carving the fundoshi, nugidana, and keshouita, plus painting, was a full week. Given that building the shimaihagi took six weeks total, these carved decorations represented a significant portion of the labor. As with the timber protecting the boat from lightning, the shimaihagi was not complete without the carvings. To people who have gone to sea for generations, and risked their lives to make a living, such beliefs are not quaint, but a part of the fabric of their culture.

An odd thing happened when it came time to hang these two large carvings on the stern of the boat. Mr. Ando, who had insisted that he never put his name anywhere on the boat, got out a brush and ink and began writing on the stern where the carvings were to be nailed. He wrote his name and address, the year and month, and then my name followed by "from the State of Vermont, America." I was touched by the recognition but I reminded him he had told me he never put his name on his boats. "It's all covered by the keshouita," he replied. "It's our secret."

(Left) The author painting Mr. Ando's carvings. *Photo copyright Catherine Wood Brooks. (Above)* The decorative plank painted and installed on the boat.

Floorboards

Mr. Ando called the floorboards of the boat *itago*, simply "boat plank," although elsewhere I have been taught the terms *sunoko* or *sashiita*.

The floorboards run athwartships and were supported by beams he called *nagiri* running fore-and-aft between the frames. The ends of the nagiri had tenons fitting into notches that we cut into the frames. The forward tenon on one end is cut long so the nagiri can be slid far enough into one frame that the other end can be dropped into place between the frames. The nagiri is then slid back and locked into the frame behind.[39]

Mr. Ando cut the floorboards out of the narrowest pieces of cedar sawn from the original log. He cut straight edges, removing the bark edge, but many of the floorboards were eventually tapered. Mr. Ando did not plane the floorboards; the rough-sawn surface would provide better traction underfoot. They were installed with the heart side of the wood facing up. He drilled a 1-sun hole into the seam between every three to five floorboards to provide a finger hole for removing them. He also marked all the floorboards with numbers so they could be reinstalled correctly.

The last detail before installing the floorboards was drilling a drain hole in the plank keel. Mr. Ando located it just forward of the forward frame and drilled a 1-sun hole on the centerline. As mentioned, fishing boats are usually hauled out of the water at the day's end by fastening a rope or cable around the toko, then left on the ramp with the bow pointing toward the sea. Therefore any water in the hull drains forward and out the hull. Mr. Ando called this hole the *janome*, and he made a plug for it out of cedar.[40]

Sacrificial Rub Rails

At the start of one of our final days, we removed the floorboards and gathered people to help us turn the boat on its side. Our regular visitors provided all the help we needed. Four of us, Mr. and Mrs. Ando, a family friend, and I, were able to tip the boat on its side and block it securely in place.[41] Mr. Ando fastened long strips of hardwood, measuring 1 sun by 1.3 sun, running along the outer edge of the bottom all the way aft. These are sacrificial rub rails called *suberi.* Ando used a hardwood called *itaya,* which could be one of two species of maple: *itayakaide* (*Acer mono*), or *itayamomiji* (*Acer japonicus*). Mr. Ando fastened the suberi to the bottom using modern, self-tapping screws.

The purpose of the suberi is to protect the hull. While these boats might have been pulled ashore on beaches or wooden planks long ago, thanks to government programs, today even the most rural fishing villages have broad concrete ramps providing access to the water. The suberi is essential because the soft cedar of the bottom would be quickly worn away if it were dragged daily across concrete. The screws holding it in place were deeply countersunk so that the heads would not be worn off. This way the suberi could be replaced when it became worn.

Paddles and Oars

Fishermen propel the shimaihagi using either a pair of paddles, called *kai*, or oars, called *kurumagai*. The paddles are not the same length; a shorter one is used aft and a longer one forward. They are both made of durable hardwood. The handle of the paddle is made of enju, the Japanese pagoda tree. The paddle handle is very thick where it attaches to the shaft of the blade, and tapers to comfortable handgrips on either end. The blade is made of the high quality oak called nara. The joint connecting the handle and blade is a wedged through-tenon.

When I saw our shimaihagi on display at the Michinoku Traditional Wooden Boat Museum in 2005, a new pair of oars was in the boat along with the paddle. These also seemed to be made of nara and they reflected the prevalent style used in the Shimokita region: very heavy handles (as a counterweight) with a hole for the thole pin (*takama*), tapering to a long, narrow blade. Throughout this region oars used a single thole pin passing through a hole in the loom of the oar. Modern oarlocks are never seen on traditional boats. These oars were each made of a single piece of wood, though this is not standard construction. Many examples of two-piece oars can be found on the Shimokita Peninsula and Hokkaido.

Pads of wood made of chestnut (*kuri*) were mounted on the boat to reinforce the places where the paddle and oars will rub against the rails. Mr. Ando called these pads of hardwood *neruba* (elsewhere they are called *kaizure*) and they protect the cap rail from wear. The paddles are inserted in loops of rope passing through holes drilled just below the neruba. Mr. Ando's older boat had a slightly different arrangement of these pads: instead of individual neruba at each rowing station his older boat had one long neruba mounted aft. He explained that this was for a *konbu* (kelp) boat; gathering kelp requires very long bamboo-handled tools that rest against this pad.

The final accessory needed for rowing the shimaihagi were two small seats that I made from scraps of cedar. These measured 1.35 shaku across by 1 shaku wide by 3.8 sun tall.

Carving detail on an isobune.

Mr. Ando pouring sake as part of a Shinto launching ceremony. He conducted the ceremony himself, with just the author and curator in attendance.

The *kamidana,* or Shinto shrine, on the back wall of the shop.

They were not fastened to the boat, but rather rested like low stools on the floorboards.

We had built the boat in just twenty-nine working days; Mr. Ando said that in his prime, working alone, he could build a shimaihagi in twenty.

Launching

In the final days of the project Mr. Ando once again surprised me. Our time together had been far from easy for me, as my actions had often driven him to varying levels of anger. I would remind myself almost daily that in working with Mr. Ando I was living, mercifully for a short while, the arduous apprenticeship that is legend in the Japanese imagination. However, as the project neared completion, Mr. Ando began suggesting I stay on and continue working with him. He proposed that he and I could build an *isobune,* the smallest type of wooden boat in the region—the kind of boat he carved bottoms for during his apprenticeship. I love these little boats: just a thick-carved bottom, two planks, a stem, and transom. They are simple, with an elegant narrow shape, and often featured a single seabird carved at the stern. On weekends I had measured several of them we found while traveling around the coast. Regardless, my one-year research visa was about to expire and my wife and I had commitments back in Tokyo. I explained this to Mr. Ando over and over again, but still he kept insisting I should stay so we could keep working together. After our various tribulations in the shop, his offer seemed a bit surreal, but it just wasn't possible for me to stay.

Mr. Ando conducted our Shinto launching ceremony. He began early in the morning on the day the completed boat was taken by truck to the Michinoku Traditional Wooden Boat Museum. He placed an offering of sake at his workshop's Shinto *kamidana,* a small model shrine hanging high on the back wall. He then set candles and salt on the bow of the boat and poured a small amount of sake on the deck. After a brief prayer, he invited me to make a similar offering of sake. He hadn't invited any of his family or my wife to witness this; after I prayed the boat was ready to be removed from the workshop and loaded onto a truck from the museum.

My wife and I followed the truck in our van for the two-hour drive from Shiranuka to Aomori City and the Michinoku Traditional Wooden Boat Museum. Our van was packed and we would be turning south as soon as the short launching ceremony at the museum was concluded. Mr. Ando followed us in his car. There was a small crowd at the museum along with local television crews and news-

Historic photo showing isobune and shimaihagi fishing off Shiranuka village. The fishermen are gathering either kelp or sea urchins. *Photo copyright Toshikatsu Hanabe.*

paper reporters. The boat was pushed into the water without fanfare, while Mr. Ando and a fisherman friend of his clambered aboard and rowed briefly in the harbor. I was not invited, but stood on shore and answered questions from the media. When he came ashore Mr. Ando and I were asked to pose next to the boat. I had already asked the reporters not to describe me as an apprentice because, frankly, I had done so little direct work on the boat I felt I wasn't justified in taking much credit for its construction. I stood patiently beside Mr. Ando as he was interviewed by a local television station. He described building the boat, not mentioning me until the end. Finally he said, pointing to me, "Any mistakes made on the boat were his."

Each of my teachers interpreted our relationship in their own way, and they could create their own stories. But fundamental would always be the unalterable divide between the roles of master and apprentice: one the purveyor of all the knowledge and skill, unquestioned in his authority; the other subservient in every way. What mattered was the form of this relationship, not the reality. Although Mr. Ando was unsparing with me, he provided me with the clearest glimpse of the often uncomfortable experience of the traditional apprenticeship. He was an uncompromising teacher, yet he had earned the right to pass judgment on me, and I do not begrudge the high standards he set.

Over the course of the summer I lived in Shiranuka, I saw just one wooden boat used for fishing: a small isobune that went out one day, along with a few fiberglass boats, to gather sea urchins. Otherwise the remnants of Shiranuka's wooden fleet lay slowly rotting on the banks of the harbor and in the few beachside boathouses. The local fishing fleet now consists of large steel squid boats operating miles offshore. Writing to me in 2009, our friend Mr. Hanabe captured perfectly the sense of an era slowly disappearing in his village, these last boats bearing mute witness to their times.

> *Remembering kelp fishing fifty years ago, I am overwhelmed with emotion now as I write my memories of that summer. My father, on whose shimaihagi I worked as a boy, is dead, as is his brother. The boat, without its master, is left behind in the boathouse and it seems to tell of the way of life of the fisherman and the village of Shiranuka. Even though the boat is obsolete, it stares at the fishing village, calmly sharing the memories of its past.*[42]

Notes

1 In addition, none of the river boatbuilders I have met, from Kyushu to Tohoku, ever drew plans for their boats.

2 He made three dugout fishing boats in the mid-1960s, two for fishermen and one for himself. In 1993 a Shinto shrine asked him to build one in order to document the process. At that time he was still using his own dugout for fishing.

3 Phoneme changes such as those between *kakko, kako,* and *kakou* are very common, and can cause confusion when trying to track down the origin of older terms. I

am indebted to Mr. Koji Matano for his research on the possible origins of this term.

4 Although Mr. Ando and Mr. Kawabata were competitors until the latter retired, Mr. Ando said they had remained friends. To this day Shiranuka is a busy fishing port and there was obviously enough work to support several boatbuilders.

5 Other boatbuilders say *wakizukuri*; *waki* means side.

6 Interview with Mr. Suezou Furukawa, Tomari Village, in October of 2005. Mr. Toshikatsu Hanabe, quoted elsewhere, described the same situation.

7 Reflections of Mr. Toshikatsu Hanabe, written in 2009 and edited by the author.

8 Perhaps no other country has so many traditional boat types copied in fiberglass by either large manufacturers like Yamaha or by independent boatbuilders who switched to this material from wood. Mr. Kotaro Horiuchi, one of Yamaha's chief designers since the1960s, explained, "In 1970 we created several local fishing boat factories. They were located at Amakusa [Kyushu], Shido [Shikoku], Ofunato [Iwate], and Gamagori [Aichi]. In these factories, we had small design and sales teams and developed local fishing boats [in fiberglass]." Yamaha's development of fiberglass fishing boats is mentioned in Mr. Horiuchi's first book *Locus of a Boat Designer,* published in Japanese by KAZI in 1987, reprinted in 2008.

9 *Brinkley's Unabridged Japanese-English Dictionary*, Sanseido, 1896.

10 *Hiba* is a variety of cypress, very similar to *hinoki,* and also sometimes called *asunaro*.

11 Equivalent to 180.39 liters, or 6.37 cubic feet. This modern *koku* is different from that used to describe the capacity of a traditional Japanese cargo ship, which is equivalent to 278.26 liters (see Chapter 14).

12 This was the first Japanese boat I built with a rabbeted stem. Mr. Ando called the rabbet *enuchi,* but woodworkers also call this type of joint *sanehagi* or *kakikomi.*

13 Many terms Mr. Ando used appeared only in my oldest dictionaries. One difficulty of rural dialects may be in part due simply to the continued use of older forms of Japanese.

14 Mr. Yuhei Yamada, an independent researcher from Hakodate, visited our workshop several times and was kind enough to share this information with me.

15 *Kusabi* is the common term for wedge. Mr. Ando actually called these *ya,* an older term I found in my 1896 dictionary.

16 Lacquer is a product derived from sap collected from the lacquer tree (*Toxicodendron vernicifluum*). Called *urushi*, it is highly toxic in its liquid state. It is used to create a hard, watertight finish on wooden tableware, musical instruments, and other decorative objects, and is also an adhesive.

17 In the West this is predicated on a softwood stopwater inserted in a hardwood backbone. In Mr. Ando's case the stopwater and the keel were both cedar.

18 I would suspect this technique comes from the West because I have not seen other Japanese boatbuilders use it, and Mr. Ando's method was almost identical to the one used by Western boatbuilders (and his largest squid boats were built with Western plank-on-frame methods). The word *akadomesen* is a combination of the words for "bilge water" (*akadome*) and "plug" (*sen*).

19 Mr. Ando's term may derive from the "head" or "top" (*kaburi*) and "inside" or "home" (*uchi*).

20 As in Urayasu, Mr. Ando distinguished boats by their beam when labeling his plank angle patterns.

21 The keel-laying ceremony is usually called the *shikizue*. In northern regions it can be called the *dainose*, although elsewhere that term refers to a less specific, workshop-blessing ceremony.

22 The standard pronunciation would be *tooshinoko,* but in the regional dialect Mr. Ando spoke it is common to pronounce *shi* as *su.* Here I spell the term as he pronounced it.

23 It took Mr. Ando, with some assistance from me, four hours to saw the seams for the two lower planks, a total of about 40 shaku of seams.

24 Mr. Nobuji Udagawa, my teacher in Urayasu, did the same thing. I never thought to ask either man why, but I suspect they believed a wire nail was less likely to split the most fragile point at the hood end of the plank. The top plank overlapped the bottom plank and covered this nail.

25 *Jiki* can mean "direct" or "direct transmission," and *gata* is from *kata,* meaning "pattern."

26 My teachers in Tokyo and Urayasu were very strict about putting the heart side of the wood toward the inside of the boat. However, the boats they built were used in Tokyo Bay, which has many fresh water rivers feeding it. Sapwood is particularly vulnerable to rot, which freshwater encourages. Shimaihagi were only used in seawater, where the salt content acts as a wood preservative. My tub boat teacher, whose boats were also used in the sea, put the heartwood facing out.

27 My teachers in Tokyo and Urayasu did not do this; instead, they used props to support the plank as they nailed. Perhaps Mr. Ando used this method because I was there to help; it would be almost impossible to execute this technique alone.

28 Nails are made of soft steel, so striking them with the chisel edge generally did little damage to the tsubanomi. My teachers rarely sharpened their tsubanomi, and when they did it was done very quickly with just a few strokes of a file.

29 In Urayasu and Tokyo these beams are called *kotsunagi*. I suspect Mr. Ando's name is related to the word *nuki*, which is a type of small horizontal beam used in house carpentry.

30 These "signatures" would make an interesting study. My taraibune teacher used to write messages on the edges of planks, which were invisible when the boat was completed; he never told the boat's owners about them. My teacher in Urayasu marked his larger boats with subtle, geometric carvings on the forward beam. My Tokyo teacher followed a family tradition and attached a copper pinwheel (*kazeguruma)* to the bow of his boats. In Okinawa my teacher carved two characters from his name in the transom. However, the Shimokita Peninsula was the first place I saw widespread use of house names identifying the owners of boats.

31 *Keshou* means "makeup," or "cosmetics," and *ita* means "plank."

32 Mr. Ando called the limber holes (openings for bilge water to drain) *ganime*.

33 *Paeonia suffruticosa,* or *botan* in Japanese.

34 My 1896 dictionary defines *aori* as the gunwale of a ship.

35 Mr. Ando's term was *kuwabara,* meaning a word or phrase repeated as a charm to protect against lightning and derived from *kuwa,* the word for mulberry. It is the Japanese equivalent of "knock on wood."

36 Similarly several people I asked in Aomori about the notorious local dialects told me these too were the result of a mixture with the Ainu language.

37 I am indebted to Mr. Juin Saito, a Shinto priest from Akita, for the information on Shinto deities and Shinto ceremonies related to boatbuilding. He has done exhaustive research on this topic. I am also grateful to Ms. Yoko Arakawa and Mr. Koji Matano for their help clarifying the symbolism of the tree peony.

38 The collection of the Michinoku Traditional Wooden Boat Museum had shimaihagi from at least two other boatbuilders from Higashidorimura. All contain representations of the tree peony but the styles are very unique. Mr. Kawabata's carvings show the leaves of the tree peony but not the flower, while a shimaihagi from Odanosawa Village built about 1950 (builder's name unknown) has the flower motif arranged in a way similar to Mr. Ando's.

39 This is a difficult joint to describe but in fact is common. Shoji screens and fusuma use the same principle. The tenons at the top have enough length and space in the groove so the panel can be raised and swung out of the joint at the bottom. The joinery of the nagiri described here works on the same principle.

40 Earlier he had told me the plug was called the *neriba* (which I could not find in a dictionary); *janome* means "bulls eye."

41 Mrs. Ando's ability to help lift a heavy boat was not surprising. She was in the shop every single day, and often helped me clean the shop and remove scrap wood. In short, if she saw something needing to be done she did not hesitate to do it. I was reminded of my first teacher's wife, as well as the wives of other boatbuilders I have met, who regularly assisted their husbands in the workshop, often performing the hardest physical work.

42 I urged the Michinoku Traditional Wooden Boat Museum to collect Mr. Hanabe's shimaihagi, which he generously agreed to donate.

The bow of the completed sabani. All the edges of the hull topside are protected by strips of apitong, an Indonesian hardwood. The sheen comes from a liberal soaking with vegetable oil and a final coat of shark liver oil.

13

The Sabani of Okinawa

While working in Tokyo in 2002 my wife and I traveled to Niigata Prefecture one weekend, where a local researcher and friends took us up the Agano River to meet some former boatmen and one boatbuilder. The most common watercraft of the region was the *sanpasen*, a long, narrow river boat. The builder we met was a local carpenter who, along with other men, had recognized in the 1980s there was only one aging boatbuilder left in the river valley. They helped him build his last boat, and the carpenter continued building boats after his teacher's death.

The sanpasen was a revelation to me. Its planks are for the most part fastened only with wooden keys called *chigiri* (in the local dialect pronounced *chikkin*).[1] This fastening is well known among furniture makers in the West, where it is called a dovetail key or butterfly key, but it is never employed in Western boatbuilding. I was fascinated by the technique and determined to learn it.

The following year, on a drive totaling eight thousand miles along the coast for further research, I found boats built on the Mogami River in Yamagata fastened this way, and I met a boatbuilder on Notojima in Ishikawa Prefecture who used the technique.[2] In addition, throughout Tohoku (the northern part of Japan's main island of Honshu) various types of semi-dugout fishing boats with thick timber bottoms—such as the *hatahatabune* of Akita Prefecture and various *mudamahagi* boats in Aomori and Hokkaido—employed these fastenings, along with iron nails.[3] I had known for some time the boatbuilders of Okinawa used similar fastenings for local fishing boats called *sabani;* there they were called by the odd name *huundu*.

Dovetail fastenings are used inside and out to join the side planking of this semi-dugout boat on Noto Peninsula, Ishikawa Prefecture.

A large derelict fishing boat found on the tip of the Noto Peninsula, with dovetail fastenings visible in her hull.

To Okinawa

Following my return to the US in late 2003, I attempted to raise funds to work with the boatbuilder I had met on the Agano River. I was not successful, and he later admitted to me he was too old to work any longer. I then turned my attention to Okinawa, in Japan's southernmost chain of islands, hoping to find a sabani builder and study with him.

The sabani, traditionally used for coastal fishing, is the iconic boat of this region. It also has the distinction of having been rediscovered in the last fifteen years by board sailors, surfers, and yachtsmen as a racing boat.[4] Without question it represents the first traditional fishing boat in Japan to have made the transition to a pleasure craft. I contacted a group of these sailors, who recommended three men all agreed to be capable of building a traditional sabani. Over the next two years I began receiving funding for the project, first from the Edwin Monk Scholarship administered by the Center For Wooden Boats in Seattle, Washington; then came a grant from the Asian Cultural Council of New York City. By this time I was corresponding with the most active of the three builders, but my attempt to work with him fell through in the spring of 2009 when he suddenly became ill. I wrote to another builder, Mr. Ryujin Shimojo, who initially declined, saying it took him six months or more to build a boat now due to a stroke he suffered three years earlier. I then received a grant from the Nippon Foundation of Tokyo to be administered by the Museum of Maritime Science.[5] The museum's curator asked Mr. Shimojo if he would reconsider. Finally he agreed, and the museum commissioned him to build an eight-meter sabani, with me participating in its construction.[6]

In November of 2009 I arrived in Tokyo and met with officials from the museum before flying to Okinawa. The curator's biggest concern was whether Mr. Shimojo and I could finish the sabani in the two-and-a-half months I could stay in Okinawa. He didn't go into much detail, except to say that for Mr. Shimojo, eighty-one years old, mid-winter was a difficult time to work. I promised to do my best and hoped Mr. Shimojo would welcome my help since my contribution might speed up the process, but we agreed that should something go wrong I could fall back on measuring two seven-meter sabani Mr. Shimojo had in his shop. With that understanding our meeting ended with the curator drawing me a crude map of how to get to Mr. Shimojo's workshop from the ferry terminal.

I flew from Tokyo to Naha, the capital city of Okinawa, where a friend gave me a ride north over the main island to Nago, the largest city on the northern coast. The tiny island of Iejima is easily visible, just a thirty-minute ferry ride from Nago's port, but with only four round-trips a day I had missed the last ferry, so I spent the night in a business hotel. The next morning I was on the first ferry to Iejima, an oval-shaped island about four miles long by three miles wide, dominated by a cone-shaped mountain towering behind the main town. Stepping off the ferry I glanced at my map and turned right. I was supposed to follow the main road until it swung inland and then take the side road running up a short hill. I glanced up and, a hundred yards away, I saw a short, stout woman standing below the crest of the hill waving her arm overhead. I broke into a trot toward her but as soon as she saw me heading her way she turned, walked up the hill, and disappeared.

The northern end of Iejima, viewed from the top of Mount Gusuku. The northern end of the main island of Okinawa is visible in the distance.

Mr. Ryujin Shimojo

A few minutes later I came around the corner to a concrete boat shop. Mr. Shimojo and his son Tomio were sitting, waiting for me. Mrs. Shimojo, the woman I had seen waving to me, was unloading a basket of snacks on a folding card table. In the shop were two enormous planks resting on widely spread sawhorses. Just outside was a four-foot high pile of cedar logs, half logs, planks, and scraps. Mr. Shimojo's large concrete, two-story house stood next to the shop, and a small machine shop stood to one side of the boat shop. I stepped up to the group, bowed, and introduced myself. The first thing I noticed was the difficulty Mr. Shimojo had getting to his feet. He used a cane to stand, and as he came forward to shake my hand I noticed one of his legs was completely stiff. When he reached me he dropped the cane so he could shake my hand with his good hand; his other arm was crooked slightly against his body and his fingers were curled into a half fist.

I had been anxious about not being able to finish this boat during my stay; meeting Mr. Shimojo and realizing the extent of his handicap made my heart sink. But in that moment, shaking my hand, he flashed the brightest of smiles and told me how much he was looking forward to building this sabani. His enthusiasm made me feel better, and I thought if he at least trusted me to do some of the work we might get the project finished in time. His son interrupted to explain that three years earlier his father had suffered a severe stroke, and this had limited his ability to work. Also winter was coming and Mr. Shimojo warned me that in the cold weather his arm tended to get stiff and painful.[7] Nonetheless, he said the next day we would start work and hew to his traditional schedule: seven days a week, interrupted only by a five-day New Year holiday. In his prime, he said, using just hand tools, he could build a sabani in forty days. Mr. Shimojo estimated he had built about one hundred fishing sabani during his career; the first twenty were boats powered by only paddles and sail. He built sabani in all sizes, from five-meter boats sailed by one fisherman to boats of seven and eight meters sailed by as many as six men.

The Shimojo family came to Iejima 120 years ago, and my teacher had lived on the island all his life. His father was a fisherman and had a large sabani, about seven meters. As a boy Mr. Shimojo fished too, and he remembers sailing alone in a smaller boat, his right hand holding the steering paddle, his left hand holding the sheet, and his teeth clamped on a fishing line trailing astern. He says no boats were built on Iejima in his youth; instead fishermen bought their boats from builders in Nago and Itoman on the main island. He credits his father with developing a unique sail shape for sabani, one with curved, rather than straight edges.

A sabani under construction in the immediate postwar years. Mr. Shimojo worked under a roof between his house on the right and a machine shop on the left. *Photo copyright Tsunemasa Shimabukuro.*

Mr. Shimojo told me he would like nothing more than to be sailing a small sabani back and forth off the beach. But he also admitted being a fisherman was hard, cold work. Many of the fishing techniques of his day involved diving into the sea to pull nets or drive fish. In addition, the narrow sabani can easily capsize. In fact, sabani sailors were experts at righting their boats, and to this day in the annual *hari* race on Iejima each boat has to be capsized, righted, and bailed before finishing.[8]

Following the War, Mr. Shimojo decided to build sabani professionally. He established his shop right at his house, at first working under a roof supported by poles. He had an intimate knowledge of the boats from his fishing days, and learned his new trade through careful observation. "I see something once and I understand it and never forget," he told me. However, these outside influences faded as he built more and more sabani, perfecting his own designs until he became the sole source for boats among the fishermen of Iejima and the nearby main island, including Nago City.

His most important design modifications came from his customers, the fishermen who used his boats and told him what they wanted. The fracturing of the craft and isolation of the few remaining builders meant each craftsman worked within the confines of his own inherited tradition. Evidence of this can be seen at today's sabani races, where the most experienced sailors can easily identify who built each boat. One would expect a comprehensive survey of all of Okinawa's remaining boatbuilders to show significant differences in technique and design.[9]

When a huge U.S. military airbase was built on Iejima following the War, small gasoline engines became available.

These were single-cylinder engines that ran pumps and generators, generally about three or four horsepower. Mr. Shimojo began installing these in sabani, and claimed to be the first in the region to do so. He bought machine tools and other metalworking equipment, another first on the island, and he taught himself how to use them. He showed me a small propeller he had machined from a solid billet of steel. His metal supply in the immediate postwar years was scrap American military equipment. "The trucks and the bulldozers were enormous," he said, referring to the postwar buildup by the U.S. "We were just natives. We had never seen such things."

Okinawans even created an entirely new boat type from scrap military hardware: the *tankubune* (tank boat). U.S. Air Force fighter planes employed drop tanks—fuel tanks carried underneath the wings that were dropped when empty—and thousands had rained down on Okinawa during the battle for the island. Islanders used them as water tanks or cut cockpits in them to make boats. On Iejima tank boats were used for octopus fishing close inshore, but in Itoman City I saw a tankubune in a museum with wooden bulwarks and an inboard engine. While talking about these boats at the guesthouse where I stayed, a visiting town official insisted I meet his friend Mr. Oshiro and see his tankubune. He was ninety-three years old and had been using his boat until just two years earlier.

U.S. Air Force P-47 Thunderbolt fighter planes, with gasoline drop tanks slung under their wings. Drop tanks were used by Okinawa fishermen to create an entirely new type of boat, called the tankubune. Iejima's most prominent geographical feature, Mount Gusuku, is visible in the background.

A tank boat in a museum on Iejima. Considered unstable, they were used primarily for octopus fishing close to shore. Some, however, were fitted with washboards and inboard engines.

Until its annexation by Japan in 1879, the Okinawan archipelago was the Ryukyu Kingdom, and to this day Okinawans regard their culture as distinct from that of "mainland" Japan. I had brought to Japan special-ordered baseball caps, embroidered with the characters for *wasen,* meaning "Japanese-style boat." They were intended as gifts for friends and contacts, and until I reached Okinawa, all who received them were delighted. Arriving on Okinawa I presented Mr. Shimojo and his son each with one, which elicited from the former my first lesson on the gulf between Japanese and Okinawan culture. Mr. Shimojo was absolutely clear, "A sabani is *not* a wasen. A sabani is a sabani." He and his son accepted my caps, but I never saw them again.

Language provided continual examples of this cultural divide. From my previous apprenticeships I had come to expect that my teachers would use unique local terms to describe boat parts, tools, and techniques. Rural Japan is a patchwork of local dialects, called *ben,* and some are notorious for their impenetrability. For most dialects, however, the divergence from standard Japanese is mostly in pronunciation, with a few unique phrasings and words. I had been warned that Okinawa-*ben* was difficult, but when I asked Mr. Shimojo if a term he used was the local dialect, he told me he did not speak a dialect, he spoke Okinawa *hougen.* Although usually defined as dialect, in truth Okinawa hougen is an entirely different language. Listening to a pair of elderly islanders, you would think they were speaking Chinese; their conversation has none of the softer tones of Japanese. While my teacher and his family spoke standard Japanese for my benefit, all of the terms relating to sabani were hougen. And, he explained, every other island in Okinawa had its own hougen, each with its own unique terms for sabani![10]

Mr. Shimojo had always lived at the same location on Iejima, but in three different houses. His childhood home, wood-framed with a thatch roof, was destroyed in World War II. The family's postwar home, a simple concrete-block building with a tile roof, was eventually replaced by a poured concrete structure. His shop was a concrete-block building replacing a lean-to roof that covered his former workspace, which had an earthen floor. We worked on a concrete floor stained with random puddles of hardened epoxy from his days building fiberglass boats. One end of the shop had a huge opening with no door. The weather wasn't severe enough to require it, plus it let in lots of light. As for securing his tools while away from the shop, Mr. Shimojo insisted there was no crime on Iejima.[11]

Initially my role in the workshop was not quite an apprentice but more than an observer. I tried to help as much as I could and Mr. Shimojo trusted me quickly with difficult and skilled tasks. He understood that I needed to learn certain techniques, like installing the huundu fastenings, yet he and his son reserved the right to do the most critical tasks themselves. As with my other teachers, I was expected to learn by observation and not by direct instruction. Mr. Shimojo expected to work without any interruption from me, and I tried to save my questions for our twice-daily breaks.

The most difficult part of our working relationship was trying to get Mr. Shimojo to explain those things he did instinctively. Several times when I asked why he did something a particular way, he responded, "Because that is the way I do it." His intention was not to dismiss my question; rather, I was asking something that seemed self-evident to him and didn't require further explanation. If I were patient, the reason would often become clear. Still, there were some questions that were never fully answered, such as exactly how he drew the shape of his planking before he had full-size patterns. While Mr. Shimojo generously invited me to copy all of his patterns and drawings, I was also aware he was not under any obligation to tell me everything.

The Sabani

The sabani is the iconic fishing boat of Okinawa for good reason. Generations of fishermen and boatbuilders refined the shape to create one of the most unique and sculptural boats I have ever seen. Sabani are distinct from all other boats of Japan, and influences on their historic development are more Polynesian than Japanese. But Okinawa is also a group of islands within an island nation, and its relative isolation has meant that, as in other distinct regions, Okinawan boatbuilders developed a craft that was ideal given their materials, technology, fishing methods, and marine environment.

Two previous publications on sabani include detailed discussions of the design and construction of these boats. One is by the late naval architect Yokoyama Akira, who was drawn to the sabani's reputation for speed. In the appendix to his book *Yacht Design* (*Yotto no Sekkei*),[12] Mr. Yokoyama mentions Okinawan boats and includes a set of lines of a sabani. He discovered a mystery in the sabani that he measured: a very slight hollow in the bottom of the boat when viewed in profile. The bottom of the boat was 15 mm higher in the middle than at the ends. Yokoyama theorized this might contribute to the sabani's high performance. He went on to describe several traditional boat types in the Tokyo region—including the *nitaribune, utasebune,* and *chokkibune*—which

(Left) Break time with the Shimojos, their cousin, and the author. Almost all conversation in the shop took place during a morning and afternoon break, when my teacher would either explain the boatbuilding process or tell stories. *Photo copyright George Kochi.* (Above) Mr. Shimojo as a young man in his shop. In the postwar years, he built over one hundred sabani using only hand tools. *Photo copyright Tsunemasa Shimabukuro.*

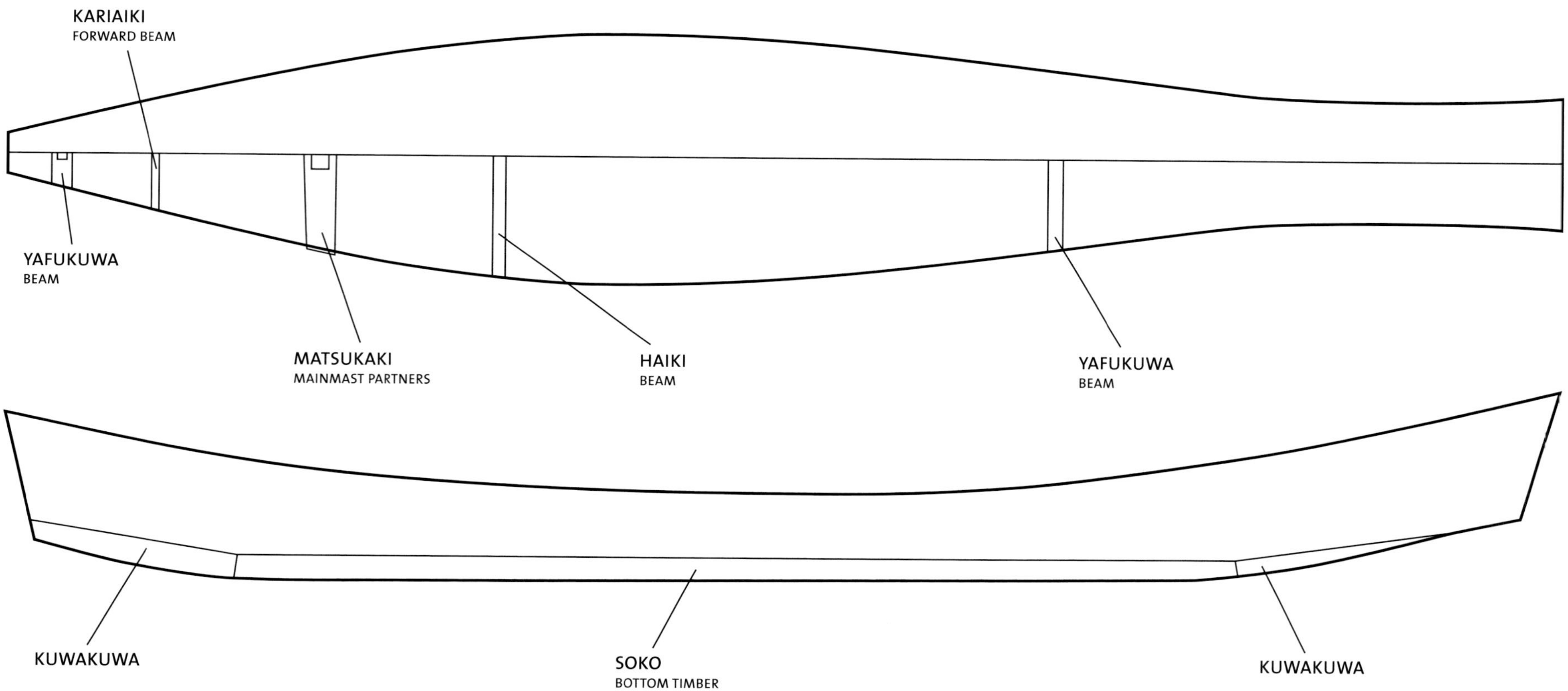

Our eight-meter sabani actually measures 8.24 meters overall, or 27.2 shaku. The beam is 1.32 meters, or 4.35 shaku. Today all sabani are referenced by their length in meters, probably because most sabani sailors are of a generation unfamiliar with the traditional measuring system. While Mr. Shimojo also referred to this boat as an eight-meter sabani, all of our work building it was done using shaku. The names of the parts here reflect terminology used on Iejima and not necessarily throughout Okinawa.

were also built with this unusual hull shape. Yokoyama theorized that sailors who came to the Tokyo region from Okinawa might have imported this idea.[13]

The second book is Shiraishi Katsuhiko's *Sabani: Canoes of Okinawa* (*Okinawa no Fune Sabani*). The author documented the construction of a traditional sabani built by an Okinawan boatbuilder he met in 1970.[14] Mr. Shiraishi's book is beautifully illustrated with sketches, and in general the methods he described match those of Mr. Shimojo. However, one significant difference is his description of bending the side planking. He describes the builder connecting the planks at either end and slowly spreading the planks in the middle. This was different from the method used by Mr. Shimojo, who joined the planks at the bow and then slowly bent them together at the stern. I spoke to several people familiar with sabani construction and none of them believed any builders ever worked the way Mr. Shiraishi described. It is hard to explain such a significant discrepancy.

These divergent views of how sabani are built illustrate the diversity within any traditional craft. We commonly talk of craftspeople as being part of a shared tradition, but as the number of boatbuilders in Japan has dwindled, they have become increasingly isolated as well. In Okinawa the three remaining sabani builders live far apart, on three different islands (Ishigakijima, Okinawa, and Iejima); they are not in contact with each other and may never have even met. More than likely their closest interaction has been seeing one another's boats. But more to the point: since they work alone, are they really part of a tradition?

The sabani's unique shape includes an unusual triangular transom and a high, flaring stern said to resemble a fish. Like other builders of traditional boats in Japan, Okinawan boatbuilders used no drawings, relying on memorized dimensions passed down from master to apprentice. Of the three elderly men in Okinawa today who can build traditional sabani, at least two (including Mr. Shimojo) were self-taught. Their fathers were not boatbuilders, nor did they apprentice with older craftsmen. Instead each worked as fishermen and, immersed in the culture of sabani, developed the intimate understanding of these boats needed to build them.

The sabani is a well-known boat type, even outside Japan. However, except for the two publications mentioned, there has been little formal research done on their history, design, and construction. Perhaps twenty or thirty historic sabani exist in museum and government collections, labeled with brief descriptions.[15] Almost all were built after World War II. Some sabani more than forty years old are still being raced, though many of these have been altered to some degree. In Itoman City and other active fishing ports it is still possible to find large fishing sabani built with inboard engines. Many of these have been coated with fiberglass.

Our first day in the shop Mr. Shimojo told me the first of what would become a list of differences between sabani and Japanese boats, each point underlining his belief that sabani were superior to any Japanese boat. His first dictum: "There are no right angles in sabani," he said, "Wasen are all angles." He was referring to the hard chine construction of Japanese boats.

The sabani's remarkable shape derives from its origins as a dugout canoe.[16] Mr. Shimojo remembered dugout sabani still being used when he was a child. He didn't think much of these precursors to the modern sabani, however. He said they were weak and usually didn't last very long. Carved from a single log, dugout boats by design expose the end grain of the log at bow and stern; end grain soaks up much more moisture, which in turn encourages rot.[17] Nevertheless, the dugout sabani I saw in the Okinawan Prefectural Museum of History in Naha displays the distinctive sabani shape, far more sculptural than the log-like shape of most dugout types.

Another great disadvantage of dugout construction is the waste of resources. Carving a typical boat or canoe from a hollow log means excavating a volume of wood equal to or greater than that of the boat itself. Dugout boats also require larger trees, and so accelerate forest depletion. Scarcity of materials created pressure to develop a different construction style. While the earliest sabani were carved using local woods, beginning even before World War II Okinawan boatbuilders had to rely on cedar (*sugi*) imported from Kyushu.[18]

Sabani represent an evolution from dugout canoes, but they really are a composite construction in which large timbers are fastened together and carved, with carved planks then added. Sabani are not true dugouts, but are also not true plank-built boats. A more correct term for them might be semi-dugout.[19] One might assume a fully plank-built boat would be superior to Mr. Shimojo's semi-dugout construction, but he sees it differently. The entire time we worked together he continually referred to the elevated level of craftsmanship required to build traditional sabani, particularly in regard to the carved nature of construction and the complex shape.

The advent of gasoline power required that sabani change. The boats became larger and wider, although the basic construction methods remained the same. Later, the largest powered sabani featured bulkheads and small cabins enclosing the engines. Some sabani even added horizontal

The launch of one of Mr. Shimojo's fiberglass fishing boats, circa 1980. The buildings behind are the boatbuilder's house and shop. The cinder-block building on the left is the shop where we built our sabani. *Photo copyright Ryujin Shimojo.*

Mr. Shimojo's homemade adze, his main tool for crafting over one hundred sabani in the postwar years.

Mr. Shimojo's hand planes, which he fitted with vertical handles after his stroke to make them easier to use.

boards at the waterline aft to stabilize the craft while under power.

The last days of fishing sabani began in the 1960s as Japanese-style boats became more popular and reached rural islands like Iejima. These were the boats Mr. Shimojo called wasen, referring to the style of plank-built boats from Japan proper, rather than from Okinawa. He began to build them, first in wood, then in fiberglass. Like the trips of his youth taken to observe sabani builders on the main island, Mr. Shimojo traveled to Kyushu and visited a manufacturer of fiberglass boats. After one visit, he came home and began building them himself. In my conversations with him he summed up what he thought of these non-native boats. "You just set up frames on the bottom and bend the planks around. It's easy. As for fiberglass, you just spread the stuff and you have a boat." Mr. Shimojo was an ardent traditionalist, and he never stopped reminding me that sabani represented a far more difficult and challenging type of boat to build.

The rising popularity of sabani racing among recreational sailors has given Okinawa's last sabani builders a chance to build traditional boats again. Mr. Shimojo built a few boats for racing teams, and has built more sabani from the leftover materials he kept. At the time we worked together there were two seven-meter sabani in his shop, along with a six-meter sabani, and a very small four-meter sabani he said had been displayed in a restaurant.

Tools

Mr. Shimojo had a large collection of both hand and power tools. Most of his sabani were built before electric power came to the island in the mid-1960s, and he proudly showed me his adze, or *teono*, literally "hand-axe." With this single tool, made from the spring of an old American military vehicle, he did the bulk of the work shaping and hollowing sabani. He had modified the adze by adding a weight behind the blade to give it more momentum. The traditional Japanese adze, or *chouna,* has a bent handle entering a socket behind the blade. The handle on Mr. Shimojo's adze was at a right angle to the blade, like a Western adze. He also had a large selection of hand planes, with both flat and curved soles he used to finish the surfaces.

As a result of his stroke, Mr. Shimojo could no longer easily use tools with both hands. He now relied heavily on a hand-held electric plane and an angle grinder with a sanding disk for both rough shaping and finish work; he called this tool a *sandaa.* Although small in stature, he could use both hand and power tools with just his right hand. Working with him was a revelation in tenacity, endurance, and talent. I was amazed at his level of skill bringing surfaces to a near perfect finish, working one handed, with these tools.

Some of the larger tools his son Tomio and I used on the project included an electric chainsaw and a large circular saw. Tomio also used an air-powered chisel early in the project to hollow the planks and later to shape the stone anchor. We occasionally used one of two large bandsaws, a table saw, joiner, and planer.

Mr. Shimojo had all the usual measuring tools, including squares and scribing tools, but like most traditional boatbuilders, he did not use a modern tape measure. For long measurements he had a series of homemade wooden rulers called *jougi*. The longest was 6 shaku. Several shorter jougi had small blocks nailed on the ends so he could reach across the hull and hook the other gunwale of the boat. He had both a modern and traditional inkline. One unique resource in the shop was a large collection of offcuts from previous sabani he had built. He saved and labeled these for patterns to double-check our work.

Design

The standard methods for measuring and drawing boats in Japan today is based on modern principles of naval architecture developed in the West. These call for dividing a hull into evenly spaced stations and recording the cross-sectional dimensions at each. Dimensions are taken from a given point, called a baseline, and recorded in a table of offsets; from this table a naval architect or boatbuilder can recreate the lines defining the shape of the boat.

The Western boatbuilder typically makes temporary molds set on the keel, and planks are then bent around these molds. Once the hull is planked, the molds are removed. Japanese boatbuilders do not use molds, but still bend the planking and check the shape of the hull at stations defined by cross-sectional measurements.[20] Boatbuilders on the main islands of Japan typically design and build boats using just three cross sections: one a fixed distance back from the bow, one forward of the stern, and one at the widest point of the hull. Typically the bow and stern sections are the same distance aft of the stem and forward of the transom, respectively. The cross-sectional dimensions give boatbuilders the information they need to lay out the lines for the bottom of the boat, along with the angle and width of the bottom and top planks. My second, third, and fourth teachers all used this method, and I expected Mr. Shimojo to do something similar.[21] Instead, I received the first confirmation of what he had told me the day we met: a sabani is not a wasen. A sabani is a sabani.

Mr. Shimojo had a series of measurements for the width of the finished hull, but the overall shape of the boat was primarily defined by the shape of the two planks comprising the sides of the hull. The basic steps of building Mr. Shimojo's sabani were: 1) cut the planks to shape; 2) bend them to form a hull of the proper width; and 3) fit the bottom to the planking. This process is just opposite from that of all other Japanese boats I have studied, not to mention the fact that all of those were built right side up while sabani are built upside down.

Mr. Shimojo told me that early in his career he laid out the shape of the planking from memory and by eye. Luckily, after returning to building racing sabani late in life, he decided to make rough drawings to record the critical dimensions of his boats, and to make full-size patterns for the side

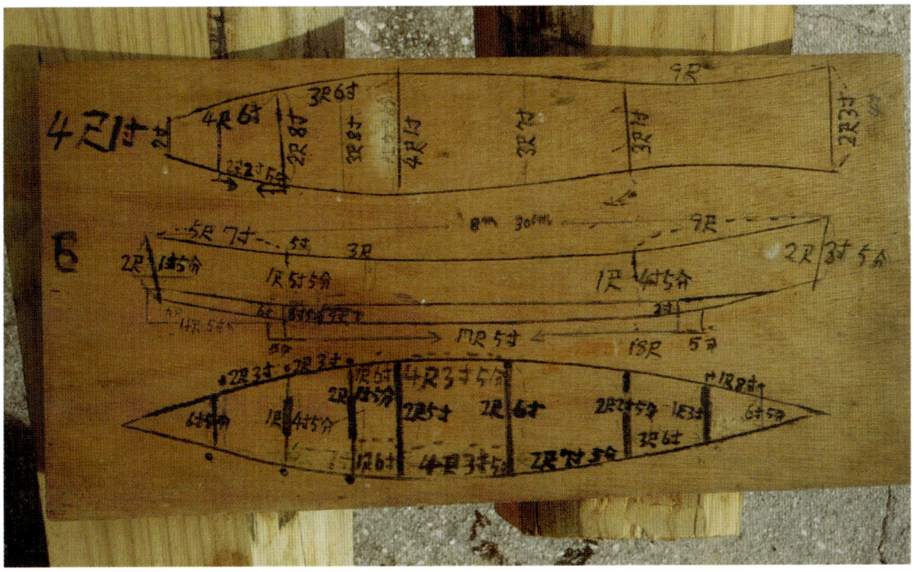

Mr. Shimojo's dimensions for his eight-meter sabani. Late in life, realizing he might forget the measurements of his earliest boats, he recorded them on sheets of plywood.

planks. He also made patterns for the plank bevels. Still, many of the details of the boat he memorized. One of the most important parts of my work involved copying this material and questioning him to make sure I understood all of his notations. Once, as we reviewed his patterns he paused in his explanation, smiling, and said that sabani were "*okashii*," meaning strange, or amusing. He is the only person I have heard describe a boat this way.

Wood

It is said the earliest dugout sabani were made of local pine until the deforestation of Okinawa forced boatbuilders to get their wood from Kyushu. This material was cedar, specifically Miyazaki cedar, prized by boatbuilders in Japan as far north as the Inland Sea.[22] Mr. Shimojo referred to his material as *obisugi* and *benkousugi*. The name obisugi comes from the town and castle of Obi, now part of Nichinan City in Miyazaki Prefecture, Kyushu. Benkousugi specifically refers to logs having two sides trimmed off, leaving the cross section to appear as a circle with two flat sides. Miyazaki cedar has a reputation for being light, easy to bend, and very strong.

Two logs are needed to build a sabani. The larger log for our boat was 2.65 shaku in diameter and Mr. Shimojo ordered it flat sawn into planks 2 sun thick. The other, smaller log, was split in half to provide material for the bottom. The planks arrived stacked in the same orientation as in the log. Mr. Shimojo did not use the two planks sawn from the center (which were the widest), but the next two adjacent planks. Choosing symmetrical planks from the log is something my other teachers did as well. I never questioned this practice but later, when we were bending the planks, Mr. Shimojo explained that given their thickness, it was important they bend with the same radius to produce a symmetrical hull. This makes perfect sense: using material taken symmetrically from the log, each plank was likely to have a similar grain structure, and theoretically would bend to the same curve. Timber movement is a real issue working with material this thick; thus another reason for matching grain and arranging pieces symmetrically would be to avoid the hull twisting. A sixty-year old sabani on display in front of the Iejima City Office has a severe twist in the hull, evidence of just how much large timbers can move.

We oriented the hull planking so the heart side of the plank faced to the outside of the boat. Mr. Shimojo said that planks aligned this way would be more likely to flare out.[23] Ideally he tried to minimize the amount of sapwood in the boat, because it is more prone to rot than the heartwood. He also pointed out that hull would have the root end of all plank material toward the bow. In the West boatbuilders sometimes utilize the natural flare of the wood at the base of the tree in order to match the sweep of the planking. Mr. Shimojo believed this was an issue not of shape but of strength; he felt the wood at the base of the tree was better able to absorb the shock of the boat plowing through the sea. He also said the leftover material from the two logs would yield enough material for a second sabani, seven meters long, and there might even be material for a third boat five meters long.

Other Okinawan woods we used included Okinawan pine for beams; *inomaki*, also called *chage*, for the huundu fastenings; and *mokkoku*, also called *motsukoken* or *iiku*, for paddles.[24] The sawmill in Miyazaki sent a large piece of *mosodake* bamboo for our nails. Mr. Shimojo would have preferred to have had cedar air-dried for at least one year. Our material was not completely dry, and he gave this as one reason we glued all the parts of the hull in addition to the fastenings. He called our glue *bondo,* after the trade name for an adhesive wood-filler, but in fact we used a urea resin-based glue from a company called Aika Kogyo.[25] For filling large gaps we mixed fine sawdust produced by our sander into the glue to form a thick paste.

We used regular soybean-based cooking oil as a lubricant for both our huundu and bamboo nails. We also dipped our chisels in this oil when we were cutting mortises. In the past Mr. Shimojo had used shark liver oil in the shop. We coated our sabani using tempura cooking oil and just after completion, when we were given a small quantity of shark liver oil, this was put on the boat as a final coat.

Planking

Before I arrived on Iejima, Mr. Shimojo and his son had already roughed out the parts for the hull using a chainsaw, and cut the two planks to their basic shape. My first day on the job focused on gluing up two pieces of cedar to each plank to give it enough width at the stern. The top piece is a large triangle forming the high stern that is a distinctive feature of these boats. Its hood (forward) end was notched into the main plank with an angled scarf so when the plank was bent, the forward end of the piece would resist springing out. We spread glue on both surfaces and Mr. Shimojo had a selection of large clamps to force the parts together. He also had many dogs (homemade iron staples) for clamping and we used these throughout the project.

The day after we glued the planking I got my first chance to install huundu, the ancient fastening for which the sabani

Side planks prior to gluing and joining with fastenings. The rise in the stern of these boats necessitated adding material to our planks.

Cutting huundu on the bandsaw. Later the sawn faces are finished with a chisel.

is famous. Mr. Shimojo had no idea where the name came from, but one theory is that it derived from *fundou*, an ancient weight it slightly resembles. Mr. Shimojo believed both name and technique came from China.[26]

Huundu are installed spanning the joint between two planks with the seam running through the narrow waist of the fastening. Mr. Shimojo mass-produced huundu, cutting a series of angled faces on a long piece of wood. The individual huundu were then cross-cut out on the bandsaw. The ends were not chiseled or sanded, but we did trim off the slight tearout left by the bandsaw blade. Mr. Shimojo tried to use vertical grain material, but this did not seem like an absolute requirement. He finished the angled faces using a sharp chisel. He told me he makes this cut at a very slight angle which, he said, could not be measured or seen; he did it entirely by feel, bearing down slightly on one side of the chisel while making the cut. The result was the angled faces of the huundu were ever so slightly tapered, the smaller face

(Top left) Each huundu is slightly different, so we used each fastening to trace its mortise, numbering each one. Then we drilled out much of the waste using a drill with a stop collar set for the proper depth. (Top right) Chiseling the mortise, working carefully toward the lines. The mark on the neck of the chisel represents the depth of the mortise. (Lower left above) The secret to the holding power of the *huundu* is cutting the mortise to the line at the corners, but leaving it slightly undersized at the waist. When installed, this leftover material act like a wedge, pulling the two planks together. (Lower right above) The huundu installed. Later it will be planed flush with the planking. Huundu are soaked in oil before being driven into their mortises with a mallet, and no glue is used.

entering the mortise first. He marked the inside face of the huundu so we could orient them correctly.

Our first huundu would be mortised 6 bu deep into the outside face of the planking, 1 shaku apart along the length of the seam. A second set of huundu would be inserted later on the inside of the planking, after the plank was hollowed, also 1 shaku apart, but laid out to land exactly between the huundu on the outside. It was essential not to chisel the mortises more than 6 bu, because we would be hollowing much of the planking to an 8 bu thickness. The huundu are slightly random sizes, so we used each one as a pattern for its own mortise. Mr. Shimojo insisted his son and I use very sharp pencils, tracing fine lines around the edges of the huundu. Huundu derive their holding strength from a precise fit and the wedging action of the four angled sides.

Before chiseling, we removed some of the material in the mortise using a large drill fitted with a stop collar. Mr. Shimojo said to check the depth of the mortise by chiseling just to the bottom of the drilled hole. I also marked the mortise depth on the back of the chisels with a pen, which I found easier to use for checking. We used a chisel 1 sun wide, working from the center of the mortise in a series of closely spaced parallel cuts. With a narrow chisel we would then clean out the waste, moving toward the outside edges of the mortise. It is extremely important to cut the sides of the mortise straight down; thus the huundu have a slight taper but the mortises do not. We cut to the line at the ends of the mortise, but along the angled sides we cut to the line only at the four outer corners. The cut runs slightly inside the line to the waist. This tiny amount of material left is the secret to how the huundu works mechanically: as it is driven tight into the mortise the four angled sides act like four wedges, each pair pulling the two adjacent planks toward one another.

Mr. Shimojo said the square ends of the huundu should just fit snugly at the top and bottom of the mortise, as a tighter fit would tend to wedge the planks apart. Before inserting the huundu in the mortise, the bottom corners are slightly chamfered with a chisel or knife. The huundu is then dipped in oil and driven in tight with a mallet. For someone making these for the first time, it is important to keep the chisels very sharp; cedar is soft and the best-looking huundu will be those set in cleanly cut mortises.

Next, Mr. Shimojo drilled holes for the bamboo nails at a very acute angle through the two pieces being joined, making sure the holes would not come out of the face of the planking. He used a 6 mm drill bit, 4.5 sun long, and drilled a hole 2.5 sun to either side of the outside huundu. This meant that when all huundu were installed inside and out, there would be a bamboo nail midpoint between each.

The bamboo nails were roughly shaped from split pieces of bamboo. The nail "heads" are the node section of the bamboo. Each nail is rounded and given a very slight taper to the point. The shaft is about 2.5 bu in diameter and 8 sun long. At the tip they are beveled like a chisel blade, not pointed, from the bark side.

To install the nails, Mr. Shimojo aligned them with the bark side facing the plank. He said the bevel would tend to make the nail curve as it was driven. We also dipped the nails in oil before carefully hammering them into the holes. Bamboo nails will not readily drive through cedar so one has to be careful, hammering only until the bamboo nail fetches up tight at the bottom of the pilot hole. Once installed, we trimmed the nails and huundu flush to the planking with a saw.

We then began hollowing out sections of the planking. The material was rough sawn and 2 sun thick. Mr. Shimojo laid his patterns carefully end to end on the planking stock. The outer edges of the patterns defined the outside of the finished planks, and on the face of the pattern were lines marking where the planking would not be hollowed, leaving extra material at the gunwale, bow, and stern, and for material to support the thwarts, the crosspieces used as seats.[27] Mr. Shimojo poked an awl through the patterns to mark the corners of the thwart risers, and after the patterns were removed we drew lines in ink to mark these edges.

When cutting the planks to size, it was deemed important to leave 1.5 sun of extra material above the edge of the pattern along the sheer (top edge of the plank). We did this because the sheer is beveled significantly. When the planks are bent and the hull completed, the gunwale is supposed to be flat (horizontal). The plank pattern marks the *inside*

(Above) Bamboo nails peg the two planks together. Mr. Shimojo believed that huundu held them together while the bamboo nails prevented them from shifting. (Right) Mr. Shimojo planing the bevel on the top edge of a plank. He holds one of his nine bevel patterns in his mouth.

face of the planking, which is not as wide as the outside face. Mr. Shimojo beveled the top edge of the planks using a series of nine patterns, starting at the bow and spaced evenly along the top edge from bow to stern. He first beveled the edges at each spot using his patterns; he and I then faired the changing bevel over the full length of the two planks.

The bottom edges of the planks were left square. Mr. Shimojo put the two planks together on edge and worked very carefully to plane these edges smooth; he said any mistakes here would create a lot of work later. He again stressed the need for the boatbuilder to be able to work by intuition. Pointing to my camera, he said a boatbuilder must have a skilled eye for the shape of the boat. "My eye understands well," he said. "Your camera can't learn this. You must train your eye."

The planks were carved to two different depths. Above the thwart riser, wood was removed to a depth of 1 sun, with the sheer left the full 2 sun thick forming the gunwale. At the bottom edge of the riser 8 bu was removed, tapering to the bottom edge of the plank, which was left full thickness. Mr. Shimojo said in the days before power tools he would chisel all the edges along the gunwale, bow and stern, and around the risers. He would make a series of saw cuts with a handsaw across the grain to the finished depth and then chop out the material between cuts with the adze. He used his selection of planes to smooth the planks to their final finish, as there was no sandpaper available. He said he could prepare a set of planks like this in one week when he was young. All of our final finish work was with electric sanders, but Mr. Shimojo claimed that a surface finished with a sharp hand plane is the most beautiful.[28]

To hollow the planking we first used a circular saw to make cuts defining the outer edges of where we would carve. Below the gunwale the saw was set to a 10-degree bevel, and we carefully checked that the depth of the cut was set to 1 sun. We used the bevel of the third plank bevel gauge and set the saw to about a 30-degree angle for the top and bottom edges of the risers. On the bottom cut we reduced the depth to 8 bu.

The next tool we used Mr. Shimojo called a *mizohoriki*: a large, powerful circular saw with a dado head blade that cut a swath about 8 bu wide. The tool was set to cut to our full depth. Because it was removing a lot of material, it was very hard to push. Mr. Shimojo's son Tomio and I shared this work. We had to leave material between each cut so the tool still had something to ride on, but we tried to remove as much as we could.

Closeup of hollowing the inside of the planking. The outline of the thwart risers were cut with a circular saw, and divots left from the dado cutter are visible.

Most of Mr. Shimojo's hand planes had tightly curved soles for hollowing material. I welcomed using these traditional tools to avoid the dust generated by power planes and sanders.

When it was no longer possible to use the mizohoriki I worked with hand tools, including planes, gouges, and chisels. Tomio used an air-powered chisel, and Mr. Shimojo used an angle grinder with 60-grit sanding disks. The clouds of sawdust generated when he used the angle grinder literally drove Tomio and me away from the boat at times. All we could do was stand outside watching while Mr. Shimojo continued sanding, disappearing ghost-like in a fog of sawdust.

During this process, I was also busy sweeping and bagging cedar shavings and sawdust. Soon one corner of the shop was piled six feet high with bags of shavings. In fact, in a nod to the traditional apprentice work, I did all of the cleaning for the entire project. A few times Mr. Shimojo's wife tried to sweep when she visited the shop, but I always took the broom from her. She would laugh and say, "That was always my job!"

Mr. Shimojo controlled the depth of our carving by drilling a series of holes, carving around them to a specific depth and marking the spot. We carved and sanded until we reached his mark.

Mr. Shimojo and the author sanding the inside of the planking. The gunwales are to the outside with the thwart risers visible near the bottom edge of the planking.

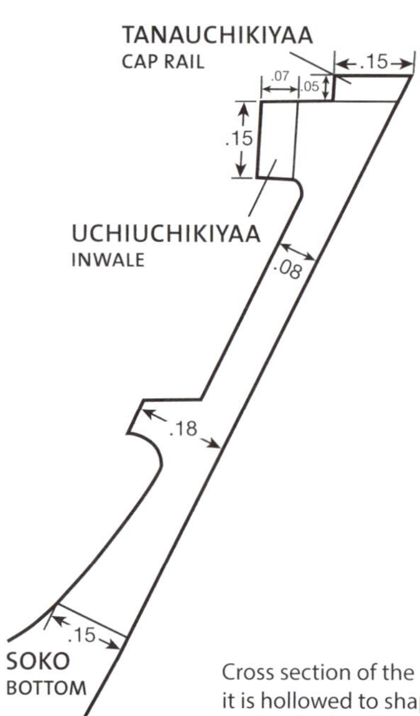

Cross section of the planking, showing how it is hollowed to shape. The step left in the middle of the plank is the support for the thwarts.

Once the planking was roughly hollowed out Mr. Shimojo drilled a series of small holes through it—just under the gunwale and just above the risers—spaced about 2 shaku apart. Next he wrapped tape on his awl as a stop 8 bu from the tip. He proceeded to carve a small depression on the inside of the planking at each hole, checking the depth by poking the awl through from the outside and feeling for the tip on the inside. Once he had carved a depression to a depth of 8 bu, he marked the bottom with a pencil; our job then was to plane and sand the surface just to the point when the pencil mark disappeared.

Tomio and I used round-bottomed planes to shape a radius under the gunwale and risers, while Mr. Shimojo used the angle grinder to get the hollowed portions ready for finish sanding. The top of the risers were planed to a thirty-degree bevel. Final sanding of the flat surface was done with pad sanders; for the underside of the gunwale and risers, and at the bow and stern, Mr. Shimojo made curved sanding pads out of pieces of styrofoam.

The last steps in preparing the planks were to bevel the inside face of the gunwale and to plane the bow and stern where the planks would meet. Finishing the surfaces had reduced the overall thickness of the planking from 2 sun (rough) to 1.8 sun. Using another pattern placed on the top edge of the gunwale, we planed material off so that the inside edge of the gunwale would be vertical when the hull was finished. Mr. Shimojo made sure the width of the top edges of the gunwale (the horizontal surface) remained consistent at 1.8 sun over the entire length. At the bottom edge of the planking we carved from the base of the risers to the bottom edge, making the entire bottom edge of the planking 1.5 sun thick. We took measurements, starting at the stern from the *outside* face of the plank, 1.5 sun to mark this edge; however, from the bow this 1.5 sun is measured from the *inside* face of the plank, tapering to zero about 10 shaku aft of the bow. We faired this transition from one side to the other keeping a constant 1.5 sun width. At the bow this edge and the bottom corner were planed very carefully. Mr. Shimojo said shifting the line this way helps give the bow the proper shape. Another bevel was planed at the stern where the two planks will meet when they are bent.

At this point in the project Tomio was working with us only part time. Mr. Shimojo, of course, was working every day, while I was working probably half the time directly on the boat and half the time cleaning the shop, measuring, photographing, videotaping, and making notes. Despite all the advantages of power tools, it still took us about a week to hollow and finish the two planks, which was about the same amount of time it took Mr. Shimojo to do this by hand, alone, over fifty years ago.

Given all the work required to hollow the planking, I couldn't help but fantasize about an easier method; specifically, building up these planks out of two layers, essentially laminating the gunwales, risers, etc. to a plank 8 bu thick. When I went to the sabani races in Itoman City I saw boats built this way. They were called *nanyouhagi*, meaning literally "southern construction" or, more loosely, the "foreign way." The name reflects influences on Okinawan boatbuilding from the south, primarily from the first European explorers of East Asia. According to a history published by the City of Itoman, nanyouhagi-style sabani were invented by Mr. Uehara Shintaro. Mr. Shintaro moved to Saipan in 1935, but he could not find the large-scale materials needed to build sabani in the traditional style, so he built them using thin boards and construction lumber. The book contends it was Mr. Shintaro who first brought this method to Okinawa.[29]

When I raised the topic of the possible advantages of this type of construction Mr. Shimojo shook his head and said one word: *"Dame"* (bad). There was no further discussion of nanyouhagi. When he later told me that a sabani, properly cared for, could last the lifetime of its owner, his inflexible opinion began to make sense to me. This longevity was the direct result of using thick, carved timbers; the extra few weeks of labor needed to build traditional sabani was more than compensated for by its extended useful life. There was also an advantage in stability, since the thick timber bottom of a traditional sabani acts like a weighted keel.

Bending the Planks

With the planking hollowed Tomio and I installed the huundu on the inside seams. Meanwhile, Mr. Shimojo carefully laid out measurements and drilled holes through the planking where we would install eyebolts for the hardware that would help us bend the planking. We also glued and nailed thin pieces of cedar to cover the end grain of the planking at the bow and stern. This precaution served to prevent the planking from drying out too quickly and cracking.[30] We set up two large sawhorses to hold the planks, carefully leveling each of them. From this point we had to be very careful about bumping and possibly moving the assembly.[31]

Mr. Shimojo told me that when building his first sabani he tried to complete the bending in one day and a plank split. From then on he took his time with this process.[32] He said we would take three days, using hot water from a diesel boiler sitting outside the shop. We would slowly soak the planks and force them to shape. We draped burlap on the planks to hold in the heat and moisture, and for the next few days Tomio and I sprayed hot water on the planks, inside and out, while Mr. Shimojo slowly tightened a complex system of chains and turnbuckles that are called *taanbakkuru*, from the English. His wife reminisced how she used to tend a large pot of water over a wood fire, carrying the hot water into the shop a bucket at a time.[33]

Beginning the bending. Temporary hooks are visible where turnbuckles are attached to bend the planking, and bars are inserted between the planks to spread the gunwale. Mr. Shimojo had a set of bars of the proper length for each size sabani he built.

A view aft from inside the boat showing the spreading bars and turnbuckles.

We clamped the bow ends of the planks together, leaving room for Mr. Shimojo to run a handsaw in between the two planks at the base of the bow. Like all my other teachers, he used the sawing method to fit parts of the boat. His name for this was *surinoko.*[34] At the bow Mr. Shimojo worked carefully sawing this joint, and he explained to me the goal was not to saw quickly, or necessarily use a lot of force. In fact the joint would be higher quality if the saw progressed slowly, leaving very closely spaced kerfs in the wood. To hold the

The bent planks seen from the bow.

The planking seen from the stern.

seam open so he could saw freely through the joint, he used a set of old handsaws with the blades broken off and the ends ground smooth. He inserted these to wedge the seam open slightly so his handsaw would not bind. He had no name for these homemade tools, but they were perfect for the job. My other teachers had used wooden wedges (*kusabi*) or caulking irons (*yatoko*) to do this, but Mr. Shimojo's recycled saws were a brilliant adaptation.

What made Mr. Shimojo's teaching distinct from that of my other teachers was his insistence on the measured pace of our work. From this point in the project he began punctuating most instructions with the phrase *yukkuri douzo,* "Please go slowly." He stressed again and again, when bending planks or fitting with the handsaw, that we needed to work methodically and not rush any task.

He also explained that no two sabani are exactly the same; each evolves distinctly into being. He alluded to the moment when we would finally turn the hull over. Only then would we finally be able to see and appreciate its shape and the boat truly be "born." Until then, not even the boatbuilder could be sure how successful his work had been. I began to understand the difference between the sabani and all the other boats I had ever made, which were essentially composed of individual parts assembled to make the larger object. Fashioning a boat from very large timbers is a very different process and, it seems fair to say, requires a different mindset and attitude.

By the third day bending the planks we began to install wooden bars called *tsuppari* that Mr. Shimojo had labeled and stored on a shelf in the shop. Tsuppari are cut to specific lengths, and when installed spread the planks apart to a precise width. He had these dimensions written on his plank drawing, and as we got closer to the finished shape he checked the measurements on the boat. I watched as he used his hook-ended wooden ruler to catch the outside of the opposite plank at the gunwale, the edge nearest the floor, and read the dimensions to the outside of the planking. Yet when he measured the width of the planks at the keel, he butted his ruler against the inside edge and read this dimension inside of the planking.

When I asked about this discrepancy, he confirmed a crucial point: that his widths at the sheer were to the *outside* of the planking, and the widths at the bottom were to the *inside* of the planking. However, nowhere on his drawings had he indicated this. His reasoning was a pragmatic solution to a boatbuilder's problem. The planks are splayed at a steep angle and at points along the sheer a ruler hooks the outside edge more easily. Conversely, at the keel where the edges cant inward the ruler won't hook, so the easiest way to measure the beam is by butting the ruler to the inside edge. Of course *he* would never confuse these dimensions, since where and when to butt or hook the ruler was automatic, while to my mind this was a convincing case for the need of precisely the kind of research I was doing. Mr. Shimojo's drawings were actually much more comprehensive than many others I have seen in Japan, but this important detail illustrates how in the Japanese tradition, drawings still require the boatbuilder's interpretation. The boatbuilder draws only for himself, with no regard to how clear his work may be to someone else. Almost every boatbuilder I have met in Japan who uses drawings omits key lines or dimensions. Crucial angles or ratios are memorized and not recorded. Someone trying to use Mr. Shimojo's drawings without this explanation would be completely confused.

As the planks came together at the stern we noticed they were not aligned, and it was necessary to run a chain diagonally from the aft end of one plank forward to the other to pull the two back into position. Mr. Shimojo used the plane to bevel the two faces meeting at the stern, which reduced the amount of material we would have to remove sawing through the joint. First we lowered the stern from the sawhorse aft down onto a low block and clamped the planking together. It was here I made my first mistake.

Mr. Shimojo said in most sabani just the lower corner of the two planks touch at the stern, but in his boats the planks come together in a seam along the bottom almost 2 shaku long. He claimed this was an innovation of his that makes the hull stronger and more beautiful. As I was sawing this seam I failed to check inside and the saw ran off into one of the planks, rather than tracking down between them. Mr. Shimojo checked for this constantly when he did surinoko and I should have learned from seeing how cautious he was. He was clearly upset when I showed him what had happened, and he took the saw from me and worked the seam until the mistake was fixed. A pall fell over the shop and we worked for several hours in complete silence, fastening the seam with three huundu and two bamboo nails. Later, while we sat having tea at break he suddenly laughed about it, telling me, "Small mistakes are okay." He also once again stressed I needed to develop an eye for the boat and, pointing to my notebook, said writing everything down might help me understand, but it wouldn't be enough to master the craft. I was grateful for the tacit forgiveness of my error.

The next day we finished bending the planking. We set up a string down the centerline where the bottom would go and found the bends in the two planks were not perfectly symmetrical. The measurement to the port side was 1.54 shaku and to the starboard side 1.49 shaku. To correct this, we placed a wooden prop at a diagonal against one plank. Because the force required to bend the plank threatened to move the whole boat, Mr. Shimojo considered pouring more hot water on one side to try to increase the curve. In the end we bolted a block to the floor, and with a turnbuckle and chain, we pulled the plank into place.

Bottom

We had now worked eleven days on the project. It was time to begin fitting the bottom, called the *soko.* We wheeled a massive piece of cedar into the shop, 18.5 shaku long, 1.8 shaku wide, and 7.5 sun thick. It would be placed heart side out from the boat, just like the side planking, with the root end of the timber facing the bow. The tree it came from was over 2 shaku in diameter and was sawn exactly in half. This timber would form the center of the sabani's bottom, with two more timbers to be joined to it on either side.

The massive timber for the bottom, first put on the boat. The bottom of our boat was made of three pieces of cedar, but Mr. Shimojo said in the old days he could find material large enough to make the bottoms in a single piece.

Mr. Shimojo scribing the bottom to fit the side planks, holding a batten at arm's length and aligning it by eye.

Using a chainfall running on a cable across the shop we hoisted the bottom timber and laid it down on the planking. Mr. Shimojo's method of scribing was very interesting: he held a batten about 5 bu wide at arm's length against the edge of the bottom timber, and tried to align the bottom edge of the batten with the edge of the planking. Because of the overhang of the bottom timber all he could do was line up the batten by sight. He then traced the top edge of the batten on the bottom timber. Our batten was only about 2 shaku long, so we did this in stages around the boat. We then took the timber off the boat, lowered it onto sawhorses, and rolled it over. Mr. Shimojo drew a line connecting his marks and, using the power plane, he planed to the line, taking off about 4 bu of material. Next we rolled the timber and hoisted it back on the boat and repeated the process. The first pass was the roughest by far; on subsequent passes we removed far less material.

Scribing the fit at the stern.

Mr. Shimojo shaping the outside of the bottom timber.

The first side timber is fit alongside the center.

We interrupted the fitting of the soko to work on hollowing its interior. Earlier, Tomio had roughed out the inside using a chainsaw. The forward end of the hollow transitioned to a V-shape near the bow where a large block of material was left for the mast step. When we started, the soko was 3 sun thick at its thinnest point; Mr. Shimojo said the finished thickness would be 2.25 sun. I was stunned by how much material had to be removed, and could not understand why we didn't just cut this material off the flat side of the timber, but Mr. Shimojo insisted this had to be done gradually as we fitted it, and so, just like with the planking, he drilled a series of holes down the centerline of the soko and carved depressions to the 2.25 thickness. He also said the distance from the bottom of the soko to the top of the gunwale, measured vertically, would be 1.55 shaku forward and 1.45 shaku aft. These dimensions would also guide how much material we needed to take off the bottom.

My notebook typically included several pages of text for each day of work. On December 1, 2009, I wrote only: "Day fifteen. Worked on soko all day." The process of measuring and fitting the center timber of the soko had required us to move it on and off the boat twenty times up to this point, and we were still not finished. I operated the chainfall, which Mr. Shimojo called the *chieingorokku,*[35] to move the timber between the boat and sawhorses, while he measured how much wood had to be trimmed. I did most of the planing. He told me in the old days these timbers were moved with a block and tackle, which he called a *kassha*. Later his wife came in and explained she was the person who operated the block and tackle. Slowly it was emerging what a significant role she played, working directly in the boatshop alongside her husband, particularly after their children were grown. During her regular visits to the shop to bring us food or tea, it became clear how well she understood the whole process.[36]

Months after the project was finished and I returned to the United States one of my contacts in Japan told me it was Mrs. Shimojo who had finally convinced her husband to teach me. I basically took over her role in the shop, doing all the cleaning, and operating the chainfall and large tools. Mr. Shimojo did most of the skilled work, but as the project wore on he let me do more, particularly when he became tired. Working seven days a week also began to wear me down as well, but I was in awe of my teacher's stamina and determination. He was basically trying to work at the pace he labored as a young man. Due to his disabilities, the two seven-meter sabani stacked along one wall of the shop had taken him over a year to build. In our case, he knew I could only stay in Okinawa for a little more than two-and-a-half months, and he understood how much I wanted to see the project through to completion.

After five full days of this work, we finished the center timber for the soko and turned to the two side pieces that complete the bottom. The wood for these pieces came from quarter sections of the same cedar log that gave us the timber for the center. The first step was to flatten the edges where they would meet the center piece. Later we would finalize this fit, but Mr. Shimojo worked very slowly and carefully with his electric plane, checking with his square, until the three pieces of the soko fit nearly perfectly. We drove two large iron staples fitted to a sling into the side piece so we could hook them with the chainfall. Unlike the center timber, which needed to be fitted to the planking only at the ends, the seam of the side timbers was a long curving arc along the planking. Our first day we took the first side timber on and off the boat ten times for fitting. In fitting the side pieces Mr. Shimojo began to go under the boat to scribe the seam on the inside as well as outside.

At the start of the process Mr. Shimojo was removing up to 5 bu of material each time he trimmed the soko; it was an enormous amount of material to remove with an electric plane. I kept thinking, while I watched and waited for his order to move the timber, that he could have carefully measured the shape he needed and cut nearly all this material off at once. As the fit got closer he would check inside and out, now trimming the soko much less, and when we put it back on the boat, we might find the gap that had been at the forward end was now tight, but there was a gap at the stern. We continued back and forth, with the fit very slowly getting closer each time. He also began to use his bevel gauge to check the fit and mark the spots that needed planing. Soon the fit was so close he used his old saw blade in the seam to feel for gaps.

At one point when he was under the boat Mr. Shimojo told me, referring to the seam "I need to see and remember where it fits and where it is open." Then he added, to my surprise, "You are wondering why this is so slow." It was one of the very few moments he paused while working to give me a detailed explanation. He pointed out that he was not able to go to the sawmill and supervise the milling of these timbers, so they came to his shop oversized. Because of his stroke he can no long use a chainsaw, and thus he had no way to cut them smaller. He said in the past he would have moved the soko on and off the boat only three or four times, trimming it with a chainsaw, and it would then be ready for a final fit.

While I may have been impatient with the process of fitting the soko, I recalled Mr. Shimojo telling me traditional sabani, if well cared of, could last the lifetime of their owners. Indeed, there were several sabani in Itoman at the race I watched that were over forty years old. An extra week of work building the boat is thus insignificant, given the longevity of the finished product. And Mr. Shimojo's slow, deliberate approach to fitting the soko would in fact be the perfect method for those trying to build their first sabani, as repeated attempts would be excellent training in developing skills or, to use his phrase, "training the eye."

That same day a local acquaintance brought an elderly ethnologist from Tokyo to the shop to meet Mr. Shimojo and see his work. Mr. Shimojo loved visitors, whether schoolchildren, old customers, relatives, or complete strangers. Mrs. Shimojo demanded we break precisely at noon every day for lunch, but our morning and afternoon breaks were random. The arrival of a visitor almost always precipitated a break. The ethnologist was particularly interested in Mr. Shimojo's description of the *noro,* or female shamans that dominate Okinawan religious life. Mr. Shimojo said our boat would be blessed upon completion by a 94-year old woman who lived nearby. She was a *yuta,* which can be translated as fortune teller, but one level below noro. As in Shinto launching ceremonies, she would use rice, salt, and sake in blessing our boat.

Our visitor, who looked oddly familiar, had a wild mane of white hair and could have been a shaman himself. He listened intently as Tomio explained that behind the Shinto torii gate in the harbor was not a shrine, but a *yutaki,* or shrine object. It was a small piece of rock, perhaps symbolizing the island's Mount Gusuku, which was also considered a scared place. Eventually our conversation about the spiritual wound down, and we returned to our work; still, it was fascinating to to be reminded of the linkages between the two operative in the craftsman's world.[37]

Eventually Mr. Shimojo was satisfied with the fit of the three soko timbers to one another and to the planking. We then placed the center timber on its side on sawhorses and stacked a side timber on top of it. The three of us all did surinoko (see Chapter 5) to finish the two straight seams. For this, we used a new handsaw and Tomio instructed me to hold the saw square to the surface or at a slight angle. It is crucial the saw handle not wander up or down, but be held steady at level of the seam. Otherwise the saw will run out of the seam and start cutting into the wood, so it is important to check often. Tomio described the process as rubbing more than cutting (he compared it to making glass lenses). Even when there is little resistance, the saw needs to advance very slowly. Tomio said as long as sawdust is coming out, the saw is cutting. One seam was already tight at the two ends, and Tomio made four passes through those areas to make a fit, then three easy passes slowly across the middle. In all we spent about an hour on each seam.

Mr. Shimojo actually relied on the surinoko technique far less than my other teachers; building a tub boat (see Chapter 9) we didn't do this at all. After building about eighty sabani Mr. Shimojo began making Japanese-style wooden fishing boats. He was disparaging of this kind of construction,

Final fit of the seam between bottom timbers, working with them stacked vertically.

The author fitting the bottom timbers by sawing through the seam. *Photo copyright Tsunemasa Shimabukuro.*

Mr. Shimojo's old saws with the teeth ground off, which he inserted into seams to hold them apart while doing surinoko.

specifically because of what he considered an over reliance on this technique to fit planks. He said excessive sawing of the seam inevitably rounds their edges, so when he built wasen he fit the planking with a plane and just made a single pass with the saw through the seam. This is another example of his isolation from tradition; he may have used techniques in common with other boatbuilders but he didn't hesitate to modify them as he saw fit.[38]

We placed all three parts of the soko together on the hull and clamped them. Still not satisfied with the fit to the side planks, Mr. Shimojo took it apart and made two more final fittings of one side piece, this time using a hand plane and removing just a tiny bit of material. He finally pronounced the soko ready for gluing.

The soko was intentionally sized to overhang the side planking by about 5 bu. Anticipating the final fit, Mr. Shimojo mentioned that given the size of the timbers they probably twisted slightly as we planed them down to size, which is reasonable given just how much wood we had removed and how this would change stresses within the material. Our final adjustment was the sixteenth time we had removed the side timber for fitting.

The three parts of the soko were glued together while it sat on top of the boat. Sheets of plastic were slipped between the planking and the soko to prevent them from sticking together, and the glue was spread quickly on all the surfaces to be joined. Eight large clamps, along with large temporary dogs both inside and out clamped the soko together. Mr. Shimojo mixed an accelerant that he called *koukazai* into his glue, and it began to harden within about twenty minutes.

Assembling the Bottom and Sides

The next day was my twenty-second on the project. We removed the clamps and dogs from the soko. Mr. Shimojo then sketched the rough outline of where we needed to plane material to begin shaping the outer face of the bottom. We began rough beveling the soko with the power planes. He marked where the huundu would go along the glued seams, while I prepared to move the timber once again to the sawhorses. The spacing of the huundu was always the same: 1 shaku between each, adjusting if necessary to avoid a knot, with holes drilled for bamboo nails centered between the huundu on the outside and inside. This put the bamboo nails 5 sun on center. We only drilled these holes about 3 sun deep. The nails were driven through the side timbers of the soko into the center, with the bark side of the bamboo facing the soko. It took us about two-and-a-half hours to mortise and insert all the huundu and bamboo nails.

The next day Mr. Shimojo shaped the mast step, using his angle grinder, while I used the round bottom plane and hollowed the interior of the soko. The dust was so choking I had taken to wearing the white surgical mask that is ubiquitous in Japan. Mr. Shimojo acknowledged the disadvantage of his angle grinder was the huge amounts of dust it created. He said his glasses prevented him from wearing a mask, which was unfortunate. I suggested we use a fan to circulate the air but he said no, he didn't want to disturb his neighbors with the dust. At about this point in the project I was trying to clean the dust from my camera lens. I was mystified because it wasn't wiping off, and then I realized the dust had gotten *inside* the lens. One of my jobs was to use the blower nozzle on Shimojo's air compressor and periodically blow the dust off him.

To check the thickness and to see if the bottom was hollowed symmetrically, Mr. Shimojo laid a straightedge across it and measured down at points 5 sun from the outer edge. He did this all the way around the soko at 1 shaku intervals and discovered one side was about 2 to 3 bu higher than the other. Working together we planed and sanded until the two sides were even. Our hand planes were not much slower than power tools, and certainly safer. As we worked Mr. Shimojo again reminisced about building sabani with just his planes and adze.[39]

With the bottom almost finished we laid out the location of the inside huundu, positioned between the outside fastenings. The huundu in the bottom were set 9 bu deep. Unlike the side planking, where we had to gauge very carefully the depth of the mortise, here we had plenty of wood.

Once the soko was fastened together we carefully laid it on top of the hull, placing some small wedges at the four corners. Though everything had fit perfectly before we assembled the soko, it had changed shape again, slightly, and there were small gaps in the seam. This was expected, and Mr. Shimojo had started his day sharpening a large, old handsaw, which Tomio took and began to run through the seam. Here the seam is at an angle, so it is more difficult to hold the saw, plus the grain of the side planking is running out in one direction while the grain of the soko is running out in the other. This is by far the most difficult place to do surinoko, because when sawing against the grain, the grain wants to pull the saw out of the seam. Plus, the face of the soko against the saw blade is wider than the plank edge, and this pushes the saw to one side. Despite his many years of experience, Mr. Shimojo constantly paused in his work, painstakingly getting down on the floor and looking inside the boat to check his progress. Due to his stroke one of his legs was nearly paralyzed, so getting under the boat and back up was a slow and precarious process; twice he fell getting to his feet.

I made mistakes here doing surinoko, as did Tomio. Even Mr. Shimojo made mistakes, but his were the most minor, because he caught them quickly and made corrections.[40] Again, he stressed this had to be done very slowly and painstakingly. Forcing the saw was bad. If the cut was tight it was better to open it slightly with a wedge. I noticed where the sawing was easy he held the blade perpendicular to the face of the planking; when it was difficult he angled the saw. The first pass down one side of the boat took forty minutes.

Mr. Shimojo spent the entire next day sawing this seam. He would oil the saw periodically and by the afternoon he was clearly fatigued. I simply stood at his side, or got under the boat to tell him how it was going. At one point I finally asked him if he wanted me to do it, to give him a rest. He waved me off, saying, "This is the hardest part of building sabani. I have to do it." He called this stage of the project *shimpai toki* (anxious time). I expected as much. After all, he had known me for just four weeks, and while he had trusted me with plenty of other work on the boat, not this, not yet. *Yukkuri douzo*.

Mr. Shimojo sands inside the bottom. The square material in the foreground is the mast step.

Mr. Shimojo sawing the seam between the bottom and planking. He controlled the opening of the seam with a wedge and two old saw blades.

Bench dogs placed one shaku apart inside and out clamp the bottom to the sides while the glue dries. The huundu fastenings for this seam are laid out on top of the assembly.

Bamboo nails pinning the bottom to the side, while a few pin the bottom timbers together.

At the end of the day Mr. Shimojo announced the fit was good, and the next day we would make a final fit with a smaller, fine-toothed saw. This final fitting took about an hour and then it was time to prepare to glue the soko to the planking. We marked where the huundu would go to fasten the planks to the bottom. Mr. Shimojo added the accelerant to the glue so we had to work fast spreading it on the mating surfaces. Mr. Shimojo, his wife, his daughter, son Tomio, another relative, and I were all involved spreading glue. We lowered the soko onto the hull one last time and Tomio pounded dogs both inside and outside the boat, making sure he placed them in between our huundu layout. The rest of us did our best to clean up any glue squeezing out of the joint. Within twenty minutes the glue was beginning to harden.

The bottom edge of the planking is a long curve in the middle, which breaks at a corner before running straight to the bow and stern. The ends of the soko were trimmed off right at these corners. Before he began to use glue, Mr. Shimojo would first fasten the bottom to the planking with bamboo nails. These pinned the bottom to the sides while he cut the mortises for the huundu. Without them, pounding the chisels with the hammer would move the bottom out of alignment. In our case the glue would hold everything together while we chiseled, so the bamboo nails would go in last.

Thirty-eight huundu fastened the soko to the planking on the outside of the hull. We had to chisel away part of the soko that was overhanging to bring the face flush to the planking where we mortised for the fastenings. Mr. Shimojo and I worked on opposite sides of the boat so our pounding chisels would be less likely to move the hull. We had removed some of the turnbuckles closest to this seam, but otherwise he said we would keep turnbuckles and other braces in place as long as we could. Holes for the bamboo nails were drilled about 3 sun, at a very steep angle from a point about 1 sun above the huundu and down into the planking.

Normally Tomio spent an afternoon with us in the shop when it was time to fasten a seam, but this day he wasn't available. Mr. Shimojo and I started at opposite corners of the boat. He would pick up his chisel with his right hand and press it into his left, which was basically paralyzed. With his right hand he would curl the fingers of his left hand around the handle. Then with his right hand he would position his left hand so the chisel was on the line. Picking up his hammer he would begin pounding the chisel. Often after three or four hammer strikes the chisel would be dislodged and fall to the floor. Slowly he would bend down, pick it up, and start the process over. We worked this way all day installing the huundu. I chiseled thirty-two mortises while he chiseled six. At no point did he complain or show any sign of frustration.

With the bottom fastened Mr. Shimojo carefully checked its shape, striking a new center line. He said he wanted the bottom to run flat from the forward end to a point about 2 shaku from the aft end, at which point he checked the size using an offcut from an earlier boat.[41] Our soko was thicker so he planed it to give the bottom a slight rise aft. From side to side he took off just a little material leaving the center about 2 bu higher than the corners. Mr. Shimojo believes a flatter bottom creates a more stable boat, but he said his customers would tell him what kind of shape they wanted.

In the old days sabani tended to have rounder bottoms, because before the War fishermen sometimes intentionally capsized their boats to ride out storms. Mr. Shimojo had many remarkable stories to tell me, but perhaps the most amazing was one about his father, who, after catching a shark four meters long was unable to get it into his boat. His solution was to capsize his sabani, right it under the shark, and then bail the boat out. The shark aboard, he sailed home!

Mr. Shimojo insisted that an eight-meter sabani, like the one we were building, was safe in almost any seas. He said the high transom meant these boats could take huge following waves safely. It was also clear he believed the sailors of his father's generation possessed phenomenal skills, and I believe him. By today's standards sabani are incredibly unstable; at least half the sabani racing teams need to rig their boats with outriggers in order to sail them. One of today's best sabani sailors, a man who has led open ocean voyages with sabani, told me, "We barely know a fraction of what the old sailors knew."

At break one day Mr. Shimojo reviewed the various types of traditional sabani from his father's era. *Hokakebune* is an Okinawan term for a sailboat, but on Iejima the generic name for a sailing sabani was *putachibune.* The largest sailing sabani, eight meters or more, were called *fukaaki*, and these were the boats fishermen sailed from Iejima to Naha, selling their catch at the regional fish market. Mr. Shimojo said with favorable winds the island's fishermen could sail to Naha in less than a day (about thirty-five nautical miles). After selling their fish, he said, they would await favorable winds before returning.

Smaller net boats were called *oikami,* while the smallest sabani of all, one-man boats as short as 12 shaku, were called *chuuaicha.* As a child and teenager my teacher sailed the latter, and told me more than once these were the happiest moments of his life.

In Iejima dialect the small timbers forming the bow and stern ends of the soko are called the *kuwakuwa* (in romanized Japanese), but pronounced "gwagwa," meaning "a small thing." The joint between the soko and kuwakuwa is basically a flat butt joint except that the face has a slight V-shape. Tomio worked fitting the aft piece while his father fitted the forward piece. They both started by making sure the plank edges were perfectly straight and at the same bevel. This made it fairly easy to get a good fit on the planking; most of the work was in fitting the butt joint. Mr. Shimojo nailed in four temporary dogs to hold the kuwakuwa tightly against the soko, and then began using a modern crosscut saw to do surinoko in the joint. It is a very tight space so the saw has to be inserted in the middle of the joint and worked down, then reversed to saw up. In less than an hour Tomio had fitted the kuwakuwa aft, but his father took his time working at the bow.

Once Mr. Shimojo was satisfied with the fit, he took the kuwakuwa and braced it against the shop doorway. Using a round-faced hammer he began pounding the face of the joint. He worked from the center out, leaving deep dents in the endgrain while avoiding the peaked centerline of the joint, and pounding more carefully when he reached the edges to avoid splitting the wood. Overall he compressed the wood about 1 bu. He finished by using the flat face of the hammer and tried to smooth out the rough surface he had created. Finally, he hand planed the surface to smooth it even further. He told me in the past he would have also hammered the face of the soko, but his arm was tired and hammering one face was enough. Mr. Shimojo called this technique *chiguchiaashi* (*chiguchi* means "cut face" and *aashi* was his pronunciation for "awase," meaning "to put

Tomio sighting down the kuwakuwa. These small timbers finish the bottom at bow and stern.

Hammering the face of the kuwakuwa where it joins the bottom. This joint is problematic, given that two faces of end grain are being joined together. Hammering the face before fastening compresses the fibers, which will swell once the boat is in the water, ensuring a watertight fit.

Huundu fastening the kuwakuwa forward. Extra material was always left on timbers and after they were fastened they were planed fair to the hull.

together") and some version of it is well known to all boatbuilders in Japan. My second teacher first taught me the method, which he called *kigoroshi*, a combination of the words for "wood" (*ki*) and "to kill" (*korosu*).

In the sabani, the endgrain of the kuwakuwa is less likely to spring back but Mr. Shimojo pounded this material far more than my previous teachers. When it was put back together he once again did surinoko, making six passes with his saw. He then spread thickened glue on the joint and along the plank seam. We clamped the kuwakuwa in place with dogs, inside and out.

The huundu fastening the kuwakuwa are spaced about 8 sun apart, a little narrower than our previous spacing, and set 7 bu deep. We also put huundu in the joint between the kuwakuwa and the soko, and inserted bamboo nails. I asked Mr. Shimojo at this point whether he thought a sabani could be fastened with glue alone. Some of my previous teachers also used glue, but they said it was mainly to help keep seams tightly closed and waterproof, and like Mr. Shimojo they used traditional fastenings as well. He actually admitted perhaps a sabani might be built using only glue, though he wasn't about to try. He laughed and told me, "In the old days if I saw light in the seams I used shark liver oil to seal it."[42] Personally I think the sabani would be a more problematic boat to rely solely on glue; the timbers are much larger and therefore the internal stresses much greater than a plank-built boat. Seasonal shrinking and swelling of large timbers could easily break a glue joint. So too could the twisting forces on the hull from the sailing rig. Glue would also be very likely to fail on an endgrain joint like the kuwakuwa.

The next day after the glue had dried Mr. Shimojo and his son shaped the kuwakuwa. Forward, this timber runs all the way to the base of the bow transom. Mr. Shimojo said that in very old sabani the planking actually came together and the kuwakuwa did not run all the way to the bow. He said this was inherently weak construction, as the planking was too thin and fragile. The kuwakuwa created a stronger timber at the base of the bow.

It was here at the forward kuwakuwa where I made my most serious mistake. I removed too much wood chiseling away material to make room to mortise one of the huundu. Mr. Shimojo discovered my error at the end of the day. He was as upset as I was crestfallen. He studied my mistake while I stood behind him, penitent. My mind raced to find some solution but he bluntly waved me off. Finally, we quit for the day and his last words to me as I prepared to walk back to my hostel was that everything would be all right.

That evening I was talking to the owner of my guesthouse about what had happened. He listened, concerned, then muttered "*Yamachichan,*" in Iejima hougen meaning literally, "to cut off the mountain." Gusukuyama is the only mountain on Iejima, located at the center and visible from all corners of the island. A spring about halfway up one slope was traditionally the island's sole source of fresh water. Not surprisingly, Gusukuyama is also considered the center of spiritual power. To cut off the mountain is to make a very, very big mistake.

It is in precisely these kinds of highly charged situations new vocabulary is branded in one's memory. The next day I came to the shop as I always did, about a half hour before Mr. Shimojo, in order to get things ready for the day's work. I took some time to study the mortise I had cut and even sketched some ideas for fixing it. Mr. Shimojo entered looking grim, and went straight to the bow and sat down. I apologized again for the mistake but he silently waved me off. After some time he told me the kuwakuwa would just have to be shaped a little smaller; but everything would be all right. Looking at my mistake with him I said quietly, "Yamachichan."

Mr. Shimojo looked up at me and burst out laughing. "Yamachichan? Do you understand that?" he asked. I pointed to the mortise and said yes, this was yamachichan. Shimojo was fiercely proud of his Okinawan heritage and delighted when I learned and used any new words in the local language. For the rest of the day he told everyone who visited the shop about what I had said. It was the sole subject of that day's lunchtime conversation with his wife. Most importantly, it had cleared another dark cloud hanging in the shop, for which I was most grateful. Mr. Shimojo was still chuckling as he carved the bow just a bit narrower, until all traces of my mistake had disappeared.

Building either Western boats or wasen involves milling parts to size, cutting them to shape, and assembling them. Thinking about my mistake made me appreciate what I would call the improvisational aspects of building sabani. Since the components are so large, and most of the work involves carving, what Mr. Shimojo said about his one hundred sabani is true: no two could be exactly alike. The aft kuwakuwa, for example, he shaped completely by eye, planing the curve where the hull transitioned from the bottom to the stern. He did not follow any drawing, rather took into account the materials, particularly the sapwood, as well as his own sense of what looked right. The thick materials give the builder tremendous flexibility. If one worked slowly and carefully, as Mr. Shimojo always stressed, there was both time and material enough to make adjustments. It wasn't until I had made a serious mistake that I could fully appreciate this.

All of my teachers were fiercely serious about their work and like Mr. Udagawa and Mr. Ando, Mr. Shimojo seemed to have a completely different persona when working than when resting. This may have been heightened by the physical toll of working every day, at a brutal pace I knew was for my benefit. A man in his eighties, partially paralyzed by a stroke, should be doing anything but working seven days a week building boats. Although he had told me it had taken him six months to build his last boat, he never once mentioned the deadline he was helping me meet nor complained about the pace of the work. For my part, if he was irritated with me for interrupting him with a question or making a mistake, I accepted it silently.

Often at lunch I could tell he was exhausted, just by how slowly he took off his shoes and came to the table. I always left lunch early so he and Mrs. Shimojo could have some time alone. I also knew he sometimes took a short nap after eating. From Monday to Friday, he would come back to the shop at one o'clock and turn on a little pink, plastic radio. Weekdays from one to two o'clock he listened to a show featuring indigenous Okinawan music. A type of *minyou*, or folk song, it is jaunty and infectious. The singing often features syncopated, high-pitched yelps, and many of the lyrics are derived from stories of fishing and farming. It is accompanied by an Okinawan three-stringed banjo called the *sanshin*—a close cousin to the Japanese *shamisen*.

Mr. Shimojo loved this music, and his family and neighbors told me that until his stroke he had been an excellent sanshin player. One day at lunch he showed me his sanshin, made of gorgeous lacquered and highly figured hardwood. "I made it myself," he said, putting it back on its stand. No matter what the mood of the morning in the shop, the first hour of our weekday afternoons was tranquilized by music from the radio, Mr. Shimojo whistling along contentedly with the traditional tunes.

The minyo show was not broadcast on weekends, but Mr. Shimojo's next door neighbor was a sanshin teacher. As long as the shop was quiet we could hear him or his students playing, the music wafting in through the open windows. Our one hour of weekday radio was the only such distraction I have ever seen in a Japanese shop. All my other teachers enforced a strict code of silence while working.

In preparation for turning the boat over we finish-sanded the hull to 100 grit and coated the exterior with a soybean-based tempura oil. The cedar soaked up the oil quickly and we put on a second coat before the end of the day. When I asked how much oil to use, Mr. Shimojo said we could put on oil until the wood stopped soaking it up. In the old days they used shark liver oil, and fishermen oiled their boats three to four times a year. Shark oil reacts with sunlight and turns completely black. It also has a powerful smell and Mr.

Fastenings in the kuwakuwa aft.

Shimojo laughed, saying that using it today would not make him popular with his neighbors.

We set up a second chainfall the next day and lifted the hull with a pair of canvas straps. Mr. Shimojo had given the bottom of the boat yet another thick coating of tempura oil while I held my camera ready to record the turning of the hull, the event he had referred to as the "birth" of the boat. I had imagined such a momentous occasion would be a slow, deliberate affair, perhaps taking us several hours. Tomio looked at me and asked, "Are you ready?" I said yes and began to take photos. Tomio then turned and pulled up on the rail of the sabani. The wet, oily hull slipped easily in the canvas straps, and within seconds the boat swung there, upright, rocking gently. We lowered the hull onto two thick blocks on the floor.

Mr. Shimojo looks at the freshly oiled hull of the sabani.

The sabani was rolled while hanging in straps, an event Mr. Shimojo called the "birth" of the boat.

Bars still spread the hull forward, while one turnbuckle pinches it aft. On the port side the huundu at the plank seam have been installed, while the starboard side is still being fastened.

Framing

Mr. Shimojo wedged three wooden bars between the rails before we removed most of the turnbuckles clamping the hull. The wooden bars held the hull shape until we installed permanent beams. One turnbuckle was left holding the planks where they narrowed near the middle. We spent the rest of the day sanding and planing the inside of the hull to fair the joint between the soko and the planking. When he was satisfied with that work, Mr. Shimojo marked the locations for forty huundu to install around the seam inside the boat, thirty-six between the soko and the planking and four connecting the kuwakuwa and the planking.

Before my arrival Mr. Shimojo and his son had roughed out the material for the bow and stern transoms, called *pijira* and *tomopijira*, and after we finished fastening the inside of the hull they carefully adjusted the clamps at the bow and stern (without removing them) so they could make room to drop the transoms into place. The faces of these two large, triangular cedar chunks were 4 sun thick, and each had mooring bits carved right from the timber. Mr. Shimojo said the heart side of the transoms should face inside, breaking with the pattern in the rest of the boat. The stern transom was made of three pieces of cedar glued together with the heart of the tree in its center. Mr. Shimojo fitted the bow transom by taking it on and off the boat and planing the sides to fit, and Tomio finished the process doing surinoko a few times down either seam. When placing it, only glue was used on the planking, but Mr. Shimojo mixed some fine sawdust with the glue and put a generous amount of this thickened mixture in the joint at the base. The leftover thickened glue he gave to me to fill small holes and indentations throughout the inside of the boat. I had been using a gouge to carve out any dead knots in the hull so these gaps were also filled with thickened glue. Any knots extending through the planking we completely cut out; I made tapered cedar plugs and glued them in those holes.

Mr. Shimojo and his son Tomio inspect the bow transom. As with most other parts of the hull they start with an oversized timber and remove a large amount of material as it is shaped and fitted.

The huundu fastening the transoms are very deep, about 1 sun, and they include a special double huundu crossing the face of the bow transom, joining it to the planks on either side. Mr. Shimojo had me make some slightly tapered cedar dowels from 5 bu square stock. With a 12-millimeter drill he bored four holes, 4 sun on center, completely through the hull and bow transom, along a line 2 sun back from the plank edge. We dipped the dowels in oil and drove them in hard, alternating the heads to either side of the boat, and cut the ends off flush. Mr. Shimojo then split the smaller end of each with a knife and drove a small cedar wedge into the cut.

The stern transom was fitted the same way, starting with marking and planing the edges and, once close, given a final fit in place by running the saw in the seam. The stern transom was also glued to the planking, and the next day Tomio fastened it with huundu. Later we inserted four dowels from either side. Both transoms had been milled leaving a large triangle of wood in the center for a mooring bitt. Tomio drilled a 1-sun hole through each of these to connect a rope.

It was the end of December and soon the seven-day-a-week schedule would end for a five-day New Year's holiday. We were all looking forward to the break. Our progress on the boat had been so good we all knew it was going to be finished on schedule. The pace in the shop became much more relaxed. We took long breaks, and Mr. Shimojo talked more about the old days.

The New Year's holiday was the only time in his entire life Mr. Shimojo simply relaxed for days on end, and he was looking forward to it. In the old days, every family raised at least one pig, he said, which they butchered for the occasion. It was also one of the few times they ate rice, instead of the staple Okinawan sweet potato. "When I see those historical dramas on television," he said, "I think to myself: we lived just like that." Our last afternoon before vacation I swept every corner of the shop while Mr. Shimojo cleaned and arranged the tools.

Five full days off! It seemed incomprehensible that I could actually sleep in for the first time in two months. Around mid-morning I walked the five minutes from my guesthouse to the shop where I found our mast delivered. It was a small cedar tree, the bark still on, lying on the concrete floor. Mr. Shimojo had placed a sprig of pine on the bow of our boat as an *Oshougatsu* (New Year) offering. I was there to trace copies of Mr. Shimojo's plank patterns, which consisted of five sheets of plywood. When laid end-to-end they represented a full-size plank, 27.44 shaku long. I set up a table with a piece of plywood over two sawhorses and rolled out the inexpensive paper I had found at a home center. Used for covering the sliding screens called *shoji,* the paper was very thin but remarkably tough, and one roll was more than enough to trace the patterns.

From the shop I headed toward the center of town to the City Hall, where an old sabani rested outside. Mr. Shimojo had not built it, but said he had made some repairs to it. It was about the same length as our sabani, but much deeper and huskier than the traditional design we were building. The planking, for instance, was about thirty percent thicker than what we were using. Large, sawn frames cut from the natural crook of the tree were installed, rising above the sheerline of the planking and supporting wash strakes, boards mounted

The author tracing the full-sized plank patterns Mr. Shimojo used to lay out the planking for his sabani.

on top of the gunwale to increase the freeboard. Most of the frames were scarfed at the bottom, but one frame forward lay against the port side planking, crossed the keel and rose nearly halfway up the starboard side where another timber was scarfed to it. The engine was gone but it showed the engine beds and the extremely wide timber available to its original builder. I found a mast step but no partners.

Mr. Shimojo had said the boat was built about sixty years ago and he thought it came from Itoman, a city at the southern tip of the main island. It may have originally been a large sailing sabani converted later to power. If so, the wash strakes were probably added at the same time to deflect spray, and there were signs the boat had stabilizing boards—horizontal timbers at the waterline aft—to keep the hull from squatting under power. Most of the old, derelict powered sabani I saw had these. Several cracks in the planking were repaired with huundu.

Leaving City Hall I headed about a quarter mile across town to a small private museum. I had not had a chance to visit it given my work schedule, but I had peeked through the locked gates during one of my evening runs. I bought my ticket at a tiny gift shop and headed for the museum proper, which was a small concrete building set in the back of a garden. The lawn was decorated with a combination of huge earthenware pots and old artillery shells. The destruction during the battle for Iejima in World War II was almost total, and so much of the cultural history was told in old photo albums. About half the artifacts were rusty implements of war, excavated in the years since 1945 when the islanders were allowed to return home. Iejima had three formal museums and all were filled with war relics, including excavated human bones.

This museum also had a very small sabani, missing part of its stern but interesting because it was built in the nanyouhagi style Mr. Shimojo disparaged. It was fastened with huundu, but in addition to the dovetail keys the planking was also edge-nailed with small wire nails. It did not have a thickly carved bottom, but a narrow plank keel with both garboard planks and sheer planks, giving it a hard chine hull reminiscent of Japanese boats. It had the triangular transoms bow and stern and the label called it a sabani. Overall it was a light and delicate boat, 17.8 shaku long, really more a hybrid of a Japanese boat and a sabani.

The day after New Year's I was walking to the ferry port when I saw Mr. Shimojo in the shop. He explained the pine branch he left on the boat was a decoration ensuring the safety of the boat and its eventual owner. In Iejima's harbors all the fishing boats were flying flags and tall sprigs of bamboo and pine for the same reason. He had sprinkled sake on the tools and the floor of the shop as another offering.[43]

On the fourth of January we started back to work. The vacation seemed to have relaxed all of us, as did the knowledge we were going to finish the boat with time to spare. The hull was finished so what remained were the gunwales, beams, thwarts, and mast.

The gunwale consists of two parts: an inwale, called the *uchiuchikiyaa*, a strip of cedar running along the inside vertical face at the gunwale; and a cap rail, called the *tanauchikiyaa,* running on top of the horizontal top edge of the planking (see drawing on p. 230). Mr. Shimojo checked the flatness of the gunwale by placing a straightedge across the boat and correcting any discrepancies with a handplane.

The inwales measured 8 bu by 1.5 sun and we milled them out of our scrap cedar. We installed them by first fitting the ends at the bow and stern and then moving toward the center. They were made of two pieces and amidships we overlapped the ends and, holding them in place, made an angled saw cut through both pieces. This created identical bevels where the two ends met and a bit of surinoko made them a tight fit. We used 7-centimeter stainless steel twist nails for fastenings. These, along with some stainless steel screws used to fasten the beams, were the only metal fasteners in the entire boat. We had to angle the nails for the inwale; otherwise they would have gone through the planking. We countersank the nail heads and filled them with our putty mix of glue and sawdust.

As mentioned above, in engine-powered sabani large sawn frames were used to support the hull, but in our boat a series of horizontal beams formed the entire framework. These consisted of three large beams mounted at the rail; two smaller beams located below the rail; and two bronze rods, 3 bu in diameter, one located under the aft beam and

All the beams in the boat are visible in this photograph, three at the sheer with one lower beam amidships.

Detail of the mast partners. Though fastened with screws, Mr. Shimojo covered them with a traditional fastening of a hardwood block trapping the beam and lashed to the planking with wire.

one across the forward face of the stern transom. The two large beams at the bow and aft at the narrowest point of the hull Mr. Shimojo called *yafukuwa* (which he pronounced *yafugwa*). The forward yafukuwa was a holdover from the days when large sabani carried two masts, and the smaller foremast would pass through this beam.[44] The aft yafukuwa has a bronze rod passing just under it and bolted with large washers outside the hull, essentially squeezing the hull at its narrowest point. The rod and beam were lashed together with copper wire.

The middle beam supports the mast and is called the *matsukaki*. Mr. Shimojo made it from a piece of Okinawan pine called *matsu*. This pale yellow wood, still available on Okinawa, is extremely hard and heavy. Mr. Shimojo told me the curved frames of larger, engine-powered sabani were also made of this wood sawn from the natural curve of the tree. All three of these major frames would have been pine, but Mr. Shimojo had a piece of Okinawan *kiri,* which he called *sendangi*, that he used to make the forward beam.[45] The aft beam was made of chage, the same wood used to make the huundu. The beams were notched over the inwale and the planking, and stainless steel screws fastened them to the rail.

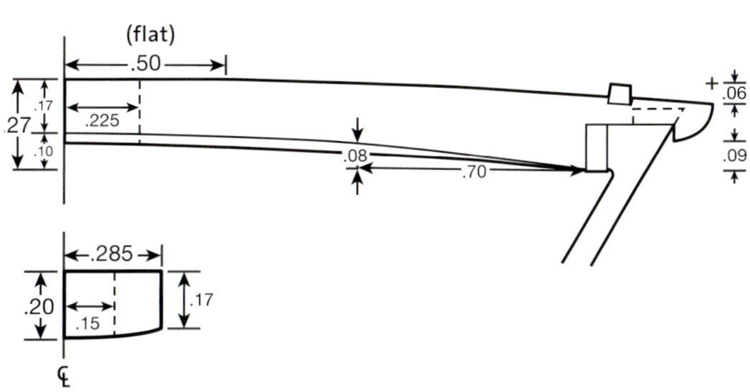

Half breadth of the matsukaki, or mast partner. The beam is cut to a curve, and the dimensions show Mr. Shimojo's method of laying out the shape of this timber.

The mast partner is fastened with complicated joinery. This beam overhangs the side of the boat and Mr. Shimojo notched it to drop into place, locking it to the rail. He did the layout for all the beams by measuring from a point at either the bow or stern of the boat and back along the rail on each side. The forward face of the mast partner, for instance, measures 5.4 shaku aft of the top corner of the bow transom. Once the beam was fitted, he cut a groove in the top of the beam right above the planking. He put screws in the base of this groove into the planking, then covered the groove with a narrow hardwood block. The block was then lashed through holes in the hull with copper wire.[46]

The cap rail is made of *apitong*, an Indonesian hardwood (*Dipterocarpus grandiflorus*). Its outer face is planed with the bevel of the hull, so its top corner extends beyond the planking and effectively forms a hard edge to protect the hull, its main function being to prevent the hardwood paddles from damaging the cedar planking. Mr. Shimojo said in the old days he used Okinawan hardwood for the cap

Forward beam, into which Mr. Shimojo cut a hole for a foremast, although this type of rig has not been seen for generations. The block at the bow held with a cord is a support for the mast when lowered.

The author fitting the thwarts while Mr. Shimojo and his son attend to other details. *Photo copyright George Kochi.*

rails, and they were much smaller, just a half-round piece of wood fastened to the hull using small bamboo nails. Our cap rail consisted of two pieces on each side, running from aft and butting to the mast partner, with a second piece from the partner to the bow.

The two smaller beams in the boat are called *haiki* and *hariaiki*. The haiki is the larger of the two, and located just aft of the mast partner. This cedar beam is sawn with a very slight crown (2 bu over its 2.3 shaku length) and the ends are mortised into two hardwood pads made of chage running vertically against the planking. The pads are mortised into the thwart riser and the inner rail.[47] The haiki is installed by inserting it into the mortise on one side of the boat then lowering it into an elongated mortise on the other side. A square wooden peg then fills the empty portion of the mortise, locking the beam in place. Mr. Shimojo also glued all the tenons before assembly.

The second, smaller beam, called the hariaiki (temporary beam) in the local dialect, Mr. Shimojo pointed out would not be mortised into the hull. The ends were angled to fit tight and it was wedged against the hull right under the inner rail, held in place with a small block of cedar nailed to the planking. He said this beam was only necessary when the boat was new, and could be removed once the planking had set to its shape (I failed to ask how long he thought this would take). He also said in the old days some beams in sabani were just pieces of bamboo wedged inside the hull and not fastened at all.

We used apitong to make rub rails, called *takuwasaa,* for the outer edges of the bow and stern. They were also fastened with stainless steel nails and they protected the fragile corners of the hull. A final piece of apitong, about 6 shaku long, was screwed to the bottom of the boat at the bow to protect the hull when beaching. Mr. Shimojo called this the *kaara*.

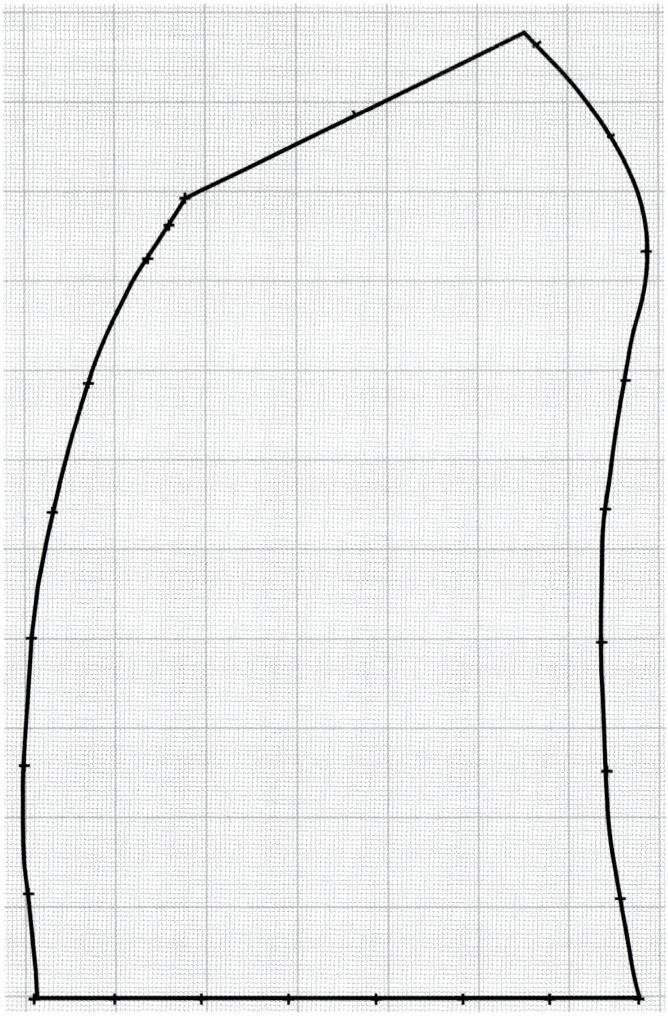

Mr. Shimojo's sail plan for an eight-meter sabani, derived from his father's design, which he said was a great innovation over sails used by fishermen before the war. Each square is 1 shaku by 1 shaku. *Drawing copyright Mr. Yoji Mori.*

Mr. Shimojo and his son worked finishing various small details on the hull while I made thwarts, called *sashika*. Each thwart was made of two or three cedar planks spanning the hull, landing on the carved risers, and held together with a pair of cedar cleats nailed across the bottom. This material was 7 bu thick and Mr. Shimojo told me the heart side of the plank should face up. He also said in the old days sabani thwarts were just pieces of bamboo lashed together. He admitted that sitting on bamboo was extremely uncomfortable, but he added fishermen didn't have much time to sit.

Mr. Shimojo fashioned small cedar blocks called *atari* that were nailed to the gunwale. He had a particular way of carving their edges and I suspect these pieces were intended to brace the cap rail and also the beam ends. Tomio also made cedar caps to cover the tops of the transoms.

Sailing Rig

The mast had been delivered as a freshly cut cedar tree. I stripped the bark using an old cleaver and Tomio gave it its final shape: beginning 1 sun square at the base, widening to 2.2 by 2.1 sun at the partners, then tapering to a round 1 sun diameter at the tip. Mr. Shimojo made a rest for the mast lashed to the bow of the boat, and said the length of a sabani's mast should equal two-thirds the length of the boat.

Mr. Shimojo set the mast in the partners and clamped it in order to determine the location for the mortises in the mast step. He then stepped back and looked at the boat carefully. He wanted the mast to stand at a right angle to the edge of the planking aft of the mast. He would make a total of three mortises in the mast step, as sabani sailors adjusted the mast angle based on the wind speed: raked aft for high winds and forward for light winds. Sabani also have a curious system of mast wedges. The mast is locked into the partners with three wedges. In high winds two side wedges are used together to make the mast lean to one side, always into the wind. The third wedge can be used in front or behind the mast to make small adjustments to the rake.

Mr. Yousuke Yamashiro of Itoman made the sail for our sabani, which he delivered and rigged after I left Iejima. It was made of cotton and stained reddish-brown with dye he made himself from the wood of the *sharimbai*, or Japanese hawthorn (*Rhaphiolepis umbellata*).[48] He worked closely with Mr. Shimojo, who never spoke of the sail without repeating how the curved edges of its design came from his father, and how extremely proud he was of it.

Sunday, January 10, 2010, was my last day working on the boat. Tomio and I oiled the entire interior, which we had sanded with 60 grit paper and finish sanded with 100 grit. I estimate we used about twenty liters of tempura oil on the boat, inside and out. Mr. Yamashiro brought by a liter of genuine shark liver oil, which we used for the final coat.

I had worked forty-eight days on the boat between November 16, 2009, and January 10, 2010.

Bailer and Paddles

Over the following week I stopped by the shop each day, and found Mr. Shimojo seated at his sawhorses working on the bailer, called the *yutui*. This tool in many ways epitomizes the sabani: a piece of sculpture, completely functional yet at the same time captivatingly beautiful. Mr. Shimojo was

Mr. Shimojo's bailer, carved from a single block of hard pine. The curve of the lip matches the curve of the bottom of the boat.

Mr. Shimojo's paddle designs. The larger one is used for steering.

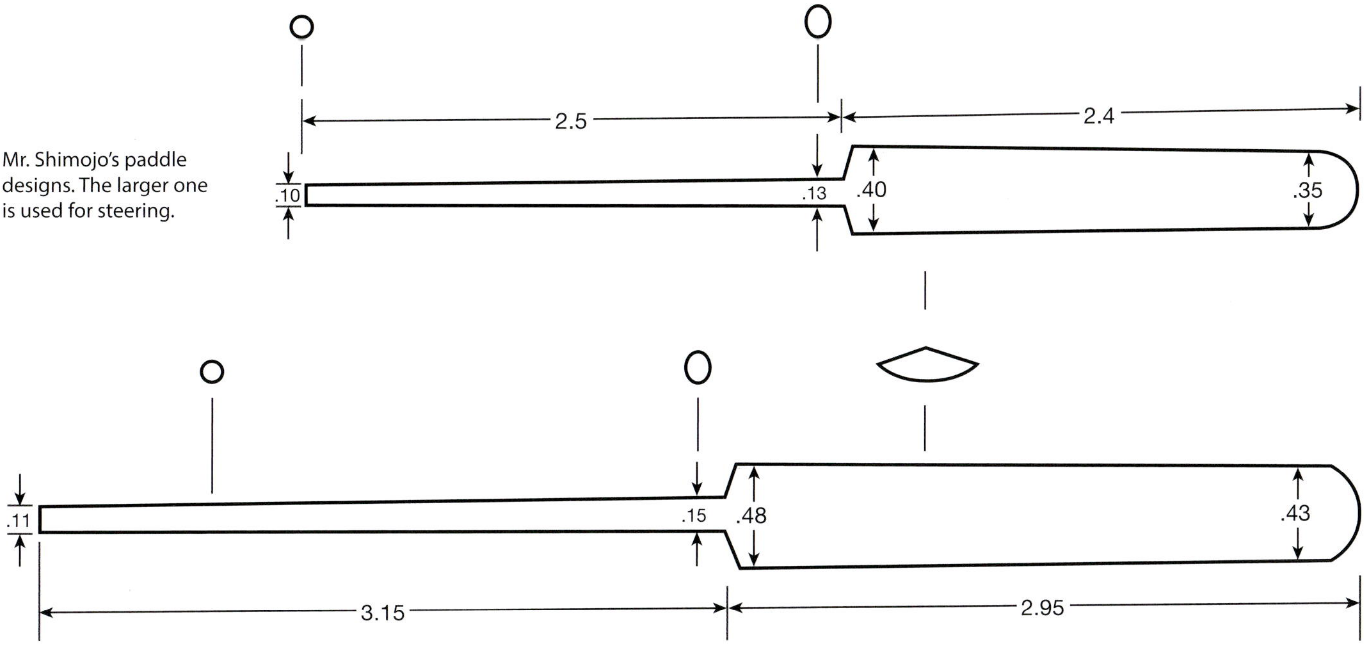

justifiably proud of his design and his skill; like his boat and paddles, he carved his mark, the two characters of his surname, into the bailer. He said that fewer craftsmen know how to make bailers than know how to build sabani. Carved from a single piece of hard pine, the bottom was curved so it fit neatly against the curved bottom of our boat. Mr. Shimojo told me fishermen would even use the yutui as a food bowl, slicing up a fish at sea and eating it raw. The skills to make these had been lost, he said, because after the war fishermen gave up wooden bailers and began using US Army helmets.

Mr. Shimojo used to make other fishing tools for sabani. He fashioned small watertight wooden boxes fishermen used to carry food and gear, and small barrels with glass bottoms for finding fish. Tomio carved a stone anchor for the boat.

Mr. Shimojo stands to the right at the launching ceremony performed by a local female shaman. *Photo copyright Staff Sergeant Emery L. Ruffin, United States Marine Corps.*

From underneath the stern, the sculptural qualities of the sabani hull are readily apparent. *Photo copyright George Kochi.*

Mr. Shimojo felt strongly that a ceremony for the completion of the boat should take place just before it left his shop, which was one month after my departure. These ceremonies are typically Shinto-based in the rest of Japan, but always follow local custom to some extent. They are not always conducted by Shinto priests; just as common are ceremonies conducted by the boatbuilders themselves, sometimes with the participation of the boat owners. Their purpose is to purify the boats by offering salt, sake, and *mochi* (pounded rice) and asking the *kami* (spirits) for the prosperity and safety of the owners.

In late January, before being shipped to the Museum of Maritime Science in Tokyo, our sabani was brought out of the shop and fully rigged. A *yuta,* or shaman, in this case a local woman in her nineties, purified the boat by sprinkling salt at the bow, amidships, and stern, and blessed it with prayers. A celebration by all spectators followed, and within days the sabani was on its way to Tokyo.

After two years on exhibit in Tokyo the boat was returned to Okinawa and launched for the first time. It was christened *Kagiroi*, an obscure Japanese term referring to the color of the eastern sky just before sunrise. The boat is now sailed by a racing team based on Zamami Island.

Parting

Mr. Ryujin Shimojo is a living bridge between epochs of Okinawan history. As a child he remembers the final days of dugout sabani carved from a single log, and he and his father fished from sabani powered by only paddle and sail. In the aftermath of World War II everything changed. His island home had been a battlefield and the traditional ways of life were altered forever. Sabani lost their sailing rigs as engines became available, fishing boats became larger, foreign designs were introduced, and fiberglass replaced wood in the boatbuilding industry. We invariably call this progress, and we measure it by all we have gained. Rarely do we pause to think about what we have lost.

As we sat drinking the Okinawan tea called *sanpincha* and eating cookies during our morning and afternoon breaks, Mr. Shimojo most often wanted to talk about his youth. The prewar Iejima he described seemed ancient: thatched-roof homes, a diet of *imo* (tubers) and fish, firewood gathered, and water carried from a communal well. Sailing a sabani was hard work as well, but it was also exhilarating. While Mr. Shimojo was grateful for all the comforts of modern life, it was clear that for him nothing could replace being at sea in a sabani—steering paddle in one hand, sheet (*tina*) in the other, and a fishing line in one's mouth. Pointing to the five-

The sabani *Ayakaji* racing. Originally built about 1960, this boat was used for fishing on Kouri Island until about 1990. The name combines the Okinawan words for "woven" and "wind." It is now sailed by students and alumnae of the University of the Ryukyus. *Photo copyright Hiroyuki Asato.*

meter boat he had built the year before, a boat he told me was perhaps his finest, he said, "If I were healthy I would take that little sabani and sail back and forth along the beach. It's a pity, really." The new generation of sabani racers has discovered an old but simple truth: sailing a sabani is fun. Looking ahead, I hope they will be able to revive the craft of building this boat; the risk of losing these skills is too great not to try.

The day before my departure, I climbed Mount Gusuku at sunset. Below me stretched the town, sweeping from the base of the mountain to the ferry port. I could pick out Mr. Shimojo's home and shop amid the blocks of concrete buildings, and to the west lay bright green sugar cane fields and neat rows of tobacco. In the distance, I could see the northwest coast of the main island of Okinawa, from the city of Nago to the island's northern tip. To the north just two small islands were visible. Mr. Shimojo's sabani had once sailed these waters, and today his fiberglass boats could still be found in many fishing ports.

Working seven days a week on the sabani I had little time to reflect on what it was like to stay on this small island and have a chance to absorb a little of its culture. Now, suddenly, standing on top the mountain I felt wistful about the experience. A stranger joined me and we began to chat. He was surprised to hear me use a few words from the local language and, as he started down, turned and said, "*Ichariba choudee.*" I asked him what it meant. "Having met," he said, "we are brothers." The last thing I learned on Iejima spoke volumes about the island and its people.[49]

The next day I was leaving Iejima and I stopped by Mr. Shimojo's house to say goodbye. His neighbor met me in the street and I asked him what he thought the boatbuilder would do now that our sabani was finished, especially in light of his health. I thought of how hard he had worked, at age eighty-one, despite his physical limitations. "Mr. Shimojo will always build boats," the neighbor assured me, "That's all he wants to do." With a smile he added, "There's no stopping him." If there is a lesson to be learned from his life, it is his incredible persistence learning how to build boats and his mastery of every challenge he faced.

As we said goodbye, Mr. Shimojo told me his experience sailing sabani as a young man is what taught him the difference between a good boat and a bad one, what made a good bow and stern. "Only then could I understand," he added. "No one today understands sabani. All the boats are fiberglass."

As for our work together he said, "Your coming made me feel good, but all your photos and notes won't prevent you from making mistakes." Then, to reassure me, he added, "I made mistakes on my early boats." I thanked him again, and made my way down the hill to the ferry. In a few minutes he and his entire family came down to the dock to see me off. This is a poignant Japanese tradition: seeing off guests at the point of physical parting, and waving until they are out of sight. As the ferry steamed past the breakwater we all waved to each other. I could see Mr. Shimojo still swinging his cane over his head, even after the others had stopped, long after I had disappeared from his sight.

Notes

1 Elsewhere in Japan these fastenings are called *tsuzumi*, the name of a two-headed drum they resemble. On the Miomote River, also in Niigata, I heard them called *ryuugo*, which refers to a dumbbell shape.

2 The Notojima boatbuilder's work is documented in a book by Akiko Deguchi and Masato Deguchi, *Building Method of the Chizi Boat, Ishikawa Prefecture, Ohchigata, Searashi, Nakajima Village* (*Ishikawa ken Ohchigata no Chizibune Nakajima machi Searashi Deno Kenzou Kiroku*), published by the Museum of Maritime Science, Tokyo, 2004.

3 In the West, boats built with thick, carved timber bottoms and plank sides are characterized as *semi-dugouts. Mudamahagi* is the Japanese equivalent of this term.

4 The best overall source of information on the sabani races in Okinawa is via the Itoman Uminchu Koubou (Itoman City Arts and Crafts Center). The center is dedicated to the preservation of the skills and artifacts of Okinawan fishing culture. Their website is available in English and has links to various racing teams and announcements of events.

5 The Fune no Kagakukan, located in the Odaiba district of Tokyo, has unfortunately been closed due to funding problems although there are plans for its reopening.

6 While Okinawan boatbuilders all build using the traditional shaku measuring system, the length of sabani are described in meters by both sailors and builders alike.

7 Coming from Vermont, the Okinawan winter was not a hardship. Although Mr. Shimojo wore a jacket every single day and often complained about the cold, I worked in a T-shirt except for a few days. In mid-January I was invited to go sailing aboard a sabani, which capsized. I spent forty-five minutes in the water and was not the least uncomfortable for it.

8 The festival boats in Okinawa are related to sabani, but designed for racing with teams of paddlers. The name *hari* comes from *haryuu* (dragon). Okinawans call these boats *haribune*, and on Iejima *paribune.*

9 Fortunately, the techniques of a boatbuilder on Ishigakijima, Mr. Yasuhiro Arashiro, have been recently documented by his apprentice, Ms. Kyoko Kunioka. A sculptor by training, she was drawn to the sabani by its complex shape and the extensive use of carving in its construction. While the wives of many boatbuilders I have met played important roles in their husband's workshops, Ms. Kunioka is the first woman I know of in Japan to become a full-fledged apprentice. Mr. Arashiro's life was also the subject of a book by Ms. Chika Yasumoto, *Sabani Breaking the Waves: The World of Boatbuilder Arashiro Yasuhiro* (*Shio wo Hiraku Fune Sabani: Funadaiku Arashiro Yasuhiro no Sekai*).

10 The Ryukyu Language Heritage Society specifically refers to Okinawa hougen as a local language rather than a dialect. While it has adopted many words from Chinese, it is believed that linguistically it is related to Japanese and that the two languages split some time around the fifth century. Here I use Mr. Shimojo's terms, which he called Iejima hougen. I am greatly indebted to Mr. Koji Matano, a boatbuilder and translator, for his help confirming technical terms in Japanese, and to Professor Wayne Lawrence of the University of Auckland, a specialist in Okinawan dialects, who also helped clarify many terms. Professor Lawrence has found significant linguistic differences can exist even between neighboring villages on the same island.

11 Mr. Shimojo never used electric lights, and on several days we quit when he said it had become too dark to work. When I asked him why there were no lights in the workshop he replied that if there were, one would be inclined to work too much.

12 Published in Japanese in two volumes by KAZI magazine of Yokohama in March, 1980. The material on sabani is found in the first volume.

13 Two of my former teachers, in Tokyo and Chiba, when building these types of boats pressed down the forward end of the bottom plank to create a concave bottom similar to what Mr. Yokoyama describes. However, they both told me the reason for the curved bottom was to bury the narrow bow deeper so the boats would track in a straight line. I have also found boats in Hyogo, Kyoto, and Iwate built this way. Mr. Shimojo insisted the bottoms of his sabani were flat.

14 Published in English and Japanese.

15 I saw historic sabani in Okinawan museums on Iejima, Iriomotejima, Taketomijima, and in Nago and Naha cities. There are also examples in museums in Ishigakijima and Amami. The only sabani I have seen in a collection elsewhere in Japan is at the Awa Museum in Chiba, east of Tokyo.

16 *Marukibune* is standard Japanese for a dugout, however Mr. Shiraishi writes in his book that the local Okinawan term for these boats is *marukinni*. Mr. Shimojo also called these *kurubune,* which literally means "carved boat."

17 In 1994 I interviewed the last builder of dugout boats in Akita Prefecture, where the bows and sterns were left solid—as much as two feet thick—to extend their lives, as it will take a long time for that much material to rot through.

18 This phenomenon is not unique to Okinawa, but has happened in other places around the world that have transitioned from dugout to semi-dugout to plank-built boats. I have long been struck by the similarities of boat evolution in Japan to that of the Chesapeake Bay in the United States.

19 The other concentration of semi-dugout types in Japan is at the opposite end of the country in the regions of Tohoku and Hokkaido. There are many distinct types of these fishing craft throughout Akita, Aomori, and Hokkaido Prefectures. They feature thick, carved timber bottoms and plank sides, and exist alongside more conventional, plank-built boats.

20 Boatbuilders in Japan usually call these stations *toubun* or, more rarely, *yokozumi*.

21 Learning to build the *taraibune* with my first teacher was a lesson in traditional barrel making more than boat-building.

22 The Inland Sea, the Seto Naikai, is a body of water separating the main island of Honshu from Kyushu and Shikoku. In 1997 I interviewed the last boatbuilder of the Gokase River in Miyazaki Prefecture in Kyushu. When I asked if he used the famous Miyazaki cedar growing locally he said, "No, the Okinawans bought all the best material." When it came to the largest timber, Mr. Shimojo complained, "The shrines get all the big trees."

23 In fact, a wooden plank is more likely to cup in the direction opposite its growth rings, away from the heart, so Mr. Shimojo's reasoning here seems faulty. Plus, the exterior face of the planking would be saturated by use, while the interior would be exposed to the sun, which would also tend to make the planks flare inward. At the time I didn't think of this and I never discussed it further with him. I am sure my comments would not have been welcome, since the apprentice has no place contradicting his teacher.

24 *Mokkoku* is Japanese Cleyera (*Ternstroemia gymnanthera*). *Inumaki* is known as Buddhist pine, but is increasingly now called *kusamaki* (*Podocarpus macrophyllus*).

25 I saw no sign of glue failure when we poured boiling water on the planking in order to bend it. A builder should choose a heat resistant glue if they follow these methods. Epoxy, for instance, weakens considerably at higher temperatures and would be inappropriate.

26 Another visitor to the shop said the word was Okinawa hougen for *hanarenai,* or "to not pull apart." In any discussion, Mr. Shimojo always insisted that influences on traditional Okinawan boatbuilding came from the south—from China or Polynesia, even from early contact with Europeans, never from Japan.

27 He called these seat supports *sashikazan,* which is Okinawa hougen. Traditional Japanese boats do not have thwarts like Western boats; most simply have floor-boards.

28 Other boatbuilders in Japan have told me this as well. Japanese furniture makers and temple carpenters also believe in the superiority of hand planing the final finish. Some argue a smoothly planed finish is more resistant to decay than one finished with sandpaper.

29 *History of Itoman City, Volume 12, Folk History*, (*Itoman Shi-shi, Shiryou Hen 12 Minzoku Shiryou*) published in 1991 by the City of Itoman. My thanks to Mr. Tsugaru Ryosuke for this reference and to Mr. Koji Matano for translating parts of the manuscript.

30 Mr. Shimojo was very careful about this throughout the project. The shop received direct sunlight all morning on the bow of the boat, which we kept shielded with a blanket.

31 In the West the workshop floor is usually wood and in a situation like this the boatbuilder would fasten the sawhorses to the floor. In Japan boatbuilders drive stakes into an earthen floor (*doma*) to keep everything secure. However, Mr. Shimojo's shop floor was concrete.

32 He said he repaired the split with huundu, and almost all the old sabani I looked at had at least one split in the planking repaired this way.

33 Mrs. Shimojo told me the shavings from hollowing the planks provided the fuel for boiling the water.

34 As we have seen, the most widely used term for this technique is *suriawase,* although in the Tohoku region of northern Japan it is sometimes called *tooshinoko.*

35 In Japanese a chainfall is called a *chieinburokku* (chain-block), so it is likely Mr. Shimojo's name reflects a local pronunciation of the term.

36 In 2000 I traveled to Sado Island to finish a tub boat my teacher was building when he died (see Chapter 9). Every day his wife would come into the workshop and critique my work and offer advice. She had worked alongside her husband, and it became obvious she knew a great deal about how the boats were made. I am sure the important

role of wives in the work of craftsmen has been greatly overlooked by researchers, myself included.

37 I later found out why the ethnologist, well-known in Japan, looked familiar. He recalls the image of his even more famous brother, the conductor Seiji Ozawa.

38 His techniques are more similar to Western boatbuilders, who fit planking with a plane only.

39 I would encourage anyone attempting to build a sabani to use hand planes. Because of his stroke Mr. Shimojo was forced to rely on his angle grinder but the health hazards of breathing sawdust should not be taken lightly. At the very least, anyone operating a sander should wear a dust mask or respirator.

40 Mr. Shimojo told me when he built sabani alone he put a large mirror under the boat so he could check his work. When his wife worked with him she would lie under the boat, a role I played for this boat. Nevertheless, even though I was watching, Mr. Shimojo still continued to check his own work.

41 Mr. Shimojo was clear that the bottom should be mostly flat lengthwise. He had never heard of any sort of hollow in the bottom of sabani.

42 Specifically, he said the dregs of the oil were thicker and better for this purpose.

43 When sake is used ceremonially it is called *omiki.*

44 The foremast raked forward, and flew a sail about one-third the size of the main sail. Mr. Shimojo does not believe there is anyone living who has sailed a two-masted sabani.

45 *Kiri,* known in the West as paulownia, is a hardwood common in Japan and mainly used in furniture.

46 I saw the same lashing technique on older sabani in museum collections. Of course those builders didn't have stainless steel screws. Mr. Shimojo essentially used modern fastenings and hid them with traditional techniques.

47 Mr. Shimojo didn't have a name for these blocks but later thought that *haikiate* (with *ate* from *ateru*, to hold) was probably correct.

48 Another traditional dye for sabani sails, as well as nets, was pig's blood.

49 This expression is commonly used throughout Okinawa. *Ichariba* means "when [we] come together" and is cognate with the Japanese *iki-au*, literally, "go-meet." *Choudee* is the local pronunciation of he Japanese *kyoudai*, meaning "brothers," or "siblings." I am indebted to Professor Wayne Lawrence of the University of Auckland for this explanation.

Notoriously difficult to handle, most racing sabani sport outriggers, not traditionally found on Okinawan boats. *Photo copyright Hiroyuki Asato.*

Michinoku-maru, a replica *bezaisen*, the type of Edo-era ship that served Japan's coastal trade for over two hundred years.

14

The Last Shipwright

On a beautiful, warm spring day during a trip along the Japanese coast in 2003, my wife and I were standing on a beach on the small island of Naoshima, located in the Seto Naikai, the Inland Sea. We were there to visit several museums, and while enjoying a sculpture garden on the beach we could not help but notice the volume of ship traffic passing the island. The view was of a veritable maritime highway. At any one moment, looking east and west, we could count over a dozen ships making their way along the sea lanes between the islands of Honshu and Shikoku.

In this book I have focused on Japan's small boatbuilding heritage, specifically my own apprenticeships with five traditional builders. However, starting in 1990 and roughly paralleling my own work in Japan, a remarkable craftsman began building a series of four replica *bezaisen*, a class of sailing cargo vessels that had once crowded Japan's ports. Unlike the boatbuilding traditions my teachers were familiar with, knowledge of the design, construction, and operation of these larger ships had all but disappeared, and would have completely were it not for the tireless efforts of Mr. Tomenoshin Niinuma, Japan's last traditional shipwright.

Maritime Japan

In Western histories, Japan is generally not regarded as an important maritime power. That status has typically been accorded based on the reach of a country's exploration and trade, or its naval might. Japan did not become a naval power until the twentieth century, and most Western scholars have viewed its previous maritime importance as reflecting its historical reclusiveness, a perception magnified by the unfortunate timing of European contact. Just as competition in the spice trade was heating up and European ships began criss-crossing Pacific waters, Japan in 1635 entered a self-imposed period of seclusion called *sakoku,* which did not end until its forced re-opening to Western diplomatic missions and trade in 1858.

However, Japan had been an important maritime power in Asia prior to the seventeenth century, when there were no shipbuilding restrictions.[1] Japanese vessels had carried on extensive trade with the Ryukyu Kingdom (modern-day Okinawa) and kingdoms in present-day Korea, China, Thailand, and Vietnam. These ships reflected technological influences from Japan's Asian neighbors, as well as the relatively recent influence of the Portuguese, who had arrived in 1543, followed by the Dutch in 1600.

The Edo period (1603–1868) began with the consolidation of government power under the Tokugawa shogunate, whose decision to restrict contact with the outside world

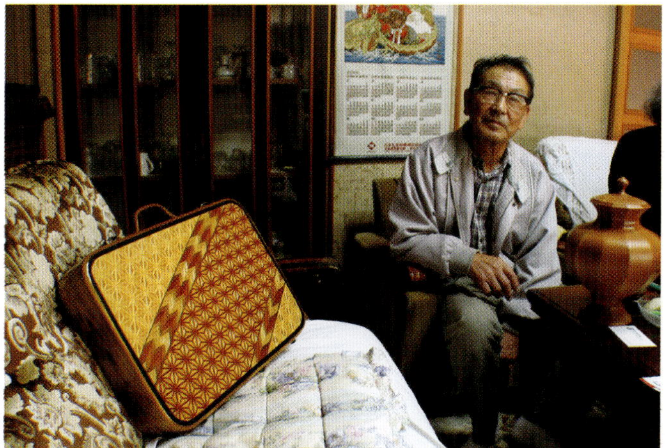

Mr. Tomenoshin Niinuma at home with two other examples of his work, an inlaid wooden valise and a bentwood vase.

was in many ways simply an extension of domestic policy, limiting any influences that might threaten its absolute control. The greatest threat was from Catholic Christianity, which it feared could subvert political and social structures. The Portuguese and Dutch had established trade at Nagasaki, on the island of Kyushu, which became the center of Japanese Christianity.

The shogunate's first edict under sakoku forbade commerce with Kyushu as a way of limiting the power of this region, and culminated with an absolute ban on all foreign travel by Japanese. Strictly controlled trade with the Dutch, Koreans, Chinese, and Ainu (Japan's aboriginal population, living mainly on Hokkaido) was allowed, but all overseas maritime activities were suspended.[2] Japan's bezaisen developed during this era of isolation. They were never intended to sail out of sight of Japan's shores; rather they sailed through a political and maritime era that looked only inward, ignoring the horizon.

Japan's geography, however, ensured the need to maintain and develop shipbuilding. The Japanese archipelago is essentially a line of mountaintops jutting from the sea, with a limited amount of arable land around them. Travel through and across the country was difficult, although a few major rivers and Japan's inland waters offered some alternate routes to the steep slopes and thick forests of the interior. Furthermore, in seeking to limit the military power of its vassals, the shogunate placed restrictions on the use of carriages and the construction of large bridges. The seas surrounding Japan were the most viable highways, and the rich maritime history of the Edo period is one of thousands of coastal traders moving goods around the country. Commerce would have ground to a halt without this vigorous coastwise trade, the modern equivalent of which we watched from the beach at Naoshima.

Naniwa-maru under sail in Osaka harbor. The lattice-work bulwarks are a distinctive feature of these ships, and no doubt this construction stiffened their hulls. Built as the main exhibit of the Osaka Maritime Museum, the ship participated in extensive sailing trials to learn how these vessels handled and performed. *Photo copyright Dr. Yutaka Masuyama.*

Sailing Cargo Vessels

Bezaisen is the most generic of several terms used to describe Edo-period coastal trading craft, one that most seamen and ship owners tended to use. Its literal origins are vague, *bezai* presumably describing the vessel type, and *sen* meaning ship. The word is also sometimes romanized as *benzaisen*. More specific terms for the coastal traders include *kitamaesen*, best translated as "northern coastal trader," the type that sailed along the Sea of Japan coast to Hokkaido. From the north the most common cargo was herring, salmon, and kelp, which would be traded for rice, salt, cotton, cloth, and sake from the mainland. Kitamaesen was also purportedly used by sailors along the more populous Pacific coast and Inland Sea as a derogatory term, since the Japan Sea coast is more rural and hence regarded as a more backward region.[3]

The trading vessels sailing between Osaka and Edo (present-day Tokyo) were called *higaki-kaisen*, from *kaisen*, a coastal cargo ship, and *higaki,* meaning "lattice," possibly referring to the lattice-like construction of the bulwarks, or reflecting a pattern that was the symbol of Osaka's merchant guilds. Most Japanese today tend to refer to all these vessels as *sengokubune*, literally "one thousand *koku* ship," a koku being a traditional volume of measurement. One koku of rice was approximately the amount required to feed one adult for one year.

It is incorrectly believed by some that rules put in place by the shogunate prevented shipwrights from building vessels suitable for the open seas as another way to enforce Japan's seclusion. Rudders, for example, were not hung on gudgeons, as is common in the West; instead the rudder stock passed through a beam. Scholars in the West have pointed out that this design, specifically mandated by the shogunate, was inherently weak. In fact, the shogunate did not enact any restrictions on shipbuilders, and the rudders of bezaisen were perfectly adapted for entering shallow draft ports because they could be raised by a capstan.[4] Bezaisen were simply never designed for offshore sailing. The shogunate's decision to cut itself off from the rest of the world meant that for the next 250 years Japan's ship design and maritime history would be dominated solely by the needs of its coastal trade.

This is not to suggest that sailing the coastal trade was without risk and its vessels less technically sophisticated. Much of Japan's shoreline is rocky and no doubt many crews and cargoes were lost. Sea chests of this period were fastened with intricate joinery and reputed to be watertight, so money and paperwork might survive the sinking of a vessel. A well-known proverb: "Only four inches from death" refers to the crews of these ships sleeping on the bottom plank of their ships.[5]

Ships used by Japan for its Asian trade were heavily influenced by foreign technologies, and illustrations of its trading fleet show round-hulled, carvel-planked ships, often using fully battened, junk-type rigs. By contrast, bezaisen were built with methods similar to those used in building smaller craft. As we have noted in previous chapters, these include a horizontal plank keel, generally twice as thick as the planking, with a hard chine hull composed of two strakes, the top strake nearly vertical over most of its length. When strakes are built up of several planks, the planks are edge fastened to each other. In some parts of Japan sawn frames are installed, but the strength of this design still comes mainly from the hull itself. In lieu of frames, horizontal beams may cross the hull at the chine and the sheer, with beam ends either tenoned through the hull and wedged from the outside or locked in place with shouldered keys. Finally, we have seen that the side planking aft often runs past the transom to form a chamber protecting the rudder.

Bezaisen reflected these same monocoque construction features, but started with a boxed keel, the sides of which gave the vessel lateral resistance when sailing to windward, and also reduced the overall draft of the vessel.[6] There were no curved frames within the hull; instead the hull was strengthened by floor timbers and massive athwartship beams at the chine and sheer. Amazingly for vessels of this size, the deck planking was entirely unfastened, which facilitated the loading and unloading of cargo.

Bezaisen hulls were hard chine, just like small craft. The box keel, however, provided lateral resistance under sail, and allowed these craft to stand upright when beached.

The large rudder, set within the protective overhang of the stern planking, extended several feet below the bottom of the hull and also contributed to the lateral resistance of the hull. The rudder could be raised or lowered, facilitating shoal-draft sailing and allowed a ship to be easily beached, where it could stand safely upright on its box keel. The single rectangular mainsail could be lowered and handled by a small crew. Often a ship's boat, or *tenma,* was carried on deck. All in all, the bezaisen's design and hull shape lent itself to efficient construction, an ability to enter small ports with shallow harbors, and easy handling by a small crew.

Mr. Tomenoshin Niinuma

Mr. Niinuma was one of nine children born to a rural family in the coastal town of Ofunato in Iwate Prefecture, a rugged, isolated region on the northeastern coast of Japan's main island of Honshu.[7] In rural postwar Japan there were very few job opportunities, and he followed his father into the boatbuilding trade, beginning his apprenticeship at age fifteen building wooden fishing boats. Ofunato is one of the best

The rudder of *Michinoku-maru,* Mr. Niinuma's most recent ship, launched in 2006. The large rudders of these vessels hung deep beneath the keel, contributing somewhat to lateral resistance when sailing. They could also be raised into the slot in the stern to enter shallow ports.

protected natural harbors along this stretch of Japan's Pacific coast, although the March 2011 earthquake and tsunami severely damaged the town. There has always been a strong local demand for fishing vessels of all sizes, as well as a tradition of shipbuilding. By the 1980s Mr. Niinuma had come to realize his generation was the last to have been trained in traditional wooden ship construction, and he began to dream of building a sailing vessel from the Edo era. At the time maritime scholarship on the subject was limited, and reference materials practically non-existent. To this day, as we have seen, traditional boatbuilders (as well as some house and temple carpenters) draw their plans on planks of wood. Although these are durable, and many original drawings from the days of bezaisen exist, shipwrights (like today's boatbuilders) typically drew only profiles of their vessels. Half-breadth dimensions were either memorized or derived from formulas, and no construction details were drawn. This secrecy was pervasive and has left Japan with incomplete documentation of the design or construction of bezaisen.

Mr. Niinuma explored elsewhere in his research, including old paintings, woodblock prints, and models, which shipowners often commissioned as shrine or temple offerings for the protection of their fleets. He began building models himself to work out an accurate design. After organizing a group of about thirty shipwrights who still possessed the necessary skills, he began to source local materials to build an authentic, full-sized replica. Initially the project was greeted with widespread skepticism and even Mr. Niinuma admits he had no idea whether the vessel would sail properly. Like his forebears, he drew the lines and construction details on wood. He was the sole designer; no naval architects or engineers were involved, and there was no modern analysis of her lines before construction commenced. Eventually a local newspaper editor took up the cause and by the late 1980s the project began to take shape. In 1991 the prefecture of Iwate decided to underwrite the project as part of the Japan Expo to be held there the following year. *Kesen-maru* was launched in 1992 and has been home-ported in Ofunato ever since. She was never actively sailed, however, and is only taken off her mooring once a year for a local festival.[8]

Kesen-maru at her mooring in Ofunato, Japan. The first of Mr. Niinuma's replica ships, she was one of just three vessels out of fifty-three in the harbor to survive the 2011 tsunami.

The Replicas

Kesen-maru is 62 feet overall and displaces 30 tons. Her mainsail is 460 square feet and she also flies a small sail on a foremast. Mr. Niinuma built her entirely of local materials: cedar for the hull; red pine for her deck, beams, and floorboards; and oak for her rudder. The 56-foot mast came from a single cedar tree. Her fastenings are all hand-forged nails, and nail heads exposed on the exterior of her hull are covered with copper plates, a technique widespread in Japanese boatbuilding. Although the ship ultimately proved to be a media and public sensation, and at least vindicated Mr. Niinuma's design, some scholars claimed she wasn't an absolutely faithful replica.[9] Amazingly, *Kesen-maru* was among just three vessels out of fifty-three in the harbor to survive the eleven-meter tsunami that swept Ofunato in 2011.

Mr. Niinuma's second ship, *Hakusan-maru,* was built in 1997 for the Ogi Folklore Museum on Sado, an island in the Sea of Japan and part of Niigata Prefecture. The museum is located just above the sleepy fishing village of Shukunegi, an important shipbuilding port during the Edo period. This time Mr. Niinuma used a 200-year old plank drawing from the late Edo period as the basis for the design, and enjoyed design support from a Tokyo research institute. He brought his team of shipbuilders from northern Japan to Sado and built the ship in just over a year. Local carpenters built a structure to house it, as there was never any intention to launch the vessel. The ship's cradle rides on tracks and in fine weather the museum rolls the ship outside and raises its sail. It also frequently serves as a set for historical dramas aired on television. Mr. Niinuma describes the Sado vessel as the most authentic of the four ships he has built in terms of materials. All wood was supplied by local loggers from the fine cedar forests Sado Island is known for. An island blacksmith provided all the fastenings and ironwork.

The largest of Mr. Niinuma's four replicas are his two most recent: *Naniwa-maru,* launched in 1999 and built for the Osaka Maritime Museum; and *Michinoku-maru,* launched in 2005 by the Michinoku Traditional Wooden Boat Museum in Aomori. Both vessels are roughly the same size, but *Naniwa-maru* was a collaboration between Mr. Niinuma and a team of maritime scholars.

Naniwa-maru is the centerpiece, literally and figuratively, of the Osaka Maritime Museum. The vessel, fully rigged, rests in a giant glass geodesic dome set in Osaka harbor, accessible to visitors via an undersea tunnel. The ship is encircled by four floors of exhibits recounting the history of Osaka, its commerce, and the development of trading ships known as higaki-kaisen.[10] Higaki-kaisen specifically refers to those traders sailing between Osaka and Edo, the most important trade route in Japan and the means by which Osaka rose to become the mercantile center of the country.

Naniwa-maru was built by Mr. Niinuma's crew at the Hitachi shipyard in Osaka, with funding for the project and the museum provided by the Port of Osaka. Some of the construction methods were modern, such as using a steambox to heat the planks and bending them around steel molds set on the keel, rather than the traditional, open-fire bending called *yakimage*. Mr. Niinuma confessed to me he believes steam-bending is a superior technique, as it heats the wood more deeply and makes it more elastic.

It was planned for *Naniwa-maru* when finished to be immediately installed in the museum, but as she came closer to completion a number of sailors, naval architects, and maritime historians insisted she should first be sailed. Since there was no one alive with any first-hand knowledge of how such vessels handled, she represented an unprecedented opportunity to explore the capabilities of this type of ship. Historically, one of the most famous voyages of higaki-kaisen was the annual "race" from Osaka to Edo. Like the square-rigged grain racers in the Australian wheat trade, the Osaka-to-Edo race was about commerce, to demonstrate the advantage of being the first to get products (in this case cotton and sake) to market. Although the single square sail is a well-understood technology, how this type of rig and hull shape performed reaching, and whether it could successfully sail upwind was a mystery. Records show the first ships reached Edo from Osaka in forty-five hours, sailing at a seven to eight knot average.

One of Japan's largest foundations, the Nippon Foundation, came forward to underwrite the extra costs of launching *Naniwa-maru* and conducting sailing trials. The team selected included the late Professor Emeritus Kensaku Nomoto of Osaka University, Professor Yutaka Masuyama of the Kanazawa Institute of Technology, and Professor Akira Sakurai of Kyushu University.[11]

The sail trim study had to take into account some unique features of the bezaisen mainsail. The massive masts of these ships are only stayed fore and aft. The lack of shrouds gives the yard much more freedom of movement. The yard is braced to a pair of windlasses located below the poop deck. Perhaps most unusual is the lack of a footrope in the sail; instead the foot of the bezaisen sail has pendants attached to a massive line laying athwartships on deck just behind the mast. A series of bowlines (usually three or four) run from the leech of the sail forward. As the researchers surmised, the rope-and-pendant arrangement was primarily for downwind sailing, while the bowlines came into play when reaching. Historically, shortening sail was done by gathering the foot of the sail and tying it around the base of the mast, lowering the yard, or a combination of the two.

Principal Dimensions of the *Naniwa-maru*	
Length overall:	29.9 m / 98' 1"
Breadth molded:	7.4 m / 24' 3"
Depth molded:	2.4 m / 7' 10"
Light weight (hull, rig, and rudder):	88 tons
Ballast:	56 tons
Crew, instrumentation, etc.:	3 tons
Total displacement at trial:	147 tons
Waterline length:	23 m / 75' 5"
Draft forward:	2.0 m / 6' 7"
Draft aft:	2.2 m / 7' 3"

The sailing trials took place in August of 1999 in Osaka harbor, a mostly sheltered body of water, in wind speeds of between ten and twenty knots. Running downwind, it seems as if the arrangement of multiple pendants controlling the shape of the foot of the sail can have a marked effect on performance. In the trials the ship ran downwind rigged two ways: in the first, drawing only the clews at either end of the foot, the way a Western square-rigger does; and in the second, using the pendants. On average the latter method yielded a ten percent higher speed. This experiment in rigging the ship's square sail in both Western and Japanese ways was also tried on a beam reach, but the researchers found drawing the foot in using the pendants was no advantage on this point of sail. They did conclude, however, the pendants were useful off the wind to a quartering reach.

Naniwa-maru's fastest point of sail was on a beam to broad reach, which surprised no one. The great mystery, however, was her windward ability. Among the few historic accounts of how these ships sailed was a statement by a master mariner that he often sailed with the wind four points off the bow. Of course this is apparent wind in the

Michinoku-maru sailing close-hauled. Note the multiple pendants attached to the foot of the sail. *Photo copyright Masaaki Kon.*

Michinoku-maru under construction, her hull partially planked. Her largest timbers were Douglas fir from Oregon and planking of local cedar. *Photo copyright Masaaki Kon.*

mariner's face, and as the researchers had already found, the layout of these vessels on deck and down-wash windflow from the single sail made any apparent wind readings suspect. Another historic document recorded a bezaisen gaining four miles to windward on a close-hauled tack of twenty miles. Although current and leeway were unknown for this event, it does correspond to a tack angle of 78 degrees, which is about what the researchers were able to perform in the sailing trials. Speed obtained was 25 to 30 percent of actual wind speed.

Tacking *Naniwa-maru* involved wearing her around from one tack to another. This particular maneuver requires precise sail handling and rudder control, so it is the most suspect component of the sea trials given a crew inexperienced with these ships. Although the sail itself is simple, the running rigging of these vessels is quite complicated. Proficiency in coordinating changes in sail trim while wearing the ship around was more than could be expected of the research crew. Unfortunately, from these trials it is impossible to know how bezaisen were handled by their original crews.

Finally, the researchers reported *Naniwa-maru's* bottom became fouled with barnacles (10 mm, or about 3/8" thick) from its launching to the time of the test period. To calculate the resulting effect on performance, they assumed a clean bottom and calculated the ship could reach an angle of 70 degrees to windward with a speed 30 percent of true wind speed, with 40 percent of wind speed possible from a beam to broad reach, and slightly less than this sailing downwind.[12]

The most recent replica bezaisen built was launched in 2005 in the northern Japanese city of Aomori. *Michinoku-maru* was commissioned by the Michinoku Traditional Wooden Boat Museum, an institution with the largest collection of historic boats in the nation.[13] These are primarily regional small craft, plus some other large vessels from throughout Asia. Mr. Niinuma had complete freedom in designing and constructing *Michinoku-maru*, a role he relished after collaborating with historians and engineers in the construction of his second and third ships. As we have seen, craftsmen are regarded as aloof and prickly personalities, and often with good reason. Their secretiveness and independence, and especially the harshness of the traditional apprentice system, seem out of place in modern times. While the historians debated whether his bezaisen were authentic replicas, and scoured documents for "proof," Mr. Niinuma regarded himself as the inheritor of a craft tradition. Although the professor may discover evidence in his research, he said, these are just pinpoints in a vast, historical darkness. Mr. Niinuma contends his own instincts are probably no different from those of an Edo-period shipwright. This is the difference, he told me, between the professor and the carpenter.[14]

Mr. Niinuma calls *Michinoku-maru* the culmination of his experience. As such, he says it is the best sailing and most useful of his four ships. Her construction, however, was under a strict budget, and much of his design work involved cutting construction costs. Her wood comes from a number of sources: Japanese cedar for the planking; Douglas fir from Oregon for her backbone; and other woods from China. The one-piece cedar mast came from the forests of Iwate Prefecture.

The traditional nails used in Mr. Niinuma's other three ships were all crafted by blacksmiths and represented a large percentage of their budgets. To cut costs on *Michinoku-maru*, he used 15 mm (5/8") galvanized lag bolts approxi-

Michinoku-maru just before launch in 2006. Some of the large beams spanning her hull are visible. She has floor timbers and beams, but no frames inside the hull.

mately a foot long to edge-fasten the hull planks. These bolts were driven at a very acute angle between adjacent planks, joining them much faster than by using more customary edge-nailing techniques. Otherwise the construction was traditional.

Mr. Niinuma called the frameless hull of traditional Japanese boat construction *zentai hantai,* which means, literally, "whole resistance," a neat equivalent of the English term monocoque. Although he had built large, wooden, plank-on-frame fishing vessels in his career—Japanese adaptations of standard Western construction—he still considers this traditional method "sensible," especially when one considers ease of construction and overall costs. It certainly is efficient; Mr. Niinuma and his fifteen-man crew built the *Michinoku-maru* in just eleven months of work, although spread out over two years. Amazingly, the sole drawing used was a 1/10th scale plan he drew on a sheet of plywood, no different from shipbuilders in the Edo period, and traditional Japanese measurements were used in construction.

Mr. Niinuma believes *Naniwa-maru* and *Michinoku-maru* are capable of carrying 150 tons, equivalent to a thousand-koku ship. Historically, larger bezaisen were built that carried twice this amount.

Michinoku-maru was built in a small shipyard in Aomori city owned by the maritime museum, and Mr. Niinuma's

Inside the cabin of *Michinoku-maru,* looking aft. The round rudder stock is visible in the center. The horizontal capstan in front of it is for raising and lowering the rudder. The deck-mounted blocks run to other capstans for the backstays.

crew lived in a house at the shipyard. They were paid a daily rate, which is typical for carpenters in Japan, who work eight hour days but can be obligated to work longer (for the same daily rate) as the deadline for completion approaches. After cutting expenses as much as possible, the final cost for *Michinoku-maru* was about two hundred million yen, or about $1.8 million U.S. dollars (at 110 yen to the dollar, the exchange rate at the time of her launch in November, 2005). Materials represented three-quarters of the total cost with labor accounting for the balance. Once again a steam box was used for bending planking but there were no building molds; the floors and beams were fitted to hold the planks as they were bent to shape.

Principal Dimensions of the *Michinoku-maru*

Length	104.7 shaku	34.55 m (113' 4-1/4")
Beam	29 shaku	9.57 m (31' 4-3/4")
Stem length	39 shaku	12.87 m (42' 2-3/4")
Mast length	92.3 shaku	30.46 m (99' 11-1/4")
Plank keel	1 shaku	30.3 cm (11-15/16") thick
Upper planking	6 sun	18 cm (7-1/8") thick
Stem	2 x 3 shaku	61 cm x 91.5 cm (1' 11-7/8" x 2' 11-13/16")
Rudder post	1 shaku	30.3 cm (11-15/16") in diameter
Decking	2 sun	6 cm (2-3/8") thick
Mast at deck	2.5 shaku	75.56 cm (2' 5-3/4") square

Historic photograph showing a bezaisen with a hybrid sailing rig. The single traditional square sail is augmented by a bowsprit with Western-style headsails, along with the gaff-rigged "spanker" on the mizzenmast. *Photo copyright Dane Owen.*

Michinoku-maru under sail in Aomori Bay. *Photo copyright Masaaki Kon.*

Since her launch *Michinoku-maru* has been sailed summers by the museum in the capacious bay at Aomori, and home ported in front of the maritime museum. In 2011 she sailed south along the Japan Sea coast, the first kitamaesen to make such a journey in over a hundred years. Mr. Niinuma told me he would like to build more of these ships, but he and his crew are getting older and quality materials are harder to find.[15]

Less than a decade after Commodore Perry sailed his fleet of iron-hulled steamships into Tokyo Bay in 1853, forcing Japan to open to the West, the Meiji government did enact shipbuilding restrictions: they forbade the construction of Japanese-style ships over 500 koku. This was to encourage the development of a Western-style merchant fleet. The Meiji government's modernization policies also confirmed the notion in Japan that its native traditions and technologies were backward and unsuited to moving the country forward onto the world stage. Bezaisen, along with sword-wielding samurai, shoguns, and the tradition-bound world they inhabited, were swept aside almost overnight, leaving the legacy of this style of shipbuilding and its culture of craftsmen to survive only in Japan's small boat traditions.

Notes

1 See *Nihon no Fune: Wasen Hen (Ships of Japan: Indigenous Designs)*, by Dr. Hiroyuki Adachi, Tokyo Museum of Maritime Science, March, 1998.

2 See Adachi, *Nihon no Fune.*

3 Interview with Mr. Tsuneo Imai, Sail Training Association of Japan, 2008.

4 See Adachi, *Nihon no Fune.*

5 Mr. Kazuyoshi Fujiwara's memoir, written in 2001.

6 In Western naval architecture monocoque refers to construction in which the strength of the vessel is in the planking, obviating the need for extensive internal framing.

7 Interviews with Mr. Tomenoshin Niinuma by the author in Ofunato, Japan (2001, 2005), and Aomori, Japan (2003).

8 Mr. Shunichi Yamamoto, "*Kesen-maru*: A *Sengokubune* Replica From Japan," *WoodenBoat* magazine, issue number 110, January/February, 1993.

9 Mr. Shunichi Yamamoto, letter to the editor, *WoodenBoat* magazine, issue number 114, September/October 1993.

10 As of publication the Osaka Maritime Museum is closed due to severe budget cuts by the Port of Osaka.

11 Dr. Yutaka Masuyama, Dr. Kensaku Nomoto, and Dr. Akira Sakurai, "Numerical Simulation of Maneuvering of *Naniwa-maru*: A Full-scale Reconstruction of Sailing Trader of Japanese Heritage," paper delivered at The 16th Chesapeake Sailing Yacht Symposium, Annapolis, Maryland, March 2003.

12 See Masuyama, *et al.,* "Numerical Simulation."

13 As of this publication, this excellent museum is closed due to funding problems.

14 Mr. Tomenoshin Niinuma, author interviews, Ofunato, Japan (2005).

15 At her launch, the average age of the crew that built *Michinoku-maru* was sixty-nine.

Michinoku-maru running downwind in Aomori Bay. She sailed half way down the Japan Sea coast as part of a summer program of cruises. She is now on static display in Aomori. *Photo copyright Masaaki Kon.*

Students in the author's winter-term class Building the Japanese Boat at Middlebury College launch their ayubune in the campus swimming pool. *Photo copyright Trent Campbell.*

Postscript to the Paperback Edition

Over the years since my last apprenticeship recorded in this book, I have had the opportunity to build several more Japanese boats, as shown on the updated p. ix map. The first resulted from a proposal to work alongside Mr. Takeshi Tsuda building a twenty-shaku ashitenma, a small workboat, for the 2012 Setouchi Triennale. This international arts festival is held on multiple islands of the Inland Sea, where I had met Mr. Tsuda, the last boatbuilder of this region, on the small island of Naoshima years before.

Sadly, after our proposal was accepted, Mr. Tsuda's health took a turn for the worse, and he was unable to participate. The organizers, however, wished to go ahead with the project, so I invited Mr. Takumi Suzuki and Mr. Koji Matano to join me in the port city of Takamatsu to build the boat. Koji, a glass artist, had long admired the sculptural qualities of Western boats and canoes, and had become an accomplished builder of them. Takumi had studied canoe-making under Koji, and also under Jerry Stelmok in Maine.

In 2014 the Mizunoki Museum of Art in Kameoka invited me to build an ayubune for an exhibition about this traditional Hozu River boat, used for catching *ayu*, or sweetfish. Although six students joined me for the project, none had ever done any woodworking. I gave short lessons on how to use each tool and demonstrated basic techniques. They then focused their attention on perfecting those skills, working diligently for hours at a stretch, with no sound except for the tools and occasional short, whispered suggestions to one another. They worked tentatively at first, but quickly gained confidence. In retrospect I am amazed at what they learned in only a few weeks and in the quality of the finished boat.

Watching my students progress was in some ways like reliving my own apprenticeships. I confess that it had taken longer for me to learn what they seemed to grasp intuitively: that it requires intense concentration to learn these skills, and tireless repetition to master them. I, on the other hand, had first wanted to impress my teachers by showing off what I knew. Nothing had prepared me for the pressures and expectations of the apprentice experience, in particular for bearing the responsibility for learning that is the student's alone.

About a hundred people attended the launching of our ayubune, which is now used by a non-profit river advocacy group teaching fishing to youngsters. While such opportunities have given me the chance to expose more people to Japanese boatbuilding, they also show that within Japan there are people interested in rediscovering the craft, and communities willing to integrate the culture of traditional boats into the local tourist business and public events.

During the 2015 winter term at Middlebury College, I led a class of fifteen students building two Japanese boats. One goal of the course was to model the apprenticeship method of transmitting knowledge. Learning by observation rather than instruction, and honing skills through trial and error, proved especially provocative to these students. Nevertheless, they rose to the challenge, and with only occasional prompting did their own problem-solving rather than always turning to the teacher to provide solutions.

In 2015 I returned to Japan for a sixth apprenticeship in Tohoku, where the tsunami struck March 11, 2011. This northern region formerly boasted the highest concentration of wooden boats in the country, which were practically all lost in that horrific destruction of life and property. I had traveled this coastline three times before the disaster and met several boatbuilders, including Mr. Tomenoshin Niinuma, the shipwright introduced in Chapter 14, and Mr. Hiroshi Murakami, now the last active boatbuilder in the region and my new teacher. Mr. Murakami specialized in building isobune, literally, "inshore boat," the smallest craft used by local fishermen. In earlier travels I have seen hundreds of them along the coastline of Iwate and Miyagi Prefectures, although in 2005 Mr. Murakami told me he had been put out of business by fiberglass boats. In an odd twist of fate, he wrote later to report that the tsunami had put him back in business; he had orders for about a dozen isobune and kakkobune, the two most common small fishing boats.

Over the last twenty years I have watched the slow, inexorable decline of wooden boats in Japan, but in Tohoku the entire boatbuilding culture was lost in a single moment. With Mr. Murakami left as the only person who could build his region's boats, I proposed working with him to record his designs, and perhaps find surviving boats and measure them. The tsunami has rendered this work especially poignant and pressing.

In 2016 I built an isobune for an exhibition on Japanese boats at the Takenaka Carpentry Tools Museum in Kobe. Just before the project began, I proposed to the curator the idea of offering half-day workshops on traditional boatbuilding each Saturday. His first reaction was to question who or why anyone would attend, but he agreed to post a notice on the museum's Facebook page. A few days later he approached me with a look of shock on his face. "All your workshops are filled," he said, "I had to stop enrollment at fifty."

At the first workshop, on wasen design, I asked the participants to introduce themselves. There were men and women, university students and retirees, several house carpenters, and amateur woodworkers. Some had traveled from Tokyo and would return for all four workshops. The next workshop was more dramatic: bending the two-inch thick bottom of my isobune over an open fire in the museum's parking lot. I was grateful this workshop coincided with a visit from Mr. Murakami, whom the museum had invited to see the exhibit. I was happy to let him direct the process and record his technique a second time. Our third workshop was on saw-fitting and edge-fastening, while our fourth was a very elaborate Shinto launching ceremony in Kobe harbor.

In 2017 I had the opportunity to build an *ukaibune*, a cormorant fishing boat, with Mr. Seichi Nasu of Gifu. I had actually been asking Mr. Nasu if I could work with him since we first met in 2003, but he had always rebuffed my requests, so it was a surprise when he suddenly offered to teach me. However, he had one major caveat: at age eighty-five he could no longer do the actual building; he would lay down the dimensions if I would do all the physical work. I didn't hesitate to accept his offer, and over a two-month period, I along with several volunteers built a forty-two foot boat, a design largely unchanged for centuries (cormorant fishing has a 1,300-year history in Gifu). It was also my first experience studying with a builder of river boats.

Since opportunities to study with traditional craftspeople are rapidly disappearing, over the last few years I have pivoted to teaching Japanese boatbuilding in as many venues as I can. I have now taught my course four times at Middlebury College and once at Bates College. I also developed a five-day boatbuilding workshop during which eight to ten students build a twenty-one foot traditional river boat.

I have also formed a partnership with America's oldest boatbuilding school, the Apprenticeshop, in Rockland, Maine; together we are working to create a boatbuilding exchange program in Japan. In 2019 the school's Director of Student Affairs and Outreach, Nina Noah, and I traveled to Japan, where we built boats with craftspeople in Niigata and Toyama. There she was able to experience first-hand the Japanese way of apprentice learning. It is our hope to create a program to bring boatbuilders to Japan to document and build boats, and ultimately bring Japanese to the Apprenticeshop to study Western boatbuilding.

Since the publication of the first edition of this book in 2015, two teachers I wrote about, Mr. Kazuyoshi Fujiwara and Mr. Nobuji Udagawa, have passed away. Beyond the personal loss, each death compels me to reflect anew on the need to transmit these skills to a new generation. Without having ever spoken to them about this directly, it feels like a promise to do this was implicit in my work with them.

Fifteen years ago, I would not have believed that any young Japanese, much less a non-Japanese, would take an interest in building wasen. Then I hoped only that this book might serve as a record of a vanished craft. Today I am far more optimistic. Like the sabani racers of Okinawa and the wooden boat enthusiasts of Wasen Tomo no Kai, others may come forward to embrace traditional boatbuilding. With the commitment of municipalities, museums, and schools, workshops and training can be offered to meet the needs of those committed to reviving the craft. This new generation of boatbuilders will unfortunately lack the opportunities afforded me to learn from incomparably skilled craftspeople; they will have to chart a new path to mastery. But their success is assured to the extent they emulate the qualities of the boatbuilding generation portrayed here: their ingenuity, resiliency, patience, and perseverance.

Douglas Brooks
April 18, 2021

Works Cited

Adachi, Hiroyuki. *Nihon no Fune: Wasen Hen* (*Ships of Japan: Indigenous Designs*). Tokyo: Museum of Maritime Science, 1998.

Brackett, Len. *Building the Japanese House Today.* New York: Harry Abrams, 2005.

Brinkley, Francis. *An Unabridged Japanees-English Dictionary.* Tokyo: Sanseido, 1896.

Brown, Azby. *The Genius of Japanese Carpentry: The Secrets of a Craft.* Tokyo: Kodansha International, 1995. Rutland VT & Tokyo: Tuttle Publishing, revised ed. 2014.

Coaldrake, William. *The Way of the Carpenter.* Tokyo: Weatherhill, 1990.

Deguchi, Akiko and Masato. *Building Method of the Chizi Boat, Ishikawa Prefecture, Ohchigata, Searashi, Nakajima Village (Ishikawa ken Ohchigata no Chizibune Nakajima machi Searashi Deno Kenzou Kiroku).* Tokyo: Museum of Maritime Science, 2004.

Hori, G. Victor Sogen. "Teaching and Learning in the Rinzai Zen Monastery," *Journal of Japanese Studies* 20:1 (1994).

Horiuchi, Kotaro. *Locus of a Boat Designer.* Yokohama: KAZI, 1987, 2008. (Japanese)

Itoman City. *History of Itoman City, Volume 12, Folk History* (*Itoman-shi Shi, Shiryou Hen 12 Minzoku Shiryou*). Itoman, Japan: Itoman City, 1991.

Makino, Kumi. *Marukobune: The Traditional Sailing Boats in the Lake Biwa Region, Japan (Biwako no Dentouteki Mokuzosen no Henyo: Marukobune wo Chushin ni*). Tokyo: Yuzankaku, 2013.

Masuyama, Yutaka , Kensaku Nomoto, and Akira Sakurai, "Numerical Simulation of Maneuvering of Naniwa-maru: A Full-scale Reconstruction of Sailing Trader of Japanese Heritage," paper delivered at the 16th Chesapeake Sailing Yacht Symposium, Annapolis, Maryland, March 2003.

Merton, Thomas. *Love and Living.* New York: Farrar, Straus & Giroux, 1979.

Needham, Joseph. *Science and Civilization in China*, Vol. 4, Part 3. Cambridge: Cambridge University Press, 1971.

Nishimura, Shinji. *A Study of Ancient Ships of Japan.* Tokyo: The Society of Naval Architects, 1931.

Odate, Toshio. *Japanese Woodworking Tools: Their Tradition, Spirit, and Use.* Newtown, CT: The Taunton Press, 1984. Fresno, CA: Linden Press, reprint 1998.

Ogi Town. *Minami Sado No Gyoroshuzoku* (*Fishing Culture of Southern Sado*). Ogi, Japan: Ogi Town Planning, Commerce, and Tourism Division, 1975.

Ono, Sokyo. *Shinto: The Kami Way.* Tokyo: Tuttle Publishing, 1962.

Pardey, Lin and Larry. *Self Sufficient Sailor.* Arcata, CA: Pardey Books, 1997.

Sato, Toshio. *Hangiri* (*Half Barrel*). Ogi, Japan: Ogi Town Planning, Commerce, and Tourism Division, 2002.

Shiraishi, Katsuhiko. *Sabani: Canoes of Okinawa* (*Okinawa no Fune Sabani*). Self-published, 1985.

Small Boat Journal, Nos. 45, 46 (1985, 1986). Bennington VT: Small Boat Journal.

Streeter, Tal. *The Art of the Japanese Kite.* Tokyo: Weatherhill, Inc., 1980.

Takusagawa, Zensuke, and Isao Yoshioka. "A Study on Ro (Oriental Sweep)," *Bulletin of the Faculty of Engineering,* 25. Yokohama: Yokohama National University, March, 1976.

Taylor, Roger C. *The Elements of Seamanship.* International Marine, 1982, reprint Mystic, CT: Flat Hammock Press, 2009.

Underwood, Horace H. *Korean Boats and Ships.* Seoul: Yonsei University Press, 1979.

WoodenBoat magazine, 100. Brooklin, ME: WoodenBoat Publications, June, 1991.

Worcester, G.R.G. *The Junks and Sampans of the Yangtze.* Annapolis, MD: Naval Institute Press, 1971.

Yamamoto, Shunichi. "*Kesen-maru*: A *Sengokubune* Replica From Japan." *WoodenBoat*, 110, January/February, 1993. Brooklin, ME: WoodenBoat Publications.

Yasumoto, Chika. *Sabani Breaking the Waves: The World of Boatbuilder Arashiro Yasuhiro (Shio wo Hiraku Fune Sabani: Funadaiku Arashiro Yasuhiro no Sekai).* Ishigaki, Japan: Nanzansha, 2003.

Yokoyama, Akira. *Yacht Design (Yotto no Sekkei).* Yokohama: KAZI, March, 1980.

Glossary-Index

I first went to Japan with only a traveler's phrasebook, and although my language skills improved with many visits over the years, I make no claim to fluency. At best I describe myself as proficient when talking about boatbuilding, and on several occasions native speakers, overhearing my conversations with craftsmen, have told me they couldn't understand a word we were saying.

One of the more personally surprising finds of my research was the variety of words used to describe the same tool or task among a people often viewed as insular and homogenous. In fact, the language environment changed markedly with the location of each apprenticeship, from the more standard Japanese of Tokyo, to the dialects of Tohoku, impenetrable even to many native Japanese, to the distinct and separately evolved language of Okinawa. Even two boatbuilders living and working within ten kilometers of each other (Tokyo and Urayasu) used some different terms. Combined with variations in boatbuilding vocabulary due to broader regional customs or boat types, documenting proper terms for even common items and techniques was a daunting task. Consequently, the glossary entries presented here must be considered "as heard," or even "as recorded," since they may possibly have been misheard.

Dictionary confirmation was equally frustrating, although interestingly, my 1896 Brinkley's *Unabridged Japanese-English Dictionary*, reprinted by Sanseido, was by far my most useful reference for boatbuilding terms. Still, although finding an entry was reasonable proof that a term is or was common and widespread, lack of an entry shed no light on whether a term was too specialized or too regional, or was simply not properly transcribed by me. To help clarify the limits of their usage I have coded some entries here with a combination of the first letter of the boat type and the first letter of the location of the project (see note below). This indicates that I heard this term used only in this location when building this boat, and so is possibly limited to that context. Terms with no code are probably more common and widespread; at the very least I heard them in other locations and with reference to other boat types. Ultimately, however, this Glossary-Index must be considered a work in progress, and I welcome the input of others in clarifying any usages.

NOTE: TS indicates a term recorded while building the Taraibune on Sado Island; BU = Bekabune built in Urayasu; CT = Chokkibune in Tokyo; SA = Shimaihagi in Aomori; SO = Sabani in Okinawa, sometimes followed by -IH for Iejima Hougen, the local dialect. Main references in text are given for the Japanese terms only. Number in **bold** indicate photos.

heartwood. See *akami*, *akama* SO-IH

heimenzu
drawing, plan view

hian SO-IH
gaff. See also *gafu*

hiba 33, 186
cypress family conifer (*Thujopsis dolabrata*), sometimes temple juniper (*Juniperus rigida*). See also *asunaro*, *hinoki*

hidake
smaller bamboo used for bucket hoops

higaki-kaisen 256, 259
traditional wooden trading ships sailing between Osaka and Edo

higashi
east

hinoki 33
cypress (*Chamaecyparis obtusa*). See also *asunaro*, *hiba*

hira SA 198
bamboo tool for spreading glue

hiraki BU 31, 147
horizontal measurement that describes the angle using the *sagefuri*; also angle of plank lean, or flare in the hull

hirameki 136
insight, having the knowledge in one's head. See also *kan de*

hiro 13
span, the distance between the fingertips of outstretched arms. See also *hitohiro*

hitohiro
span, same as *hiro*, with hito meaning "person." See also *hiro*

hiwata
caulking TS. See also *makihada*

ho **64**
sail. See also *hoashi*, *hoashizuna*

hoashi (or *hoashizuna*)
sheet

hobashira
mast. See also *bou*, *hashira* SO-IH

hobikisen 64
literally, "sail pulling boat," a small *utasebune* still sailed on Lake Kasumigaura for tourists

hokakebune SO-IH 239
sailboat. See also *putachibune* SO-IH, *hosen*

hoonoki SA 186
magnolia (*Magnolia hypoleuca* or *Magnolia obovata*)

horsepower. See *bariki* SO

hosen
sailboat. See also *putachibune*, *hokakebune* SO-IH

hozuna
halyard. See also *minawa* SO, *tina* SO-IH

huundu SO-IH 217, **227**
dovetail fastening. See also *chigiri*, *chikkin*, *ryuugo*, *tsuzumi*

I

ichiwari TS 118
describes ten degrees of outward flare of the side of a tub boat

iiku SO-IH 226
flowering evergreen (*Cleyera japonica*) sacred to Shinto. See also *sakaki*

ikatsuribune 183
a larger boat for catching squid, *ika*

iku SO-IH
paddle, from wood name *iiku* (*Cleyera japonica*)

inomaki 226
conifer native to southern Japan (*Podocarpus macrophyllus*). See also *kusamaki*, chage SO-IH

inwale. See *uchiuchikiyaa* SO-IH

ireko **58**, **60**
socket for the pin of a sculling oar

iri SO-IH
west

irigu SO-IH
plug, mortise. See also *umeki*, *yoji* (Tohoku)

isobune SA 64, **182**, 212
inshore fishing boat; in Tohoku a small boat with carved bottom and plank sides. See also *kakkobune*

ita 215
wooden plank, on boat

itago SA **185**, 211
floorboards. See also *sunoko*, *sashiita* BU

itaya 186, 211
maple, either painted maple or mono maple, as short for *itayakaede* (*Acer mono*), and *itayamomiji* (*Acer japonicus*)

itazumen. See *itazu*

itazu **1–2**, **10–11**, **165**, **225**
plank drawings

J

janome SA 211, 215
drain hole

jikigata SA 200
spiling plank. See also *zuchigata* SA, *kataita* CT, *kaikata* TS

moji (or *mojiri*) **42**
a square-tipped chisel with T-handle for turning to make rough holes.
mokkoku 226
flowering evergreen (*Ternstroemia gymnanthera*); also called Japanese Cleyera and so taken to be *Cleyera japonica*
momigiri
drill powered by a stick-handle one rubs between the palms of the hands
mooring bit. See *kanzashi*
mosodake 226
inferior species of timber bamboo. See also *madake*
motsukoken. See mokkoku
mudamahagi 183, 217
semi-dugout construction in which bottom plank is carved from a very thick board, with side-planking attached (Tohoku and Hokkaido)
mulberry. See *kuwa*

N

nagiri SA 211
beams running fore-and-aft supporting the floorboards
nail. See *kugi*; chart, p. 40; nail pouch, *kugibukuro*; nail set, *kugishime*
namaki (or *namagi* SO-IH)
green wood
namezure TS
runners on bottom of taraibune
nanyouhagi 231
"southern ocean construction," referring to a non-Japanese method of boat construction
nara 186, 211
Japanese oak (*Quercus serrata*). See also *kashi, akagashi, shirogashi*
nawanosumi CT 164
lofting technique, literally, from *nawa* (rope) and *sumi* (ink)
ne BU 135
planking bevel
nedoori CT
faying surface between planks or the seam between planks
nejiribou SA 195
"twist bar," a board used to distribute pressure across the width of a plank being bent
nejitaga TS
twisted hoop
neko CT 175–**76**
cleat for sculling oar rope
neriba SA 215
drain-hole plug
neruba SA 211
pad for *kai*. See also *kaizure* TS
nettou
boiling water. See also *oyu*
nibumi BU **127**, **142**
top of rail
nishi
west
nitaribune CT 152, 169
small cargo lighter
nokke-zukuri BU 9, 125
boat construction in which the planking meets flush at the chine. See drawing p. 9
nokogiri 24–**25**, 47, **131**
handsaw
nomi 25
carpenter's chisel
noribeka 125
smallest bekabune, used only for seaweed harvesting
noshiro CT
nail set with handle
nugidana SA **185**, 206
narrow plank on the outside plank at the gunwale; similar to *koberi*, but not a rub rail
nukiita 170
almond-shaped repair patch in hull
nutmeg. See *kaya*

O

oak. See *nara, kashi, akagashi, shirogashi*
oar. See *ro, kai* (paddle), *yafu, iku* SO-IH
obinoko **35**, 186
bandsaw. See also *bando*
obisugi 33, 226
cedar of high quality, from Obi, a town in Miyazaki Prefecture. See also *sugi, benkousugi*
ogakuzu BU
sawdust
oharai CT 164
Shinto purification
oikami SO-IH 239
small net boats
okiza CT 175–**76**
softwood pad in beam (*toko*) for sculling oar post (*rogui*)
omojiki BU
forward face of stem

sailboat. See *hokakebune*, *putachibune* SO-IH
sakaki 72
  flowering evergreen (*Cleyera japonica*) sacred to Shinto. See also *iiku* SO-IH
sanbuta CT
  foredeck
sandaa 224
  angle grinder with sanding disk SO, from English "sander"
sanehagi. See *enuchi, kakikomi* CT
sanpasen 217
  long, narrow river boat (Agano River, Niigata)
sapwood. See *shirata*
sashigane **29**
  carpenter's square. See also *magarigane, kane* SA
sashiita BU
  floorboards and removable washboards at bulwarks. See also *sunoko*, *itago* SA
sashika SO-IH 246
  thwart. See also *suwooto* SO
sashikazan SO-IH 251
  thwart riser
saw (handsaw). See *nokogiri*; coarser (medium) saw for fitting, *chuume* BU; finer saw for fitting, *koba* BU; dado saw, *mizohoriki*; saw sharpener/sharpening, *metate*; saw vise, *hasami*; sawhorse, *dai* SO
seizai 35, 128, 186
  sawing, referring to a sawmill, *seizaiki* or *seizaisho*
sekobune **57**
  multi-oar chase boat for whaling
sekou TS
  assistant to a craftsman (Mr. Homma)
senban
  lathe. See also *rokuro*
sendangi 245
  chinaberry (*Paulownia tomentosa*)
sengaiki 87, 183
  outboard motor
sengokubune 256
  generic term for traditional wooden trading ships; literally "one thousand *koku* ship," a reference to cargo capacity
shakkanhou 13
  traditional system of Japanese measurements. See chart p. 13
shaku 13
  traditional measurement equal to 10 *sun*; 11 15/16 inches; 303 millimeters. See chart p. 13
shakuri (or *shakuri-kanna*)
  a plough plane, rabbet plane
sharimbai 247
  Japanese hawthorn (*Rhaphiolepis umbellate*)
shazuchi TS
  small mallet
sheer plank. See *uwadana*
shiageganna (or *shiage*) 26
  finish plane
shigotoba 19
  workshop, used for boatbuilder's shop
shikasa SO-IH
  wedge. See also *kusabi*, *ya* SA
shiki 9, 14, **95**, 133, 155
  keel plank, bottom. See also *soko* SO, *ura* TS, *sufu* SO-IH
shikasa SO-IH
  wedge. See also *kusabi*, *ya* SA
shikisan BU
  floor timber
shikisueru 137
  keel-laying ceremony. See also *shikizue*
shikizue BU 70–**71**, 148, 164
  keel-laying ceremony. See also *shikisueru* BU
shimaihagi **21**, **64**, **79**, **181**
  fishing boat type of Aomori Prefecture SA, literally, "four planks put together." See drawing p. 185
shimaki 118
  bamboo insert inside a hoop (Osaka cooper)
shimeigi TS 100, **110**
  wooden punch used to set bamboo hoops. See also *tagashime*
shimetsukeru 45
  to clench nail BU, from *shimeru* (to fasten) and *tsukeru* (to put together)
shinai
  drafting batten, from *shimau* (to bend)
shinsuishiki **68**, 70, **73**, **120**, **145**, **248**
  launching ceremony, literally, "enter water ceremony." See also *funeoroshi*, *shinzouoroshi* BU
shinzouoroshi BU
  launching ceremony, literally, "enter water ceremony." See also *shinsuishiki*, *funeoroshi*
shirakashi 33
  evergreen oak (*Quercus myrsinifolia*), literally "white oak" (not to be confused with *Quercus alba*). See also *kashi*
shirata 35, 92, 128, 155, 214, 227
  sapwood
shiri CT 159
  the knees supporting plank ends aft, literally, "buttocks"

U

Floating World Editions

Floating World Editions publishes books that contribute to a deeper understanding of Asian cultures. Editorial supervision: Ray Furse. Editorial support: Catherine Wood Brooks, Wayne Hileman, and Willem de Lange. Book and cover design: Michelle Landry, Digital Dragon Designery. Map by Benjamin Meader, Rhumb Line Maps. Production supervision: Bill Rose. Printing and binding: Toppan Leefung Printing Limited. The typefaces used are Garamond Premier Pro, Myriad Pro, The Sans and Trajan Pro.